Internet Research, Theory, and Practice: Perspectives from Ireland

Edited by Cathy Fowley, Claire English, and Sylvie Thouësny

R esearch-publishing.net

Published by Research-publishing.net
Dublin, Ireland; Voillans, France
info@research-publishing.net

© 2013 by Research-publishing.net
Research-publishing.net is a not-for-profit association

Internet Research, Theory, and Practice: Perspectives from Ireland
Edited by Cathy Fowley, Claire English, and Sylvie Thouësny

The moral right of the authors has been asserted

Typeset by Research-publishing.net
Cover design: © Raphaël Savina (raphael@savina.net)

Fonts used are licensed under a SIL Open Font License

ISBN13: 978-1-908416-04-9 (Paperback, Print on Demand, Lulu.com)
ISBN13: 978-1-908416-05-6 (Ebook, Kindle Edition, Amazon Media EU S.à r.l.)
ISBN13: 978-1-908416-08-7 (Ebook, PDF file, Open Access, Research-publishing.net)

British Library Cataloguing-in-Publication Data.
A cataloguing record for this book is available from the British Library.

Bibliothèque Nationale de France - Dépôt légal: juin 2013.

Table of Contents

Section 3. Research and Reflections on Educational Practices

Section 4. Research and Reflections on Irish Resources

Notes on Contributors

Editors

Dr Cathy Fowley's doctoral research explored new theoretical frameworks to study the relationship between authors, readers and technology in young people's blogs and their management of privacy issues. These frameworks are now being adapted to computer assisted language learning as well as autobiographical writings. Her research interests are at the intersection of writing and technology, in the field of digital literacies and older people's uses of the internet. She lectures in French through technology in the School of Applied Language and Intercultural Studies in Dublin City University; as part of the DCU Intergenerational Learning Programme team, she also designs and teaches modules on social media, digital skills, and lifewriting for older students.

Dr Claire English's research explores the use of media technologies in everyday life. She completed her PhD research in 2013 at the School of Communications, Dublin City University. Funded by the Irish Social Science Platform, this research conducted a qualitative examination into the use of online social media sites in everyday life in Ireland between 2008 and 2012. This multi-method qualitative research examined conceptions and practices of citizenship among participants during this time. Her research interests include audience studies, media and society, uses of online social media, gender, citizenship and deliberative democracy.

Dr Sylvie Thouësny holds a PhD in second language acquisition from Dublin City University, Ireland. Her current research focuses on language learner modelling to assist second language teachers in the provision of strategic and effective corrective feedback adapted to each individual. This field of research mainly draws on disciplines such as applied linguistics, natural language processing, human-computer interaction, intelligent computer-assisted language learning, and dynamic assessment. Her publications can be consulted on her website (http://icall-research.net/). Additionally, she is a Computational Linguistics Consultant for Appen Butler Hill, currently working on speech recognition projects. Furthermore, she is the founder and

President of Research-publishing.net, a not-for-profit association committed to making edited collections of research papers a freely available public resource (http://research-publishing.net/).

Reading Committee

Dr Debbie Ging is a lecturer in the School of Communications. She teaches Media Studies, Film Studies and Cultural Studies with a focus on gender and sexuality, and her research is concerned with diverse aspects of gender in the media. Debbie is currently chair of the MA in Film and Television Studies. She is a member of the International Advisory Board for the journal Men and Masculinities (http://jmm.sagepub.com/), the Editorial Board of Gender, Sexuality and Feminism (http://www.gsfjournal.org/) and the EROSS research group in DCU (http://www.dcu.ie/eross/index.shtml). Debbie is co-editor of Transforming Ireland: Challenges, Critiques, Resources (Manchester University Press, 2009) and is author of the recently published Men and Masculinities in Irish Cinema (Palgrave Macmillan, 2012).

Dr Deirdre Hynes is a Principle Lecturer in Information and Communications at Manchester Metropolitan University. Her PhD, 'Digital Multimedia Use and Consumption in the Irish Household Setting' (2005, unpublished), focused on issues surrounding the use and uptake of internet in Irish households across household composition, class, gender and age. She reviews for several journals. She has published widely in the field of technology and domestication and has recently co-edited a collection of papers on football and communities. Her current research focuses on female football fans and issues surrounding disenfranchisement, exclusion and empowerment. She is a passionate Liverpool fan and regular match-goer.

Dr Kylie Jarrett is Lecturer in Multimedia at the Centre for Media Studies at the National University of Ireland Maynooth. She has been researching the political economy of the commercial Web for over a decade, investigating sites such as *ninemsn, YouTube* and *eBay*. She has most recently co-authored *Google* and the *Culture of Search* (2012, Routledge) with Ken Hillis and Michael Petit that explores the metaphysical cultural imaginary underpinning the search engine's economics. Her current research uses Feminist theories of work to explore consumer labour on the internet.

Margaret Kelleher is Professor of Anglo-Irish Literature and Drama, University College Dublin and former Director of An Foras Feasa, NUI Maynooth. She is the current Chairperson of the International Association for the Study of Irish Literatures and a member of Science Europe's Humanities Committee. In 2011 she received a Senior Fellowship Project from the Irish Research Council to work with colleagues in An Foras Feasa to create an electronic version of the Loebers' Guide to Irish Fiction 1650-1900, a free, publicly accessible digital resource now live at http://www.lgif.ie.

Dr Orla Murphy is a lecturer in the School of English at University College Cork, in the national, inter-institutional Digital Arts and Humanities PhD program, and co coordinator of the MA in Digital Arts and Humanities at UCC. Her research is focused on intermediality, on how the text is, was, and will be transmitted; how we read, represent, and share knowledge in new networked and virtual environments. She is co chair with Fredrik Palm, HUMlab Sweden, of the information visualisation working group in NeDiMAH.eu (Network for Digital Methods in the Arts and Humanities) and vice chair of the EU COST (Cooperation in Science and Technology) CoSCH.info working group on algorithms and representing 3D. Her PhD (2006) examined the 3D (re) modelling of medieval sculptural heritage in Ireland using laser scanning. It is openly accessible online via UCC's Institutional Repository, CORA.

Dr Minako O'Hagan is a Senior Lecturer in the School of Applied Language and Intercultural Studies (SALIS). Since joining SALIS in 2002, she has expanded her main field of research Translation Technology into Video Game Localisation which combines translation and new media. She has secured internal and external funding, including Proof of Concept funding from Enterprise Ireland and served as an external expert assessor on European projects such as eCoLoMedia. Her PhD supervision covers a range of technology-oriented emerging research areas, including an eye-tracking study of abusive subtitling of Japanese anime, an ethnographic study on young bloggers and Facebook translation crowdsourcing. Her recent publications include Linguistica Antverpiensia New Series - Themes in Translation Studies: Translation as a Social Activity - community translation 2.0 (O'Hagan [ed.], 2011) and a co-authored monograph Game Localization (O'Hagan & Mangiron 2013, forthcoming).

Dr Brian O'Neill is Head of the School of Media at Dublin Institute of Technology, Ireland. His areas of research include media literacy, policymaking and public interest issues in media and communications related to children and youth. He has written widely on media technologies and media literacy for academic journals as well as for organisations such as UNICEF and the Broadcasting Commission of Ireland. He is a member of the Management Committee of COST Action ISO906 - Transforming Audiences, Transforming Societies and Chair of the International Association for Media and Communication Research (IAMCR) Audience Section. He leads the policy work package for EU Kids Online (EC Safer Internet Programme) and is also a member of Ireland's Internet Safety Advisory Council.

Authors

Dr Marie-Thérèse Batardière is a lecturer in French at the University of Limerick (UL). A faculty member of the language department since 1985, she co-founded an Erasmus student exchange between UL and her former university in Angers in 1989 and has been a strong advocate for an interdisciplinary and multicultural approach in the classroom since then. Her PhD thesis, completed in 2002 at Trinity College Dublin, focused on the second language development of university learners experimenting with immersion in the target language. She has also been involved for many years in the field of education; first delivering in-service training for secondary-school teachers of French and, more recently, designing and coordinating a language module for postgraduate student-teachers at UL. As new technologies became available, she made a point to incorporate computer-mediated-communication tools into her teaching. This leads her to participate in projects on technologically enhanced language learning.

Kenny Doyle is a research postgraduate student and Assistant Lecturer in Sociology at Waterford Institute of Technology. He currently teaches introduction to sociology courses in both the Arts and Social Care courses. His education background is a mixture of technology and the humanities as he holds a certificate in computing from Waterford Institute of Technology as well as a degree in English and Sociology from University College Dublin. His primary research interests are technology and social change with a particular emphasis on digitally networked technologies, surveillance, social interaction and the internet. His secondary research interests are governance, security, consumerism and globalisation. His current research, entitled *Surveillance Privacy and Technology: Contemporary Irish Perspectives*, was completed to satisfy the requirements for a Masters in Sociology.

Dr Heike Felzmann is a lecturer in ethics in the Department of Philosophy, School of Humanities at NUI Galway and is a member of the Centre of Bioethical Research and Analysis (COBRA). Her main research areas are health care ethics, professional ethics and research ethics. She was the principal investigator on a recent national review of Irish research ethics committees for the DCYA. She has been a member of a DCYA working group tasked with the development of research ethics guidance for children's research and of the Research Consent Subgroup for the HSE National Consent Advisory Group. Since 2006 she has been a member and vice chair of the NUI Galway University REC. She has ample experience with providing research ethics training for research ethics committees, researchers and postgraduate students throughout Ireland.

Dr Noel Fitzpatrick (doc ès lettres, université de Paris VII) is Dean of the Graduate School of Creative Arts and Media (www.gradcam.ie), Head of Research at the School of Art, Design and Printing at the Dublin Institute of Technology and Director of RADICUL. He is also programme chair for the Creative Arts Masters Platform. He teaches Critical Theory, Philosophy and Aesthetics to undergraduate students at the school and supervises Postgraduate students in the College of Arts and Tourism. Noel holds postgraduate seminars in Phenomenology, Hermeneutics and contemporary French Philosophy at the Graduate School of Creative Arts and Media (www.gradcam.ie). Noel also managed a translational research in Natural Language Processing 'Comenius2.0' (2009-2011) with the National Digital Research Centre (www.ndrc.ie).

Dr Clodagh Harris is a lecturer in the Department of Government, University College Cork. Her research interests include deliberative democracy, political participation and the scholarship of teaching and learning in political science. With colleagues elsewhere on the island she has established and convenes the Political Studies Association of Ireland's (PSAI) specialist groups on participatory and deliberative democracy and teaching and learning in politics. Clodagh is a member of the International Scientific Advisory board of 'We the Citizens', which recently piloted Ireland's first Citizens' Assembly and a member of the International Observers' committee of the G1000, Belgian Citizens' summit. Dr. Harris is one of the key authors of 'Power to the People: Assessing Democracy in Ireland', New Island: Dublin (2007), the first comprehensive audit of the state of democracy in modern Ireland. This project was funded by Atlantic Philanthropies. She has published in leading international journals such as Representation, European Political Science, PS Political Science and Politics and the Journal of Political Science Education.

Sonia Howell is a former doctoral fellow with An Foras Feasa and the School of English, Media and Theatre Studies, NUI Maynooth. Her doctoral thesis, entitled "Partners in Practice: Contemporary Irish literature, World Literature and the Digital Humanities", was funded by a 3 year doctoral scholarship, provided by the Higher Education Authority under the PRTLI4 "Humanities, Technology and Innovation" scheme, awarded to An Foras Feasa (NUI Maynooth). Since commencing her doctoral research, she has presented at a number of international conferences in both digital humanities and Irish studies, including the 2010 Digital Humanities Conference and the International Association of Irish Literatures Conference in 2010 and 2012. She is a member of the editorial board for Breac, an online digital journal for Irish Studies and is incoming editor of The Bibliography of Irish Literary Criticism database.

Michael Hynes is a doctoral candidate in the School of Political Science and Sociology at the National University of Ireland Galway. His current research interests are virtual mobility technologies, tools, and options for promoting more sustainable consumption behaviour in transportation, as part of the wider ConsEnSus project (www.consensus.ie). The ConsEnSus Project is a four year collaborative research project with Trinity College Dublin examining key areas of household consumption, and is funded by the EPA under the STRIVE Programme 2007-2013. Michael holds a Master's Degree in Information Technology from the National University of Ireland Galway and a first class Bachelor of Science Degree in Information Technology from OSCAIL, the Irish National Distance Education Centre.

Catherine Jeanneau is the Administrator of the Language Resource Area at the University of Limerick. Prior to 2011 she worked as Research and Development Manager of the Language Support Unit, which aimed at implementing a learner support strategy and providing customised services outside of formal classroom time, with a particular emphasis on non-traditional and mature students in language learning. She obtained two Maitrises from the Université d'Angers (France) in English language and culture and French as a foreign language and is now conducting her postgraduate studies on online language-learning communities and their impact on language teaching, learning and support. Her research interests include second language acquisition, technology and language learning and learner autonomy.

Dr John Keating is the Associate Director of An Foras Feasa: The Institute for Research in Irish Historical and Cultural Traditions where he supports and leads the research, educational and operational activities of the Institute. He was seconded to this role in 2007 from the Department of Computer Science and NUI Maynooth, where he has lectured since 1990. He holds a BSc in Mathematics and Experimental Physics, an MA in Education, and a PhD in Experimental Physics. His research interests are varied, and include digital humanities, humanities computing, document encoding, hyperspectral segmentation, systemic functional linguistics, educational technology, and software engineering. John has a strong track record of securing competitive funding from international and national funding agencies including science, humanities and social science. He has also received funding support from companies, with a view to co-funding mutually beneficial research in the areas of digital humanities and educational technology.

Margaret Liston is an independent researcher in Philosophy. She holds a BA honours degree in English and a first class honours degree in Philosophy from the National University of Ireland, Galway. Her current research topic examines the concept of judgement in digital hermeneutics. Her undergraduate thesis (2000) focused on WVO Quine's reductionism using scientific notation thereby limiting the interpretation of quantum phenomena. Margaret also has a strong interest in creative writing. Her first short story was published in Phoenix Short Stories, 1996, edited by the late David Marcus. The story received critical acclaim in both the Irish and English Times Literary Supplement (August 7th 1996). In 1998 Margaret co-founded the former Jonathan Swift International web-base satire competition.

Dr Vanessa Liston is a Research Associate in the Department of Political Science, Trinity College Dublin, Ireland. Her research interests are deliberative democracy, Web 2.0 communications and political innovation. Vanessa has a background in Music, Multimedia Systems and Management Consulting. Her PhD (2008) focused on the impact of democratic structures within NGOs on citizens' attitudes and behaviour in Kenya, East Africa where Vanessa supported the early development of a successful community primary school. From this varied background in participatory development, education, technology and the arts Vanessa has developed an interest in the relationship between technology use, knowledge and political development. Vanessa has won awards from the Irish Research Council for the Humanities and Social Sciences (IRCHSS) and private industry and has published in international journals on civil society and political activism.

Dr Gloria Macri is a researcher and part-time lecturer/tutor at Dublin City University (DCU) and NUI-Maynooth. She was a Government of Ireland Scholar (IRCHSS Postgraduate Scholarship) and completed her PhD in the School of Communications at DCU in 2012. Her doctoral research focuses on the process of shaping and negotiating of diasporic identities of Romanians in Ireland in online space. She has a keen interest in research activities and has been so far extensively involved in various international academic research projects, such as EU-EIGE project on Women and the Media in European Union (2013) and MEDIVA (FP7 project between 2011-2012) project on strengthening the media's capacity to reflect diversity and thus foster a better understanding of immigrant integration processes. Her research interests include the following topics: migration, cultural identities, diaspora communities, online communication, youth, and social media.

Dr Ann Marcus-Quinn works at the University of Limerick and was the Open Educational Resources advocate with the National Digital Learning Repository (NDLR) from 2006 until 2012, at the Centre for Teaching and Learning, University of Limerick. Her research interests include Open Educational Resources (OERs), usability, instructional design and the use of information and communication technology at post-primary level.

Dr Oliver McGarr is a Senior Lecturer in the Department of Education and Professional Studies at the University of Limerick. He contributes to the undergraduate and postgraduate initial teacher education programmes as well as the continuing professional development programmes run by the department. His research interests include the pedagogical use of information and communication technology (ICT), the adoption of ICT in post-primary schools and initial and continuing teacher education.

Angela Nagle is a PhD candidate at Dublin City University and an Irish Research Council postgraduate scholar. She has been published in a variety of non-academic publications including the Atlantic, the Irish Times, Press Europe, the Irish Examiner and the Irish Left Review and has written on topics such as cyberutopianism, online anti-feminism, online protest movements, as well as, more broadly, culture and politics. Her research is focused on misanthropic, misogynist and anti-feminist tendencies within online subcultures and counterculture and the resistance to the feminisation of online media and she recently delivered a talk to Feminist Open Forum on all of the above. She received her BA from NUI Maynooth and an M(Phil) in Popular Literature from Trinity College Dublin. This is her first peer reviewed publication.

Jeneen Naji is currently Digital Media Faculty in both the Centre for Media Studies and the Department of Computer Science at the National University of Ireland, Maynooth where she lectures on the B.A. and B.Sc. in Multimedia. Previous to this she was Multimedia Faculty in the Higher Colleges of Technology in the United Arab Emirates and before this she taught in the Department of Creative Media in Dundalk Institute of Technology. Jeneen holds a B.A. (hons) in Imaginative Writing & Theatre Studies from Liverpool John Moore's University in the U.K. and a M.Sc. in Multimedia from Dublin City University in Ireland. She is currently completing her PhD with Dublin City University, conducting research into the impact of the digital apparatus on poetic expression.

Niall O'Leary is DHO Project Manager (IT) with the Digital Humanities Observatory. A graduate of University College Dublin's MA in Film Studies, Niall was a scriptwriter in the audiovisual industry for several years. In 1997 he graduated from Trinity College Dublin with a MSc in Multimedia Systems. From writing, he became more involved in development work, becoming Web Development Specialist at Dublin City University. In this role he developed several major online systems. While at DCU he also lectured on writing for the screen, Internet technologies and Web programming. Since moving to the DHO, he has helped develop many Digital Humanities projects, including St Patrick's Confessio Hyperstack and DHO: Discovery. He maintains a keen interest in teaching and film. Correspondence concerning this article should be addressed to Niall O'Leary, Digital Humanities Observatory, Royal Irish Academy, 19 Dawson Street, Dublin 2.

Mark O'Toole is an Information Systems Project Manager for Kilkenny County Council. His research interests include deliberative democracy, Web 2.0, collaboration, Knowledge Management, Content Management, Data Visualisation, Open Source software and Business Intelligence. Mark has worked professionally on the web since 1995. In 2008 he completed an MSc in Internet

Systems for which his thesis examined the potential applications of social media technologies to organisational knowledge management. Mark also holds an MBA from Dublin City University. Since 2008 Mark has been an advocate within government circles for the use of social and collaborative technologies to improve the quality of both government services and of government interactions with citizens. He speaks regularly on the topic to staff from across various government organisations in Ireland and curates a blog on government use of social media: www.rialtas.net.

Jennifer Patterson is currently completing a research postgraduate study with the Department of Applied Arts at Waterford Institute of Technology. Her research uses a multi-disciplinary approach (sociology, psychology and media studies) to examine the area of adolescent online communication and negative social interactions such as cyberbullying, trolling, indirecting and sexting. She is a graduate of Environmental Health from Dublin Institute of Technology and a graduate of Applied Social Studies in Social Care from Waterford Institute of Technology. She has spent several years working within the Education sector in both primary and secondary schools, as well as working in residential child care and the intellectual disability sector. Her current research interests include adolescent culture with particular emphasis on their networked lives.

Having graduated with a MSc in Communications in 1997, **Anne Rice** has worked for ten years in the community and voluntary sector on a number of research projects, including emigration research, art therapy research, and community feasibility studies. She is currently completing her PhD and she is particularly interested in the role of social networking websites such as Facebook in young people's lives. Her research focuses on (as outlined in this book chapter) the meaning of online friendship to youth social capital. Beyond this chapter her research offers fresh insights into the relationship between social networking, young people and the family. These include technology and the emergence of a new level of global social capital, the gender split in parental knowledge and monitoring of children's online lives, and the invaluable role of new technology for residents of rural areas such young carers and the elderly.

Nina Shiel is a PhD Researcher in Comparative Literature in the School of Applied Language and Intercultural Studies, Dublin City University. She gained BA (Mod) (2001) and M.Litt (2007) in Trinity College Dublin, followed by MA in Comparative Literature in DCU (2011). At the end of her MA she was awarded the SALIS Founders Medal for Academic Excellence for the highest overall grade achieved by a graduate student in the School. Her doctoral research into literary representations of virtual worlds is supported by the Irish Research Council (Humanities and Social Sciences). She is a member of the Comparative Literature Association of Ireland Executive Committee. In addition to the relationship between image and text, her research interests include contemporary adaptations of myths, literature and technology, and bridging the assumed gap between humanities and sciences.

Aja Teehan is the Senior Technology Officer at An Foras Feasa, the Institute for Research in Irish Historical and Cultural Traditions. Specialising in Digital Humanities, she is involved in the practical application of developed theory in relation to the production of digital humanities artefacts. Particular research interests include document and data modeling, ingestion into repositories, and tool design for the creation, management and investigation of digital cultural artefacts. Also active in practical DH projects, most recently she was the DH consultant on the IRCHSS-funded Loeber's Guide to Irish Fiction project. She is also the course coordinator for An Foras Feasa's MA in Digital Humanities and is involved in the development and delivery of many of the modules therein, such as AFF602 Software Methods and XML Technologies for Humanities Research, and AFF606 Text and Textuality.

Etáin Watson is a lecturer in Italian in Dublin Institute of Technology. She is a graduate of the University of Dublin, Trinity College, University of Sussex and University College Dublin. She has also studied at postgraduate level in the Universities of Sassari and Cagliari, Sardinia, and at undergraduate level in the University of Pavia, Italy. She was awarded Italian government scholarships to undertake both undergraduate and postgraduate studies. She is interested in the theory of second language acquisition, the use of innovative technology in enhancing foreign language learning, Italian cinema, and Sardinian and Irish folklore. She has published papers in academic journals in Ireland, Italy, Iran and America. She has presented papers at international conferences in Italy, Spain, Iran and Albania.

Dr Sharon Webb is the Digital Repository of Ireland's Requirements Analyst, based in An Foras Feasa at NUI Maynooth. She finished her PhD, a study of associational culture and the development of Irish nationalism, 1780-1830, with the construction of a software information environment, which was funded by the HEA under the PRTLI4 Humanities, Technology and Innovation award to An Foras Feasa, in 2011. Her thesis can be described as a digital humanities project as it entailed software development as well as historical research and reflects her background in history and computer science. It describes advances and developments in Irish nationalism during the late eighteenth and early nineteenth century within a twenty-first century digital framework. Sharon is the course coordinator and lecturer for AFF260 Humanities Computing I, an undergraduate course at NUI Maynooth.

Acknowledgements

We would like to warmly thank everyone who participated in this project so aptly entitled Internet Research, Theory, and Practice: Perspectives from Ireland, which indeed was an enriching experience for us as editors. It was a great endeavour that required a team-driven effort to complete, but due to everyone's perseverance and determination, it was completed to extraordinary standards.

We would especially like to thank the authors without whom this project would not have existed; they responded with enthusiasm to our initial idea, and their contributions built this idea into an exhaustive picture of internet research in Ireland, throughout disciplines and traditions.

We would also like to thank our wonderful Reading Committee for their tireless toil to make this project the best it possibly could. They were incredibly generous with their time and expertise, and their encouragement certainly helped us more than we can say.

Finally, another special thank you to Catherine Cronin for writing a foreword introducing this project to researchers in Ireland and worldwide.

Go raibh mile maith agat
Cathy Fowley, Claire English, and Sylvie Thouësny

Foreword

Created by humans, for humans, the Internet resides intimately with us – and before long, perhaps, within us. From 2000 to 2012 the number of Internet users rose from less than 0.4 billion to 2.4 billion (about one-third of the world's population)[1]. This continues to rise; predicted estimates of the number of Internet users in 2020 range from 4 to 5 billion[2]. The Internet is becoming increasingly wireless, mobile and geographically dispersed. We are also moving closer to an Internet of Things[3] as opposed to simply computers, as objects from appliances to buildings to roads are equipped with digital sensors and communicative capabilities.

Many metaphors have been used to describe the Internet, its growth, and its role in our lives: the Internet as a network, an organism, a non-hierarchical space, the ultimate panopticon. Both utopian and dystopian views of the Internet abound in the popular press, on topics such as social networking among young people, the future of privacy, the future of reading, online education, teleworking and more.

Scholarly, evidence-based Internet research is of critical importance. The field of Internet research explores the Internet as a social, political and educational phenomenon, providing theoretical and practical contributions to our understanding, and informing practice, policy and further research.

This new collection, Internet Research, Perspectives from Ireland, is a unique and welcome work. The editors have compiled a diverse range of new scholarly, peer-reviewed research, spanning the fields of education, arts, the social sciences and technology. The authors provide academic perspectives, both theoretical and practical, on the Internet and citizenship, education, employment, gender, identity, friendship, language, poetry, literature and more. The collection comprises a rich resource for researchers and practitioners alike.

---

1 International Telecommunications Union (2013) http://www.itu.int/en/ITU-D/Statistics/Pages/stat/default.aspx; Internet World Stats (2013) http://www.internetworldstats.com/stats.htm

2 Microsoft (2013) http://blogs.technet.com/b/trustworthycomputing/archive/2013/02/06/linking-cybersecurity-policy-and-performance-microsoft-releases-special-edition-security-intelligence-report.aspx; Intac (2010) http://www.intac.net/the-internet-in-2020/

3 Ashton, K. (2009). That 'Internet of Things' Thing. *RFID Journal* http://www.itrco.jp/libraries/RFIDjournal-That%20Internet%20of%20Things%20Thing.pdf

The locus and focus of the collection is Ireland – in this the collection is unique. All of the authors are based in Ireland. They are self-described Digital Humanities scholars, as well as researchers in literature, languages, psychology, philosophy, sociology, political science, information technology and media studies. They explore the global in a local context. Thus the collection provides a vital resource for researchers in Ireland, hoping to learn from and build on country-specific Internet research, as well as an important node in the global network of Internet research.

I applaud the researchers and editors for publishing this work, and more so for publishing it openly. Enabling open access to this research will only increase its value, now and for years to come.

Catherine Cronin
Lecturer and Academic Coordinator
Department of Information Technology
National University of Ireland, Galway

1 Introduction on Internet Research, Theory, and Practice: Perspectives from Ireland

Cathy Fowley[1], Claire English[2], and Sylvie Thouësny[3]

1. Project context

In 2007 and 2008 we started our doctoral research, each with a specific topic, but all related to technology and the internet – in the fields of education, communications, and humanities. For two of us, the locus was twofold: we were researching particular spaces on the internet, linked to the everyday life of young people in Ireland. This geographical anchoring proved to be problematic: nowhere could we easily identify internet research from Ireland. We knew some scholars who were indeed researching areas related to the internet, but an overview was impossible to find. At the same time, another member of our group became involved in open access publishing.

Open access to research literature may simply be described as the practice of making scholarly materials or peer-reviewed articles available via the internet to anybody, anywhere. More specifically, it allows the democratisation of research and the distribution of knowledge to those who are not affiliated to universities or institutions, without any monetary barriers to overcome. The benefits of open access are invaluable not only for the readers but also for the writers. While the former may freely access the material to further explore the domain, facilitate collaboration, or merely broaden the extent of their knowledge, the latter, i.e., the authors of articles published under an open access model, will have the opportunity of reaching a larger population of

1. Dublin City University, Dublin, Ireland; cathy.fowley@dcu.ie

2. Dublin City University, Dublin, Ireland; claire.english3@mail.dcu.ie

3. Dublin, Ireland; sylvie.thouesny@icall-research.net

How to cite this chapter: Fowley, C., English, C., & Thouësny, S. (2013). Introduction on Internet Research, Theory, and Practice: Perspectives from Ireland. In C. Fowley, C. English, & S. Thouësny (Eds.), *Internet Research, Theory, and Practice: Perspectives from Ireland* (pp. 1-8). Dublin: © Research-publishing.net.

potential readers, as well as increasing international recognition and visibility with respect to citations (Bernius, Hanauske, Dugall, & König, 2013).

This project started in January 2012 with a call for papers issued to all Irish third-level institutions. The sheer number of submissions received showed that there was indeed a thriving internet research community, albeit scattered and often unaware that others were also researching digital issues. The final collection is a snapshot of internet research on the island of Ireland and by publishing this collection of papers under the golden road approach – all texts going through a quality assurance process (blind-peer review) and being openly accessible online on the publisher's website –, our aim is to contribute to and freely diffuse internet research from Ireland to the world wide web.

2.   What is internet research?

In September 2000, the newly-formed Association of Internet Researchers (AoIR) held its first international conference, entitled "the State of the Interdiscipline", highlighting a new locus of research, and a "focus on the Internet as a distinct interdisciplinary field for research" (http://aoir.org/conferences/past/ir-1-2000/). Internet research was gradually established as a discipline, whose focus and/or locus is the internet (Rall, 2007). Within a decade, the internet became part of everyday life, and barriers between the "virtual" and the "real" were slowly eroded, leading to a seamless experience for most young people in Western societies of the 21st century. At the same time, the internet as a locus of research found its way in many traditional disciplines; however, internet research throws a different light on methodologies, and research strategies are not always easily transferred (Markham & Baym, 2009). The first section of this publication in particular highlights some of the issues which focus the attention of humanities researchers online, from textual practices to the ethics of research on the internet, and following chapters consider the specificities of the internet with regards to societal or educational practices. In each case, the researchers or practitioners are keenly aware of methodological and ethical issues inherent to internet research. They also all have in common their relationship to a specific geographical space, whether they are based in Ireland and research universal issues, or research specifically Irish issues.

Although the internet has been heralded – and indeed also criticised – for creating new types of communities (Baym, 2010; Rheingold, 2000), it has also been proven to consolidate links within physical communities (Wellman, Quan-Haase, Boase, & Chen, 2003). In the words of Haythornwaite and Kendall (2010), "early on, the question was whether community could exist online; now the question may be whether it can exist without online" (p. 1086). Thus, the increasing seamlessness of online and offline life, and the strength of physical as well as virtual communities led us to this volume, where physical geography and local issues meet internet research in the humanities and social sciences.

3.   Humanities and social sciences, and interdisciplinary research

In internet research more than anywhere else, humanities and social sciences meet and meld to help investigate areas related to art, writing, and society. From its inception, the field has reflected the interdisciplinarity of its nature, and this volume illustrates this in its four separate sections. The first section entitled "Research and reflections on ethics and digital culture" is thus mostly concerned with theoretical issues, ethics and digital texts. The second section "Research and reflections on societal practices" observes how people behave and integrate new concepts and online technologies into their social practices, asking questions about gender, citizenship, friendship, work and privacy within daily life in Ireland. The third section labelled "Research and reflections on educational practices" focuses on learning and teaching methods in second and third level environments – from the presence of digital divide in secondary schools to the use of internet-based tools and platforms for language learning. In the final section named "Research and reflection on Irish resources", each chapter describes and analyses a specific digital resource within an Irish context.

3.1.   Section 1 – Research and reflections on ethics and digital culture

Section 1 presents chapters dedicated to theoretical thinking and reflections linked to the emergence of humanities disciplines on the internet. One of the crucial issues to have arisen is that of which ethical guidelines and thinking to apply in a field which belongs both to humanities and social sciences traditions. *Heike Felzmann* outlines the main ethical concerns which have arisen in internet research, from the specific relationship between researchers, participants and the technology to expectations and requirements of privacy, and from confidentiality and anonymity issues to the assessment of vulnerability online. She then situates these concerns in an Irish context, reviewing existing Irish research ethics documents. *Cathy Fowley*'s chapter echoes these concerns and issues, whilst relating them to an ethnographic study of young Irish bloggers. She outlines the issues as well as the approaches and ethical solutions which can be found within the qualitative research tradition, examining in detail issues of privacy management amongst the participants in her study. While the first two chapters deal with aspects of ethics in internet research, the following three chapters are all concerned with textual aspects of humanities and the internet. *Jeneen Naji*'s chapter examines poetry in the digital medium, and she uses theories of translation in order to analyse the impact of the move from analogue to digital, as well as the impact of interactivity on the traditional characteristics of poetry. *Nina Shiel*'s chapter is also concerned with digital texts, and introduces the concept of ekphrasis to computer-generated graphics and their representation, with examples from social media, interactive fiction and electronic literature. *Noel Fitzpatrick*, for his part, is concerned with issues of digital reading, which he compares to prelectio, a pre-reading of texts for salient information. The concept of pharmakon is thus offered as a means of revisiting the technology of writing and positing a positive pharmacology.

3.2.   Section 2 – Research and reflectionson societal practices

Through the means of semi-structured focus group discussions, *Jennifer Patterson*, in chapter 7, opens the section on societal aspects and explores male adolescents' thoughts and opinions on the viewing of violent content in either fantasy worlds or real life. After reflecting on the meaning of the word violence, she examines whether violent media play a role in gender representation, and more specifically, whether violence can function as a model to affirming one's masculinity. *Claire English*, in the following chapter, presents findings from a qualitative study which analyses adults' use of online social media in discursive practices of citizenship. She investigates participants' attitudes towards posting and discussion, and explores whether online social media sites may act as online public spheres and create a space for rational debate. In a similar vein, *Angela Nagle* investigates public spheres and the online arena of political debate. Her focus, however, is placed on women's experience of online life, misogyny, and verbal abuse. Accompanied with shocking examples, she illustrates the situation of some female journalists and internet users and argues that, although a few women have started challenging the optimistic expectations of the cyberfeminists of the 90s, there is still a need for such a discourse. *Anne Rice*, on the other hand, claims that online, nowadays, we are all friends. She considers the outcomes of online friendship for young people with respect to social capital, i.e., resources individuals gather through their relationships. Discussing the benefits of friend bonding and friend linking, she illustrates how the traditional concept of youth friendship is evolving. *Gloria Macri*, in chapter 11, further discusses spaces for debate and bonding. She presents a case study of an online ethnography examining the development of an online Romanian community in Ireland. She investigates whether the online community represents the online dimension of the Romanian diaspora in Ireland, or whether it represents a community in its own right. In another area of research, *Michael Hynes* discusses and examines the environmental impact of one's carbon footprint when deciding to telework in Ireland. Gathering evidence from a multinational company, he analyses participants' self-reflection and self-assessment to estimate the environmental impact of teleworkers and argues for a need to develop enriched indicators. The final chapter in this section is a reflection on dataveillance, i.e., the subtle and pervasive surveillance of people through the application of information technology. Investigating citizens' awareness of these practices, *Kenny Doyle* discusses privacy and surveillance, and identifies the participants' positions.

3.3.   Section 3 – Research and reflections on educational practices

Ann Marcus-Quinn and *Oliver McGarr*, in chapter 14, start the third section with a reflection on the use of technology and online resources in educational settings. They design and develop open educational resources for the teaching of poetry at post-primary and secondary levels to capture collaborative designs and development processes. Raising the problematics of the digital divide, they demonstrate that access to technology in Irish schools is not always an issue per se. Rather, the challenge for these schools is how to embrace technology and make use of the resources available. While the previous chapter focuses on the teachers' use of technology, *Marie-Thérèse Batardière*'s study investigates, from the students' point of view, the use of technology, and more specifically, the use of an online discussion forum during an intercultural exchange. Drawing on both qualitative and quantitative data, the author highlights the students' adopted patterns of behaviour when completing tasks, and explores the perceived benefits of an online discussion task with respect to language acquisition. Continuing the discussion on the use of technology, *Catherine Jeanneau* in chapter 16 questions whether the use of social media is changing teaching and learning practices in third-level education and if Irish students are ready to adopt these new tools. To address these questions, she explores online practices of staff and students in a language learning context. While her data reveals that students have no strong opposition to the use of technology and social media in their learning environment, she demonstrates that preconceptions, however, exist and continue to prevail. *Sylvie Thouësny*, on the other hand, shows that although internet-based tools may be useful in theory to help language learners complete their tasks, in practice, these tools' functionalities are not systematically adopted by learners. More precisely, she investigates, at university level, the students' use of an internet-based word processing tool while engaging in a written task, and observes how they intervened and interacted with their teacher after being provided with comments on their written performance. The concluding chapter in this section outlines practical aspects of using internet resources in a foreign language classroom. Following an action research methodology, *Etáin Watson* in chapter 18 discusses and documents activities and conclusions reached from using the internet as a learning support in her language classes.

3.4.   Section 4 – Research and reflection on Irish resources

The fourth and final section of this collection of papers focuses on Irish resources. *Sharon Webb*, *Aja Teehan*, and *John Keating*, in chapter 19, begin with a discussion on how digital tools may be used to create multiple representations of a doctoral dissertation, and discuss one approach to present interactive "born-digital" theses that move beyond static scholarly texts. *Niall O'Leary*, in the following chapter, provides an insight into the wide-ranging scope of the "Digital Humanities Observatory: Discovery" application, an online gateway to Irish digital collections and resources. He details the challenges encountered in building the infrastructure of the system and explains how the application can offer researchers new ways of visualising data from humanities content. *Sonia Howell*, in chapter 21, offers a practical and critical account of "The Bibliography of Irish Literary Criticism", a bibliographical database developed by humanities and information and communication technology researchers. More specifically, she investigates the content of the database as well as the searches it permits, and argues that paying attention to issues with respect to dissemination and sustainability is essential to ensure the ongoing viability of the digital database. *Vanessa Liston*, *Clodagh Harris*, *Mark O'Toole*, and *Margaret Liston*, in the final chapter of this section, show how political knowledge resources can be drawn from citizens' everyday communications. They present the SOWIT project, an e-supported deliberation process, which aims to not only improve political communications, deliberations, and active reflections between citizens and public representatives, but also provide them with new digital political artefacts and objective data.

4.   Conclusion

The articles presented in this edited book illustrate the broad diversity of internet-based studies in an Irish context, as well as the interdisciplinarity which distinguishes much of its outputs. From digital humanities in the strictest sense – through the creation and use of digital objects and resources to a close examination of digital texts, from ethical issues to societal issues – through the lenses of gender or nationality, from empirical research to practitioners reports, the chapters are a snapshot of internet research in Ireland. Our contributors come from many third-level institutions on the island – universities as well as institutes of technology, east and west, north and south –, thus illustrating a geographical space linked to digital spaces. It is our hope that this open access publication will enable students, researchers and practitioners to gain a broader understanding of these areas of research in Ireland, and will foster communication and cooperation among internet researchers.

References

Baym, N. K. (2010). *Personal Connections in the Digital Age*. Cambridge: Polity Press.

Bernius, S., Hanauske, M., Dugall, B., & König, W. (2013). Exploring the Effects of a Transition to Open Access: Insights from a Simulation Study. *Journal of The American Society for Information Science and Technology, 64*(4), 701-726. doi:10.1002/asi.22772

Haythornwaite, C., & Kendall, L. (2010). Internet and Community. *American Behavioral Scientist, 53*(8), 1083-1094. doi: 10.1177/0002764209356242

Markham, A. N., & Baym, N. K. (2009). Introduction: Making Smart Choices on Shifting Ground . In A. N. Markham & N. K. Baym (Eds.), *Internet Inquiry: conversation about method* (pp. vii-xix). Thousand Oaks: SAGE publications.

Rall, D. N. (2007). Considering internet scholarship – in theory and practice. Southern Cross University: Lismore.

Rheingold, H. (2000). *The virtual community: Homesteading on the electronic frontier* (Revised edition). Cambridge, MA: MIT Press.

Wellman, B., Quan-Haase, A., Boase, J., & Chen, W. (2003). The Social Affordances of the Internet for Networked Individualism. *Journal of Computer Mediated Communication, 8*(3), np. Retrieved from http://jcmc.indiana.edu/vol8/issue3/wellman.html

Research and Reflections on Ethics and Digital Culture

2 Ethical Issues in Internet Research: International Good Practice and Irish Research Ethics Documents

Heike Felzmann[1]

Abstract

This chapter discusses the main research ethical concerns that arise in internet research and reviews existing research ethical guidance in the Irish context in relation to its application to internet research. The chapter begins with a brief outline of high profile cases in the early history of the internet that highlighted specific emerging ethical concerns regarding the new medium and the first development of ethical guidance in this context. Important research ethical concerns in internet research are then presented. These include: (i) understanding the specific relationship between researchers, participants and the online materials, and the ethical significance of contributors' potential lack of awareness of research conducted on their online interactions, (ii) clarifying privacy expectations and ethical requirements regarding the access to and use of online materials, (iii) implementing ethically appropriate consent processes in the online medium, (iv) doing justice to confidentiality, anonymity and data protection requirements and (v) clarifying vulnerability of participants, and potential risks and benefits arising from research participation. In the final part of the chapter existing Irish research ethical guidance documents are reviewed in relation to the relevance of their guidance for the conduct of internet research.

Keywords: research ethics, internet research, privacy, informed consent, confidentiality, vulnerability.

---

1. Philosophy, School of Humanities & COBRA, NUI Galway, Galway, Ireland; heike.felzmann@nuigalway.ie

How to cite this chapter: Felzmann, H. (2013). Ethical Issues in Internet Research: International Good Practice and Irish Research Ethics Documents. In C. Fowley, C. English, & S. Thouësny (Eds.), *Internet Research, Theory, and Practice: Perspectives from Ireland* (pp. 11-32). Dublin: © Research-publishing.net.

1.   Introduction

Researchers conducting internet research frequently encounter challenges in relation to research ethics review. Internet research can pose new challenges in relation to the ethical conduct of research and research ethics committees are frequently unsure how to adapt standard research ethical requirements to the realm of internet research. As the other chapters in this volume have made clear, internet research is an extremely wide field that allows for a huge variety of approaches and research methodologies. Accordingly, an article on internet research ethics has to be selective and will leave out many issues that might be of interest to researchers using the internet as a medium or subject matter for research.

An additional caveat regarding this paper is the fact that, at the time of writing, only limited research ethical guidance is in place in Ireland, and none of the guidance that exists directly addresses ethical issues in internet research. Accordingly, the majority of the following discussion is based on international discussions of ethical research in internet research. In the final part of the chapter the existing Irish documentation will be examined in relation to its application to some prominent issues in internet research.

2.   The development of internet research ethics

When use of the internet became more widespread in the 1990s, researchers' attention began to be drawn to the research potential of this medium. This included a wide range of research concerns, from an interest in understanding the use of the medium and the new possibilities of online activities and interaction that it created, to using it as a large and easily accessible repository of quantitative and qualitative data, and also to its potential as a novel medium for the recruitment of research participants and a medium for the fast and low cost delivery of surveys and other research instruments. At the same time, increasing attention was being paid to determining what constituted good ethical practice in social science research. Internet research was one emerging area of research and the development of guidelines on ethical issues in internet research soon followed.

Among the earliest concerns highlighted in the field was the issue of potential harm that could arise in research on online interaction of internet-based communities. In the early days of the internet, the potential real life impact of virtual interactions was not always understood clearly. However, with increasing experience of the new modes of interaction, evidence accumulated that, despite their virtuality, online interactions had very real emotional effects on participants. Several much-discussed popular magazine articles that described the experience of harm resulting from internet interactions indicated that a reassessment of the presumed harmlessness of 'virtual' internet interaction was warranted. This in turn highlighted that internet research itself could not be assumed to be entirely risk free. In her 1985 *Ms. Magazine* article *The strange case of the electronic lover*, van Gelder (1985/1991) discussed a case of assumed online identity, where a male psychiatrist posed as a disabled and disfigured female "Joan" over a period of several years. In 1993 Dibbell wrote a much discussed magazine article on *A Rape in Cyberspace* in the *Village Voice*, describing the reverberations of an instance of 'virtual rape' in a virtual context, *LambdaMOO* (Dibbell, 1993). Both of these articles made clear that virtual events and interactions had the power of engendering very real and intense emotional experiences and similar observations have continued with the development of increasingly sophisticated modes of online interactions which, if anything, further intensify the experience of reality and immersion in those virtual contexts (Craft, 2007; Wolfendale, 2007).

Among the first attempts at providing guidance on internet research ethics were the 1996 special issue of *The Information Society* (King, 1996), the 1999 American Association for the Advancement of Science (AAAS) workshop on *Ethical and Legal Aspects of Human Subjects Research on the Internet* (Frankel & Siang, 1999) and the 2002 guidelines by the Association of Internet Researchers on *Ethical decision-making and Internet research: recommendations from the AoIR ethics working committee* (Ess & AoIR, 2002). According to Frankel and

Siang (1999), relevant ethical issues in internet research included "[t]he ability of both researchers and their subjects to assume anonymous or pseudonymous identities online, the complexities of obtaining consent, the often exaggerated expectations, if not the illusion, of privacy in cyberspace, and the blurred distinction between public and private domains" (pp. 1-2). The AAAS document in particular proved influential in shaping what is considered good ethical practice in internet research.

3. Core ethical concerns in internet research

The following section will provide a brief introduction to the main research ethical concerns arising in common forms of internet research, with particular emphasis on its potential impact on human participants. It is important to acknowledge the significant methodological variety in internet research; the concerns discussed here are necessarily selective. The underlying assumption of this chapter is that the basic ethical concerns in internet research can be understood in terms of general research ethical concepts used in social science research (see also Elgesem, 2002). However, the various contexts of internet research raise some specific issues that require the reconsideration and problematisation of standard ethical practices; how much they stretch existing research ethical practices and requirements is open to debate (Frankel & Siang, 1999; Pittenger, 2003).

3.1. The relationship between researchers, participants and online materials

The internet allows researchers to reach large numbers of research participants who may be widely dispersed geographically, and to do so at a much lower cost than traditional research approaches (Frankel & Siang, 1999). This makes it a potentially very attractive medium for the recruitment of participants. However, much research conducted via the internet merely employs traditional research methodologies in the online medium (Pittenger, 2003). This mainly requires minor adaptations regarding recruitment and delivery to the characteristics of the online medium. As long as researchers clearly present themselves as researchers and recruit participants transparently via non-intrusive channels, the ethical challenges arising in such research are mostly comparable to those encountered in traditional research mediums.

However, additional challenges arise when the relationship between researchers and participants is not established clearly from the outset, or when it uses channels that potential participants do not expect to be used for research. The internet makes it significantly easier for researchers not to have to present themselves as researchers in order to access interesting data . It facilitates easy access to vast amounts of materials that the authors may never have envisaged as permanently available, it allows researchers to view interaction without leaving publically visibles trace of their presence, and it makes possible easy data mining by researchers in contexts dedicated to purposes far from research.

As Eysenbach and Till (2001) highlight in relation to qualitative health research, the role of researchers could range from (i) 'passive analysis', where researchers analyse the textual materials on specific internet sites without actively intervening in the context which they are analysing, (ii) 'active analysis', where researchers intervene actively in a particular context to evoke relevant responses, but without identifying themselves as researchers, and (iii) 'forms of active recruitment', where researchers identify themselves as such and use the internet as a medium of recruiting participants and collecting information, which are clearly identified as research activities.

While deception in relation to the 'true role' of researchers is not unique to the online environment and is not uncommon for example in certain types of ethnographic research, it is generally considered ethically problematic in contemporary research ethics and requires stronger ethical justifications (Pittenger, 2003).

3.2. The blurring of the distinction between public and private information

Usually, in traditional research ethics there is the assumption that a fairly clear distinction exists in ethical requirements between public and private information. Use of material that is in the public domain does not require individual informed consent, whereas research that collects data outside the public domain is considered private and permission needs to be sought from the originators of the data for any use of that data. However, the internet is a peculiar case because the boundaries between the public and the private are frequently blurred in the minds of users, especially in relation to social interactions and personal communications in a wide range of online contexts.

What characterises all such sites is that on the one hand, material is not only openly accessible but also archived over extended periods of time; on the other hand, people write their contributions often under the assumption of relative privacy and react negatively to perceived intrusions (Frankel & Siang, 1999; Sixsmith & Murray, 2001). Even for a more recent service like *Twitter* which, in comparison to the original chat rooms, is set up more clearly as a medium of individual public 'broadcasting', in practice the very same issues arise, as evident in a lively discussion on the topic in Zimmer (2010b) where respondents expressed strongly diverging views on whether research on contributions on public *Twitter* accounts would require consent by account owners.

There has been much debate about how exactly to conceptualise privacy. Eysenbach and Till (2001) and Bruckman (2002) claim that the traditional dichotomies between public and private or published and unpublished become blurred in the case of the internet and become much more akin to a continuum than a dichotomy. Nissenbaum's (2004) conception of 'privacy as contextual integrity' is particularly promising in this context. She claims that within each context of interaction, participants have certain expectations about how participants in this context will behave in relation to the use and distribution of information. Contextual integrity demands "that information gathering and dissemination be appropriate to that context and obey the governing norms of distribution within it" (Nissenbaum, 2004, p. 101). Behaviour that breaches these context-specific expectations by broadcasting information further or to different audiences counts as breach of privacy.

In a similar vein, Bruckman (2002) proposes to consider most communications on the internet as 'semipublished' and 'semiprivate'. There is considerable evidence that, even though technically speaking contributions shared in internet chatrooms may be of a public nature, many participants consider them a strictly private space and can be extremely reluctant to allow researchers access to their interactions. A participant of an online support group quoted in King (1996) expressed her upset at finding out that their support group interactions were being analysed by researchers: "When I joined this, I thought it would be a support group, not a fishbowl for a bunch of guinea pigs. I certainly don't feel at this point that it is a safe environment [...] and I will not open myself up to be dissected by students or scientists" (p. 122).

Hudson and Bruckman (2004) conducted a controlled experiment where they compared chatroom activity in reaction to various forms of disclosure of researchers' presence and activity. They found that any type of explicit disclosure that researchers were present and intending to study the chatroom activities (whether merely announcing their intention, asking for opt-in or opt-out consent) led to significant hostility. Under the research announcement conditions, the researchers were kicked out four times more frequently than under the non-announcement condition.

Eysenbach and Till (2001) list a number of factors that determine whether an online space is perceived as a private space in which members are not likely to seek the kind of 'public visibility' that would qualify their contributions as public in nature: (i) some form of subscription or registration is required to gain access to the forum, (ii) the number of perceived users of the forum (see also Hudson & Bruckman, 2004), (iii) the implicit or explicit group norms, including statements who the target group is and what the purpose of the forum is.

With the explosion in the use of *Facebook* as a medium of social networking, privacy has become a widely considered issue. On the one hand it can be argued that the widespread use of social networking sites has increased the awareness and understanding of average users regarding the control and limitations of privacy. As Lange (2007) shows in relation to the use of social networking functions on *YouTube*, users manage their social networks in relation to privacy concerns in a quite sophisticated and individualised manner.

On the other hand, as Zimmer (2010a) shows in his discussion of the ethical shortcomings of the Harvard-based T3 project, significant complexities exist regarding privacy on complex networking sites like *Facebook*. In fact, the T3 research project breached several privacy rules despite having undergone significant scrutiny. In particular, the layered and relational character of *Facebook* privacy settings made information accessible to researchers which was not generally publicly accessible, but was mistakenly perceived as if it was (Zimmer, 2010a).

3.3.   Concerns about informed consent

Informed consent is one of the cornerstones of research ethics. Most research with human participants requires researchers to obtain participants' explicit consent to participate in the research, on the basis of a comprehensive process of information about the research project. In order to be able to give meaningful informed consent, participants need to (i) have the ability to reflect on the information, (ii) make their decision voluntarily without being put under any pressure to participate or make decisions quickly, (iii) have been given all relevant information on the research and its potential implications, (iv) have understood that information, (v) made a conscious decision to participate and expressed it unambiguously to the researcher. For the use of traditional research methods in an online environment, e.g., the recruitment of participants in an online environment for online surveys, online interviewing or online focus groups, the standard ethical requirements regarding consent apply. Conducting informed consent in an online environment poses some specific challenges: in the absence of face-to-face interaction it is more difficult for the researcher to ascertain whether the participant is in principle able to consent and has indeed understood the information provided to them (Frankel & Siang, 1999). However, these problems are not unique to the online environment, and challenges to achieving meaningful consent are present in most research settings (Walther, 2002).

The waiving of consent requirements is a possibility under some circumstances, and there may be clear rules in place, depending on the jurisdiction in which the research is being conducted. Bruckman (2002) suggests that consent requirements for use of online material might be waived if this material (i) is officially, publicly, permanently archived, (ii) no password is required to archive access, (iii) no site policy prohibits it, and (iv) the topic is not highly sensitive (for similar positions see also Pittenger, 2003; Sixsmith & Murray, 2001; for a more simplified understanding of the problem see Rodham & Gavin, 2006).

As indicated above (Hudson & Bruckman, 2004), even requesting consent can lead to negative reactions in online settings. However, this is not inevitable. Scharf (1999) shows how she achieved explicit research consent by participants in a chatroom dedicated to breast cancer support, a very sensitive topic. She took particular care to gain credibility as genuinely interested participant as well as researcher in the chatroom from an early stage, and later used an individualised approach to specifically request explicit consent to quote from each individual participant whose contributions she wanted to include. This individualised, and 'private' approach by somebody who had already gained credibility appeared significantly more acceptable to participants than general public announcements requesting or announcing research access to the forum as a whole. However, as Eysenbach and Till (2001) report, credibility as established forum participant in itself might not always protect participant-researchers from negative reactions when asking for permission to research.

An additional concern is the role of gatekeepers of online fora for consent. In many research fields, gatekeepers play a significant role in determining access of researchers to particular populations. In relation to online research, Bruckman (2002) suggests that gatekeepers should be given a role for consent only in relation to those for a where the forum rules assign this role to the gatekeeper, or where the population studied is a particularly vulnerable population. However, many online communities are very fluid in terms of membership (Frankel & Siang, 1999; King, 1996; Sixsmith & Murray, 2001), so that the gatekeeper's relationship with community members might be less established and therefore less authoritative than comparable gatekeeper roles in real life.

3.4. Confidentiality, anonymity and data management

Confidentiality as an ethical concern is generally a strict requirement for anybody handling other persons' personal data, and strict legal requirements are in place in most jurisdictions. Researchers are not entitled to use or share potentially identifiable personal data without the participant's agreement, and uses of personal data for particular purposes have to be authorised by the participant. The requirement of confidentiality is closely related to that of anonymity, but they are not identical. Confidentiality is concerned with the issue of accessing and sharing personal information only on the basis of authorisation by the person concerned, whereas anonymity is concerned with making sure the person whose data is being used is not identifiable to others from the research data. Confidentiality is also closely linked to the requirement of security of data storage.

One significant concern in relation to confidentiality is data security, beginning with the potentially unsecure transmission of electronic data, to lack of awareness of the kind of identifying information available to the researcher, to unintentional sharing of information e.g., through shared email accounts (Frankel & Siang, 1999), to finally the potential for compromising confidentiality at a later stage of research through data multiplication, loss or insufficiently secure storage, or even the problematic legal status of certain computer files as public records (Pittenger, 2003). As already indicated, the distinction between public vs. private data is blurred in the case of many types of internet communications. This has implications for the treatment of confidentiality and anonymity. Internet researchers cannot rely on an easy classification of data as public or private, but have to assess carefully the particular characteristics of their research area, and the specific attitudes that participants are likely to have to the use of their data.

One of the concerns in relation to confidentiality and anonymity is the use of pseudonyms in communications on the internet. While the real life identity of participants is in most cases hidden to researchers, this does not mean that using these pseudonyms, e.g., *Twitter* names, in reporting on research data is unproblematic (King, 1996; Sixsmith & Murray, 2001). As Bruckman (2002) highlights, pseudonyms function like real names and therefore should be treated in a similar manner. Especially in the case of well-established online identities, users may care deeply about the reputation of their online identities, and may experience the reference to their original pseudonyms in research as intrusive as real-life identification. On the other hand, the personal investment in their online persona might also have the opposite effect: if participants take particular pride in their online presence or activities they may feel disenfranchised if they are not explicitly referred to by their pseudonym. Bruckman (2002) and Hudson and Bruckman (2004) point out that the strategy regarding anonymity should depend very much on the forum studied, and might range from scrupulous anonymisation of any potentially identifiable material to the opposite: taking care to identify explicitly the participant's contributions as theirs.

This issue can be considered in a slightly wider context, insofar as it points to uncertainties regarding the appropriate attitudes towards materials that are not created as research materials. Ess (2007) highlights the tension between viewing the originators of such materials as participants in human subject research who deserve protection, or rather as artists or authors who deserve credit and are entitled to copyright protections. In a similar vein Roberts, Smith, and Pollock (2004) explain their particular approach of managing the issue of anonymity or authorship through individual consent.

3.5. Vulnerability, risk and benefit

Concern about participants' vulnerability is a particularly significant research ethical concern; prevention of harm to participants is generally considered to be the main rationale for the requirement of research ethics review. Internet research raises a number of concerns regarding vulnerability and harm, but also regarding potential benefit that other forms of research might not be able to achieve. Some of the concerns regarding risk of harm have already been addressed in the section on privacy and confidentiality. In addition, particular concerns regarding vulnerable participant groups arise. The internet is frequently used as a medium of support for persons who may be subject to mental or physical vulnerabilities, impairments or disabilities.

Accordingly, research on the internet has the potential to reach vulnerable populations, persons with disability or other populations that may not otherwise be sufficiently represented in research, and thereby achieve greater inclusiveness (Bowker & Tuffin, 2004; Frankel & Siang, 1999). This has the potential to lead to the creation of a more substantial knowledge base regarding those participant groups, which in turn could feed into the improvement of services. It may also have the added advantage of allowing those participants to represent themselves on different terms than may be possible in face-to-face contexts, especially in relation to overcoming stereotyping and stigma. From its early days, the internet has also served as a medium of research on sexuality (Binik, Mah, & Kiesler, 1999), risky health behaviour like recreational drug use (Barratt & Lenton, 2010) or other issues like gambling (Griffiths & Whitty, 2010) that people would be reluctant to address if they were not anonymous, but that might have significance for understanding human behaviour or targeting public health interventions.

However, tapping into the internet as a resource of knowledge on vulnerable groups also comes at a risk. Unwittingly becoming the subject of research may be experienced as a traumatic violation of personal integrity for members of vulnerable groups, as for example in the much criticised research by Finn and Lavitt (1994) on self-help groups for survivors of sexual abuse. In the case of most research with vulnerable participants, the researcher is considered to have a special duty of care to participants. In internet research, the identification and management of potential problems or participant distress becomes much more difficult if participants are anonymous internet users who may not disclose their vulnerability status (Frankel & Siang, 1999) or just break off interaction and be inaccessible to any further query or intervention.

A particular area of concern in relation to harm is the issue of researching the internet use of minors. Vulnerable children and teenagers may use internet facilities in problematic or risky ways, from posting inappropriate photos or comments on social networking sites, divulging drug use or under-age sexual activity, to cyber-bullying, or the use of pro-anorexia, self-harm or suicide websites. On the one hand, achieving a better understanding of these phenomena through research is desirable; on the other hand, conducting research with minors on these issues could be considered ethically problematic. Difficulties regarding parental consent would be a significant obstacle to such research, not just because of general issues of anonymity, but especially because children may be very hesitant to even inform their parents about their internet presence and activities (Stern, 2004). Child protection concerns are an additional issue. Child protection guidelines might require researchers to intervene if they become aware of children who are at risk of significant harm, but to do so in online contexts is likely to be extremely challenging. Even the prospect that child protection interventions might be attempted is likely to make potential participants extremely hesitant to allow researchers access. Moreover, accessing such sensitive materials without transparent and explicit consent would pose the familiar problems of privacy.

4. Irish research ethics guidance documents and their application to internet research

First of all, Irish internet researchers need to be aware that their research might be subject to research ethics review requirements. In comparison to other jurisdictions, especially in the English speaking world, the Irish research ethics landscape is still comparatively lightly regulated. Outside of the EU Clinical Trials Directive (Irish Statute Book, 2004), there are currently no binding national regulations in place in relation to research ethics review. However, that does not mean that research ethics review is entirely optional. All health research involving patients or staff of the Irish Health Service Executive (HSE) is expected to be reviewed by a HSE Research Ethics Committee (REC). The Irish Health Information and Quality Authority (HIQA) now has the responsibility for the governance of health RECs, and is in the process of developing standards for those RECs. In the academic sector, most institutions in Ireland have RECs that review research conducted by their employees and students. Institutions differ in whether they regard research ethics review as compulsory for all research and in the level of scrutiny that different types of proposals need to undergo, but generally speaking researchers are expected to undergo research ethics review for all research projects that involve human subjects.

What does this mean for internet research? As Walther (2002) outlined in his paper, many research methodologies on the internet do not meet the criteria of human subject research and are not likely to pose any risk to persons whose data is being considered in research. However, as much of the literature reviewed above indicates, it is important not to be cavalier about the level of risk that may be involved in internet research. Especially in disciplines that may have less experience with considering ethical concerns typical to social science research, like engineering, computer science or linguistics, the landscape of relevant ethical challenges to consider – outside clear health and safety concerns – may be largely unfamiliar to researchers. Accordingly, it is essential for internet researchers to clarify with their local research ethics committee whether the research they are conducting falls under its remit, even if at first sight it does not appear to them to pose obvious ethical problems.

Data protection is an important concern in internet research, due to the easy transfer and multiplication of electronic data. In the Irish context, the *Data Protection Act 1988 and the Data Protection (Amendment) Act 2003* are the main laws dealing with data protection (Data Protection Commissioner, n.d.). These do not specify specific concerns for research, but state general requirements for dealing with personal data. The detailed discussion of legal requirements is outside of the scope of the present chapter, but some general concerns with relevance to research data will be briefly outlined here. According to the Data Protection Acts, "personal data" is defined as "data relating to a living individual who is or can be identified either from the data or from the data in conjunction with other information that is in, or is likely to come into, the possession of the data controller" (Data Protection Commissioner, n.d., p. 2). As already indicated above, much of the data collected in internet research may not be personal data in the strict sense, and might therefore not be considered to fall under these requirements. However, as this definition clarifies, researchers need to be aware of the potential overall identifiability of data collected, even though it may have been originally collected as anonymous or pseudonymous data.

In relation to data security, the Data Protection Acts require researchers and other data controllers to have sufficient security measures in place to prevent any unauthorised access to potentially identifiable personal research data. The more sensitive the data, the more restrictive the requirements regarding access control. Internet research by its very nature deals with electronic data which is easily transferable and carries the risk of allowing unintended access to non-authorised persons.

Professional ethics codes are another frequently useful source of research ethical guidance. However, in relation to internet research, most of the existing professional ethics codes in the Irish context (for example An Bord Altranais, 2007; Medical Council Ireland, 2009) do not contain items with specific relevance to internet research; their statements on consent, confidentiality, and harm/risk minimisation are of a more general nature and are primarily focused on professional service delivery rather than research; those parts in the medical and nursing documents that address the conduct of research focus mostly on clinical trials research. Internet-based health research as discussed for example by Eysenbach and Till (2001) is not (yet) recognised as a research area worthy of special consideration in these documents. The recently published draft HSE *National Consent Policy, Part 3 – Research* (NCAG, 2012) is specifically targeted towards issues arising in relation to consent in health research and contains many helpful clarifications regarding a wide range of concerns relating to consent, but again does not cover concerns specific to internet research.

Psychology is probably the academic discipline most likely to engage in internet research involving interaction with human participants or the analysis of potentially sensitive data. Unlike the codes of other professional organisations, the Psychological Society of Ireland Code of Ethics (PSI, 2011) addresses a number of ethical issues with a degree of specificity that allows for the reflection on its implications for internet research. Section 1.2.7 of the code states, in line with the Irish data commissioner, that the researcher has the responsibility to ensure anonymisation or destruction of data as soon as identifiability is not required any more for the task for which data was collected, which has implications for electronic data management practices.

Other sections in the code address the issue of privacy which was outlined above as being particularly relevant for research on online communities. Section 1.3.17 seems to assume a clear distinction between public and private behaviour and explicitly exempts public behaviour from consent requirements in relation to taking audio, video and photographic records. However, Section 1.2.2 states to "[t]ake care not to infringe, in research or service activities, on the *personally or culturally defined private space* of individuals or groups unless clear and appropriate permission is granted to do so" (PSI, 2011, p. 6, emphasis added), thereby highlighting that what is private for a particular person or in a particular context may not always be clearly identifiable by an outsider and that the perception of what is private can differ between persons and cultures. Section 1.3.9 states that informed consent needs to be sought for all research activities which involve "obtrusive measures, invasion into the private lives of research participants, risks to the participant" (PSI, 2011, p. 7). While it remains unclear which level of intrusion triggers a demand for informed consent, the literature on research in online communities has highlighted that the threshold for perceiving research interventions as intrusive might be significantly lower than frequently assumed. Finally, section 3.3.14 might be understood as a note of caution in relation to using novel research approaches, as e.g., some approaches to internet research: "Seek an independent and adequate ethical review of the balance of risks and potential benefits of all research which involves procedures of unknown consequence, or where pain, discomfort, or harm are possible, before making a decision to proceed" (PSI, 2011, p. 12).

One of the specific areas of research where explicit ethical guidelines exist in Ireland is the area of research with children. The recently published *Guidance for developing ethical research projects involving children* by the Department for Children and Youth Affairs (DCYA, 2012) and also a comprehensive section in the HSE *Draft National Consent Policy* by the National Consent Advisory Group (NCAG, 2012) address some specific requirements of conducting research with children in the Irish context. Research with children also needs to conform to the requirements of the *Children First* guidelines which state relevant child protection requirements (DCYA, 2011). Two major concerns in relation to children's research are children's protection from risk and the appropriate realisation of informed consent, which requires the involvement of all relevant stakeholders and the provision information in an appropriate format.

Due to the special protection of the family under the Irish constitution, the current consensus is that any social research with children under 18 strictly requires parental consent. As already indicated above, the accidental inclusion of children who are not identified as such is a real possibility in internet research that is conducted with participants whose real life identity is not ascertained during the research (Ess & AoIR, 2002; Frankel & Siang, 1999; Hudson & Bruckman, 2004). This poses a number of ethical concerns. Informed consent is one prominent concern in this context insofar as children might participate in online studies without parental consent. Guidelines for children's research stipulate that generally the threshold for acceptable risk in children's research is much lower than for research with adults. Accordingly, even if the subject matter itself might not be considered inappropriate, risk assessment for adults might come to different results if the intended participants are children rather than adults. In relation to risk, the *Children First* guidelines are also significant, insofar as children's researchers are required to be competent in assessing and adequately responding to child protection issues by alerting relevant agencies in the case of children at risk of significant harm or abuse (DCYA, 2011). They might require children's researchers, under some circumstances, to make such disclosure against the children's wishes, thereby breaching confidentiality. In research with participants whose real identities remain unclear, however, no such response to emerging child protection concerns will be possible. However, as the DCYA (2012) guidance document states, it is also essential that research addresses topics that are relevant to children's lives and actively engages children's viewpoints, including on potentially difficult or problematic issues. Research in relation to aspects of children's internet use might be very appropriate and valuable; however, relevant safeguards need to be put into place and researchers have to make sure that their research is in compliance with child protection requirements.

An additional area of research for which guidelines for ethical research have been put into place is the area of disability research. The National Disability

Authority (NDA) guidelines identify issues in disability research (NDA, 2009). The most pertinent in the context of online research are probably the issues of accessibility and inclusiveness of research. For some forms of disability, the internet as a research medium might be more accessible for research participants than traditional face to face or pen and paper research (Bowker & Tuffin, 2004). The internet as communication medium might allow participants to circumvent physical access problems, fatigue, or verbal communication difficulties. At the same time, internet research can only access persons with disabilities for whom written communication is a suitable mode of communication. One particularly important point in the NDA (2009) guidelines is the importance of inclusiveness and participation. Accordingly, it is essential that internet research on disability be conducted with a view to facilitating active and respectful involvement of participants with disability, and particular care will be required in planning an ethical approach to using materials created by persons with disabilities.

5.   Conclusion

As this chapter has shown, there are numerous ethical concerns that need to be considered in conducting internet research, most prominently the question of the public or private nature of online materials, the moral status of online identities, requirements and suitable practices of informed consent, data management, concerns around harm, benefit and vulnerability and the inclusion of participants that require particular protections. This paper has also identified a number of Irish documents that can provide guidance on issues arising in internet research. However, these guidance documents do not explicitly address internet research as such. Accordingly, Irish researchers in this emerging field should refer to international documents that outline good practice, from the AAAS and AoIR guidelines to emerging national and professional guidelines and to ongoing specialist discussions of emerging issues, for example in the journals *Ethics and Information Technology* or *Journal of Information Ethics*, and analyse carefully the implications of the Irish guidance documents to ensure they are working within the boundaries of acceptable practice in Ireland. Because of the specific characteristics and challenges of the internet as research medium, Irish internet researchers might take the publication of the present volume as an opportunity to create a forum of discussion of their research and its challenges. If it appears that certain challenges occur frequently in a particular area of research, they should bring these to the attention of their professional associations or other representative bodies, to ensure that these issues will be addressed in future statements of good practice and research ethics guidance documents. While this chapter could not do justice to the wide range of internet research methodologies and topics, each with their own set of ethical concerns, it has hopefully given readers an idea of common ethical concerns in internet research that will allow them to further reflect on the complexities of ethical issues encountered in their own research.

References

An Bord Altranais. (2007). *Guidance to nurses and midwives regarding ethical conduct of nursing and midwifery research.* Retrieved from http://www.nursingboard.ie/ GetAttachment.aspx?id=322b92ac-60f6-48c6-8ec6-88c087a8013f

Barratt, M., & Lenton, S. (2010). Beyond recruitment. Participatory online research with people who use drugs. *International Journal of Internet Research Ethics, 3*(1), 69-86. Retrieved from http://www.ijire.net/issue_3.1/6_barratt_lenton.pdf

Binik, Y. M., Mah, K., & Kiesler, S. (1999). Ethical issues in conducting sex research on the Internet. *The Journal of Sex Research, 36*(1), 82-90. doi: 10.1080/00224499909551971

Bowker, N., & Tuffin, K. (2004). Using the online medium for discursive research about people with disabilities. *Social Science Computer Review, 22*(2), 228-241. doi: 10.1177/0894439303262561

Bruckman, A. (2002). *Ethical Guidelines for Online Research.* Retrieved from http://www. cc.gatech.edu/~asb/ethics

Craft, A. J. (2007). Sin in cyber-eden: understanding the metaphysics and morals of virtual worlds. *Ethics and Information Technology, 9*(3), 205-217. doi: 10.1007/s10676-007-9144-4

Data Protection Commissioner. (n.d.). *Data Protection Acts 1988 and 2003: A Guide For Data Controllers.* Retrieved from http://www.dataprotection.ie/documents/forms/ NewAGuideForDataControllers.pdf

DCYA. (2011). *Children First - National Guidance for the Protection and Welfare of Children.* Dublin: Department of Children and Youth Affairs. Retrieved from http://www.dcya.gov.ie/documents/child_welfare_protection/ChildrenFirst.pdf

DCYA. (2012). *Guidance for developing ethical research projects involving children.* Dublin: Department of Children and Youth Affairs. Retrieved from http://www.dcya.gov.ie/documents/Publications/Ethics_Guidance.pdf

Dibbell, J. (1993, December 21). A Rape in Cyberspace or How an Evil Clown, a Haitian Trickster Spirit, Two Wizards, and a Cast of Dozens Turned a Database Into a Society. *The Village Voice*, 36-42. Retrieved from http://loki.stockton.edu/~kinsellt/stuff/dibbelrapeincyberspace.html

Elgesem, D. (2002). What is special about the ethical issues in online research? *Ethics and Information Technology, 4*(3), 195-203. doi: 10.1023/A:1021320510186

Ess, C. (2007). Internet Research Ethics. In A. Joinson, K. McKenna, T. Postmes, & U. Reips (Eds.), *The Oxford Handbook of Internet Psychology* (pp. 487-502). New York: Oxford University Press.

Ess, C., & AoIR ethics working committee. (2002). *Ethical decision-making and Internet research: Recommendations from the AoIR ethics working committee.* Retrieved from www.aoir.org/reports/ethics.pdf

Eysenbach, G., & Till, J. E. (2001). Ethical issues in qualitative research on internet communities. *British Medical Journal (BMJ), 323*(7321), 1003-1005. doi: 10.1136/bmj.323.7321.1103

Finn, J., & Lavitt, M. (1994). Computer-based self-help groups for sexual abuse survivors. *Social Work with Groups, 17*(1-2), 21-46. doi: 10.1300/J009v17n01_03

Frankel, M. S., & Siang, S. (1999). *Ethical and Legal Aspects of Human Subjects Research on the Internet: A report of a Workshop, June 10-11, 1999, Washington, DC.* New York: American Association for the Advancement of Science. Retrieved from http://www.aaas.org/spp/sfrl/projects/intres/report.pdf

Griffiths, M., & Whitty, M. (2010). Online behavioral tracking in Internet gambling research: ethical and methodological issues. *International Journal of Internet Research Ethics, 3*(1), 104-117. Retrieved from http://ijire.net/issue_3.1/8_Griffiths_Whitty.pdf

Hudson, J. M., & Bruckman, A. (2004). "Go Away": Participant Objections to Being Studied and the Ethics of Chatroom Research. *The Information Society: An International Journal, 20*(2), 127-139. doi: 10.1080/01972240490423030

Irish Statute Book. (2004). *European Communities (Clinical Trials on Medicinal Products for Human Use) Regulations, 2004* (S.I. No. 190 of 2004). Retrieved from http://www.irishstatutebook.ie/2004/en/si/0190.html

King, S. A. (1996). Researching internet communities: proposed ethical guidelines for the reporting of results. *The Information Society: An International Journal, 12*(2), 119-128. doi: 10.1080/713856145

Lange, P. G. (2007). Publicly Private and Privately Public: Social Networking on YouTube. *Journal of Computer-Mediated Communication, 13*(1), 361-380. doi: 10.1111/j.1083-6101.2007.00400.x

Medical Council Ireland. (2009). *Guide to professional conduct and ethics for registered medical practitioners* (7th ed.). Retrieved from http://www.medicalcouncil.ie/Public-Information/Professional-Conduct-Ethics/The-Guide-to-Professional-Conduct-and-Ethics-for-Registered-Medical-Practitioners.pdf

NCAG. (2012). *National Consent Advisory Group: National Consent Policy. Part 3 – Research* (Draft Document for Consultation). Retrieved from http://www.hse.ie/eng/about/Who/qualityandpatientsafety/Patient_Safety/National_Consent_Advisory_Group/ncag3.pdf

NDA. (2009). *Disability Research Series 13: Ethical Guidance for Research with People with Disabilities.* National Disability Authority. Retrieved from http://www.nda.ie/cntmgmtnew.nsf/0/232F61AE5397A93D802576650052B3B9/$File/EthicalGuidanceforResearchwithPeoplewithDisabilities.pdf

Nissenbaum, H. (2004). Privacy as contextual integrity. *Washington Law Review, 79*(1), 119-158. Retrieved from http://digital.law.washington.edu/dspace-law/bitstream/handle/1773.1/61/volume79.pdf

Pittenger, D. J. (2003). Internet Research: An Opportunity to Revisit Classic Ethical Problems in Behavioral Research. *Ethics & Behavior, 13*(1), 45-60. doi: 10.1207/S15327019EB1301_08

PSI. (2011). *The Psychological Society of Ireland: Code of Professional Ethics* (Revised November 2010). Retrieved from http://www.psychologicalsociety.ie/page/file_dwn/25/PSI%202011-12%20Code%20of%20Ethics.pdf

Roberts, L., Smith, L., & Pollock, C. (2004). Conducting Ethical Research Online: Respect for Individuals, Identities and the Ownership of Words. In E. A. Buchanan (Ed.), *Readings in Virtual Research Ethics: Issues and Controversies* (pp. 156-173). Hershey, PA: Information Science Publishing.

Rodham, K., & Gavin, J. (2006). The ethics of using the internet to collect qualitative research data. *Research Ethics, 2*(3), 92-97. doi: 10.1177/174701610600200303

Scharf, B. F. (1999). Beyond Netiquette: The Ethics of Doing Naturalistic Discourse Research on the Internet. In S. Jones (Ed.), *Doing Internet Research: Critical Issues and Methods for Examining the Net* (pp. 243-256). London: Sage Publications.

Sixsmith, J., & Murray, C. D. (2001). Ethical issues in the documentary data analysis of Internet posts and archives. *Qualitative Health Research, 11*(3), 423-432. doi: 10.1177/104973201129119109

Stern, S. R. (2004). Studying adolescents online: a consideration of ethical issues. In E. A. Buchanan (Ed.), *Readings in Virtual Research Ethics: Issues and Controversies* (pp. 274-287). Hershey, PA: Information Science Publishing.

Van Gelder, L. (1985/1991). The strange case of the electronic lover. Reprinted in C. Dunlop & R. Kling (Eds.), *Computerization and Controversy: Value Conflicts and Social Choices* (pp. 364-375). Boston: Academic Press.

Walther, J. B. (2002). Research ethics in Internet-enabled research: human subjects issues and methodological myopia. *Ethics and Information Technology, 4*(3), 205-216. doi: 10.1023/A:1021368426115

Wolfendale, J. (2007). My avatar, my self: Virtual harm and attachment. *Ethics and Information Technology, 9*(2), 111-119. doi: 10.1007/s10676-006-9125-z

Zimmer, M. (2010a). "But the data is already public": on the ethics of research in Facebook. *Ethics and Information Technology, 12*(4), 313-325. doi: 10.1007/s10676-010-9227-5

Zimmer, M. & commentaries (2010b, February 12). Is it ethical to harvest public Twitter accounts without consent? *Michael Zimmer.org*. Retrieved from http://michaelzimmer.org/2010/02/12/is-it-ethical-to-harvest-public-twitter-accounts-without-consent/

3 Studying Young People's Blogs: Ethical Implications

Cathy Fowley[1]

Abstract

A s internet research was gradually established as a discipline, whose focus and/or locus is the internet (Rall, 2007), ethical issues came to the fore. These issues, often centering around the shifting concept of privacy and ownership of text, consider new practices and communications online, and increasingly, the conduct of ethical research within various sites on the internet. This chapter draws on a five year study of young people's blogs in Ireland which used an ethnographic approach to two different groups of bloggers, varying in age from 17 to 23. Ethical issues were identified from the start of the project, and indeed included at design stage; some of the issues arose from the multidisciplinary nature of internet research, and these will be examined in this chapter in the first place; current recommendations available to the internet researcher will be addressed, as well as the ethical practices of researchers in the field of blogging. Several approaches and ethical solutions will be reported from within the qualitative research tradition. This chapter will then examine issues which have been identified as "conceptual gaps" by Zimmer (2010), illustrated in light of this ethnographic study of young Irish bloggers, in particular the concept of privacy.

Keywords: ethical practices, ethical issues, privacy, ownership of text, blog.

1. Dublin City University, Dublin, Ireland; cathy.fowley@dcu.ie

How to cite this chapter: Fowley, C. (2013). Studying Young People's Blogs: Ethical Implications. In C. Fowley, C. English, & S. Thouësny (Eds.), *Internet Research, Theory, and Practice: Perspectives from Ireland* (pp. 33-54). Dublin: © Research-publishing.net.

1.   The ethics of internet research

The interdisciplinary aspect of most internet research brings its own ethical issues, due to the difference in the approach to ethics from various disciplines, such as social sciences, which take their model from medical science, or literary studies, which considers people as authors and treats them as such (Ess & the AoIR ethics working committee, 2002). For researchers from the field of humanities, these conflicting frameworks should be acknowledged in the case of a cross-disciplinary research project.

Social sciences ethical norms are derived from the ethical norms of the medical field. The basic ethical principles are seen as autonomy, beneficence, and justice (Greig & Taylor, 1999). One of the main issues is that of informed consent of participants in a study, and of the duty of the researcher to do no harm. Whereas these basic ethical principles of research cannot be denied, the advent of a new cultural context has led to the belief that "[o]nline research is marked as a special category in which the institutionalized understandings of the ethics of research must be re-examined" (Hine, 2005, p. 5).

Within a tradition of literary studies, Serfaty (2004) contends that a literary approach to blogs frees the researcher of certain ethical considerations, as the text is studied rather than the author, and is in fact a "self-contained, self referential artefact" (p. 10). She also decided to avoid any contact with the diarists she studied in order to avoid any possible relationship, which she sees as detrimental to the quality of the research, as she feels that informing the participants "ultimately amounts to granting them the right to oversee the research project" (Serfaty, 2004, p. 12).

The literary approach to studying online texts considers the participant in internet communication as an author and the text as a published literary artefact (Ess, 2002). A social sciences approach to the same study will consider the author as a participant in the research project, and as such will grant her some protection in ethical guidelines. Bruckman (2002) argues that the 'semi-publishing' of material online by 'amateur artists' offers new challenges and requires new approaches to ethical dilemmas, dealing with liminal spaces between public and private.

Both approaches are also subject to emerging netiquette, and sometimes heralded by the use of Creative Commons[1] convention in blogs. Indeed bloggers in general follow emerging rules of netiquette, which do not allow for copying or republishing without crediting the original author, by name and through hyperlinks to the text quoted. Similarly, when a blog post is picked up by print media and the content in used offline, it is seen as plagiarism if the blog is not quoted as the original source. This has led some bloggers to insert a Creative Commons license in their blogs, which allows sharing and non-commercial use with attribution.

In any case, ethical approaches are complicated by several other issues if the participants/authors are children or young people, who warrant increased protection: the authors of the blogs in this study could be regarded as a vulnerable group in social sciences disciplines, where research involving children and young people is governed by its own set of rules (Greig & Taylor, 1999). Mixing these two aspects brings out a third set of ethical issues, particular to the study of young people online, which merits special consideration.

Recent developments in youth research have changed assumptions about transitions between youth and adulthood, and notably led to the gradual replacement of the terms 'adolescence' and 'adolescents' by the terms 'youth' and 'young people', as well as the introduction of the new term of 'young adult' (Bois-Reymond & Chisholm, 2006). This trend is notably echoed in literature, which now discerns between children's literature and the newer genre of young adult fiction. It is now accepted that youth encompasses a wide range of ages and stages of development, and that it extends into ages which had previously been considered as adult; this longer youth period tends to mix within the same category people of very different ages and psychological and psychosocial development: a ten year old child does not have the same

---

1. http://creativecommons.org/

understanding as a twenty year old woman. However, some young people, albeit not children, remain legally minor, and ethical issues regarding them occupy a grey area.

Informed consent is one of the main issues in research with children and young people, who are traditionally represented as vulnerable groups in social sciences. Obtaining consent from young people is a relatively new notion, as children for a long time were considered mere objects of research, reflecting their historical place in society (Greig & Taylor, 1999). However, within the past decades, it has been recognised that children should have a say in research that involves them.

> "Researching youth also brings research ethics – a professional challenge – to the forefront in considering how young people can and should be informed and included as active research subjects in studies about youth" (Chisholm, 2006, p. 18).

The Declaration of Helsinki (1964) states that not only is consent to be sought from a legal guardian, but also from children themselves. Informed consent from adolescents seems to be a grey area. In England, the Family Law Reform Act of 1969[1] states that, in the medical field, children from 16 to 17 years old are presumed to be competent to consent to treatment, and a similar situation exists in Ireland. When it comes to consent online, the office of the Irish data commissioner's website[2] advises that

> "[t]he minimum age at which consent can be legitimately obtained is not defined in the Data Protection Act, 1988. Section 2A(1) of the Acts states that consent cannot be obtained from a person who, by reason of age, is likely to be unable to appreciate the nature and effect of such consent. Judging maturity will vary from case to case" (para. 1-2).

---

1. http://www.legislation.gov.uk/ukpga/1969/46

2. http://www.dataprotection.ie/viewdoc.asp?m=m&fn=/documents/guidance/3gm5.htm

It goes on to refer to the General Practice Information Technology[1] (GPIT) guide in the medical area, which defines the age of consent at 16. The Office of the Data Commissioner adds that for marketing purposes, 14 can be considered as a reasonable consent age, and that companies should ensure that the individual understands the implications of giving consent.

1.1.   Directives and guidelines

Elgesem (2002) refers to the the guidelines published by the body for research ethics in Norway, regarding ethical research in social sciences and the humanities, which identifies two broad categories of conflict of interest: those dealing with the integrity of the research process, and those dealing with the integrity of research subjects. Elgesem (2002) posits that online research ethics can be drawn from offline research ethics, with some proviso, which refer to the problematic private/public dichotomy. The presence of a fragmented audience online is a major difference and is linked to the expectation of a "limited and homogeneous audience" (Elgesem, 2002, p. 202) by online participants, even when the fora are not password-protected and could thus be seen as widely public. The issue of privacy, which has been deemed irrelevant for published texts (Serfaty, 2004) thus becomes an issue of perceived privacy.

1.2.   AoIR recommendations

The Association of Internet Researchers published in 2002 a set of guidelines from their ethics working group, guidelines which became a major source of information for internet researchers (Ess & the AoIR ethics working committee, 2002). Whilst they acknowledged the existence and validity of various ethical frameworks, they also highlighted some major questions relevant to internet research, amongst which the various venues which can be found and researched and the different ethical expectations which their users may have. Similarly, they advised to ascertain whether the participants in the project should be considered more as authors or as research subjects, as this perception also

---

1. http://www.icgp.ie/go/in_the_practice/information_technology

carries different ethical expectations. Whether offline or online, children should be afforded increased ethical protection, and this was also reflected in the AoIR guidelines. These were the guidelines which were followed at the time of research. However, online researchers are constantly confronted to new spaces, new norms, and new ethical problems. The Association of Internet Researchers has thus published a new set of guidelines, stressing the importance of context, whilst also identifying some areas which are specific to internet research.

1.3. Research ethics committees

Markham and Baym (2009) conducted research in the perception of internet research ethical issues amongst Institutional Review Boards (IRBs) in the United States. Most were found to have no guidelines whatsoever on internet research (62%); in the qualitative study carried out along with the questionnaire, the need for education of IRBs was a recurring theme; issues of data security and consent were most problematic for IRBs, and most frequently mentioned were consent and privacy issues which are difficult to comprehend in a new space. Some initiatives have been led by educators and researchers in an effort to adapt guidelines and recommendations to the study of online communities: a program led by Bruckman (2002) had thus enabled undergraduates to learn how to conduct ethical research in online communities, with an emphasis on the protection of human subjects.

European universities seem to encounter the same problems in adapting to new contexts of research, and some have issued specific guidelines: University of Bristol, UK Kids Online in the London School of Economics for example have guidelines for internet research and internet research with children and young people. In many cases however, the public/private divide seems to be the main guideline which can be applied to online research: texts which are publicly available are thus exempt from ethical review, except in the cases of vulnerable populations. Indeed the study of blogs brings these issues to the fore, as blog posts are often considered public texts, by the audience as well as bloggers who seek public recognition.

2.   Research on blogging: researchers in practice

For Herring, Scheidt, Wright, and Bonus (2005), blogging is seen as many things by many people. For journalists, it is about news from an alternative source, for scholars it is about research and knowledge sharing, but for many private individuals, it is about expression and self-empowerment. Their study endeavours to find the properties of blogs at a moment in time, and categorise them as a new genre, situated with respect to offline genres and the broader genre ecology of the internet.

It is now argued that the time has gone for the relevance of the word blog (Bruns & Jacobs, 2006; Efimova, 2009b). Indeed a lot of the misunderstandings within the blogging world and misinformation in the print media come from an overuse of the word, with no strict definition: newspapers now commonly introduce a blog section to their online editions, and indeed some introduce blog sections to their paper edition. Some predict that the word will soon only be used with a qualifier, as in research blogging, community blogging, or diary blogging (Bruns & Jacobs, 2006), and it is increasingly necessary to define the type of blog which is the object of research (Efimova, 2009b; Nowson, 2006). Indeed when it comes to ethical issues in research on blogs, this definition becomes essential, if only to ascertain the different levels of expectations of privacy from the blogger's point of view.

Moreover, different approaches are taken by researchers from different disciplines and traditions. In some cases, the blogger is seen solely as an author. Serfaty (2004) studies personal blogs, where bloggers are seen as authors, and thus exempt from consent according to humanities and literary studies traditions. She also acknowledges their identity as potential participants, yet denies their participation as threatening the integrity of the research. The ethical approach she takes is to treat bloggers as literary authors, and thus she does not ask for consent, and does not attempt to conceal their online identities. Hendrick (2012) also sees the blogger as an author or intellectual, indeed she is a blogger herself, and sometimes part of a blogging community which she studies. Hendrick (2012) does not ask for consent, nor does she anonymise her data, as she follows criteria led out by Pace and Livingston (2005) exempting from consent material which is publicly archived, is not password protected, is not sensitive, and no state or site policy prohibits its use.

Efimova (2009a), in her PhD research, considers bloggers as public intellectuals; she points out the fundamental difference between the knowledge or professional blogger and the academic, in which the blogger cites other blogs and links back to them, thus creating a web of knowledge, whereas the academic anonymises sources. Efimova (2009a) treats the bloggers from her study as public intellectuals, and thus asks no permission, but disseminates the results of her research through her blog, while linking to the bloggers cited, thus choosing an ethical approach that follows ethnographic sensibilities.

Different ethical choices are taken by researchers who study young people's blogs (Brake, 2009; Fowley, 2011). Brake (2009) feels an ethical and moral obligation towards the young people whose blogs he studies. Not only does he ask for consent from the bloggers, but he acts as an educator, pointing out the potential problems in allowing a researcher to publish part of their blog posts. Indeed, despite their consent, he does not reproduce text from the blogs, because "several of those who make their weblogs available freely online (and would be prepared to have them publicised in an academic study) may come to regret that choice later in life" (Brake, 2009, p. 76).

3.   Conceptual gaps in research ethics

As outlined by the AoIR recommendations, and illustrated by the examples above, researchers are guided not only by rules, recommendations and best practices, but also by their own moral compass, and their knowledge of the context in which their research is based (Ess & the AoIR ethics working committee, 2002).

Zimmer (2010) identifies several issues which epitomise the differences between offline and online research. I used his idea of conceptual gap and correlate it with my own ethical choices. Indeed as an internet researcher attempting to fill in the required forms for my university's Research Ethics Committee, I came across those conceptual gaps, relating to the issues of consent, anonymity, harm and privacy. The following section will thus match those concepts to issues encountered in my research, after defining the type of ethnography which was chosen.

The research identified and followed two groups of young bloggers in Ireland: the first group, which will be referred to in this chapter, was formed around a few young people who had attended a summer school together; their blogs became a means of keeping in touch with their friends, as well as recounting their daily lives. At the heart of the second group were two young bloggers who managed their friendship at a distance, as well as interacting with others. All the blogs were on the *LiveJournal* platform, which was most popular for young people at the time.

The methodological choice of ethnographic tools and methods was a result of the theoretical lens used to approach the study; however, it was also heavily influenced by the ethical approach that underpinned the study.

> "Consider this tentative axiom: methods first, ethics follow. This axiom focuses attention on the fact that ethics are embedded in one's everyday method of approaching, understanding, evaluating, and producing academic texts about a social phenomenon. To say methods first; ethics follow is to emphasize that all methods decisions are in actuality ethics decisions and that all ethics decisions are in actuality methods decisions" (Markham, 2006, p. 7).

As the internet becomes more enmeshed in daily life, and the demarcations between online and offline relationships become increasingly blurred, many have called for ethnographies which follow the participants offline and online throughout their daily lives (boyd, 2008). I did not however follow this trend in this research project, where, on the contrary, I ensured that the ethnography remained online only, and this for several reasons. I was guided first of all by ethical considerations, due mainly to the nature of the study and of the age of the young bloggers (Fowley, 2011). When the study started, in 2005, few young people had started blogging in Ireland, and the search for the initial bloggers had to start online. Whereas it may have been easy to move an ethnography project from an offline context to an online context, it seemed ethically dubious to initiate contact with young people online and then attempt to meet them offline.

3.1. Consent

There are two problematic aspects to the issue of consent in internet research. The first is linked to the issue of authenticity, and the other one to access to the offline identity of the participant. The oft-quoted *New Yorker* cartoon states that on the internet, no one knows if you're a dog. Indeed, if bloggers for example have chosen to blog under a pseudonym, it can be difficult, time-consuming, and sometimes impossible to ascertain the 'real' identity of the author; naturally, no one knows how old you are either, at least in theory. However, young people in particular tend to be mostly truthful in the representation of their age (Scheidt, 2006). Indeed most young people now live a seamless life between online and offline, where their network of friends follow them from one space to the other (boyd, 2008; Ito et al., 2008; Palfrey & Gasser, 2008). Even if the age of the blogger can be ascertained, the identity remains that which they have chosen, and if they have chosen to link their blog to an email address bearing a similar pseudonym, only their online identity can be verified, and only their online identity can give consent to take part in the research.

This problem is naturally more acute in the case of online only ethnographies, and was amplified by my reluctance to request personal information. I felt that such an attempt would be contrary to best practice and indeed to current recommendations to parents and children or teenagers, who are advised never to reveal any personal information to a stranger on the internet. This was also the reason for the methodological choice of an online only ethnography: I had found these young peoples' blogs online, and thus all communication remained online. This choice of course also implied that I would not have access to their parents for consent, which in turn influenced the data sampling, as I chose not to interact with anyone under sixteen without parental consent. The permanence of the digital text meant that I did however have access to some parts of the blogs when the writer was under sixteen, in the case when the blog had been started before that age, with the consent of the now-sixteen or eighteen year old blogger.

3.2. Anonymity

It should first of all be noted that the participants were anonymous from the outset, as they did not blog under their own name, nor did they usually reveal their full name or address. However, a pseudo, or in this particular case a *LiveJournal* name, is often used on different fora and is as such part of the online person (Bruckman, 2002); the use of this pseudo can thus be seen as a failure to anonymise the research by the participants. I decided to use double pseudonyms, and asked the bloggers if they wished to choose a new pseudo themselves, so that they could retain some power over their texts and their presence in the research. Some decided to create their own names, others did not answer the message sent to them, and were randomly allocated a new pseudonym.

However, it could be argued that anonymity is not always possible, even if the bloggers use pseudonyms, as their life stories contain elements relating to events, places and people which may help to identify them. If Lally (2009) is aware of the 'tyranny of distance' linked to internet research, in my case, I was very much aware of the tyranny of proximity; Ireland is a small country, with a small population, where the famous 'degrees of separations' are fewer than in more populated areas. Whyte (2006) points out that, when it comes to research on specific populations, it is practically impossible to guarantee anonymity in Ireland. This local issue amplified another anonymity problem online, due this time to the power of search engines. If texts are quoted in a publication, these excerpts can be entered in search engines and the blog from which they were selected can thus be found. A significant number of the quotes were taken from blogs which are no longer publicly accessible. When excerpts from the blogs were chosen, the bloggers were advised of which part of their text was being cited and were also advised to lock the relevant entry if it was still public. Even though in more conventional settings, this might be construed as perverting data, in an emergent social space where younger people can lack adult guidance, it should be a moral imperative for the researcher to educate and protect the young participants in a study.

3.3.   Harm

This concept, and its adaptation to online spaces, can be linked to the concept of privacy, anonymity, and space. Some sensitive information, some texts of a very personal nature, when taken out of context, can be met by a public for which they were not intended. This breach of the expectation of privacy could indeed lead to harm for the participants, in the case for example of young people who may be openly gay online, but not offline.

Another ethical issue, this time of concern to the researcher, is the possibility of encountering disturbing texts. These could possibly be relating an obvious danger for a blogger, such as depression, risk of suicide, incidence of abuse or even relating the possibility of danger to the public, suggested by rantings and threats of violent action. Bearing in mind that information posted on internet sites is not always truthful, and that in some cases the text belongs more to fiction than autobiography, some practical steps are however possible: contact with the platform security officer is the first step to take, as the companies have requested personal details when the blog/social network page was set up. If the matter is more urgent, contact should be attempted through the platform with the named friends of the adolescent who are likely to know her in real life, or to have access to personal information such as telephone number or address, and they should be requested to contact the person, their family, or a relevant official body. These issues are being discussed regularly amongst internet researchers, and some propositions have been made in the US for an anonymous online support forum for young people.

3.4.   Privacy

The AoIR recommendations highlight the concept of *expectation* of privacy in various online spaces (Ess & the AoIR ethics working committee, 2002). The binary private/public concept is no longer of use when it comes to the internet, and this issue is at the heart of many moral panics and many misunderstandings. Different venues carry different expectations, some fora are open, others require registration and password and as such are *felt* as more private. The motivation of the writer can also influence this perception and expectation of privacy: whereas some bloggers consider blogging as a form of publishing, expecting to be cited as authors, others regard their blogs as personal artefacts which they expect a small selection of readers to share. In knowledge blogs, the aim is dissemination of knowledge. For diary-style blogs, the content is different, as is the intent, and instead of publication of 'one to many', the aim is for 'one to some'.

4.   Publicly available data

Several Resesarch Ethics Committees in Ireland consider that publicly available data is exempt from ethics approval, and texts freely available online tend to be categorised as such. Indeed this attitude is also prevalent when it comes to so-called Big Data, among which is the growing mass of personal data collected by various social media sites. The availability of this Big Data has been seen as the new currency, and its mining and analysis has become the subject of much research. However, the lack of contextualisation has been flagged by danah boyd (2010), who stated that "Just Because It is Accessible Doesn't Mean Using It is Ethical" (Section "Methodologically sound approaches to big data", para. 5).

The conceptual gaps identified by Zimmer (2010) were thus all obvious throughout the research. However, despite a concerted ethical reflection, and the integration of ethical principles in the research design, issues emerged as soon as the presence of the researcher became known to the participants. These would eventually be separated into the two groups mentioned earlier, the first group, built around the first blogger I had encountered, Saila, included her friends Homi, Corcra, Planet and Disco (girls) as well as Brightears and

Fry (boys). The other group, for the purposes of my study, was of two girls, Myriam and Jen, although they regularly interacted with a large number of other bloggers.

5.   When public is not public

In autumn 2005, I had identified *LiveJournal* as the place where I was most likely to find young Irish bloggers. The previously popular *diaryland.com* counted no Irish blogs any longer, and it proved extremely difficult to find blogs hosted on the *Blogger* platform or on personal sites. Some of the blogs I had studied in the past had now migrated to *LiveJournal*, which offered an internal search engine. In October 2005, I created a blog on LiveJournal, and wrote my first entry. This was a public entry, as would be all the entries I would write until I selected the blogs for the study. The first entries were thus personal reflections on my budding research, and little stories about my children or domestic misadventures; I had simultaneously created a second blog on the *Blogger* platform, and for the first year, I simply published the same posts on two different platforms.

Saila's blog was the first blog I started reading, eventually navigating from her posts to her readers' blogs, following the links embedded in their user-names. I also started reading Jen's blog, following links to Myriam's blog. Throughout this phase of the research, the act of reading a blog became laden with meaning which I had not envisaged, more similar to the act of lurking than reading, as I was to discover when I started communicating with the authors. The word 'lurking' entered the internet language very early on, from the time of MOOs[1] and MUDs[2] and discussion boards, and refers to the act of reading without notifying the others of your presence. This 'reading alone' act is seen at best as very bad manners, at worst as slightly sinister or threatening to the author or the group. It does also signal texts on the web as a conversation, where

---

1. MUD Object Oriented

2. Multi-User Dungeon

all protagonists should make themselves known and participate. The blogs I discovered through the search engine and that I started reading were all publicly available to readers, but although I read, I did not comment until late in November 2006.

In November 2006, I wrote an entry on my blog which explained my presence on the platform and referred to my research and planned research questions. The same week, I commented on a number of blogs, from both groups, asking the authors if they would like to participate in the study, with a link to the explanatory blog entry. Whilst in ethnographic terms, this was an entry into the field, to the young people whose blogs I had been reading, it felt like de-lurking. The reactions to my presence varied: Saila and Corcra, whose blogs had a mixture of locked entries and public entries, agreed immediately to participate in the study, and both of them engaged in some conversation with me; Saila sent me an email immediately, and I responded through email as well, Corcra responded on her blog, but also gave me her email address in her response, so that any further conversations could take place outside the blog. Both wrote about their participation and about the study itself. In the event, I chose not to correspond by email, but to keep all communication on the same platform, through the *LiveJournal* internal messaging function.

I very rarely commented on the blogs after this first contact, so as not to intrude in personal conversations between the bloggers and their friends. Instead, all communication about the thesis and questions related to the research were posted on my own *LiveJournal* blog, I followed those entries with private messages to the young bloggers, with a link to the entry in question. In the first group, Saila and Corcra responded to all the messages, which were often ignored by the other bloggers. Homi's blog was also a mixture of private and public, and she also gave me access to all her entries, but she kept this initial communication in the comments section of her blog. All of them also included me in their Friends lists, thus granting me access to their private, locked entries. Planet, Disco and Brightears, whose blogs were public, engaged as well in their responses, and left their settings unchanged, as well as Fry, whose blog was mostly public. The two girls who form the second group both accepted immediately and gave access to most of their private entries, although Jen did point out that "anything really personal is squirreled away in filters anyhow", from which I assumed that some entries were not meant for my eyes.

Table 1. GROUP 1 - Public/private settings before and after first contact

Name	Gender	Public/ private entries	Response	Public/ private entries after contact
Saila	F	Mixed public/private	Yes	No change Private entries opened to researcher
Homi	F	Mostly private	Yes	No change Private entries opened to researcher
Brightears	M	Public	Yes	No change
Planet	F	Public	Yes	No change
Fry	M	Mixed public/private	Yes	No change Private entries opened to researcher
Disco	F	Public	Yes	No change
Corcra	F	Private	Yes	No change Private entries opened to researcher

These final participants were not however the only bloggers whom I initially contacted. Within the group of friends named on profile pages, a further seven either declined or declined to answer. Two gave negative responses, both in answer to my comment; one explained that she had links to my university, and immediately locked her journal, posting a "Friends Only" page, with a black and white picture and the words "I am a private person, this journal is now Friends Only". Another girl simply answered "hem, no thanks", but left her journal setting public. Five bloggers ignored the comment and request and never answered, either on their comments page or on my blog. One girl did not answer, but locked her journal, with no announcement on the first page. One boy did not answer me directly, but instead locked his journal and posted a "Friends Only" page, which consisted of a black rectangle with two white letters: F.O., which I took to be a message to the researcher who had caused him to lock his journal. One other boy ignored the message, left his old public entries as they were, but subsequently set all other entries as private, and the last three bloggers ignored the message and continued as they had before. I never included any of their entries in the study, yet their behaviour on first contact caused me to reflect deeply on ethical issues in research and also on the question of privacy, which became a crucial question in this research. Whereas none of the bloggers who agreed to participate in the study changed their privacy level after being contacted, as outlined in Table 1 above, this was not the case for those who refused or ignored my request: four of those remaining seven bloggers changed their settings, 'locking' their journal or part of their journal, as outlined in Table 2 below. This reactive take up of the privacy affordance seemed from the start to signify the emerging digital literacy of the young people involved, who had known about the lock facility but had not identified or seen the need for the privacy affordance until the sudden appearance of my comments and messages, seen as the intrusion of an unwanted reader.

Table 2.   Public/private settings after refusals

Name	Gender	Public/ private entries	Response	Public/ private entries after contact
LJSweet.	F	Public	No	Private
LJBigSam	M	Public	No answer	Private
LJSparrow	F	Public	No answer	Private
LJLuciakiss.	F	Public	No answer	No change
LJBalin	F	Public	No	No change
LJStevenSmith.	M	Public	No answer	No change
LJBudda	M	Public	No answer	No change for old entries. Private for new entries

My presence, not only as a researcher, but as an adult and a stranger, had attributes of voyeurism. Even the most enthusiastic participants asked me where and how I had 'found' them. The explanation of my selection methods was however accepted as a valid one. Nevertheless, my presence was a catalyst for some, notably those who did not want to participate, as it influenced their privacy levels and indeed changed their expectations of privacy on the *LiveJournal* platform, if not online in general.

One of the grey areas comes from the nature of the blog as life-writing. Whereas authenticity may not be an issue in young people's blogs, too much truth may be one. Ethical issues online are often played around the complex and shifting concept of privacy, which in blogs can be linked to life narratives. Eakin (2004) reflects on the ethics of life-writing in relation to others:

> "because we live our lives in relation to others, our privacies are largely shared, making it hard to demarcate the boundary where one life leaves off and another begins" (Eakin, 2004, p. 8).

> "While our lives are increasingly on display in public, the ethics of presenting such revelations remains largely unexamined" (Eakin, 2004, p. 1).

These issues also impact on research: whereas I asked for consent from the bloggers that I had selected, and I kept an open communication channel with them, I was also conscious of the presence of others in the text, and my own text has removed the names of anyone mentioned, as well as place names which might make the bloggers and their friends identifiable. The grey area is that of the active readers who comment on the blogs; it would have been impossible to contact each and every one of them and ask them for consent; consent was only sought by the blogger, the 'owner' of the place as it were. As for the commenters who are not part of the sample, their names were thus replaced by initials, but their comments were nevertheless quoted.

6.   Conclusion

Contextual gaps and ethical grey areas have been illustrated here by the reactions of young bloggers after first contact with an unknown adult, the researcher. Even though privacy settings existed on the platform, it can be argued that the affordance of privacy is at times a hidden affordance, thus not necessarily obvious to young users. The identification and realisation of privacy affordances often necessitated a first experience where the need for managing privacy was made obvious, as in an encounter with an unexpected person. The realisation of these affordances can thus be assimilated to different levels of digital literacies, which should be kept in mind by researchers.

As a researcher, I felt that the guiding concept should be that of contextual integrity introduced by Nissenbaum (2010) to account for the puzzling issue of privacy in public, but which can be adapted to the area of internet research:

> "The underlying thesis is that social activity occurs in contexts and is governed by context-relative norms. Among these, informational norms govern the flow of information about a subject from one party to another, taking account of the capacities (or roles) in which the parties act, the types of information, and the principles under which this information is transmitted among the parties. We can think of contextual integrity as a metric, preserved when informational norms within a context are respected and violated when they are contravened" (Nissembaum, 2010, p. 14).

Contextual integrity calls for the *appropriate* flow of information, in a context-sensitive manner, reminiscent of the call of the AoIR ethics working group for sensitivity to the expectations of the digital venue. An ethical reflection does not however stop at the design stage of the research, or the choice of relational boundaries. All through the research process, there appear instances and events which call on the researcher to reflect again and again on the ethics of her research.

References

Bois-Reymond, M., & Chisholm, L. (2006). Young Europeans in a changing world. *New Directions for Child and Adolescent Development, 2006*(113), 1-9. doi: 10.1002/cd.164

boyd, d. m. (2008). *Taken Out of Context: American Teen Sociality in Networked Publics.* PhD Thesis. University of California, Berkeley. Retrieved from http://www.danah.org/papers/TakenOutOfContext.pdf

boyd, d. m. (2010, April 29). Privacy and Publicity in the Context of Big Data. *WWW.* Raleigh, North Carolina. Retrieved from http://www.danah.org/papers/talks/2010/WWW2010.html

Brake, D. R. (2009). *As if nobody's reading'?: the imagined audience and socio-technical biases in personal blogging practice in the UK.* PhD Thesis. London School of Economics. Retrieved from http://etheses.lse.ac.uk/4/

Bruckman, A. (2002). Studying the amateur artist: A perspective on disguising data collected in human subjects on the Internet. *Ethics and Information Technology, 4*(3), 217-231. doi: 10.1023/A:1021316409277

Bruns, A., & Jacobs, J. (2006). Introduction. In A. Bruns & J. Jacobs (Eds.), *Uses of Blogs* (pp. 1-9). New York: Peter Lang.

Chisholm, L. (2006). European youth research: Development, debates, demands. *New Directions for Child and Adolescent Development,* 11-21. doi: 10.1002/cd.165

Declaration of Helsinki. (1964). *British Medical Journal 1996, 313*(7070), 1448-1449. doi: 10.1136/bmj.313.7070.1448a

Eakin, P. J. (Ed.). (2004). *The Ethics of Life Writing.* Cornell: Cornell University Press.

Efimova, L. (2009a). *Passion at work: blogging practices of knowledge workers* . PhD Thesis. University of Utrecht.

Efimova, L. (2009b). Weblog as a personal thinking space. In *Proceedings of the 20th ACM conference on Hypertext and hypermedia - HT '09. Torino, Italy,* p. 289. Retrieved from http://dl.acm.org/citation.cfm?id=1557963

Efimova, L., & De Moor, A. (2005). Beyond Personal Webpublishing: An Exploratory Study of Conversational Blogging Practices. In *HICSS '05. Proceedings of the 38th Annual Hawaii International Conference on System Sciences, 2005* (pp. 107a). Retrieved from https://doc.novay.nl/dsweb/Get/Version-22432/HICSS05_Efimova_deMoor.pdf

Elgesem, D. (2002). What is special about the ethical issues in online research? *Ethics and Information Technology, 4*(3), 195-203. doi: 10.1023/A:1021320510186

Ess, C., & the AoIR ethics working committee. (2002). *Ethical decision-making and Internet Research: recommendations from the aoir ethics working committee.* Retrieved from www.aoir.org/reports/ethics.pdf

Ess, C. (2002). Introduction . *Ethics and Information Technology 4*(4), 177-188.

Ess, C. (2009). *Digital Media Ethics.* Cambridge: Polity Press.

Fowley, C. (2011). *Publishing the Confidential: an ethnographic study of young Irish bloggers*. PhD Thesis. Dublin City University. Retrieved from http://doras.dcu.ie/16577/1/PhDCathyFowleyFinal.pdf

Greig, A. D., & Taylor, J. (1999). *Doing Research with Children*. London: Sage Publications.

Hendrick, S. F. (2012). *Beyond the Blog*. PhD Thesis. Umeå: Umeå Universitet.

Herring, S., Scheidt, L., Wright, E., Bonus, S. (2005). Weblogs as a bridging genre. *Information Technology & People, 18*(2), 142-171. doi: 10.1108/09593840510601513

Hine, C. (2005). Virtual Methods and the Sociology of Cyber-Social-Scientific Knowledge. In C. Hine (Ed.), *Virtual Methods*. Oxford: Berg.

Ito, M., Horst, H., Bittanti, M., boyd, d. m., Herr-Stephenson, B., Lange, P. G., Pascoe, C. J., & Robinson, L. (2008). *Living and Learning with New Media: Summary of Findings from the Digital Youth Project*. Chicago: The MacArthur Foundation. Retrieved from http://digitalyouth.ischool.berkeley.edu/files/report/digitalyouth-WhitePaper.pdf

Lally, E. (2009). Questions of the local and the global in Internet research: a response to Annette Markham. In A. N. Markham & N. K. Baym (Eds.), *Internet inquiry: Conversations about method*. Thousand Oaks: Sage Publications.

Markham, A. N. (2006). Ethic as Method, Method as Ethic: A Case for Reflexivity in Qualitative ICT Research. *Journal of Information Ethics, 15*(2), 37-54. Retrieved from http://markham.internetinquiry.org/writing/jie.pdf

Markham, A. N., & Baym, N. K. (Eds.). (2009). *Internet inquiry: Conversations about method*. Thousand Oaks: Sage Publications.

Nissenbaum, H. (2010). *Privacy in Context: technology, policy, and the integrity of social life*. Stanford: Stanford University Press.

Nowson, S. (2006). *The Language of Weblogs: a study of genre and individual differences*. PhD thesis. Edinburgh: University of Edinburgh. Retrieved from http://www.era.lib.ed.ac.uk/bitstream/1842/1113/1/thesis.pdf

Pace, L. A., & Livingston, M. M. (2005). Protecting Human Subjects in Internet Research. *Electronic Journal of Business Ethics and Organization Studies, 10*(1), 35-41. Retrieved from http://ejbo.jyu.fi/pdf/ejbo_vol10_no1_pages_35-41.pdf

Palfrey, J., & Gasser, U. (2008). *Born Digital: Understanding the First Generation of Digital Natives*. New York: Basic Books.

Rall, D. N. (2007). *Locating Four Pathways to Internet Scholarship*. PhD Thesis. Southern Cross University.

Scheidt, L. A. (2006). Adolescent diary weblogs and the unseen audience. In D. Buckingham & R. Willett (Eds.), *Digital generations: Children, young people and new media*. London: Lawrence Erlbaum.

Serfaty, V. (2004). *The Mirror and the Veil: an Overview of American Online Diaries and Blogs*. Amsterdam, New York: Editions Robopi.

Whyte, J. (2006). *Ethics in Research with Children*. Seminar, St. Patrick's College.

Zimmer, M. (2010). "But the data is already public": on the ethics of research in Facebook. *Ethics and Information Technology, 12*(4), 313-325. doi: 10.1007/s10676-010-9227-5

Poetic Machines: From Paper to Pixel

Jeneen Naji[1]

Abstract

This chapter investigates digital methods of signification in order to examine the impact of the digital medium on poetic expression. Traditional poetry criticism is problematised with reference to its suitability for application to online works in order to develop a comprehensive ePoetry rhetoric that explores not only what is being said, but also crucially how it is being said. Theories of translation are also used as a context in which to analyse the transposition of poetry from analogue to digital. This framework then forms the basis for a study that explores the move from print to pixel by analysing qualitative ePoet interviews as well as their corresponding ePoems. This is done through an examination of the translation process from analogue to digital within the context of Holmes (1994) translation theories. In particular this chapter also looks at the impact that interactivity and the digital environment have on the traditional characteristics of poetry as proposed by Orr (1996), such as story, structure, music, and imagination and how this impacts on poetic expression. This chapter then concludes that as the movement from paper to pixel has expanded the possibility for poetic expression, so too has it expanded the scope for undermining such expression.

Keywords: translation, digital, poetry, flash, signification, interactivity, communication.

---

1. NUI Maynooth, Maynooth, Ireland; jeneen.naji@nuim.ie

How to cite this chapter: Naji, J. (2013). Poetic Machines: From Paper to Pixel. In C. Fowley, C. English, & S. Thouësny (Eds.), *Internet Research, Theory, and Practice: Perspectives from Ireland* (pp. 55-74). Dublin: © Research-publishing.net.

---

1.   Introduction

Currently the pervasiveness of digital technology and access to the Internet means there exists online a wealth of digital poetry or ePoetry , some animated, some static, some interactive, some linear. Landow (2006) tells us that when Bush (1945) conceptualised the Internet in *The Memex* in his seminal paper *As We May Think* he created what are essentially *poetic machines*: machines that work "according to analogy and association, machines that capture and create the anarchic brilliance of human imagination. Bush, we perceive, assumed that science and poetry work in essentially the same way" (Landow, 2006, p. 13). It is at this intersection of science and poetry that this research finds itself and it is these *poetic machines* creating ePoetic works of analogy and association that are the realisation of our electric dreams.

The methods of this chapter are two-fold. Firstly it examines the process of translation of an ePoem from print to pixel. Using Holmes' (1994) translation theory as a framework, this process allows a comparison of analogue and digital forms which informs us of the true extent of the impact of the digital medium on poetic expression. Secondly this chapter compares and identifies the characteristics of ePoetry in relation to traditional poetry theory using Orr's (1996) temperaments of poetry as a framework. Traditional poetry criticism is problematised with reference to its suitability for application to online works in order to develop a comprehensive ePoetry rhetoric that explores not only what is being said, but also crucially how it is being said.

However to truly see the relevance of these theories we must look for evidence of them at work in the creation of ePoetry and the best way to do this was to conduct interviews with the creators of some of these ePoems, the ePoets themselves. Consenting ePoet candidates were e-mailed interview questions as a word document which they then filled in and sent back. Out of the seven interviews quoted in this paper, two were not conducted through e-mail. The interview with Dylan Sheehan was conducted through youtube messaging but was otherwise similar to the others. Also the interview with Claire Allan Dinsmore was conducted by Megan Sapnar in July 2002 for the website *Poems That Go* (Sapnar, 2002). When quoting from the interviews I have listed the candidate's name, the year of the interview and the number relating to the question asked: (Ong, personal communication, 2009, q. 1) refers to Monica Ong's response to question 1 of her interview which was conducted in 2009.

The ePoets whose responses are quoted in this paper:

- Nick Robinson translated Anderton and Robinson's (2008) poem *A Servant. A Hanging. A Paper House.* into a Flash[1] piece.
- Monica Ong translated Givens and Ong's (2007) poem *Fallow* into a highly interactive Flash piece.
- Sam Tootal along with Chris Turner make up the eMedia duo who call themselves SamuelChristopher, Sam Tootal gave responses on the video and audio based eMedia translation of Billy Collins poem *Hunger* (Collins & SamuelChristopher, 2006).
- Dylan Sheehan made a video and audio based eMedia translation of his own poem *Ten Doors Closing* (Sheehan, 2006).
- Young-Hae Chang Heavy Industries is an eMedia duo made up of Marc Voge and Young-Hae Chang, they responded to questions regarding *The Last Day of Betty Nkomo* (Young-Hae Chang Heavy Industries, 2004) a Flash piece they created for International AIDS day.
- Mateo Parilla translated Heather Lee Schroeder's poem *In Praise of an Elevator* into a Flash piece (Schroeder & Handplant Studio, 2008).
- The Claire Allan Dinsmore interview was conducted by Megan Sapnar in July 2002 for the website *Poems That Go* and it discusses her piece *The Dazzle as Question* (Dinsmore, n.d.), a Flash ePoem she created herself.
- Bill Dorris was a digital media lecturer in the Department of Communications in Dublin City University, he is a poet and ePoet and created *The Burning* (Dorris & Kuypers, 2008) in Adobe Flash with the poet Janet Kuypers who wrote the poem and also provided some imagery and audio for the ePoem.

---

1. Flash or Adobe Flash is a multimedia authoring software used to create a large proportion on interactive online content with a strong visual focus.

2.   ePoetic translation –
translation as communication

McLuhan (1962) purports that the modern reader is involved in total translation of sight into sounds as they look at the page; in this case McLuhan is referring to a reader translating from print into oral words in the mind. For the purposes of this paper, this can be equally applied to the translation of poems from print into online visuals in the eMedia. This then is translation as communication and it is in this manner that I refer to translation, in a similar sense to Hatim and Mason (1997). They look upon translation "as an act of communication which attempts to relay, across cultural and linguistic boundaries, another act of communication (which may have been intended for different purposes and different readers/hearers)" (Hatim & Mason, 1997, p. 1). The ePoet, through the ePoem, is communicating to the creader[1], perhaps the intended communication differs from that actually received but that point is outside my research question. This chapter focuses on the process of creation of the ePoem, the translation of the poem from paper to pixel.

It is important to note that the ePoetry with which this research is concerned starts out as written or print poetry; the poem's initial form was analogue on printed-paper. It is essential to look at what happens next, the process of translation of the printed text into visual motion graphics with audio and interactivity, in order to understand what ePoetry is. It is comparable to the creation of music videos, where music comes first; so too in ePoetry does the poem come first (Vernallis, 2004, p. x). One exception however is that of generative ePoems: in these instances the computer code generates the poem, each experience is unique based on a series of variables at each instance of play. The code will use variables such as words to generate a poem, so in a

---

1. With reference to the ePoetry examples I discuss in this research, the term viewer, player, reader, or user no longer adequately encompasses the active role that will need to be played. Though some of the ePoems provide minimal interactivity such as simply a click to play, others allow the freedom to explore the poetic environment to such an extent that the result is an experiential literary experience. This could involve reading, playing, viewing, listening or linking. So we are left searching for a term for an active individual who might perform any one or all of these activities. Also another factor in affirming the inappropriateness of using the term reader for ePoetry is that in computer terminology 'to read' means to copy data from one storage medium or device to another. This is different to print terminology when 'to read' means to decipher and interpret the letters and signs of a document (Morris, 2006, p. 15). So for the purposes of this research rather than interpose constantly the terms viewer, reader, user, I will use the term creader. This is a combination of the words creator and reader to refer to what Barthes (1970) termed the active reader.

sense a generative ePoem still exists in print first, but not to the same extent as a definite written poem which is later translated into ePoetry.

Similarities can be found in the process of translating a poem from one language to another and the process of translating a poem from print to digital. In order to identify these similarities and/or differences, I will apply poetry translation theory to the process of ePoetry creation using ePoet interview responses as evidence.

Holmes (1994), a poet and a translator of poetry provided what is widely considered the most systematically theoretical map of processes involved in poetic translation[1]. We can apply Holmes' (1994) model of translation to ePoetry translation if we interpret language A, the source text, to be a piece in standard textual language and language B, the target text, to be the piece translated into digital multimedia form. The transfer mechanism is then both the ePoet and the software applications of choice (such as Flash) with or without the collaboration of the poet. In this case the translator first decodes the piece to allow for assimilation and interpretation and then recodes the piece into a new mode. Whether this new mode is from one language to another such as for example French to Spanish or analogue to digital it does not affect the model.

2.1. Holmes' forms of translation

Holmes (1994) outlines the following four approaches that translators have traditionally come upon as solutions to the problem of form of the metapoem. Firstly there is a *mimetic* form where the original form is kept (most similar to original). This approach tends to have the effect of re-emphasising, "by its strangeness, the strangeness which for the target-language reader is inherent in the semantic message of the original poem" (Holmes, 1994, p. 27). Then there is the *analogical* form; here the translation seeks functionally to parallel the

---

1. Holmes (1994) is credited with starting the attempt to map translation studies as an academic field of study in his article *The Name and Nature of Translation Studies* (Holmes, 1994, p. 67). Holmes broke the field into two main areas, *pure* and *applied*. The pure deals with the description of translation and the development of corresponding principles to help describe and explain it, this is the main area this research deals with. Applied is more practical and deals with activities such as translator training and developing practical translation aids such as dictionaries and term banks (Baker, 2001, p. 278).

form in the original's poetic tradition. Both of these are "form derivative [...] determined as they are by the principle of seeking some kind of equivalence in the target language for the outward form of the original poem" (Holmes, 1994, p. 26). There is also the *organic* form or "content derivative", this form starts with the same semantic content but allows it to form its own unique shape rather than the form of the original. And finally there is the *deviant* or *extraneous* form where the metapoem is cast into a form that is in no way implicit in either the form or the content of the original (most dissimilar to original) (France, 2000, p. 31).

Some extracts from the interviews point us to how we should categorise the electronic metapoems. "The words and structure are unaltered from the reading that we received by Billy Collins. We've obviously given it other levels of subjective meaning by virtue of the fact we set it to sound design and images" (Tootal, personal communication, 2009, q. 11). This comment regarding *Hunger* (Collins & SamuelChristopher, 2006) leads us to set it in the category of an organic translation according to Holmes' (1994) theory: the content is similar to the original poem but the form is different. In this case the content of the poem is the same but the form has changed from print text to digital video and audio.

Similarly Sheehan when asked about his piece *Ten Doors Closing* (Sheehan, 2006) answers, "I think the finished product fairly represents the original idea. The poem its self [sic] is essentially unchanged" (Sheehan, personal communication, 2009, q. 8), this would also lead us to categorise the piece according to Holmes' theories as an organic translation. Parilla comments that, "the essence of the poem is the same. Of course, there are new nuances anf [sic] others have been diluted" (Parilla, personal communication, 2009, q. 12); this also points us to categorising his ePoem *In praise of an elevator* (Schroeder & Handplant Studio, 2008) as organic. In fact most of the examples of ePoetry examined in this research fall into this category except for *The Last Day of Betty Nkomo* (Young-Hae Chang Heavy Industries, 2004): although the words were indeed written first, they were in fact written specifically for this piece and still appear as written words although they are now digital written words and the rhythm and audio is new. There is however no added imagery, unlike the other pieces, and therefore it could be categorised as *analogical*, whereby the translation seeks to functionally parallel the form in the original's poetic tradition.

2.2. The specificity of poetry translation

Holmes (1994) emphasises the innate difference between the translation of prose and poetry due to the ambiguity inherent in poetry as opposed to the more single-minded nature of prose (p. 9). It is this chameleon like quality of poetry that makes its translation such a complex task.

According to Holmes (1994) the basic problem that the poetry translator (who has set out to create a text that is closely related enough to the original to be called a translation and that also displays enough of the basic characteristics in the target language to be called a poem) faces, is the fact that the translator not only has to shift the original poem to another linguistic context but also to another literary intertext and socio-cultural situation (p. 47). The range of choice presented to the translator ranges from the *exoticizing* to the *naturalizing* plane, and the *historicizing* to the *modernizing* plane[1]. In these planes a translation can range from being the most different (*exoticizing*) or similar (*naturalizing*) to the source text. Moreover a translation may take a historical (*historicizing*) form or contain historical content as opposed to a modern, contemporary form and/or content (*modernizing*).

Ong is an example of an ePoet dealing with such problems by situating *Fallow* (Givens & Ong, 2007) in a historical context and specific socio-cultural situation. Evidence to support this can be seen in the response: "When I read *Fallow* (Givens & Ong, 2007), I sense a voice of longing, lingering in a time passed. I ended up visiting many antique shops in the rural part of Hudson Valley where I collected vintage postcards. I think there is something about old correspondences, letters and belongings that evoke that same longing" (Ong, personal communication, 2009, q. 10). In fact in Givens and Ong's (2007) piece we can see graphics of these same vintage photos, postcards and letters

1. Though in my writing I use British spelling when Holmes coined these terms he used American spelling so to remain accurate to his terminology when I use these terms I retain his original spelling and italicise the term in order to note this.

all which contribute towards placing the translation within a specific historical and socio-cultural context. Her response as well as the visuals of the piece itself show us that her ePoetry translation is situated with the socio-cultural situation of Hudson Valley, 1950 or 1960s rural America in the state of New York.

Interestingly the use of Asian traditional music as audio for *The Last Day of Betty Nkomo* (Young-Hae Chang Heavy Industries, 2004) situates it within a different socio-cultural situation. This is also reflected in the literary intertext as the text is reminiscent of a Japanese haiku, although the linguistic context is modern western English. It seems to be the case in most of the ePoems that the choice of music and/or graphics contribute to placing the piece in a socio-cultural situation and increased poetic impact can be arrived at by the combination of the socio-cultual situation, the linguistic context, and the literary intertext. However, as in the screenshot below (Figure 1) of *A Servant. A Hanging. A Paper House* (Anderton & Robinson, 2008), it is not as obvious in this piece what part the music, graphics, or text have to play regarding the socio-cultural situation, literary intertext, or linguistic context.

Figure 1.   A Servant. A Hanging. A Paper House (Anderton & Robinson, 2008)

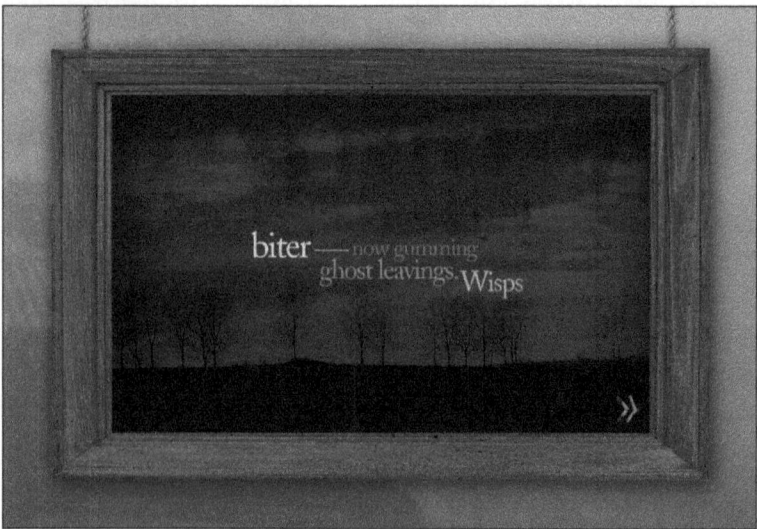

The choice of song is crackly and old but it is impossible to make out the words. The text is modern English, which give us the literary intertext. The graphics contribute to the same historical feeling by showing some scratches and water damage stains, the visuals show remote rural countryside but more than that is hard to discern.

2.3. Holmes' serial and structural planes

Holmes (1994) also proposes that when a poem is translated it takes place on two planes, a serial plane and a structural plane. The serial plane deals with translating sentence by sentence and the structural plane deals with the overview translation "on which one abstracts a 'mental conception' of the original text. This mental conception is then used as a kind of general criterion against which to test each sentence during the formulation of the new translated text" (Holmes, 1994, p. 82), so that when translating a poem it is not enough to translate the individual elements but also the overall sense of the piece.

Likewise there is clear evidence in the ePoet interview responses to link to Holmes' (1994) structural and serial planes. The structural plane deals with the overview translation and nearly all interviewees mention reading the poem in its entirety first and then begin to deal with the poem line by line or couplet by couplet. So we start with the structural plane and then move to the serial plane which Holmes states deals with sentence by sentence or what Chang calls "keyframe by keyframe" (Chang, personal communication, 2009, q. 7) or as the ePoet Dorris suggests "word by word" (Dorris, personal communication, 2011, q. 7).

For example, many respondents stress the importance of immersing oneself in the poem at the beginning of the process. Such as "The poet sent me the poem. I read it carefully, out loud, repeatedly" (Ong, personal communication, 2009, q. 4). Also Robinson "The first thing I did was read the poem that was emailed to me and reflect on the overall themes and my own personal interpretations. Then I isolated each two-line segment and read it several times while writing down any imagery that came to mind" (Robinson, personal communication,

2009, q. 7). Despite the majority of respondents stating they were trying to put the poet's interpretation across it is also clear that the majority spent some time developing their own interpretation before beginning work. Samuel Tootal states this explicitly when he tells us "It is entirely our interpretation of the poem" and that he and his partner worked "Line by line" (Tootal, personal communication, 2009, q. 7). This is a particularly evocative piece so perhaps this freedom from worrying about the poet's interpretation liberated them and allowed them to concentrate on evoking their interpretation.

Translation theory can thus be useful when we examine the changing form from print to pixel. Through Holmes' (1994) model of translation it was ascertained that many different aspects of a translation can be studied: process, forms, levels, and planes. Translation theory is thus a useful prism with which to examine and unlock the creation of specific ePoetry examples. However, traditional poetry theory can also be applied to ePoetry examples.

3.   Poetry structure - Orr's temperaments

The new poetic experiences of the ePoems – while not derived from text, but rather from eMedia enhancements of text, such as via motion graphics or video – nonetheless conform to the characteristics common to analogue poetry, as discussed, for example, by Orr (1996). Orr (1996), in his paper *Four Temperaments and the Forms of Poetry* proposes four categories or as he calls them *temperaments* to poetry (p. 270) and these are not dissimilar to Aristotle's (1996) analysis of a tragedy[1]. These are: Story, Structure, Music, and Imagination. Orr (1996) also suggests that the dynamic tension of a poem is brought about through a marriage of contraries that occurs through the contrast of each of these temperaments and it is this aspect of Orr's (1996) theory in particular that lead me select them as the most appropriate for this research.

---

1. Aristotle (1996) suggests a structure for the breakdown of poetry to enable analysis. He believed tragedy, like poetry to be imitation. With reference to this research it is interesting to note that the elements which Aristotle lists as comprising a tragedy, are echoed in many theories on what constitutes poetry and as such I believe are relevant to this reserach. In fact Miller (2004) notes, "Aristotle's remarks on dialogue have stood the test of time, and are as applicable to interactive media as they were to Greek drama" (p. 110). As well as this the "principles discussed in The Poetics have been applied not only to stage plays, but also to movies, TV shows, and, most recently, are finding their way into interactive narratives" (Miller, 2004, p. 75).

It is clear by evidence of ePoet responses that Orr's (1996) poetry criticism theory can not only be applied to traditional analogue poetry, but also to ePoetry. However the question remains to what extent? This section tackles this issue by outlining each of the temperaments and then, using ePoet interview responses and ePoetry examples, illustrating their application to ePoetry. This then allows for a problematising of Orr's (1996) theory in relation to ePoetry and concurrently, a rationale towards a revision of poetry criticism for the digital realm.

3.1.   Story

According to Orr (1996), Story is the beginning, middle, and end (pp. 271-277). It is an element which is essential for a human connection, though less imperative for a poem than for a film or novel (Orr, 1996, pp. 271-277). Nonetheless it is still important for a story to be told, conflict must seek a resolution. If not immediately apparent we will always seek the story in a work of art such as a painting or poem. In some of the ePoems considered in this research, story does not exist in the traditional sense, such as a clear beginning, middle and end. In these cases the authors have made an effort either graphically or otherwise to situate their piece in a recognisable location or space. In Arnall's (2002) sense an ePoem is "an open, explorable environment" rather than a narrative. The creader's response can then be to create their own narratives by associating their own personal experiences of such an environment to the ePoem and so too will they begin to associate emotions, leading to an evocative piece.

A number of the interviewees commented on just such a process in relation to their own ePoems. Ong in discussing her ePoem *Fallow* (Givens & Ong, 2007) mentions that she "brought a visual space to the words, a sort of setting in terms of landscape – not a literal one but perhaps one that taps into the reader's landscape of memory" (Ong, personal communication, 2009, q. 3). She also speaks of the "emotional space" (Ong, 2009, q. 11) of her ePoem and states that she likes "creating a poetic space that is just as engaging or transformative as a book" (Ong, 2009, q. 1). In both *Fallow* (Givens & Ong, 2007) and *Hunger*

(Collins & SamuelChristopher, 2006) media elements are used to suggest spaces that people would recognise and therefore relate to in a subtle way. The "stills we used are urban compositions we're interested in in general, the kind of thing you glance at whilst travelling around a town or city" (Tootal, personal communication, 2009, q. 9). This is the equivalent of setting it within a story or context that people can connect and identify with. Similarly Sheehan talks of using the London Underground as a setting that is an "instantly recognisable and everyday place to most Londoners I wanted to inject an element of 'myth' to something so taken for granted" (Sheehan, personal communication, 2009, q. 5). This recognisable place allows the creader to become a character in the story of the poem and so allows for a greater emotional connection, personal interpretation, identification and emotional evocation.

3.2. Structure

Orr's (1996) temperament of Structure is the pattern of the poem, the element most often (but not always) recognisable in poetry (pp. 271-277). In fact sometimes it is even the lack of a structure compared to prose that makes poetry recognisable as what its is.

Interestingly, structure seems to be an area left most often unchanged in the ePoetry pieces by the translators. With reference to *Hunger* (Collins & SamuelChristopher, 2006) Tootal states that the "words and structure are unaltered from the reading that we received by Billy Collins" (Tootal, personal communication, 2009, q. 11), thus they did not alter or change the words or structure of the original poem written by Collins that they translated into eMedia. Parilla also reports, "I respect the original groups [sic] of lines" and "aspects that must be respect [sic] are the reading, order, the rhythm" (Parilla, personal communication, 2009, q. 16). This is echoed by Ong's opinion that "the media art needs [sic] come from the poetic content and be carefully considered. Artist Ben Shahn always emphasized that 'form is the shape of content'" (Ong, personal communication, 2009, q. 16). Similarly Dinsmore tells us that "form is an extension of content" (Sapnar, 2002). Robinson explains that when he was communicating with the poet Anderton she told him "the 'meaning' of the poem is reflected in the shape of the poem" and as a result Robinson tried to maintain as much as possible the original structure of the poem by working line by line, "I treated each line as a 'frame' that I wanted to stand on its own as an appealing visual" (Robinson, personal communication, 2009, q. 7).

3.3. Music

The next temperament, Music, is the interaction of syllables, syntax and sounds inherent in reading or reciting which create the poem's aural and rhythmical structure (Orr, 1996, pp. 271-277). This is the sound of the words that contribute to a rhythm in the poem.

Orr's (1996) temperament of music does not refer to music as in songs or soundtracks when applied to traditional analogue poetry, but in eMedia translations the concept can expand to include not only this, but anything (such as motion graphics) which contributed to the rhythm of a piece, including of course the original interaction of syllables, syntax, intonation, etc. from the original poem. The music of a piece seems in the ePoetry examples I have so far looked at to be essential, the omission of such leads to a dull, flat and unengaging piece. To support this view there is much to be found in the interviews.

Tootal for example states that he and his partner Turner are "very interested in creating depth and texture to our work and when it is moving image you suddenly have the world of audio to delve into. Sound is so important to us, to any moving image creators and filmmakers. Work can live or die on the audio content and for us with *Hunger* it needed that added depth, a sense of mystery. Audio is the character of the environment" (Tootal, personal communication, 2009, q. 8). Tootal in this instance is describing how audio or sound is afforded as much weight as an actor in a play. Sheehan also uses audio in his piece, "many of the sounds are the normal workings of the Underground, we block them out in day-to-day travels. The screeching of metal wheels on metal tracks and the mechanical rhythm of the escalators and the announcements over the public address system" (Sheehan, personal communication, 2009, q. 6). These comments from ePoets outline the extensive expressive and communicative potential of audio in ePoetry.

Though I have been applying Orr's (1996) temperament of music to audio in ePoetry, in its original interpretation it relates to the rhythm of a poem. Dinsmore stresses the importance of rhythm in poetry both traditional and eMedia and the changing of such can impact the meaning of the piece. When discussing her piece *The Dazzle as Question* (Dinsmore, n.d.), she observes, "setting up a rhythm was one of the most important things for me. The meaning inferred by that rhythm, placing emphasis in time. When reading a poem for instance, the meaning can be construed very differently depending upon how the work is read – where the emphasis is placed, lull – each nuance of elocution lending meaning to the distinct content of each particular word, and thus to the work as a whole. I wanted to further the levels upon which this piece functioned by lending the 'reading' a voice beyond how the words would tell if the piece were, say, straight prose" (Sapnar, 2002).

3.4.   Imagination

Orr's (1996) final temperament, that of Imagination, deals with the themes or metaphors of a piece, the ideas, and thoughts. Much from the respondents' answers on this topic can be extracted. The temperament of Imagination is the ideas and thought process of the poet, the metaphors and imagery at use, the flow of image-to-image or thought-to-thought (Orr, 1996, pp. 271-277).

Robinson reveals that he was being careful not to pigeonhole reader's interpretation but believed the poem to be about languish (Robinson, personal communication, 2009, qq. 12-13). This mirrors the original poet's intentions as Robinson cites communication with her in which she (the poet) states, "the images, hopefully, enfold the reader in a world of feeling and atmosphere that is not literal. This is not a 'literal' poem, it is a poem that opens doors within, and I cannot control what doors it opens for each reader (I am a big believer in not trying to write for other peoples [sic] interpretations" (Robinson, personal communication, 2009). While the eMedia translator is aware of the themes of a piece they are also anxious to be careful to allow space for the creaders to form their own interpretations of the themes of the piece.

3.5. A marriage of contraries – rationale for using Orr

Orr (1996) suggests that these four temperaments together form a marriage of contraries and that while each of these temperaments is capable of creating the unity we call a poem, he believes that "for a poem to have the stability and dynamic tension that comes of a marriage of contraries it must fuse a limiting impulse with an impulse that resists limitation" (p. 270). This reflects Barthes's (1970) analysis of culture and his concept of *trope*, by referring to literary texts using this concept he emphasized the importance of difference in the creation of meaning[1]. Gottdiener (1995) posits that according to Barthes both metaphorical[2] and metonymical[3] tropes rely on contrasts or difference and that this is how meaning arises (p. 27). Similarly Orr's (1996) dynamic tension, which is brought about through the contrasts or difference of conflicting temperaments allows the true emotional meaning of poem to be evoked.

Orr's (1996) marriage of contraries however can refer not only to the conflict of temperaments but it can also refer to what I feel is most apparent in the ePoems and that is the emotional impact or dynamic tension that comes from a marriage of contraries of the visuals and the audio (p. 270). Often jarring audio is combined with beautiful graphics (or vice versa), which accentuates the impact of the piece. For example in *The Last Day of Betty Nkomo* (Young-Hae Chang Heavy Industries, 2004) the audio of the piece is some quite intricate music and yet the visuals are simple black and white Monaco font. The opposition of these two elements gives a unique style and emotional impact to the ePoem.

---

1. According to Barthes (1970) a trope is a figure of speech in relation to the system of signification in the field of semiotics (mentioned in Gottdiener, 1995, p. 27).

2. Associative.

3. Juxtapositional or contiguous.

3.6.   eTemperaments – Orr's theory revised

While it is clear that Orr's (1996) temperaments still come into play much as they did in analogue poetry, nonetheless it is also clear that there is considerably more potential for variation within these when dealing with ePoems. This is due to the fact that in the electronic medium the ePoet is afforded a greater range of tools to use than in print. To adequately communicate the varying nuances and the potential for expanded possibilities of temperaments in the electronic realm as opposed to print, I will refer to them as *eTemperaments*, that is, Orr's (1996) temperaments expanded in electronic form.

For example, story or narrative in the digital medium have changed as there are now multiple levels and sequencing possibilities, especially in relation to implicit narratives, driven by the content and sequencing of visual displays with or without reference to text. Rhyme is now demoted, as visual and repetition and tensions become dominant, and the focus is no longer on the text read as a linear narrative. Intonation is potentially expanded as multiple readings or voices are possible simultaneously or sequentially, and other audio aural effects can be incorporated. All these factors when brought into play in a studied, practised and balanced manner can contribute to a far more immediate, semiotically and experientially richer poetic experience for the creader than would have originally been possible in print form. However as there is potential for an enhanced experience so too is there the risk of a greatly inferior poetic experience if the ePoem is translated without consideration of the overall experience.

It is important to note is that in the original analogue poems the dynamic tension in the text could not be undermined by any eTemperaments, yet in the ePoem this is imminently possible. For example in the ePoem *I didn't know infants in arms until* (Petrosino & Weychert, 2006) the dynamic tension of the piece is undermined by the use of interactivity which requires the creader to click after every line and so jars the rhythm of the ePoetic experience.

In general it can be argued that the role of eTemperaments has become much more complex with the additional individual possibilities for enhancing or diminishing any particular element contributing to even one of these temperaments. For example in relation to music, Orr's (1996) traditional contributing elements (such as the interaction of syllables, syntax, and sounds inherent in the reading or reciting of the poem which create its aural and rhythmical structure) now have been greatly augmented by the addition of eMedia elements such as sound effects and audio as well as the rhythm contributions created by the use of video, motion graphics and interactivity. The ways in which these individual elements may interact with each other to enhance or diminish the poetic experience are obviously immense and will no doubt provide the basis for years of further ePoetic evolution to come.

4.   Conclusion

Overall, the move from analogue to digital poetry has expanded the possibility for poetic expression. However, it has also expanded the scope for undermining such expression, resulting in the possibility of a lack of dynamic tension.

For example it is clear that interactivity can be a double-edged sword and ought not come at the cost of the music or overall meaning of the ePoem[1]. However it is also clear that allowing the creaders to construct their own experience using the ePoetic machine allows for a more personalised and therefore more memorable, affective and engaging piece. An exploratory ePoetic environment similar to that of *Fallow* (Givens & Ong, 2007) allows creaders to construct their own ePoetic experience through the piece. Considering also the scope for expanded creader interaction that is now available through the use of haptic screens and gesture technologies such as respectively the *iPhone* or the *Nintendo Wii*, much more complex and rewarding creader interaction can potentially be provided.

Essentially technology can and will change, but the use of this technology to create new literary experiences is something that ePoets can and will become more expert in. The interdisciplinary use of cultural theory to study emerging

---

1. The interaction of syllables, syntax, and sounds inherent in the reading or reciting of the poem, which creates its aural and rhythmical structure (Orr, 1996, p. 274).

forms allows us to create a contemporary hybrid framework more appropriate for analysis of emerging cultural and technological forms. Just because things have changed does not mean we completely disregard what has gone before, in fact what emerges now builds on previous models. As Branston and Stafford (2010) state, "'old' approaches to different sets of power still produce valuable ways of exploring media forms for use in these times" (p. 3). Similarly Buzzetti and McGann (n.d.) tell us "present work and future developments in digital scholarship evolve from critical models that we have inherited". However that is not to say that these critical models do not merit revisiting and reviewing in light of recent cultural and technological developments. Nonetheless this chapter has shown that there is merit in using traditional translation and poetry theory as a framework to analyse the process of creation of ePoetry. This process unlocks the ePoems for our use and contributes to a deeper understanding of the impact of the digital medium on literary expression.

References

Anderton, L., & Robinson, N. (2008). *A Servant. A Hanging. A Paper House* [Online]. Retrieved from http://www.bornmagazine.org/projects/servant/

Aristotle. (1996). *Poetics*. London: Penguin Books.

Arnall, T. (2002). *Interaction and narrative lecture, channel 4, London*. Retrieved from http://www.elasticspace.com/interaction/narrative/14.html

Baker, M. (Ed.). (2001). *Routledge Encyclopedia of Translation Studies*. Oxon: Routledge.

Barthes, R. (1970). *S/Z*. Paris: Editions de Seuil.

Branston, G., & Stafford, R. (2010). *The Media Student's Book* (5th ed.). London & New York: Routledge.

Bush, V. (1945). As We May Think [online]. Retrieved from http://www.theatlantic.com/magazine/archive/1945/07/as-we-may-think/303881/ [accessed 26/03/2013]

Buzzetti, D., & McGann, J. (n.d.). *Electronic Textual Editing: Critical Editing in a Digital Horizon* [Online]. Retrieved from http://www.tei-c.org/About/Archive_new/ETE/Preview/mcgann.xml

Collins, B., & SamuelChristopher. (2006). *Hunger* [Online]. Retrieved from http://www.bcactionpoet.org/hunger.html

Dinsmore, C. (n.d.). *The Dazzle as Question* [Online]. Retrieved from http://www.studiocleo. com/projects/dazzle/a.html

Dorris, B., & Kuypers, J. (2008). *The Burning* [Online]. Retrieved from http://homepage. eircom.net/~wdorris/theburning.html

France, P. (Ed.). (2000). *The Oxford guide to literature in English translation.* New York: Oxford University Press.

Givens, R., & Ong, M. (2007). *Fallow* [Online]. Retrieved from http://www.bornmagazine. org/projects/fallow

Gottdiener. M. (1995). The System of Objects and the Commodification of Everyday Life: The Early Baudrillard. In D. Kellner (Ed.), *Baudrillard: A Critical Reader* (pp. 25-40). Oxford: Blackwell Publishers.

Hatim, B., & Mason, I. (1997). *The Translator as Communicator.* London & New York: Routledge.

Holmes, J. (1994). *Translated! Papers on Literary Translation and Translation Studies* (2nd ed.). Amsterdam & Atlanta: Rodopi.

Jankowski, N. W. (2006). Creating Community with Media: History, Theories and Scientific Investigations. In L. A. Lievrouw & S. Livingstone (Eds.), *The Handbook of New Media: Updated Student Edition* (pp. 56-74). London: Thousand Oaks & New Delhi Sage Publications.

Kellner, D. (Ed.). (1995). Baudrillard: A Critical Reader. Oxford: Blackwell Publishers.

Landow, G. P. (2006). *Hypertext 3.0 Critical Theory and new Media in an Era of Globalization* (3rd ed.). Maryland: The John Hopkins University Press.

McLuhan, M. (1962). *The Gutenberg Galaxy.* Toronto: University of Toronto Press.

Miller, C. H. (2004). *Digital storytelling: a creator's guide to interactive entertainment.* Oxford: Focal Press.

Morris, A. (2006). New Media Poetics: As We May Think/How to Write. In A. Morris & T. Swiss (Eds.), *New Media Poetics: contexts, technotexts, and theories.* Cambridge, Massachusetts: The MIT Press.

Orr, G. (1996). Four Temperaments and the Forms of Poetry. In G. Orr & E. Voigt (Eds.), *Poets Teaching Poets: Self and the World.* Ann Arbor: University of Michigan Press.

Petrosino, K., & Weychert, R. (2006). *I didn't know infants in arms until* [Online]. Retrieved from http://www.bornmagazine.org/projects/infants_in_arms

Sapnar, M. (2002). *Interview with Claire Alan Dinsmore re Dazzle as Question.* Retrieved from http://www.poemsthatgo.com/gallery/summer2002/dazzle/interview.htm [accessed 02/06/2009]

Schroeder, H. L., & Handplant Studio. (2008). *In praise of an elevator* [Online]. Retrieved from http://www.bornmagazine.org/projects/praise/

Sheehan, D. (2006). *Ten Doors Closing* [Online]. Retrieved from http://www.youtube.com/watch?v=yIy540QP0N0

Vernallis, C. (2004). *Experiencing Music Video*. New York: Columbia University Press.

Young-Hae Chang Heavy Industries. (2004). *The Last day of Betty Nkomo* [Online]. Retrieved from http://www.yhchang.com/BETTY_NKOMO.html

5 A Second Level Pictorial Turn? The Emergence of Digital Ekphrasis from the Visuality of New Media

Nina Shiel[1]

Abstract

The increasing visuality of our culture was observed in 1994 by Mitchell, who coined the term 'pictorial turn' to describe the interest in the visual taking place in culture and discourse (Mitchell, 1994). Since then, this process has increased further, particularly in all the areas of digital/new media. This chapter will consider this development from the perspective of literary studies. Its approach will be centred on the concept of ekphrasis, usually defined as a textual representation of a visual representation. This essay will expand from theories of ekphrasis towards a little researched area of visual/textual studies: computer-generated graphics and their representation. Briefly touching on examples from social media, interactive fiction (IF) and electronic literature, this chapter will proceed to consider the representation of the digital visual in print texts. Brief examples in terms of prose fiction will be taken from Stephenson's (1992) *Snow Crash* and (2011) *REAMDE*. Finally, the essay will analyse Redmond's (2008) poem *MUDe* as an example of digital ekphrasis that brings most of its features together. It will be argued that in a digital context, ekphrasis must move beyond the visual and, instead, represent the entire experience, thereby bringing the word and image closer together.

Keywords: ekphrasis, visuality, virtual worlds.

1. School of Applied Language and Intercultural Studies, Dublin City University, Dublin, Ireland; nina.shiel3@mail.dcu.ie

How to cite this chapter: Shiel, N. (2013). A Second Level Pictorial Turn? The Emergence of Digital Ekphrasis from the Visuality of New Media. In C. Fowley, C. English, & S. Thouësny (Eds.), *Internet Research, Theory, and Practice: Perspectives from Ireland* (pp. 75-93). Dublin: © Research-publishing.net.

1.   Introduction

In the 1980s and early 1990s, visionaries such as William Gibson and Neal Stephenson imagined a global information network, to be experienced as a fully graphical, fully immersive artificial environment. While a network did develop during this time, what came out was not an immanent and immediate full-body virtual reality experience, but the internet: a stream of text and images framed by the computer screen, at a distance from the reader/viewer. Virtual reality, simulated sensory input by means of a headset and artificial limbs such as gloves, remained a trendy direction of research for a time until gradually fading out in the general lack of interest and suitable applications.

In its place, another sort of electronic immersion emerged as virtual worlds, graphical interactive environments intended for a multiplicity of users, formed on the screens. In these, users came to inhabit worlds other than their present reality through emotional and narrative immersion (Castronova, 2006). The dream of an intimate connection with the virtual by means of a phantom touch has given way to engagement of the visual sense, which has become the primary means of perceiving a virtual environment. The virtual is not to be touched; it can only be seen, or, secondarily, heard. Therefore, it would initially seem that a gap is destined to remain between the user and the environment, like that between a painting and its viewer.

The visuality of today's internet does not simply manifest in virtual worlds. The increased overall visuality acts as a status symbol. Since first becoming available to the general public at the beginning of the 1990s, the internet has rapidly grown from being a curiosity to becoming a household essential, comparable to the television or the telephone. This has enabled the growth of computer processors and the bandwidth required for transfer of data, which, for their part, have made possible the handling of more and more complex graphics. In the beginning, everything was based on simple ASCII text. Later, simple 9-bit graphics appeared. Later still, more complex graphics and digital photography became possible. Those of us who remember patiently accessing the internet through a dial-up modem will also recall the slow stage-by-stage downloading of images in the second half of the 1990s, in striking contrast to today's high speed connections and near – or fully instantaneous appearance of image-heavy websites. In the area of games, a drive for more and more complex and believable (as opposed to 'realistic') graphics is continuing and is set to continue into the future. Thus, the digital image has come to signify progress, hi-tech, top of the line.

This trend is visible throughout today's information technology. From black and white, fully textual beginnings, software interfaces have embraced colours and pictures. On the web, news sites and online magazines employ large images, complex graphs and a steadily increasing amount of video. Social networking has transformed from the early textual blogging communities such as *LiveJournal* (www.livejournal.com) towards restricted textual updates such as those on *Twitter* (www.twitter.com), with a maximum limit of 140 characters, and *Facebook* (www.facebook.com), where users tend towards short updates, photos and videos. Wholly image-focused social networks, such as *Tumblr* (www.tumblr.com) and *Pinterest* (www.pinterest.com), are on the rise. This visuality of digital media is constantly available. No longer restricted to bulky desktops, which may have been only accessible at workplaces or at schools, the near-constant stream of images is enabled by mobile technology such as smartphones and tablets.

This essay will consider the visuality of the internet from the perspective of literary studies, specifically in terms of the relationship between word and image, which have been seen as separate from each other, and, consequently, opponents, for at least 250 years. If the apparent threat of domination of the image in the digital media presents a challenge to the position of the word, how is the word responding to this challenge? Below, I will discuss some of the forms the word, as a building block of literature, has taken to adapt to the new domain. This is not happening solely within the digital media itself, but also in the 'old', print media. Novels, short stories, and even poetry, are having – or choosing – to incorporate elements from digital media. These include representations of the visuality of digital graphics and the overall interactive experience of virtual worlds. In literary studies, verbal representations of the visual are often analysed through the concept of ekphrasis. Once a rhetorical device in Antiquity, it later became adopted in a new guise for literary studies in the 1950s. Here, it will be applied to ask how word stands against the digital image. Having considered examples of digital ekphrasis both on- and offline, this essay will close by briefly analysing Redmond's (2008) poem *MUDe*.

2.   The ambivalence of the image

The association of the digital image with progress and the subsequent apparent proclivity towards it over text is remarkable, considering that in studies of the relationship between word and image, the image has traditionally held the second place. It has been considered more primitive than the word, a feminised 'Other' to be feared and to be captivated by in the process of the gaze. Word and image have been regarded as fully separate from each other since the time of Lessing, who in his *Laocoon* of 1766 (translated into English in 1836: Lessing, 2009/1836) severed any pre-existing connections between the two by arguing that words are best suited for representing other words, images to represent images, and that on no account should the two be mixed. A visual depiction cannot duplicate speech, nor can a text imitate a picture. Therefore, Lessing (2009/1836) felt that any kind of attempts of one to represent the other would be pointless.

The duality of fascination/fear has had a key role in academic perceptions of the image. In 1994, shortly after the internet had become available to the general public, Mitchell coined the concept of a 'pictorial turn', a new interest in the visual in the public culture and in academic discourse (Mitchell, 1994). A large part of his argument was based on the mass media of the time, but he already brought into play information, or what he called 'cybernetic', technology. In his study, he notes that the latter has created new forms of visuality with significant power upon the spectator. Mitchell (1994) hints here at what has been further discussed by Bolter (1996, 2001): how the dominance of the visual in digital media also reaches out to inform the 'old' media, such as print newspapers, in their increasing reliance on the image.

One of the central concepts to Mitchell's (1994) 'pictorial turn' is the realisation that a picture presents "a complex interplay between visuality, apparatus, institutions, discourse, bodies and figurality", which, at the time, meant the discovery that *spectatorship* could be considered at least as complex an issue as *reading* (p. 16). He connects the pictorial turn to a number of European philosophers such as Wittgenstein, Derrida and the Frankfurt School, noting that the fascination with the visual is mixed with unease, or outright fear, of the visual. Mitchell (1994) writes, "we still do not know exactly what pictures are, what their relation to language is, how they operate on observers and on the world, how their history is to be understood, and what is to be done with or about them" (p. 13).

The ideas of separation and mutual opposition of word and image evolved to take a key role in the concept of ekphrasis. Present in literary scholarship since the 1950s, it, too, has seen a considerable increase of interest in the past two decades. Ekphrasis refers to a verbal representation of a visual image, not simply by means of straightforward *description* but also by means of *evocation*, often using poetic language or extra details and/or appealing to the reader's own memories or other familiar associations. This lets the reader 'see' the intended visual in their own imagination. This concept began in Classical Antiquity as a rhetorical device, used in emotive delivery intended to evoke any kind of visual, from significant events to festivals, people, places and objects (Webb, 2009). The ideal was that the listener of the oratory would feel as though they were personally part of the scene evoked and experience emotions appropriate to the 'simulated' situation.

In modern literary studies, ekphrasis has become associated specifically with works of visual art and their representations in literary texts, particularly in poetry. It has also become intrinsically linked to the ambivalent status of the image in comparison with the word. In a seminal work on ekphrasis, Heffernan (1993) places the assumed opposition between word and image at the core of this concept, as the word struggles to represent the visual image. For him, this rivalry between the two is also inherently gendered. The act of spectating is active, while the object of the gaze is passive and still. Following old-fashioned gender rules and the tradition of male poets to feminise the objects of art that acted as vessels for their emotions, in gendered ekphrasis the active male spectator subjects the passive, silent, female object of his gaze to his power and judgement. The passive visual only achieves any semblance of activity or voice through the interpretation of the text produced by the spectator, who has been inspired by the encounter. The object's message, or any interpretation, is under the writer's full control. This, of course, diminishes the supposed danger presented by the visual, which, despite its assumed passivity and silence, paradoxically possesses the dangerous power to enchant and captivate its spectator.

This potential danger of the visual is developed in another direction by Mitchell (1994) in his concept of the 'ekphrastic fear', which refers to the disquiet at the prospect of the merging of the visual and the textual. With this, Mitchell (1994) effectively prioritises human imagination over a straightforward visual depiction. If the verbal were able to fully reproduce the visual that it seeks to represent, there would be no function left for the verbal. It would be rendered obsolete, essentially non-existent. Likewise, no room would remain for imagination, as experiencing the visual in a text would no longer be a matter of a personal mental process of associations, familiarities and interpretations. In such circumstances, the visual would become invasive. To avoid this, the borders between the text and image must remain in place, and the two must treat each other as rivals and 'others'.

If the image presents such a threat, why is it so attractive? This question is addressed by Krieger (1992), who links ekphrasis with a semiotic desire to the general preference of the visual over the verbal. Manifesting as an 'ekphrastic impulse', this semiotic urge strives towards what Krieger (1992) calls a 'natural sign', a theoretical (and impossible) sign which is that which it represents. A word for 'apple' would be represented by an actual apple. An actual physical apple is understood far more quickly than the word 'apple' even by a native speaker. The verbal always, inevitably, mediates the visual. As with Mitchell's (1994) ekphrastic fear, if such a natural sign existed, representation would become meaningless. Histories, fiction and visual artistic representations would effectively cease to exist. Rather than presenting the ekphrastic opposition as a struggle, Krieger (1992) sees it as a stillness in a text. To him, ekphrasis stills the flow of linguistic narrative into a moment of quiet, like the static, silent object of visual art at the heart of its inspiration.

Until now, ekphrasis has been mostly applied to static works of art such as statues and paintings. Most typically, such artworks are viewed in a gallery or a museum setting, which creates an additional formal layer to the viewer's encounter with the visual. Like the narrative in Krieger's (1992) suggestion, the viewer stops his or her own motion to view the artwork, always remaining detached from it. Although the artwork is tangible and physical, the viewer's experience is monosensory: only vision is used. Touch is forbidden, other senses are unnecessary.

Digital visual art, on the other hand, differs in a number of respects. Primarily, it is non-tangible to the user's physical body, but her/his graphical avatar may be able to interact with it in a variety of different ways. No longer simply a viewer, the *user* may be able to control the digital visual, not simply by gazing at it and offering it a guise and voice according to his/her own agenda, but in a concrete manner, by giving commands by means of a controller such as the mouse, keyboard, or a sensor that reads gestures. In many cases, this control 'creates' the artwork anew each time: for instance, when a cursor is guided on the screen of a digital poem to make the elements move, or when the user's avatar moves through a virtual landscape and progresses his/her own personal narrative by completing quests and advancing plot in an online game. If the immersion of the virtual environment is sufficiently strong, the avatar, as the user's proxy, enables the user to directly experience the emotions and reactions appropriate to the situation and setting. By interacting with the environment, the user enters into a dialogue that would be unreachable with a non-digital artwork.

The experience of a virtual environment is not simply visual. In a manner that might give pause to Lessing (2009/1836) and Krieger (1992), the user interface of a massively multiplayer online (MMO) game blurs textual commands, communication and input with strong visuals, and also with significant auditory input, in the form of background music, sound effects, in-game dialogue and voice over internet communication with other players. This form of visual art is not still or silent: it shifts and changes and imbues the user with an illusion of movement or touch, as the avatar runs, fights or handles equipment, other avatars or even virtual 'food'. It forces the user to make decisions in terms of plot or engagement with other users. Not being sentient, a MMO or another virtual world will never be as active as its user, but neither does it sit back in its own passivity like a painting or a statue. By offering the user direct rather than indirect control and by enabling interactive dialogue and the (illusionary) freedom of (illusionary) movement, the participatory nature of the digital visual decreases the fear of the unreachable otherness of the image and makes it considerably more appealing.

3.   Responses of the word

As discussed above, the word encounters and attempts to match the representational power of the image in the concept of ekphrasis. The first mention of ekphrasis in a digital context occurs in the first edition[1] of Bolter's (2001) work. He raised the possibility of a digital ekphrasis, but, following his observation that culture was becoming dominated by images, he saw a reversal the ekphrastic process in the new media and in its influence. Using examples from traditional and new media, he proposes that, rather than words striving to represent images, images are now used to represent words. Bolter's (2001) argument is supported by what might be termed 'legacy iconography'. Nowadays, a decreasing number of users know why the sign for 'save file' in the Windows operating system is a dark rectangle with a smaller white rectangle and a white dot inside it – a floppy disk. Original representation of the command in terms of appropriate technology approaches Krieger's (1992) desire for the natural sign very closely, but, by now, few users have ever even seen a floppy disk. The sign has transformed from its original signification to a representation of an idea, an action.

---

1. Bolter (1991).

Much of digital text centres on hypertext, which refers to segments of interconnected texts linked to each other by means of hyperlinks. Although the concept of hypertext lies at the heart of all websites, the term itself is little used now. It was in wider use in the 1990s, as the first academic enquiries into digital texts, images and their interrelations took place. Using the definitions of Krieger (1992) and Mitchell (1994), Tolva (1996) has put forward that a hypertext cluster of linked fragments of text acts in an ekphrastic way. Rather than simply describing such a spatial textual structure, it evokes one through uses of text colours and the reader's experience, as the reader moves through segments of texts using hyperlinks, distinguished from the rest of the text by their colour.

In interactive fiction, a form of online literature made possible by hypertext, the reader progresses through the narrative by following links, which typically present two or more alternative paths. Starting out in the 1980s as adventure games, in the 1990s this form found some more literary applications. Joyce's *Afternoon*, written in 1987 and published in 1990, is considered to be the first example of the so-called 'hypertext fiction'. Cooper's (1994) *Delirium*, the first novel to be serialised on the internet, presented four different narrative pathways to the reader. *Delirium* was subsequently published in print in 1998, but reviews found it confusing. The popularity of interactive fiction faded towards the end of the 1990s, but recently, new manifestations of this literary form have emerged in the form of browser games such as the complex, mock-Victorian *Fallen London*[1]. It follows the principles of interactive fiction by telling a story, personal to the player, within the constraints of her/his choices. It employs very evocative intertextual language, which succeeds in creating a sense of personal involvement through the use of the second person address, details, allusions, references and similes. The game also steps out of its immediate borders by having some of the notable non-player characters post in-character messages to their own in-character social media accounts. This enables the players to communicate with the characters of the setting even outside the formal boundaries of the game itself.

1. Originally known as *Echo Bazaar*, *Fallen London* (http://fallenlondon.storynexus.com/) is part of the Storynexus initiative, which allows users to create their own interactive textual worlds and narratives within them.

Such interactivity between a literary setting and its reader is also present in the 2010 real-time adaptation of Romeo and Juliet on *Twitter*, when some of the characters actively solicited suggestions and answers to questions from the audience[1]. It could be argued that in the latter circumstance interactivity with the audience is illusionary, as everyone knows how the story must end, but this is equally applicable to most interactive literary material. The reader has a certain amount of freedom and choice, but the nature of the work as strictly or weakly narrative dictates how much influence the reader actually has[2].

Kashtan (2011) argues that in interactive fiction, ekphrasis is the characteristic mode of visual representation, as online text seeks to (re-)create and evoke the experience of this typically ludic form of writing/reading, which allows the reader/user to select his/her own path through the text. He points out that the heavily textual interactive fiction manifests the cultural ambivalence with images, by reacting against, or distinguishing itself, from the far more popular graphical games. Kashtan's (2011) main proposal is that interactive fiction offers indirect visual experiences dependent on the player's imagination, rather than unmediated, explicit visual experiences as a painting or a graphical game would do. In this way, an IF text becomes an ekphrastic text, especially if we consider Hollander's (1995) suggestion of notional ekphrasis as a form of ekphrasis pertaining to a fictional artwork. Interactive fiction, like an ekphrastic text, does not only describe, but evokes, something visual. Kashtan (2011) supports this by referring back to the original ekphrasis as practiced in the Classical world as a practice of making the listener/reader 'translate' the intended powerful visual, from its representation in words, into an imaginary visual representation in the listener's mind's eye[3].

Another feature of Classical ekphrasis – its interdependence between the

1. The performance of Romeo and Juliet (http://www.guardian.co.uk/culture/2010/apr/12/shakespeare-twitter-such-tweet-sorrow) was 'staged' by Mudlark and the Royal Shakespeare Company.

2. The opposite of a strictly narrative interactive story or a game is the form known in the world of game design as 'sandbox'. Rather than following through the various options of a pre-determined plot, it focuses on exploration, social interaction and construction of items and houses in-game.

3. Kashtan's (2011) source for Classical ekphrasis is Koelb (2006). This work is heavily based on the groundbreaking article by Webb (1999), which was expanded into a full length study in 2009.

deliverer of the ekphrasis and its receiver – is employed by Lindhé (2010), who sees this dialogue as an integral way to consider the interactivity of digital material. Ekphrasis fully comes into being when its receiver forms a vivid visual in her/his mind in response to a powerful verbal delivery, thereby requiring a two-way communication. In her exploration of electronic literature, she focuses on installations created using computer technology and intended to be 'read' by the same means. One of the best known examples of such works is Screen, created in the Brown University CAVE virtual environment[1]. CAVE works, when experienced directly, involve a headset to create immersion, with strong visual and auditory elements. The 'reader' is no longer an outsider, a passive observer, but becomes an essential part of the 'text' due to interactive elements. In this sense, such experiential forms of 'electronic' literature[2], as well as full virtual worlds, link back to interactive fiction, which also places the reader at the centre of things by offering choices and a degree of control throughout the process of reading, thus offering a fuller sense of an experience. In her analysis, Lindhé (2010) focuses on the element of touch, interactivity and the near-bodily intimacy with the form of art that does not keep the viewer gazing at a distance in a power play, as traditional static art does, but invites the viewer into a close contact with, and within, it.

The intimacy between the digital and the reader/user can also emerge in less subtle ways. Much of digital literature addresses the reader directly, in the second person. This is particularly the case in any ludic material, whether an IF text or an MMO game, which casts the reader in a role within the setting. This device is not unknown from pre-digital print literature, but the influence of digital material has seen it increase in use, not only online but also in certain print texts[3]. Recent examples of this include the novels *Halting State* and *Rule 34* by Stross (2008, 2011), both of which deal with blurring boundaries of on-

---

1. A video of Screen can be viewed on *YouTube*: http://www.youtube.com/watch?v=WOwF5KD5BV4&feature. Brown University offers a module in CAVE writing, which enables non-programmers to create visual and verbal texts using this technology. In Ireland, the Dun Laoghaire Institute of Art, Design and Technology has a CAVE laboratory.

2. The Electronic Literature Organisation defines 'electronic' or 'digital' literature as "works with important literary aspects that take advantage of the capabilities and contexts provided by the stand-alone or networked computer". The website of the ELO, featuring this definition, can be found at http://eliterature.org/, see also Hayles (2008).

3. It has, for instance, been used by Calvino (1981) in his *If on a Winter's Night a Traveller*.

and offline existence, and also the poem *MUDe* by Redmond (2008), analysed below. This device was also used by Jennifer Egan in her short story, *Black Box*, published in several self-contained instalments on Twitter in May 2012[1]. Unlike in the instances of social media used as appendices to game worlds or as a 'stage' for interactive theatrical performance, in the case of 'Black Box' no input was sought from the audience. Yet, the format of the second person narrative casts the reader as the main character of the story, seeking to ekphrastically invoke appropriate visuals and reactions in the reader, specifically from the reader's point of view.

Aside from the second person address, which aims to engage the reader immediately as a central cast member of the work, by channeling through the reader the visuals and the entire participatory experience, print texts have adopted several other strategies to represent the digital image. Print literature has represented the digital visual since well before the latter's general public availability, since the time of the emergence of the cyberpunk genre with Gibson's (1984) *Neuromancer*. As actual technology has rapidly reached and often also surpassed, or bypassed, the technologies represented in literature, literature has responded in two ways. Some texts, such as Stephenson's (2011) *REAMDE*, have chosen to work with currently available technology in their setting, without outwardly confining themselves to a particular year. Others, such as the works mentioned above by Stross (2008, 2011) and Brin's (2012) *Existence* , have sought to remain ahead of the curve by imagining a move away from terminals towards sleek 'augmented reality', computer-generated text and visuals overlaid on actual reality, accessed by spectacles, contact lenses or implants.

Common to all verbal representations of the digital/virtual in prose texts is the dependence on some form of technology. The alternate world, in and out of which the characters pass, is not a mystical Otherworld, but a layer of existence artificially generated by technological means. The examples considered below are taken from the works of Stephenson (1992), whose *Snow Crash* holds a

---

1. First published on *The New Yorker* Fiction account, twitter.com/NYerFiction, the story is also available on *The New Yorker* blog: http://www.newyorker.com/online/blogs/books/2012/05/jennifer-egan-black-box.html.

seminal position in the area of text and the digital visual. He deals with the same themes in *The Diamond Age* (Stephenson, 1995) and in *REAMDE* (Stephenson, 2011).

In *Snow Crash* (Stephenson, 1992), artificiality is enhanced by regular emphases in the text, either straightforwardly in verbs of technology or visuality such as 'render', 'represent' and 'appear' and in adjectives such as 'imaginary', 'computer-generated' and 'not real'. At times, borders between the virtual and real are blurred, for example when the main characters Hiro and Y.T. phone each other. The question 'Where are you?' is with a return question, 'In Reality or the Metaverse?' (p. 191). When Hiro enters or exits the Metaverse, the novel's virtual environment, we hear that 'He turns off Reality' (p. 388) or that it is 'Time to get immersed in Reality' (p. 285). In *REAMDE*, which sets part of its narrative in an online game called T'Rain, the protagonist Richard retorts a colleague's lament about the difficulties of 'physically' moving in-game resources across the virtual landscape: 'Not "physically" [...] You guys always make that mistake. It's a game, remember?' (Stephenson, 2011, p. 171).

The artificiality of the virtual landscape is linked with the awareness of the issues relating to the visual. The plot of *Snow Crash* is centred upon the eponymous virtual 'drug', an information virus, which appears as an image of a scroll of nonsensical text. Its viewing in the virtual environment does not only infect the user's computer but also damages the user's brain. Although Hiro's point of view protests that 'You can't get high by looking at something' (Stephenson, 1992, p. 39), the ekphrastic danger of gazing at a fascinating object appears to be underlined here. However, the graphic combines both image and text, which, together with the frequent mentions throughout the text that the visuals of the Metaverse have been 'written' into existence by means of programming code, indicates that the relationship between the word and image is not as straightforward as traditional ekphrasis would have it. The apparent dangers of the visual are also present in the much more recent *REAMDE*. As a consequence of a 'palette drift' in the graphics, the players of T'Rain end up battling each other as two opposing factions based on their colour schemes of preference. This mocks the typical division into Good and Evil in the fantasy genre, on which the novel's game is modelled. Here, on the other hand, the concepts of 'good' and 'evil' lose all meaning as the users prefer to align themselves with colour schemes. The sheer absurdity of a division based on something as apparently trivial as colour palettes emphasises the power of the visual image.

In these texts, passages that may be termed as ekphrastic occur as intense, dynamic, evocative descriptions of the virtual environment[1]. These scenes are typically seen through a character's eye, with verbs of looking and seeing in frequent use. In addition to verbs of seeing, the passages also typically include several verbs of action and movement. The virtual scenes are themselves active within a constantly dynamic work of art, rather than still paintings or statues. This sense of movement in text reflects the same element present in digital texts. Similarly, works such as those constructed by the CAVE method and which involve wearable technology directly involve the movement of our own bodies in the creation of the digital experience. Installations of electronic literature typically rely on movement in their presentations of words and images. In interactive fiction, the reader proceeds through the segments of the narrative using the underlying hypertext.

4.   Representing digital text, representing imaginary visuals: John Redmond's MUDe

An example of digital ekphrasis, as employed within the print domain, comes from the Irish poet John Redmond in his poem 'MUDe', published in a collection of the same title in 2008. The poem is written in the form of four sessions of online gameplay, interspersed with personal memories. In his explanatory notes attached to the poem, Redmond (2008) notes that the particular fictional MUD of the poem is a 'Dungeons and Dragons' themed fantasy online environment, entirely text-based. As Redmond (2008) observes, text-based online games are

---

1. Some examples of these include, in *Snow Crash*, pp. 23-25, 33-39, 50-52, 405-408; and in *REAMDE*, pp. 591-594, 737-739 and 764-766.

a (dying) minority in the genre dominated by graphical games. However, many conventions of MUDs, such as certain idioms and terminology, division of characters into players and automated non-players, as well as many features of in-game communication by means of textual channels, have been preserved in the graphical games. This, combined with the intense visuals of the text, would make the representation of this textual online world indistinguishable from a graphical one, were the authorial intention not known.

Although technology tends to be emphasised in prose texts representing the virtual, it receives no outright mentions here. The artificiality of the scenes and events narrated is, instead, indicated by means of symbols and fonts denoting typed commands and out-of-character communication, as well as by the contrast of mundane matters such as employment and different time zones discussed on these channels. As some of the player characters are harassed by an orc tithe-collector and his fire spirit minion, one of the players, Oompah, logged on from her office, remarks: "*#Oompah: Because my boss just came in and me help him spell 'insubordinate'*". The player communication is denoted by the hash symbol and the italic font. While Oompah remains distracted by real world matters, another player, Godsend, displays newcomer behaviour by impolitely demanding instructions on how to play the game and 'loudly' (using all capital letters) 'shouting' abuse at other players. Immersion, so important in texts like *Snow Crash*, in which virtual characters are forbidden to try to touch each other for fear of breaking immersion, is of no concern to the players here. Ironically, the main character, the 'you' addressed by the poem, using the ludic second-person device, is fully immersed not only in the game but also in his own tragic memories triggered by the events and exchanges in the game. This ekphrastic appeal to emotional memories and associations, the merging of the boundaries between virtual and the real, familiar from the prose texts discussed above, also reflects the mutual two-way communication of the user and the game.

Throughout the poem, the main character is visited, seemingly in-game, by 'your ten-year-old self' and anxious relatives, with whom the player relives his childhood home and the trauma of his father's suicide in the sea. The poem contrasts the finality of a real-life death with the reversible nature of a death of a game character. The poem opens with 'As you move, you turn living again' and proceeds to chronicle the main character's resurrection, another death in a battle against the fire spirit, another resurrection and another near-demise, saved by the temporary reboot of the server on which the game is hosted. These events are often associated with a sensation of falling, ekphrastically brought to life by descending irregular lines, consonance and assonance, and generous use of white space.

Right from the first line of the poem, a sense of movement runs throughout it. Aside from the scenes of falling and the cycle of death/resurrection, player and non-player characters constantly 'arrive', 'leave', move around and fight. In each area of the game, available directions for movement are presented: 'Obvious directions: east, down' (Redmond, 2008, p. 30). At times the desired movement is not possible: the command '>east' is typed, but there is 'No such exit' (Redmond, 2008, p. 27). The 'you' of the main character wrestles, falls, throws things, climbs, fights, drinks, explores, swims. It is worth emphasising again that in the poem, these actions are assumed to take place on a computer screen. Not real, they are visualised by the player, from whose point of view the poem is written. As the poem passes on to the reader, the reader must, for her/his part, visualise the events anew.

Although the poem's game is meant to consist purely of text, strong visuals are delivered as the main character's memories merge with the game areas. These most recognisably 'traditionally' ekphrastic paragraphs, seeking to bring alive vivid visuals, appear as semi-prose, differentiated by even lines amidst the rest of the free-form poem. The descriptions are of significant sites: the main character's childhood home, the nearby barn, pub and the sea, here resituated within the game and brought to life in a visceral manner. "When you walk, the surface twitches and your legs vanish below the knee", "the entrance – a large rectangle of daylight – leans an ambivalent shoulder against the darkening banks of hay", and "As the suddenly visible walls blister with self-understanding, a scorched ladder floats into the inferno" (Redmond, 2008, pp. 28-33). As visualisation, imagination and memories unite the act of looking, present in the beginning of the poem at the start of a new 'life', is no longer enough. Fear, relief, annoyance, discomfort and amusement are all present. The poem shows that in a digital context, ekphrasis can no longer be said to apply to representations of the purely visual only: it becomes a verbal representation of the whole experience of the digital.

5.   Conclusion

Examining the various responses of the word to the increased presence of the image in the current digital mass media offers an intriguing set of insights into the relationship between the two. Despite the long-held notion that word and image are separate, even rivals, the treatment of the word in the digital media and that of digital media in the realm of word indicate that their relationship in this context may be more amicable. Digital ekphrasis, which we may term a verbal representation of the digital/virtual *experience*, rather than simply that of a digital visual, offers a mutual dialogue between the immersive visual and the user. This creates a sense of a more balanced power dynamic and of a certain freedom. Although the user is not physically 'there' in the virtual environment, the use of vivid evocative language in the manner of Classical ekphrasis, the use of the second personal address, and the ability to experience not only vision, but also hearing, movement and strong emotions, create a strong simulation of personal participation, the very aim of ekphrasis in the ancient times. This is in contrast to many modern theories of ekphrasis, which perceive it as a process of detachment and outside observation, a one-way channel of antagonistic power struggle, and a moment of still reflection in the text. Even if, as the borders between the image and text blur, like they do in instances of the merging of the virtual and the real, we might feel a trace of Mitchell's (1994) ekphrastic fear, perhaps we will also be sufficiently excited about the new possibilities afforded to embrace the little-considered core of ekphrasis: inspiration.

Author note: This research is supported by the Irish Research Council (Humanities and Social Sciences).

References

Bolter, J. D. (1991). *Writing Space: The Computer, Hypertext, and the History of Writing* (2nd ed.). Hillsdale, New Jersey: Lawrence Erlbaum.

Bolter, J. D. (1996). Ekphrasis, virtual reality, and the future of writing. In G. Nunberg (Ed.), *The Future of the book* (pp. 253-271). Berkeley and Los Angeles: University of California Press.

Bolter, J. D. (2001). *Writing space: The Computer, hypertext, and the history of writing* (2nd ed.). Hillsdale, NJ: Lawrence Erlbaum.

Brin, D. (2012). *Existence*. New York: Tor Books.

Calvino, I. (1981). *If on a Winter's Night a Traveller*. London: Harcourt Brace & Company.

Castronova, E. (2006). *Synthetic Worlds*. Chicago and London: University of Chicago Press.

Cooper, D. A. (1994). *Delirium*. Time Warner Electronic Publishing (TWEP).

Cooper, D. A. (1998). *Delirium*. New York: Hyperion Books.

Gibson, W. (1984). *Neuromancer*. London: Victor Gollancz Ltd.

Hayles, N. K. (2008). *Electronic Literature: New Horizons for the Literary*. Notre Dame, IL: University of Notre Dame Press.

Heffernan, J. A. W. (1993). *Museum of words: The Poetics of ekphrasis from Homer to Ashbery*. Chicago: University of Chicago Press.

Hollander, J. (1995). *The Gazer's spirit: Poems speaking to silent works of art*. Chicago: University of Chicago Press.

Joyce, M. (1990). *Afternoon*. Eastgate Systems. Retrieved from http://www.wwnorton.com/college/english/pmaf/hypertext/aft/index.html

Kashtan, A. (2011). Because it's not there: Ekphrasis and the threat of graphics in interactive fiction. *Digital Humanities Quarterly, 5*(1). Retrieved from http://digitalhumanities.org/dhq/vol/5/1/000101/000101.html

Koelb, J. H. (2006). *The Poetics of Description: Imagined Places in European Literature*. New York: Palgrave Macmillan.

Krieger, M. (1992). *Ekphrasis: The Illusion of the natural sign*. Baltimore, Maryland: The Johns Hopkins University Press.

Lindhé, C. (2010). 'Bildseendet föds i fingertopparna': Om en ekfras för den digitala tidsåldern. *Ekfrase, 1*, 4-16.

Lessing, G. E. (2009/1836). *Laocoon: An Essay upon the limits of painting and poetry* [Translated by E. Frothingham]. Mineola: Dover Publications Inc.

Mitchell, W. J. T. (1994). *Picture theory: Essays on verbal and visual representation*. Chicago: University of Chicago Press.

Redmond, J. (2008). *MUDe*. Manchester: Carcanet.

Stephenson, N. (1992). *Snow Crash*. New York: Bantam Books.

Stephenson, N. (1995). *The Diamond Age*. New York: Bantam Books.

Stephenson, N. (2011). *REAMDE*. London: Atlantic Books.

Stross, C. (2008). *Halting State*. London: Orbit.

Stross, C. (2011). *Rule 34*. London: Orbit.

Tolva, J. (1996). 'Ut pictura hyperpoesis' Spatial form, visuality, and the digital word. *Hypertext 96: The Seventh ACM Conference on Hypertext, Washington DC, March 16-20 1996*. Retrieved from http://www.dilip.info/HT96/P43/pictura.htm

Webb, R. (1999). Ekphrasis Ancient and Modern: The Invention of a Genre. *Word and Image, 15*(1), 7-18. doi: 10.1080/02666286.1999.10443970

Webb, R. (2009). *Ekphrasis, Imagination and Persuasion in Ancient Rhetorical Theory and Practice*. Farnham: Ashgate Press.

6 Digital Reading: A Question of Prelectio?

Noel Fitzpatrick[1]

Abstract

Digital reading as superficial reading is examined by demonstrating that technologies act as placeholders for different types of memory, artificial memory and true memory. This chapter argues that the affordances of digital technologies enable certain types of reading activity, digital reading, but hinders others, such as deep reading. In particular, there is a tenuous relationship between digital reading and scanning for information in the printed text, a form of reading traditionally known as *prelectio*. This latter is a pre-reading of the text for salient information, not for deep understanding: it is, rather, a scanning or skimming of the text. Since the development of digital reading, there has been a debate about the role taken by digital technologies in the acquisition of reading as an activity. This chapter will, through the analysis of the recent works of Stiegler (2010) and the research group Ars Industrialis, challenge the outright rejection of the digital technologies of reading. Instead, by revisiting the technology of writing as a cure and a poison, as a *pharmakon*, a positive pharmacology will be proposed. By re-examining the philosophical problematic of reading and writing, the first step of this positive pharmacology will be to identify the necessary curative aspects of the technology.

Keywords: digital reading, prelectio, narratio, lectio, Generation M, cognitive overflow, pharmakon, Stiegler.

---

1. The School of Art, Design and Printing, Dublin Institute of Technology, Dublin, Ireland; noel.fitzpatrick@dit.ie

How to cite this chapter: Fitzpatrick, N. (2013). Digital Reading: A Question of Prelectio? In C. Fowley, C. English, & S. Thouësny (Eds.), *Internet Research, Theory, and Practice: Perspectives from Ireland* (pp. 95-110). Dublin: © Research-publishing.net.

---

1. Introduction

This chapter sets out to counter a train of thought which posits the technologies of digital reading as the root of a decline in reading and as the cause for the development of surface reading. It questions the claim that the technologies themselves lead to a type of reading which remains on the surface and hinders readers from developing more reflective reading practices. In order to counter this argument, the chapter highlights the principal reasons for rejecting digital reading as a form of pre-reading exercise, a *prelectio*. Then this chapter examines the relationship between different types of reading and contextualises the philosophical problematic of reading by investigating current writing within the work of French philosopher Stiegler (2010). The chapter attempts to determine the first steps in the revisiting of digital technologies of reading as a positive remedy to enable the development of deeper reading.

There is a wealth of research dealing with digital literacy. In America the debate has focused on the decrease in reading habits and the growth of digital forms of reading (Cartelli, 2012). In the US, it is claimed that *Generation M* are reading less and less printed texts. The term *Generation M* was used to describe the generation of 8-18 year olds as a media generation and it came from the title of a report written in 2005, which investigates the use of media by this age group (Roberts, Foehr, & Rideout, 2005). *Generation M* are reading less and less, we are told, but at the same time they are reading more and more online, using media other than the printed text. However, digital reading is a specific form of reading, a specific form of *tekhnē*, and therefore requires specific analysis.

In order to come to a fuller understanding of the impact of digital technologies on reading, we need to revisit the form of reading which takes place on screen. This chapter will argue that there is a specific form of reading, a *prelectio*, which is enabled by the form of the text on screen. Whether this form of reading is detrimental to more sustained deep reading is a moot point within literacy studies. The outright rejection of digital technology has become more prevalent through a series of recent publications where the analysis of the detrimental effect of digital reading is embedded within a discourse which highlights the negative effects of technology. Bauerlein (2008), in his book *The Dumbest Generation: How the Digital Age Stupefies Young Americans and Jeopardizes Our Future*, rejects internet technologies, as is evident from the provocative title. Bauerlein (2008) argues that a decline in reading is directly linked to two main factors: the decrease in print reading and the growth of digital texts. He also argues that there is no transfer from digital reading to print reading, going so far as stating that digital reading does not develop strong reading skills (Bauerlein, 2008, pp. 93-111).

Another example is Carr (2011) in his book *The Shallows: What the internet is doing to our Brains*; Carr (2011) takes a slightly different slant but one which, nonetheless, rejects digital reading, identifying it as a form of surface reading. His analysis of his personal experience of reading in the digital age details the development of his addiction to skimming along the surface, a pathological internet usage. He describes this addiction as a form of inattention, skipping from screen to screen, and not allowing the time or space for reflection and deeper reading. Both authors illustrate a tendency at the moment to view the technological tools of digital reading as a 'scapegoat': a *pharmakos*.

2. Surface reading and deep reading

However, the specific form of reading which Carr (2011) and Bauerlein (2008) refer to as surface reading has its parallel in another form of surface reading which has a long history in relation to reading and education: the *prelectio*. In the study of rhetoric, *prelectio* can be dated back to the first century, to Quinitilian, and then extends through monastic traditions to John of Salisbury (1180) and Bernard de Chartes (c.1130). In order to comprehend what is at stake in drawing a parallel between surface reading in digital technologies and *prelectio*, it is necessary to give a brief historical account of the latter. In the monastic tradition techniques were developed to decipher texts without reading in detail. Thus, it is argued that word separation and *prelectio* were part of the development of silent reading (Saenger, 1991). The monks were amongst the first to establish canonical word separation. At that time, romance latin of the early biblical texts had fallen into disuse, and texts were blocks, *scriptura continua*, without punctuation or word separation. The texts were read out loud; hence, the lack of punctuation. Saenger (1997) in his book *Space Between Words: The Origins of Silent Reading* demonstrates that the practice of canonical word separation led to the growth of silent individual reading in the monasteries. Word separation, therefore, became the norm. The reading of the text to first establish word separation was a scanning for information in the text, not for its meaning: the monks skimmed the surface of the text in order to separate out the words before engaging in a deeper reading. This initial scanning for information or pre-reading of the text was an essential part of the process of deciphering the morphological structure of text; the ability to move from *prelectio* to *narratio* or *lectio* was central to the reading process in the monastic tradition: one enables the other and is not exclusive of the other. The movement is from a pre-reading for information to a detailed reading for meaning, from scanning to semantics, from *prelectio* to *lectio*.

Reading as *lectio* was a silent reflective activity, associated with learning and meditation. Saint Augustine (AD 397/1955) points to the relationship between reading and meditation. The reader's eye glances from the page to an inner eye of reflection and meditation:

> "Thus he spoke, and in the pangs of the travail of the new life he turned his eyes again onto the page and continued reading; he was inwardly changed, as thou didst see, and the world dropped away from his mind, as soon became plain to others. For as he read with a heart like a stormy sea, more than once he groaned. Finally he saw the better course, and resolved on it" (Saint Augustine, AD 397/1955, book 8, chapter 6, para. 15).

Prelectio, lectio and *narratio* were seen as part of the approach to the pedagogy of reading (Minnis, 1994). The parallel is, therefore, a movement from scanning to comprehension which constitutes an inherent relationship between both forms of reading: surface reading enables deeper reading, they are not mutually exclusive reading activities. The type of reading involved in the implementation of word separation in the monastic tradition is akin to techniques used in natural language processing, which are widely used ; texts are parsed and analysed in terms of the smallest unit or n-gram. The text is analysed in terms of its surface characteristics: spaces, full stops and punctuation markers, which, it can be argued, is a form of surface reading of texts. However, in natural language processing the movement from the statistical surface information to the deeper semantics has been much more difficult than initially thought. The semantics of the semantic web today remain a goal of artificial intelligent systems but remain unattainable.

3.   Digital reading and inattention

Hayles (2007) sets out to understand why students in third level education are reading less and less in the humanities. She demonstrates that there is a cognitive divide between generations. *Generation M* are finding it more difficult to read novels because of their inability to attend to the texts for sustained periods of reading. Hayles (2007) argues that there is an opposition between the types of attention involved in different media, print and digital, and that reading as an activity requires deep attention while the use of digital technologies necessitates hyper-attention. The skipping from screen to screen reflects a more profound problematic of inattention:

> "Deep attention, the cognitive style traditionally associated with the humanities, is characterized by concentrating on a single object for long periods (say, a novel by Dickens), ignoring outside stimuli while so engaged, preferring a single information stream, and having a high tolerance for long focus times. Hyper-attention is characterized by switching focus rapidly among different tasks, preferring multiple information streams, seeking a high level of stimulation, and having a low tolerance for boredom" (Hayles, 2007, p. 187).

The hyper-attention involved in switching rapidly from task to task is, therefore, a form of inattention, leading to the inability to concentrate for sustained periods of time. Hayles (2007) points to the development of a generation in America where deficit hyperactivity disorder (ADHD) is on the increase. *Ritalin*, the drug used to treat children with ADHD stimulates the brain so that the activity is increased, the drug acting as a cortical stimulant. Hyperactivity is therefore sustained, to avoid boredom setting in. If Carr (2011) and Bauerlein (2008) highlight hyper-attention or inattention as part of digital reading, Hayles (2007) links it to a wider issue in relation to digital technologies and the development of other forms of inattention. However, Hayles (2007) does not dismiss technologies as the 'scapegoat' but attempts to offer examples of how hyper-attention and attention could be developed as specific pedagogical strategies, where e-learning or blended learning could harness the technologies of hyperactivity for positive use. The emergence of serious games, for example, highlights the positive learning opportunities afforded by the use of gaming technologies in education. Positive aspects thus include the ability to handle multiple tasks and to strategise. Hyper-attention and attention should not therefore be seen as mutually exclusive; ADHD may be an extreme point on the continuum of inattention, yet hyper-attention linked to digital technologies could be used to engage new generations into more sustained attention. She concludes by stating:

> "Whether inclined toward deep or hyper-attention, toward one side or another of the generational divide separating print from digital culture, we cannot afford to ignore the frustrating, zesty, and intriguing ways in which the two cognitive modes interact. Our responsibilities as educators, not to mention our position as practitioners of the literary arts, require nothing less" (Hayles, 2007, p. 198).

The design of reading activities in higher education must include educational opportunities which enable the two cognitive forms to interact. However, the problematic of reading in the twenty first century is not just about cognition. Reading has also become part of a powerful and commercially successful 'reading industry', a term coined by Giffard (2009) to describe an industry which seeks the traces we leave on the web as part of our daily reading activity and offers them as a good to be bought, sold and monetised.

4. Digital reading as a form of surface reading

The relationship between *prelectio* and digital reading is that both are based on reading for information and not reading for content. The type of reading offered by early pre-web screen reading is akin to the monastic *prelectio* for word separation. As Giffard (2009) points out:

"Before the web, in the practice of reading on a screen, the text is not the objective of the reader. Rather is it a control reading, a certain way to decipher and survey the informations (sic) and operations of the computer. And reading is submitted to another activity that is the real goal. Credit card, word processor, phototypesetting are examples of such a "reading on a screen". Umberto Eco has said "word processor e una machina molto spirituale" but reading functionalities of word processor are not spirituals at all" (Section "Digital reading is reading", para. 4).

Reading on screen is akin to the *prelectio*, reading for information, a control reading to ensure that the information being portrayed is correct or incorrect. This functional reading is not a spiritual one of meditation i.e., *lectio*. Giffard (2009) argues that this form of reading for information is inherent in any screen reading and is now so widespread as to be second nature to our relationship with digital technologies. The affordances of the technologies in place lead to the predominance of a *prelectio*.

Embedded in 'digital reading' is a form of hyper-attention because the reader is distracted from the principal task at hand. The model of comprehension of the text is interrupted by the technology itself; there is a distraction built into the very interface of the digital technology being used. The reader is cognitively aware of choices being made or not made at the same time that reading takes place. This leads to what is referred to as cognitive overflow. Reading in itself is a highly challenging cognitive activity – a young child learning to read is the proof of how challenging it can be – and in addition to this complex cognitive activity, digital reading intersperses supplementary cognitive demands such as hyperlinks. Hyperlinks, which may or may not be clicked on, act as a distraction from the principal task at hand. In addition, there is the distraction inherent to the very interface, the technology, the screen renewing, the backlight, the layout of the page on screen and often the use of poor typography. The challenges of reading online lead to distraction:

> "As opposed to the relative linearity of printed text, the very appearance of digital information at once presents both new richness and new challenges for the online reader. The fluid, multimodal nature of digital information enables online readers to become immersed in a subject, both visually and verbally. Even as this presentation of material in several different modes provides the reader with multiple points of entry into a subject, it also opens the door to great distraction. It further requires that the reader understand how to evaluate visual information and make meaning in and across several different modalities" (Wolf & Barzillai, 2009, p. 135).

All of these lead to a distraction within the distraction, a type of hyper-attention which leads to a surface reading of the text, and this constant distraction is an object of criticism, as discussed above. The distraction impinges on the reader's ability to move from surface to deep reading, a reading that enables reflection and understanding, and which for Saint Augustine (AD 397/1955) allowed the development of the spirit. But Giffard (2011) also posits a positive alternative to this deterministic vision of technology:

> "Evoquons enfin une autre orientation de Carr et ce qu'il faut bien appeler sa vision déterministe de la technique. L'auteur semble prisonnier de l'hypothèse de McLuhan selon laquelle le medium définit le message. D'autre part, il n'envisage pas la possibilité que le lecteur, par un régime d'exercices appropriés, puisse conquérir son autonomie par rapport au dispositif technique, voire le détourner. Le formatage de la lecture par l'internet est la logique qui s'impose à l'exclusion de toute autre" (Giffard, 2011, section "Une vision déterministe de la technique", para. 1).

> *Lastly to mention Carr's other orientation and which must be called his determinist vision of technology. The author seems to be a prisoner of*

McLuhan's hypothesis according to which the medium is the message. In addition, he does not envisage the possibility that through a mechanism of appropriate exercises the reader could attain their autonomy in relation to the technological dispositive, or even overcome it. The formatting of reading by the internet is a logic which imposes itself to the exclusion of any other.

In opposition to the outright rejection of digital reading as a form of surface reading Giffard (2011) is proposing to go beyond Carr's (2011) deterministic view of digital technologies and offers positive alternatives.

5. Reading and writing: the positive pharmakon

To further explore how this positive alternative may develop, it is necessary to place the debate within a philosophical context of the notion of the text: reading and writing as a form of problematic. Whilst this is a well-rehearsed argument within contemporary philosophy it is necessary here to revisit a recent development in the understanding of writing as a *pharmakon* (Ricoeur, 2004). Stiegler (2010) has developed what he terms a positive pharmacology or therapeutic. In the quotation from Giffard (2011) above we can glimpse how this positive pharmacology could come to fruition in relation to digital reading. The criticism which is made of Carr's (2011) position could be summarised in terms of an over emphasis upon the negative aspect of digital reading which leads the positing of surface reading, the *prelectio*, as the ultimate end point of all digital reading.

In the background to Stiegler's (2010) analysis of a positive pharmacology is the analysis of writing as a *pharmakon*. Stiegler (2010) retraces the philosophical debate in relation to reading and writing as problematic back through Derrida (1981) to Plato. There is an irony here, as Plato was opposed to writing as a *pharmakon*, something which was not good for the brain and not good for memory. Analyses of digital reading show a similar reticence: digital reading, it is argued, leads to a form of reading which is also bad for the brain because it leads to a form of hyper-attention. Derrida (1981) in his work *Dissemination* wrote a long essay entitled *Plato's Pharmacy*. This text has become a central part of the canon of philosophical texts in relation to the development of Derrida's (1981) shift from grammatology to deconstruction. In this essay Derrida (1981) gives a sustained micro-reading of Plato's (370 BC/1985) *Phaedrus*, with a critique of Plato's position on writing as a *pharmakon*, that is, a cure and a poison. *Pharmakon* is the etymological root of pharmacology, the study of cure as poison and poison as cure. Writing, for Plato, is a poison in the sense that writing divorces speech from meaning. The absence of the interlocutor leads to a position whereby the text could say what the writer did not intend it to say. Writing enables the misconstruction of meaning; the absence of the speaker leads to untruth. Derrida (1981) describes this as the phonocentric position that Plato holds. Writing is also a poison in relation to memory/reminding:

> "The fact is that this invention [writing] will produce forgetfulness in the souls of those who have learned it because they will not need to exercise their memories […], being able to rely on what is written, using the stimulus of external marks that are alien to themselves […] rather than, from within, their own unaided powers to call things to mind […]. So it's not a remedy for memory, but for reminding, that you discovered (*oukoun mnēmēs, alla hupomnēseōs, pharmakon hēures*). And as for wisdom […], you're equipping your pupils with only a semblance […] of it, not with truth" (Plato, 370 BC/1985, 274e-275b, cited in Derrida, 1981, pp. 104-105, emphasis in original).

The *pharmakon* is here played out in its ambiguity, it is not a cure for memory (mnemes) but for reminding (hypomnesis), this latter refers to the act of technical regurgitation, an artificial memory, a mechanism of reminding. It is therefore to repeat without thought. The distinction which Plato/Socrates makes is between memory and artificial memory. True memory takes the form of the dialectic, *dialogos* through which truth can disclose itself as *alethea*. For Plato writing does not enable anamnesis, true memory, but enables a mechanical repetition which does not lead to the truth. Writing is a form of hypomnesis, an artificial holding place of memory, a mechanism for repetition and not thought. This is where the ambiguity of the word *pharmakon* comes to the fore. Derrida's (1981) critique of Plato and by extension of all Western metaphysics is grounded in his criticism of Plato's rejection of writing. However, more recently with the work of Stiegler (2010) this criticism was revisited, and the opposition between anamnesis and hypomnesis as outlined by Derrida (1981) now leads to a positive pharmacology, the remedy. Derrida (1981) never envisaged the curative aspect of pharmacology, the positive pharmacology which Stiegler (2010) posits. Stiegler (2010) develops an understanding of the *pharmakon* as cure and poison, building upon Derrida's (1981) identification of the semantics of remedy that are present in Plato's text:

> "we hope to display in the most striking manner the regular, ordered polysemy that has, through skewing, indetermination, or overdetermination, but without mistranslation, permitted the rendering of the same word by "remedy", "recipe", "poison", "drug", "philter", etc. It will also be seen to what extent the malleable unity of this concept, or rather its rules and the strange logic that links it with its signifier, has been dispersed, masked, obliterated, and rendered almost unreadable not only by the imprudence or empiricism of the translators, but first and foremost by the redoubtable, irreducible difficulty of translation" (Derrida, 1981, p. 77).

The *pharmakon* as cure and poison demonstrates the difficulty of language to hold a primacy of meaning, a unity of signification. Indeed the *pharmakon* demonstrates the dispersal of the signifier which is the very basis of Derrida's (1981) deconstruction. Derrida's (1981) primary challenge is that Plato's critique of writing as used by the Sophists relates to the idea that it is essentially a poison for reminding and not for memory.

For Stiegler (2010), writing is the very condition of thinking itself, a process of meta-categorisation which is essential to a reflective, recursive process:

> "Le *pharmakon*, qu'est l'écriture – comme *hypomnésis, hypomnématon*, c'est-à-dire mémoire artificielle – est ce dont Platon combat les effets

empoisonnants et artificieux en y opposant *l'anamnésis* : la pensée "par soi-même", c'est-à-dire *l'autonomie* de la pensée" (p. 13, emphasis in original).

The pharmakon, which is writing – as hypomnesis, hypomnematon, that is to say artificial memory – is that of which Plato fights the noxious and artificial effects by opposing it to anamnesis: thinking for oneself, i.e., the autonomy of thought.

Writing is poisonous because it is a form of artificial memory which leads to forgetfulness, memory is exteriorised in the *tekhnē* itself as a form of mnemotechnics. The affordances of technology for digital reading lead to a form of forgetfulness, all technology leads to a form of forgetfulness. Digital technologies function as placeholders for memory, in the same way as, for Plato, writing functions as placeholder for speech. For Stiegler (2010), there is an inherent link between the development of technologies and a proletarianisation of knowledge which leads ultimately to a loss of knowledge:

"A cet égard, le *pharmakon* constitue un facteur de prolétarisation de l'esprit (de perte de savoir) tout comme la machine-outil prolétarisera les corps des ouvriers producteurs (les privera de leur savoir-faire)" (p. 40, emphasis in original).

In this way, the Pharmakon constitutes a factor of proletarnisation of the spirit (loss of knowledge) just as the machine-tool proletarised the bodies of the manual workers (Which took away their know how).

The consequence of the *pharmakon* is the loss of knowledge. The concept of forgetfulness which Plato highlights in relation to writing is developed and expanded by Stiegler (2010) in relation to all forms of technology. For Stiegler (2010) the loss of knowledge leads to the pharmacological situation representative of the contemporary situation in the West: financial, political and social crisis. However, it is necessary to point out that this should not be misconstrued as a rejection of the technology of writing or technology itself.

Stiegler (2010) is mindful of the current of thought which uses technology as the scapegoat, as a *pharmakos*, for all the failures and shortcomings of society, a current of thought which rejects the technologies (of the spirit). This trend does not take into account that the very spirit itself is at the origin and constitutive of the *pharmakon* or the pharma-logico:

> "Rien n'est plus légitime que ces luttes philosophiques contre ce qui, dans la technique ou la technologie, est toxique pour la vie de l'esprit. Mais face à ce qui, dans le *pharmakon*, constitue la possibilité d'un affaiblissement de l'esprit, ces luttes choisissent aussi d'ignorer la constitution originairement pharma-logique de l'esprit lui-même. Elles choisissent d'ignorer la pharmacologie de l'esprit en faisant du *pharmakon* en général un *pharmakos* : un bouc émissaire – celui des pratiques sacrificielles en Grèce ancienne polythéiste, que l'on trouve également en Judée, ou ce *pharmakos* est chargé, comme le sera le Christ, de toutes fautes qu'il emmène vers une région inaccessible" (Stiegler, 2010, p. 40, emphasis in original).

> *Nothing is more legitimate than the philosophical disputes against that which, in the technic or the technology, are toxic for the spirit. But against which, in the pharmakon, constitutes the possibility of the weakening of the spirit/mind, the disputes choose to ignore the original pharma-logic constitution of this spirit itself. They choose to ignore the pharmacology of the spirit by making the pharmakon in general a pharmakos: a scapegoat, the scapegoat of the polytheist ancient Greece, which is also found in Judea, where the pharmakos is charged, as will Christ, with all the faults that he brings him to an inaccessible region.*

Stiegler (2010) contends that technology is part and parcel of who we are and writing is a form of technology which enables reflection to develop, that there are elements of technology which are poisonous to the mind, but there is a pharmacology of the spirit. It is possible to envisage a positive pharmacology of the spirit which entails the development of technology as primary, secondary and tertiary retention. The process of individuating ourselves, becoming who we are through differentiation takes place through the constant development of technology. This is a process of becoming, an ontology of becoming which is inherently present in the technologies that we develop. In this short essay we do not have the time to develop these key concepts further. However, the relationship between different forms of memory which leads to Plato's dismissal of writing as remedy for reminding is overcome by Stiegler's (2010) analysis of the relationship between different types of retention, primary, secondary and tertiary. Stiegler's (2010) analysis points to the short circuit which is afforded by writing as hypomnesis. Hypomnesis is constitutive of anamnesis. In Plato's terms the remedy for reminding is constitutive of true memory itself.

6.   Conclusion

The recognition that the relationship between the nefarious and curative aspects of the *pharmakon* is necessary as the first step towards identifying the curative aspects of the *pharmakon*. The simple accusation that the *pharmakon* as technology is the root of all evil is one which Stiegler (2010) rejects outright. We cannot be for or against technology: technology is an inherent part of who we are and who we are becoming. The question itself therefore borders on the nonsensical, akin to being for or against the sun. The opposition between *pharmakon* as cure and as poison has led to a misunderstanding in relation to the development of writing. For Stiegler (2010), anamnesis is inherently linked to hypomnesis and hypomnesis to anamnesis. The critique, therefore, of digital reading as a reading which leads to cognitive overflow and hyper-attention and hence to surface reading, as Carr (2011) proposes, misses the extent to which the technic of artificial memory is embedded in the very technologies themselves which form part of who we are. The simple dichotomy of print reading as deep attention and digital reading as hyper-attention leading to surface reading is one which needs to countered. The opposition between writing as a form of artificial memory and speech as a form of true memory has led the philosophical debate to revisit the *pharmakon* as possibility for positive development. This is the first step towards a positive pharmacology, a new therapeutics, a pharmacology which attempts to go beyond the noxious effects of the poison and moves towards the remedy. In relation to hyper-attention and deep attention there is the possibility of re-harnessing the technologies of reading to enable deep reflection to take place. Hence, for example, whilst the industry of reading offers technologies which monetise reading activities, developments in computational linguistics are offering new approaches to textual analysis and reading, where the tools of discourse analysis enable large corpuses to be indexed and available for new types of literary analysis. Carr (2011) and Bauerlin (2008) offer a pessimistic vision of digital reading for the future and, more importantly, demonstrate an understanding of the brain which does not take into account the plasticity of its development. Wolf (2007), however, offers a more optimistic approach to the development of the brain and reading:

> "Thus the reading brain is part of highly successful two-way dynamics. Reading can be learned only because of the brain's plastic design, and when reading takes place, that individual brain is forever changed, both physiologically and intellectually" (p. 5).

The future of digital reading, if we accept the analyses of Giffard (2011) and Stiegler (2010), is reliant on the ability to revisit the very technologies of reading as a mechanism of re-harnessing thought, rearming thought. By revisiting the inherent design and typographic problems present in digital text we are offered an opportunity to rearm thought through the technologies of thought itself. The positive pharmacology is one which accepts the *pharmakon* as a poison but embraces the *pharmakon* as a possible means of therapeutic development.

References

Bauerlein, M. (2008). *The Dumbest Generation: How the Digital Age Stupefies Young Americans and Jeopardizes our Future*. New York: Penguin books.
Carr, N. (2011). *The Shallows: what the internet is doing to our brains*. New York: Norton and Company.

Cartelli, A. (2012). *Current Trends and Future Practices for Digital Literacy and Competence.* Hershey, PA: IGI Global.

Derrida, J. (1981). *Dissemination.* Chicago: University Press of Chicago.

Giffard, A. (2009). *Digital Reading, industrial reading* [weblog]. Retrieved from http://alaingiffard.wordpress.com/2009/07/11/digital-reading-industrial-readings/

Giffard, A. (2011). *A propos du livre de Nicholas Carr* [weblog]. Retrieved from http://alaingiffard.blogs.com/culture/2011/11/a-propos-du-livre-de-nicholas-carr.html

Hayles, N. K. (2007). Hyper and Deep Attention: The Generational Divide in Cognitive Modes. *Profession*, 13, 187-199. doi: 10.1632/prof.2007.2007.1.187

Minnis, A. J. (1994). The Medieval Concept of the Author. In D. Graddol & O. Boyd-Barrett (Eds.), *Media Texts: Authors and Readers* (pp. 161-165). Oxford: The Oxford University Press.

Plato. (370 BC/1985). *Phaedrus* (Phèdre. Greek text with French translation by Léon Robin). Paris: Edition Belles Lettres Budé.

Ricoeur, P. (2004). *Memory, History, Forgetting* (Translated by Kathleen Blamey and David Pellauer, originally published in France in 2000). Chicago: University of Chicago Press.

Roberts, D. F., Foehr, U. G., & Rideout, V. (2005). *Generation M: Media in the Lives of 8–18-Year-Olds.* A Kaiser Family Foundation Study. Retrieved from http://www.kff.org/entmedia/upload/Generation-M-Media-in-the-Lives-of-8-18-Year-olds-Report.pdf

Saenger, P. (1991). The separation of words and the physiology of reading. In D. R. Olson & N. Torrance (Eds.), *Literacy and Orality* (pp. 198-214). Cambridge: Cambridge University Press.

Saenger, P. (1997). *Space Between Words: The origins of silent reading.* Standford: Standford University Press.

Saint Augustine. (AD 397/1955). *Confessions* (Newly translated and edited by Albert C. Outler). Retrieved from http://www9.georgetown.edu/faculty/jod/augustine/conf.pdf

Stiegler, B. (2010). *Ce qui fait que la vie vaut la peine d'être vécue: De la pharmacologie.* Paris: Flammarion.

Wolf, M. (2007). *Proust and the Squid: The Story and Science of the Reading Brain.* New York: HarperCollins Publishers.

Wolf, M., & Barzillai, M. (2009). The importance of deep reading. *Educational Leadership*, 66(6), 32-37. Retrieved from http://www.ascd.org/publications/educational-leadership/mar09/vol66/num06/The-Importance-of-Deep-Reading.aspx

Section 2.

Research and Reflections on Societal Practices

Constructions of Violence and Masculinity in the Digital Age

Jennifer Patterson[1]

Abstract

This chapter examines a specific aspect of digital media use, namely the viewing of violent content amongst a male adolescent cohort aged 15-17 years. It is a qualitative study that examines the online practices of fourteen male adolescents, with particular emphasis placed on their understanding of violence. The participants offer the researcher two examples of extreme violence for discussion; one is set in the fantasy world of online gaming and the other footage of a murder that occurred in 2007. The example of 'real life' violence was accessed by the participants via a video clip uploaded to *YouTube*. It is through the participants' subsequent reflection upon these examples, that we gain some insights into their ongoing construction of violence, and the corresponding underlying theme of masculinity. By determining the participants' understanding of violence, it becomes apparent how this shared meaning may act as a benchmark against which they measure all other portrayals of violence. Thus explaining how participants were more comfortable with what they view as 'acceptable' levels of violence evident in the *Call of Duty* or *Grand Theft Auto* series.

Keywords: adolescents, masculinity, online gaming, violence, snuff movie, YouTube.

1. Department of Applied Arts, Waterford Institute of Technology, Waterford, Ireland; jennifer.patterson3@btinternet.com

How to cite this chapter: Patterson, J. (2013). Constructions of Violence and Masculinity in the Digital Age. In C. Fowley, C. English, & S. Thouësny (Eds.), *Internet Research, Theory, and Practice: Perspectives from Ireland* (pp. 113-133). Dublin: © Research-publishing.net.

1.   Introduction

In the last decade alone, society has witnessed unprecedented changes that have enabled more and more aspects of our lives to be coordinated through electronic flows of information (New Scientist, 2012). In essence these changes have become more personal, and as a result more intimate, creating an almost osmotic effect between two realms, that in previous generations were treated as though they were distinctly separate – the 'technical' and the 'social' (Stalder, 2006). To communicate via a mobile phone, a gaming console, a laptop or personal computer is no longer considered a fad, it has now become the norm. The rationale for this study emerges from this context of change, and the resounding concerns this generates within educational institutions. The present study is a direct response to a specific secondary school who wanted to understand the digital existence of their male pupils, and it endeavours to address some of those concerns surrounding their online preferences.

2.   Assessing identity, gender, media and violence in adolescence

Growing up in our technology rich society is a collection of young people, a generation of digital pioneers undertaking a journey that is inherently luminal; theirs is a world that traverses both the on and offline realms; a world that offers the liberty of adult-free spaces with the security of family life. Such liberty or what the postmodern theorist Bauman (2000) refers to as 'fluidity' brings with it responsibility that is also inherently problematic by the absence of a definable structure or stability. The previously restrictive boundaries of time or space are no longer a concern within this newly constructed 'Internet Galaxy' (Castells, 2001). The technologist Prensky (2001) favoured the term 'digital natives' to describe these pioneers and categorising them as those born after 1980 and who are ""native speakers" of the digital language of computers, video games and the Internet" (p. 1, emphasis in original). Not only are they becoming competent native speakers of this new digital language, they are also fostering competency in their endless networked connections to each other (boyd, 2007). It is through these networked connections that new avenues for identity creation and visual outlets of self-presentation are been cultivated. The work of psychologist Erikson (1986) isolated identity as one of the key challenges in adolescent development. Concepts such as identity and gender are social constructions that are intricately entwined and difficult to separate. In today's modern world, identity and gender are neither fixed nor passive static constructs; instead they are subject to continual change, reworking and reaffirmation through various social institutions and practices. A continuous process that enables us to create what may be referred to as a "reflexive biography" (Elliott & Urry, 2010; Giddens, 1991, p. 54).

Of significant importance to adolescent identity are the patterns of power relations between masculinity and femininity that are widespread in society, as Connell (2005) states "[o]ne of the most important circumstances of young people's lives is the gender order they live in" (p. 13). By his rejection of the notion that biology plays a dominant role in determining gender, Connell (2005) endorses masculinity as a construct particular to a certain period of time and place. He is not alone in this endorsement, numerous theorists also stress the importance of recognising that "gender is a matter of learning and continuous "work" rather than a simple expression of biologically given gender difference" (Butler, 1990; Elliott & Urry, 2010; Giddens, 1991, p. 63; Mac an Ghaill, 1994). Secondary schools in particular as one of the formal institutions unconsciously involved with the active construction of masculinity, follow strict gender regimes noticeable to their pupils (Connell, 2005). Salisbury and Jackson (1996) suggested in their work that schools are both influenced and reflective of the macho values of the social world outside them, as well as being "a place where masculinities are actively made, negotiated, regulated and renegotiated" (p. 10). The authors posit that it is through three interrelated levels that this influence of macho values may transpire in the school environment; the institutional level, hidden curriculum level and the official curriculum level. In the institutional level gendered values may be conveyed through styles of leadership or management and also through the threat or absence of appropriate discipline and authority. In the hidden curriculum macho values may be shared through whispers, ritual insults, sexist jokes and bullying, amounting to what Salisbury and Jackson (1996) considered the unofficial curriculum. The official curriculum on the other hand is often considered to be blind to the personal and social forces that may help shape male student's lives.

Lynch and Lodge (2002) examined the practice of gender socialisation in the Irish education system. Their study contrasted the control and surveillance of dress and appearance in girl's schools in comparison to boys. The findings pointed towards secondary schools as sites for determining patterns of gender inequality. This resonated through a form of control exerted over uniforms, make-up and jewellery in the segregated girl's schools, whereas in the boy's school this pervasive level of monitoring and surveillance was not evident. Connell (2005) focused on social practices like organised, competitive sport, specifically football, as an important site of masculinity formation. The popular practice of football is presented to adolescent males as "a site of camaraderie, source of identity, an arena of competition for prestige and a possible career" (Connell, 2005, p. 15). In this manner, football reinforces the ideals society holds for the embodiment of masculine traits. Ging (2005) examined how mass media functions as a 'manual on masculinity' for secondary school boys, providing them with sources of reference for constructing a catalogue of acceptable male behaviour. Her empirical study found that throughout the boys' accounts of masculinity, contradictions existed between being tough or rejecting violence and also between the ability to express emotions or to remain stoic. The participants in her study were very conscious of the performative nature of masculinity and how it was controlled in their daily lives. Ging (2005) also noted that much of the appeal of video gaming for adolescent males was its connection to the manner in which it may affirm their masculinity to others.

De Róiste and Dinneen's (2005) study highlighted that boys were most likely to refer to computer-related activities and girls to watching TV and listening to music as their favourite forms of leisure activity. Sixty per cent of the boys reported frequent gaming, either daily or most days, as opposed to only 13 per cent of girls. In a similar vein, Goldstein (1998) suggests that the social purpose of violent media is to show one's peers "that they are man enough to take it" (p. 215). Another Irish study that examined gender identity in Irish school children, Lodge and Flynn (2001) noted that their participants tended to define themselves "in ways which reflected traditional gendered expectations of behaviour, attitudes and characteristics" (p. 190). O'Connor (2009) in his analysis of Irish young people's narratives concluded that adolescents were still holding strong onto "a rather stereotypical gendered framework underlying their friendships and aspects of their lifestyles" (p. 110).

Every new medium introduced into the communication process has been included in a long running debate regarding its influence on the behaviour of young people (Kaplan, 2012; Wartella & Jennings, 2000). For Critcher (2008) what mattered most was the content, if the content "is seen as criminal or violent or horrific. It constitutes a danger to children who cannot distinguish between reality and fantasy" (p. 65). The belief that exposure to harmful content can influence the unknowing masses can be traced back to Plato's era (Heins, 2001). Since then academic debates have been rife with claims that media acts as an external social force possessing the ability to influence or shape peoples identity by providing them with a new perspective through which to view life (McQuail, 2005; Potter, 2011; Potter & Riddle, 2007).

Many media critics assessed the viewing nature of television audiences as one of passivity, suggesting it dulled the senses and created a sedentary culture of non-participation surrounding its viewers (Putnam, 2000). Indeed Putnam (2000) posited that the advent of television into American life had directly contributed to the downturn in social capital and civic participation within communities. Adorno and Horkheimer (1979) were the original authors of the 'media effects' argument claiming that media is a powerful force shaping the consciousness of the public. Some advocates of the 'media effects' argument support the idea that it is through the media that people learn behavioural scripts (Strasburger & Wilson, 2002). Rosenberg and Santa Barbara (2002) inform us that the narratives found in media violence often contain a number of commonalities: "These include (1) polarisation of conflict by dividing the world into good and evil, (2) dehumanisation of the enemy characters, and (3) conflict resolution through violence" (cited in Nevins, 2004, p. 9). To apply this argument to adolescents suggests that those presented with conflict in their own lives may select an aggressive behavioural script to guide their behaviour in resolving the situation.

Several media theorists have however opposed this argument, stressing that it was the audience that holds the power over the media (Fiske, 1987; Gassner, 2007; Wilson, 2009). For instance cartoons are considered four times more violent than other types of programmes, yet Gunter and Wober (1988) found that viewers did not perceive them in that way. Morrison (1999) discussed violent films with British viewers and found that they did not rate the film *Pulp Fiction* as violent even though it had been given an 'adult only' rating by the film censor. Instead the viewers saw the film as less violent and less threatening because the violence was surrounded by humour. The core of Fiske's (1987) 'active audience' theory is immersed in the social experiences and cultural knowledge that audiences use to interpret and respond to the media. Gender is also as an important social factor in determining how audiences will respond to certain media as a study by Koukounas and McCabe (2001) confirmed. Their examination of gender differences in emotional response to violent film used the eye blink startle response; male participants reported more positive feelings, curiosity, and entertainment in response to the violent film, whereas women reported more disgust, anger, boredom, and greater startle reaction to the violent material.

Following the findings of these previous studies, this chapter will now examine how constructions of violence could influence male adolescent engagement with media content, and in turn their interpretation of that content.

3.   Method and analysis

The researcher was initially approached by the Guidance Counsellor of a boys school in the Waterford area. The school in question was seeking to gain an understanding of their pupils' online habits and, for that reason, a qualitative design was adopted as it would provide the flexibility necessary to probe deeper into participants' thoughts and opinions on various topics. The methodology consisted of three semi-structured focus group discussions with a sampling framework that utilised purposive sampling, gathering fourteen participants ranging from 15-17 years. Focus groups were chosen as they are deemed less intimidating for adolescents, and facilitate better discussion than one-to-one interviews (Heary & Hennessy, 2002; Hoppe, Wells, Morrison, Gillmore, & Wilsdon, 1995; Mauthner, 1997).

The discipline of social psychology instructs us that group discussions often make explicit what is considered (in)appropriate interview interaction. That it is only through interrupting, correcting, or disagreeing with one another, that participants shed more light upon what is considered to be normative (Condor, Figgou, Abell, Gibson, & Stevenson, 2006). Using focus groups to gain insight into the group dynamics of participant's subcultures in action is deemed of particular value by Hyde, Howlett, Brady, and Drennen (2005). However, the authors also forewarn of a fundamental issue the researcher may struggle with when immersed in focus group research "trying to distinguish when reports should be taken as truthful or untruthful" (Hyde et al., 2005, p. 2592). It is often the case that a certain degree of 'performance' may occur in group discussions, especially with young males interacting with a female researcher, when they may use the group environment to assert their individual masculinity. However, rather than discount their contributions outright as acting or performing, Frosh, Phoenix and Pattman (2002) suggest the researcher understands this behaviour as a revelation of the differing facets of identity construction (p. 32). Thus, it is better to consider this issue as a mode of gendered work in action rather than an authentic expression of gender identity.

All focus groups were conducted within the school itself and access to participants was arranged via a school gatekeeper. The focus group discussions were structured around the following areas: online activity, video gaming, bullying, schoolwork and digital media. Conducting discussion groups with adolescent males is often considered somewhat unproductive, especially given the "stereotype of grunting adolescent boy" (Frosh, Phoenix, & Pattman, 2002, p. 23). Many concerns are raised with conducting unstructured or semi structured style interviews with boys, ranging from a general lack of engagement with the research process, to managing disruptive participants who have been temporarily liberated from the disciplinary constraints of their teachers (Frosh et al., 2002). However, in the present study the participants were found to interact enthusiastically and contribute in a coherent and constructive manner.

This study was granted ethical approval from the Ethics Committee of Waterford Institute of Technology. Prior to the study, informed consent was obtained from both the participants and their parents and all three focus groups were recorded and fully transcribed for analysis. The transcriptions amassed a wealth of raw data, which was then analysed using a social constructivist approach to uncover thematic content that highlighted key experiences and issues important to participants. Analysis involved the repeated reading of interview transcripts and coding the text data by hand in order to reduce it and generate findings. The scope of this chapter will limit the discussion to one of the main study findings that emerged, constructions of violence, and to a brief examination of its corresponding underlying theme of masculinity. Findings are accompanied by illustrative quotes from the participants who were allocated pseudonyms to protect their anonymity.

3.1.   Constructing violence in fantasy and reality

Certain terms are ambiguous in meaning, and also subjective; the word 'violence' falls into this category. What one person understands as violence may vastly contradict the understanding of another. This may explain why many studies will postulate a positive link between violent games and aggression (Anderson, 2004; Barlett, Harris, & Bruey, 2008; Bushman & Huesmann, 2006; Engelhardt, Bartholow, Kerr, & Bushman, 2011) and yet a corresponding number will find no definitive link (Collwell & Payne, 2000; Durkin & Barber, 2002; Ferguson et al., 2008; Williams & Skoric, 2005). In order to construct a shared understanding of the concept of violence, participants were asked to offer the researcher an example of what they considered to be an extreme act of violence. While the researcher initially posed an open ended question designed to elicit data on the theme of violence, the participants themselves determined the remaining direction of the discussion. Across the three focus groups, participants disclosed the same examples, one located amidst the fantasy world of video gaming, the other a violent video clip uploaded onto *YouTube*.

3.2.   Massive multiplayer online gaming (MMOG)

Online gaming has become the newest chronicle in the gaming narrative uniting players from across the world into a private sphere of collective experiences. It is a realm that operates outside the boundaries of physical space and time, and one which is indifferent to individual traits or physical characteristics. Players can engage in their game of choice with numerous others, opening new levels of interaction to the overall playability of the game. Kerr, Kücklich, and Brereton (2006) refer to these playability options as "intra-personal play" – competing against the computer and themselves, and "inter-personal play" – competing against other people (p. 20). Participants in this study shared a significant preference for inter-personal game playing, following time spent immersed in intra-personal play.

> **Graeme**: Play it through... but then it gets repetitive... story doesn't change... so then you just go online.

> **Ian**: You play single player until you get the hang of the controls and then... like a team death match.

> **Interviewer**: So you prefer to play with multi-players than single player then?

> [Chorus of yeahs]

> **Niall**: Yeah cos you can play along with your mates or whatever like... people from around the world.

MMOG's such as *Call of Duty* (CoD) have been noted as a prominent feature of adolescent male gaming habits (Griffiths, Davies, & Chappell, 2004). The majority of participants in this study also followed this trend with top preference going to the *Call of Duty* series; *Modern Warfare* (2, 3 and 4), *Black Ops*, *Zombies* and *World at War*. Their second preference was the *Grand Theft Auto* (GTA) series, GTA (1 and 3) and *San Andreas*. Games such as *Halo*,

Gran-turismo, *Tiger Woods Golf* and *FIFA* also received a mention but not to the same extent as CoD or GTA. Participants told how the majority of players they encountered within the online gaming arena were male, with the only the occasional female player. They also reported a mixed age range amongst fellow players, not solely adolescent boys. Considering that the participants only interaction with fellow gamers was in an online context, there was no way of knowing for sure the true identity of these gamers. However, research conducted by the Entertainment Software Association (ESA) would appear to confirm the participants' initial observations. According to the ESA the average game player was found to be male and aged thirty years (ESA, 2012). The research also detailed a further demographic breakdown of gamers, finding that 32% of gamers were under 18 years, 31% of gamers were aged between 18-35 years and 37% of gamers were in fact 36+ years.

CoD is a first-person shooter game set during World War 2 and is played through the perspective of a serving army soldier. GTA on the other hand is set in modern fictional cities where players take on the role of a criminal who attempts to rise up the ranks of organisational crime by completing tasks. When discussing with participants the particular attributes they sought from a game, the following were mentioned: challenging plot, competitive element, options for game-play such as solo games or playing online and overall entertainment appeal. Yet violent content was completely omitted, the following discussion explores the rationale behind this:

> **Keith**: I never played the ManHunt games but they're supposed to be really, really bad now.
>
> **Interviewer**: In what way?
>
> **Keith**: You can see everything that's going on, like if you cut your man's head off you can see the blood going everywhere.
>
> **Interviewer**: Ok, but does that not normally happen in games when you cut people's heads off?

Keith: It does, but it's not that bad.

John: It's a bit over the top.

Interviewer: Is it the detail then?

John: Yeah, yeah, yeah.

Niall: And there's no sense to it your just going around killing people.

John: There's no plot or anything.

Interviewer: So random killing for the sake of killing?

John: Yeah, yeah, yeah.

The *ManHunter* games are notorious within the gaming world for violent content. For this reason they have been banned in several countries worldwide, sometimes causing moral panics: in the UK in 2004, a copycat *ManHunter* style murder was preliminarily identified as the cause for a 17 year old fan to murder his 14 year old friend with a claw hammer (BBC News, 2004a). However, police later confirmed that the motive for the attack was robbery and a copy of the game was found in the victim's home and not the assailants (BBC News, 2004b). It is noteworthy that participants in this study did not appreciate the credible detail of the bloodshed, or the randomness of the kills. Suggesting that random violence isn't the primary draw, the game must include a level of competitiveness or progression through levels as previously mentioned.

3.3.   Three men and a hammer

The second example of excessive violence the participants referred to was in a video they had accessed via *YouTube*. The video contained footage of a murder committed in the Ukraine, which they informed the researcher was entitled

Three men and a hammer. Media coverage referred to it as the *Dnepropetrovsk Maniacs*, a real life horror story that broke in 2007 after the video was leaked onto the internet from one of the perpetrators' mobile phones. Many of this studies participants had viewed the video, which has since been removed, and spoke of the sheer brutality of it. They stated concerns for the level of violence, leading to most of them to discontinue viewing.

> **Evan**: It was this video that was put up on the Internet about these three Russian men in a forest and they bagged this guy and then beat him to death with a hammer.

> **Graeme**: And they used a screwdriver, was so bad.

> **Niall**: I turned on the thing [video clip] and turned it off after a few minutes, it was sick.

> **Graeme**: That would be the kind of violence we would see something wrong with.

The video is effectively a 'snuff movie' showing scenes of a murder committed by three 19 year old Ukrainian teenagers. News reports at the time claimed that the youths had committed at least 19 murders in a one month period (Unian, 2007). The video itself was filmed by one of the offenders and shows the murder of one victim who, after been kidnapped and covered with a hood, was taken to an isolated wooded area and killed with a hammer. All study participants were fully aware of this video, some had attempted to watch it, but all agreed it was an example of extreme violence to which none of the participants could watch in full.

This would appear to contradict the desensitisation theory, that heavy viewing of violent content over time conditions individuals to accept violence as normal, dulling their sensitivity to aggressive behaviour in real life. Exploring the argument that young people have become increasingly desensitised to media violence seemed to be a natural direction to follow. On a very basic level many participants felt that they had become desensitised to gaming/media violence but that this degree of desensitisation did not necessarily correlate with real life violence.

> **Evan**: We don't play Modern Warfare thinking this would be fun to do on a Saturday afternoon in real life.

The disturbing nature of the video, coupled with witnessing a real life murder, is by most standards cause for concern. Bearing in mind that these murders occurred in 2007 indicating that participants were aged between 11 and 12 years when they initially viewed it. Several years on and they were still able to share some very vivid memories with the researcher, memories that had stayed with them since that initial viewing.

4. Discussing violence and gendered frameworks in the digital world

In developing a sense of identity, individuals will draw upon the culturally available references within their immediate environment. Media such as games or videos help to act as such reference points (Ging, 2005). The participants in this study revealed how they had a collective preference for male-orientated genres of gaming. Close examination of their favourite games uncovers a strong sense of masculinity established in the symbolic display of action, guns and violence within these games. Gender representation within video games often appears blatantly stereotypical, male characters predominate in the role of 'brutal gangster' or 'grunting soldier' whereas female characters are seen as more helpless and 'sexually provocative' as is the case with the *Tomb Raider* character Lara Croft and the prostitutes in *Grand Theft Auto: Vice City* (Gauntlett, 2008, p. 68). It is the mass consumption of these games that acts an agent for reproducing a normative gender divide (Connell, 2005).

Kirkland (2009) states that the gaming environment provides a traditional masculine space for the rehearsal of predominantly male activities such as navigating complex spaces, the destruction of enemies, overcoming obstacles, which he claims replicate male drives to kill, conquer and colonise. Whereas, Kline, Dyer-Witheford and de Peuter (2005) use the term "militarised masculinity" (p. 247) to describe the gaming industry's tendency to construct game play around gender-coded violence and combat appealing to young male players. These ideas resonate with Connell's (2005) ideal type of masculinity, entitled 'hegemonic masculinity', which can now be delivered through the global culture of video gaming (Giddens, 2006, p. 463). It appears then that online gaming could play a strong role as an instrument of gender socialisation.

In contrast to the world of online gaming, Gauntlett's (2008) analysis of gender representations online examined the popularity of *YouTube* clips and concluded that online outlets for personal representations such as the aforementioned site allow for a level of diversity not encountered through other forms of media. He adds that "representations of women and men on YouTube are less glossy and stereotypical, and are correspondingly more real, varied and imaginative" (Gauntlett, 2008, p. 73). *YouTube* is now one of the predominant websites that participants stated they 'hang out' in, although they encountered the *Three Men and a Hammer* video through this site, the overt themes of dominance and control that were evident in the video repulsed study participants. Their inability to view the video in its entirety was an outward display of their repulsion, rejection and condemnation of such extreme acts of violence.

One of the objectives of this study was to address concerns stemming from the use of violent media, as violent, criminal or horrific content that cannot be distinguished from reality is seen to constitute a danger to children and adolescents (Critcher, 2008). There is no question that the participants in this study could differentiate between reality and fantasy, and were able to police their own viewing in terms of violent content. The participants could easily have pretended to have seen the *Three Men* video, after all they were well aware of the contents of the video by that stage, but instead they did not feel the need to do so. They also could have 'performed' or embellished the facts of the examples they provided, however the consensus that emerged across the three groups did not support this. There is a strong possibility that a level of 'performance' could transpire within one group, but the chances of it occurring across all three groups would have been unlikely. Therefore, the researcher accepted the details the participant's provided as factual based on that deduction, thus contradicting Goldstein's (1998) finding on the social purpose of violent media as a means of conveying an outward display of hardness to one's peers.

In this study participants shared examples of real and virtual acts of violence that they deemed offensive, signifying a genuine disdain for extreme violent acts in both realms. This generated an understanding of how this group of adolescent males collectively constructs a meaning for violence. Through establishing this meaning, it becomes clear how it can act as a benchmark against which to measure all other portrayals of violence, thus explaining how participants were more comfortable with what they view as more 'acceptable' levels of violence, evident in CoD or GTA. Decoding the meanings that young people apply to culturally available references, such as digital media, should enable a deeper knowledge of their online preferences and practices to emerge.

5.   Conclusion

As was demonstrated in this chapter, gender socialisation and the acquisition of macho values occur through a variety of means. These may be directed through participation in the education system (Lodge & Flynn, 2001; Lynch & Lodge, 2002; O'Connor, 2009; Salisbury & Jackson, 1996), via a sporting activity like football (Connell, 2005) or through the consumption of popular media (De Róiste & Dinneen, 2005; Ging, 2005). Not ignoring how these individual strata may overlap in the lives of adolescents, the 'unofficial curriculum' of the school environment undoubtedly contains many lessons on online gaming tactics or tales of football victories. These agents of socialisation exist in part to instil and shape the values and beliefs that assist in guiding our individual biography.

It was the key undertaking of this chapter to examine if violent media possessed the ability to function as a valid script for masculinity. In terms of the meaning making process, participants displayed an awareness that lived experiences of violence differ vastly from media portrayals. They rejected the idea that a correlation existed between media violence and real life violence. As we discovered, immersion within the digital environments of online gaming has lead to the creation of an informal arena for a collective masculine consciousness. As participants are willing to partake in online activities it is likely they are more open and passive to the reception of this inconspicuous form of gender socialisation. The author is not inferring that this could influence their behaviour directly as the 'media effects' argument suggests, rather that it directs their socialisation increasingly towards more stereotyped masculine scripts. When it came to raising concerns over violent content, it is worth bearing in mind that these adolescent males were not easily brainwashed by the pseudo-macho values that certain media contain. In fact considering their many interactions with masculine media scripts, the participants appeared to endorse the 'active audience' theory. They openly rejected the themes of dominance and control they witnessed in the snuff movie and rebuffed the senseless violence of the *ManHunter* game. While it is true that media may contain a certain power by imprinting their values upon their audience, as this study has demonstrated, that relationship is a two way process. Audiences also possess the power to reject such blatant overtures. While young adolescent males may regularly interact with digital media containing violent narratives, this study evidenced that some of that content does disturb them.

In truth, we are only starting to understand how adolescents make sense of the many electronic flows of information that surround them. The exponential growth in unregulated daily video uploads to the internet, and *YouTube* in particular, brings the risk of accidental exposure to unsuitable content. There is an overriding concern for many adult observers of adolescent online activity that there exists a risk that young people may stumble across unsuitable content. Therefore it is envisaged that this research may contribute some useful knowledge to addressing that concern.

References

Adorno, T., & Horkheimer, M. (1979). *Diaclectic of Enlightment.* London: Verso.

Anderson, C. A. (2004). An update on the effects of playing violent video games. *Journal of Adolescence, 27*(1), 113-122. doi: 10.1016/j.adolescence.2003.10.009

BBC News. (2004a, July 29). Game blamed for hammer murder. *BBC.* Retrieved from http://news.bbc.co.uk/2/hi/uk_news/england/leicestershire/3934277.stm

BBC News. (2004b, August 5). Police reject game link to murder. *BBC.* Retrieved from http://news.bbc.co.uk/2/hi/uk_news/england/leicestershire/3538066.stm

Barlett, C. P., Harris, R. J., & Bruey, C. (2008). The effect of the amount of blood in a violent game on aggression, hostility, and arousal. *Journal of Experimental Social Psychology, 44*(3), 539-546. doi: 10.1016/j.jesp.2007.10.003

Bauman, Z. (2000). *Liquid Modernity.* Cambridge: Polity Press.

boyd, d. m. (2007). Why Youth (Heart) Social Network Sites: The Role of Networked Publics in Teenage Social Life. In D. Buckingham (Ed.), *Youth, Identity, and Digital Media: MacArthur Foundation Series on Digital Learning* (pp. 119-142). Cambridge, MA: The MIT Press.

Bushman, B. J., & Huesmann, L. R. (2006). Short-term and long-term effects of violent media on aggression in children and adults. *Archives of Pediatrics and Adolescent Medicine, 160*(4), 348-352. doi: 10.1001/archpedi.160.4.348

Butler, J. (1990). *Gender Trouble: Feminism and the Subversion of Identity.* London: Routledge.

Castells, M. (2001). *The Internet Galaxy: Reflections on the Internet, Business & Society.* Oxford: Oxford University Press.

Collwell, J., & Payne, J. (2000). Negative correlates of computer game play in adolescents. *British Journal of Psychology, 91*(3), 295-310. doi: 10.1348/000712600161844

Condor, S., Figgou, L., Abell, J., Gibson, S., & Stevenson, C. (2006). 'They're not racist...' Prejudice denial, mitigation and suppression in dialogue. *British Journal of Social Psychology, 45*(3), 441-462. doi: 10.1348/014466605X66817

Connell, R. W. (2005). Growing up Masculine: Rethinking the Significance of Adolescence in the Making of Masculinities. *Irish Journal of Sociology, 12*(2), 11-28.

Critcher, C. (2008). Making waves: Historic aspects of public debates about children and mass media. In K. Drotner & S. Livingstone (Eds.), *International Handbook of Children, Media and Culture* (pp. 91-104). London: Sage Publications.

De Róiste, Á., & Dinneen, J. (2005). *Young People's Views about Opportunities, Barriers and Supports to Recreation and Leisure*. Dublin: National Children's Office. Retrieved from http://www.dcya.gov.ie/documents/publications/Summary_Recreation_ResearchFINAL.pdf

Durkin, K., & Barber, B. (2002). Not so doomed: Computer game play and positive adolescent development. *Journal of Applied Developmental Psychology, 23*(4), 373-392. doi: 10.1016/S0193-3973(02)00124-7

Elliott, A., & Urry, J. (2010). *Mobile Lives*. New York: Routledge.

Engelhardt, C. R., Bartholow, B. D., Kerr, G. T., & Bushman, B. J. (2011). This is your brain on violent video games: Neural desensitisation to violence predicts increased aggression following violent video game exposure. *Journal of Experimental Social Psychology, 47*(5), 1033-1036. doi: 10.1016/j.jesp.2011.03.027

Erikson, E. H. (1986). *Identity: Youth and Crisis*. New York: Norton.

ESA. (2012). *Sales, Demographic & Usage Data. Essential Facts about the Computer and Video Gaming Industry*. Entertainment Software Association. Retrieved from http://www.theesa.com/facts/pdfs/ESA_EF_2012.pdf

Ferguson, C. J., Rueda, S. M., Cruz, A. M., Ferguson, D. E., Fritz, S., & Smith, S. M. (2008). Violent video games and aggression: Causal relationship or by-product of family violence and intrinsic violence motivation? *Criminal Justice and Behavior, 35*(3), 311-332. doi: 10.1177/0093854807311719

Frosh, S., Phoenix, A., & Pattman, R. (2002). *Young Masculinities: Understanding Boys in Contemporary Society*. Hampshire: Palgrave Macmillan.

Fiske, J. (1987). *Television Culture*. London: Methuen & Co.

Gassner, P. (2007). The end of the audience: How the nature of audiences changed. *Global Media Journal African Edition, 1*(1), 120-129. doi: 10.5789/1-1-51

Gauntlett, D. (2008). *Media, Gender & Identity: An Introduction* (2nd ed.). London: Routledge.

Giddens, A. (1991). *Modernity and Self-Identity: Self and Society in the Late Modern Age*. Cambridge: Polity Press.

Giddens, A. (2006). *Sociology* (5th ed.). Cambridge: Polity Press.

Ging, D. (2005). A 'Manual on Masculinity'? The consumption and use of mediated images of masculinity among teenage boys in Ireland. *Irish Journal of Sociology, 14*(2), 29-52. Retrieved from http://doras.dcu.ie/4544/1/ging_ijs_14_2_2005.pdf

Goldstein, J. H. (1998). *Why We Watch: The Attractions of Violent Entertainment*. Oxford: Oxford University Press.

Griffiths, M. D., Davies, M. N. O., & Chappell, D. (2004). Online computer gaming: a comparison of adolescent and adult gamers. *Journal of Adolescence, 27*(1), 87-96. doi: 10.1016/j.adolescence.2003.10.007

Gunter, B., & Wober, M. (1988). *Violence on Television: What the Viewers Think*. London: John Liby.

Hoppe, M. J., Wells, E. A., Morrison, D. M., Gillmore, M. R., & Wilsdon, A. (1995). Using focus groups to discuss sensitive topics with children. *Evaluation Review, 19*(1), 102-114. doi: 10.1177/0193841X9501900105

Heary, C. M., & Hennessy, E. (2002). The use of focus group interviews in pediatric health care research. *Journal of Pediatric Psychology, 27*(1), 47-56. doi: 10.1093/jpepsy/27.1.47

Heins, M. (2001). *Not in Front of the Children: "Indecency," Censorship, and the Innocence of Youth*. NewYork: Hill and Wang.

Hyde, A., Howlett, E., Brady, D., & Drennen, J. (2005). The focus group method: Insights from focus group interviews on sexual health with adolescents. *Social Science and Medicine, 61*(12), 2588–2599. doi: 10.1016/j.socscimed.2005.04.040

Kaplan, A. (2012). Violence in the Media: What effects on Behaviour? *Psychiatric Times, 29*(10), 1.

Kerr, A., Kücklich, J., & Brereton, P. (2006). New media – new pleasures? *International Journal of Cultural Studies, 9*(1), 63-82. doi: 10.1177/1367877906061165

Kirkland, E. (2009). Masculinity in Video Games: The Gendered Gameplay of Silent Hill. *Camera Obscura, 24*(2 71), 161-183.

Koukounas, E., & McCabe, M. P. (2001). Emotional responses to filmed violence and the eye blink startle response: A preliminary investigation. *Journal of Interpersonal Violence, 16*(5), 476-488. doi: 10.1177/088626001016005006

Kline, S., Dyer-Witheford, N., & de Peuter, G. (2005). *Digital Play: The Interaction of Technology, Culture, and Marketing*. London: McGill-Queen University Press.

Lodge, A., & Flynn, M. (2001). Gender Identity in the Primary School Playground. In A. Cleary, P. NicGhiolla, & S. Quin (Eds.), *Understanding Children, State, Education & Economy* (Vol. 1). Cork: Oak Tree Press.

Lynch, K., & Lodge, A. (2002). *Equality and Power in Schools: Redistribution, Recognition and Representation*. London: Routledge Falmer.

McQuail, D. (2005). *McQuail's mass communication theory* (5th ed.). London: Sage Publications.

Mac an Ghaill, M. (1994). *The Making of Men: Masculinities, Sexualities and Schooling.* Buckingham: Open University Press.

Mauthner, M. (1997). Methodological aspects of collecting data from children: Lessons from three research projects. *Children & Society, 11*(1), 16-28. doi: 10.1111/j.1099-0860.1997. tb00003.x

Morrison, D. E. (1999). *Defining Violence; The Search for Understanding.* Luton: Luton University Press.

New Scientist (2012). Editorial: The Singularity is upon us? Not so fast. *New Scientist, 215*(2884), 3. doi: 10.1016/S0262-4079(12)62469-5

Nevins, T. (2004). *The Effects of Media Violence on Adolescent Health: A research report written for Physicians for Global Survival (Canada).* Retrieved from http://www.pgs.ca/ wp-content/uploads/2008/03/effectsofmediaviolence_final.pdf

O'Connor, P. (2009). Irish young people's narratives; the existence of gender differentiated cultures? *Irish Journal of Sociology, 17*(1), 95-115. doi: 10.7227/IJS.17.1.7

Potter, W. J. (2011). Conceptualizing Mass Media Effect. *Journal of Communication, 61*(5), 896-915. doi: 10.1111/j.1460-2466.2011.01586.x

Potter, W. J., & Riddle, K. (2007). A content analysis of the media effects literature. *Journalism & Mass Communication Quarterly, 84*(1), 90-104. doi: 10.1177/107769900708400107

Prensky, M. (2001). Digital Natives, Digital Immigrants Part 1. *On The Horizon - The Strategic Planning Resource for Education Professionals, 9*(5), 1-6.

Putnam, R. D. (2000). *Bowling Alone. The collapse and revival of American community.* New York: Simon & Schuster.

Rosenberg, J., & Santa Barbara, J. (2002). *Media and Entertainment Violence and Children.* Physicians for Global Survival (Canada).

Salisbury, J., & Jackson, D. (1996). *Challenging macho values: practical ways of working with adolescent boys.* London: Falmer Press.

Stalder, F. (2006). *Manuel Castells: The Theory of the Network Society.* Cambridge: Polity Press.

Strasburger, V. C., & Wilson, B. J. (2002). *Children, Adolescents, & the Media.* Thousand Oaks: Sage Publications.

Unian. (2007, July 24). *Three 19 Year Old Youths Committed 19 Murders in Dnipropetrovsk During A Month.* Unian. Retrieved from http://www.unian.info/news/204617-three-19-year-old-youths-committed-19-murders-in-dnipropetrovsk-during-a-month.html

Wartella, E., & Jennings, N. (2000). Children and Computers: New technology – old concerns. *Children and Computer Technology, 10*(2), 31-43. Retrieved from http://futureofchildren. org/futureofchildren/publications/docs/10_02_01.pdf

Williams, D., & Skoric, M. (2005). Internet fantasy and violence: A test of aggression in an online game. *Communication Monographs, 72*(2), 217-233. doi: 10.1080/03637750500111781

Wilson, T. (2009). *Understanding media users: from theory to practice*. Oxford: Wiley-Blackwell.

8 The Public Sphere and Online Social Media: Exploring the Use of Online Social Media as Discursive Spaces in an Irish Context

Claire English[1]

Abstract

Online social media have become integral to individuals' media and communication repertoires globally. They provide spaces to meet with friends, reconnect with old acquaintances and gather around shared topics of interest. This chapter presents findings from a qualitative study into the role of online social media in the lives of 25 to 30 year olds in Ireland. The wider research project asks how these sites are enmeshed into everyday life. This chapter focuses on the use of these online social media sites for discursive practices associated with Habermas's (1989) conception of the public sphere, as a space of rational debate among private individuals. Here I report on empirical research carried out between 2008 and 2012 drawing on insights gained from semi structured interviews and online observation carried out with eleven participants. The study aims to gain an insight into their use of online social media focusing here on their attitudes towards posting, online discussion and conceptions of online social media as a discursive space.

Keywords: online social media, citizenship, public sphere, media and everyday life, audience studies, internet research.

1. Dublin City University, Dublin, Ireland; claire.english3@mail.dcu.ie

This chapter draws on research undertaken as part of the Irish Social Science Platform (ISSP). Please note that the latter was funded by the Higher Education Authority's PRTLI Cycle 4, the European Regional Development Fund, Irelands' EU Structural Funds Programme and the Department of Jobs, Enterprise and Innovation.

How to cite this chapter: English, C. (2013). The Public Sphere and Online Social Media: Exploring the Use of Online Social Media as Discursive Spaces in an Irish Context. In C. Fowley, C. English, & S. Thouësny (Eds.), *Internet Research, Theory, and Practice: Perspectives from Ireland* (pp. 135-155). Dublin: © Research-publishing.net

1.   Introduction

Web 2.0 and social media in particular have come into sharp focus within debates surrounding public engagement and citizenship as possible elixirs to a perceived democratic deficit in contemporary society. However, it is all too easy to valorise technology, viewing it as a 'magic bullet' which will alter greatly the way in which citizens engage with public life. If we examine only the technical features or the content of such media and eliminate the user from the equation an incomplete picture may be formed. Following research which emphasises the need to examine the role of the internet in civic participation (Dahlgren, 2000; Dahlgren & Gurevitch, 2005; Hirzalla & Van Zoonen, 2010; Wellman & Haythornwaite, 2002) this study investigates how online social media is utilised by citizens in everyday life to engage with civic life in an Irish context. This chapter focuses on one aspect of a wider research project, namely participants' use of online social media in discussion of formal political events.

The context for this particular study is Ireland. The past ten years have seen major changes for the generation of Irish citizens now in their late twenties. The highs of the Irish 'Celtic Tiger' economy have given way to a phase of economic meltdown where the confidence and expectations of prosperity and stability have been replaced by mass unemployment and a resurgence of emigration[1]. Members of this age group are often cited as being disengaged from politics and public issues; this research asks whether online social media sites play a role in this group's participation in discursive civic practices?

Running parallel to this, the dissemination of vast amounts of information of various genres and questionable quality is often viewed as a distraction to citizens, corrosive to the public sphere. The structure of the home as a private space can be seen as increasingly permeable through the use of media technologies. Just

---

1. Unemployment figures published by the CSO put the unemployment rate in Ireland at 14.4% for October 2011 (Quarterly National Household Survey: Quarter 3). This is an increase of 9.6% since January 2008 when this research began when the rate was calculated at 4.8%. This reporting period was deemed of most relevance to this research as it corresponded to the period of empirical research. In terms of emigration the CSO released figures in September 2011 which show increases in the level of emigration from Ireland, especially among Irish nationals (Population and Migration Estimates April 2011). In the year from April 2010 to April 2011 76,400 people emigrated from Ireland in total with 40,200 of these being Irish nationals, a rise from 27,700 in the previous year. In terms of age 25 to 44 year olds were the largest cohort to emigrate with 34,400 leaving the country in this period.

as the public sphere has infiltrated this once perceived private space of the home, its inhabitants have gained power to influence events within the public sphere through the use of information and communication technologies (ICTs). In terms of more recent ICT development, new forms of social reality are emerging: where national, regional and cultural boundaries are breaking down, technology is the only remaining boundary, and it allows for forms of social reality whereby shared experience is permitted across thousands of kilometres (Morley, 2007). Online social media in their different incarnations allow for a variety of interactions among users. From 'one to one' interactions in an instant messaging session, email and private messages on social networking sites; 'one to many' interactions through blogs, social media posts and comments on various media websites through to 'many to many' interactions on forums, group and community web pages. These sites create spaces where people can connect with each other, gather together and where discussion can occur (Baym, 2000). Boyd and Ellison (2007) identify the power in these interactions for users as the ability to collapse time and space, reflecting McLuhan's (1964) ideas on the impact of technology on society. In what can be held as a technological determinist stance these interactions are seen to alter practices of communication, collaboration, information dissemination and social organisation (Benkler, 2006; Castells, 1996; Rheingold, 2000). Negroponte (1995) thus described how internet technology would create a new "global social fabric" which would replace any technology which went before it (p. 183).

Within this research the conception of the public sphere emerges from Habermasian theory as a space where a collective of private individuals can gather to share information and ideas and engage in debate surrounding matters of public concern. Habermas (1989) saw the bourgeois society of the late 17th and 18th centuries as providing a model for the ideal public sphere where issues relating to the state and public policies could be discussed in accordance with Kantian ideals of procedural rationality[1]. Utopian perspectives view the internet as having a potential for the enhanced provision of such a space, where people can construct their identity independently of their demographic

---

1. Procedural rationality posits that where discussions take place the emphasis is on the strength of an argument as opposed to a person's social status and background.

profile, providing a potential for debate irrespective of the social situations of the individuals involved (Benkler, 2006; Negroponte, 1995; Turkle, 1996).

Habermas (1989) tends to idealise the public sphere of the 17th and 18th centuries in his work, defining the public sphere as "the public of private individuals who join in debate of issues bearing on state authority" (cited in Calhoun, 1992, p. 7, emphasis in original). The origins of this idea can be seen to stretch back as far as Classical Greece[1]. The Grecian model of a public sphere coupled with Immanuel Kant's idea of 'procedural rationality' can be seen as the foundations of Habermas's (1989) formulation of the public sphere. This ancient model of the public sphere resurfaced during the Renaissance period and Habermas (1989) sees this template for society as surviving in some form through the Enlightenment to the emergence of contemporary democratic society. Critiques of Habermas's (1989) concept of the public sphere have come from a variety of standpoints, and point out the exclusions evident in the structure of Habermas's (1989) romanticised vision of the 18th Century public sphere where access was limited to upper class, property owning, white males. Fraser (1985, 1992) has argued for a broadening of access and an expansion of the scope for valid topics of discussion, to include the politics of everyday life as well as formal politics at the level of the State. She argues that the public sphere is not a singular entity but is constituted of a multitude of public-spheres or 'counterpublics' made up of those members of society excluded from Habermas's (1989) conceptualisation of the public sphere.

Democracy and citizenship require the provision of a space where citizens can gather and discuss public issues, a fact which continues to be drawn on in much of the literature concerning the potential for the internet to play a role in the strengthening of citizenship and democracy (Dahlgren, 2009; Hirzalla & Van Zoonen, 2010; Livingstone, Couldry, & Markham, 2007; Rheingold, 2000). In contemporary society there may be the potential to establish this type of public sphere through the internet. Thus, Habermas's (1989) concept

---

1. In the Greek instance society was demarcated along lines of the state (*polis*) and the private realms of free citizens (*idia*) and also public life (*bios politicos*) and home life (Habermas, 1989, p. 3). The public sphere in the Greek sense was formed on the basis of discussion where heads of households could engage in discussions of all aspects of public life. Their status as the head of a household was the criterion for gaining entry to the public sphere (Habermas, 1989).

of the public sphere becomes an ideal reference point within which to examine the use of online social media in an Irish context. These sites provide spaces where discussion can take place. They are spaces which have the potential for groups of private individuals to come together and examine the actions of public figures. However it would be naive to posit that this type of discussion is taking place based solely on the structural features of these technologies (Papacharissi, 2011).

The united public sphere envisaged by Habermas (1989) may have given way in the 'information age' to arenas of public debate which are based on the discussion of shared interests and the sharing of information. Gitlin (1998) hypothesises on the fragmentation of the public sphere into a collection of 'public sphericules' made up of a variety of interest groups. He views the development of computer technology and in particular the personal computer and the internet as contributing to the emergence of these sphericules of distinct interests. Public discussion is viewed as focusing on local and personal issues and displaying them to the world. These developments can be viewed as creating a sense of a 'globally interconnected world' relating McLuhan's (1964) conception of the 'global village'. The structure of this online mediascape is problematic, from a production perspective niche audiences are defined with content tailored and directed accordingly. Within this type of environment the chances for the development of a unified arena of discussion are slim. While online social media often enable the easy development of distinct interest groups it is unclear whether the emergence of a multitude of publics can lead to the creation of a singular public defined by Gitlin (1998) as

> "an active democratic encounter of citizens who reach across their social and ideological differences to establish a common agenda of concern and to debate rival approaches" (p. 173).

In terms of the media consumed in contemporary society, the perceived danger is that the creation of highly distinct niches of interest can have a cocooning effect, wrapping people in the areas of their own passion and interest with little exposure to alternative viewpoints and debate; this could eventually manifest in the loss of a sense of the 'imagined community' (Anderson, 1991) of the nation, which authors such as Morley (1996) saw as a central function of shared media experiences.

2.   Methods

There are a number of approaches which researchers can take in qualitative studies of internet use. Research can be situated in the online setting examining the interactions of users and content created by them (Baym, 2000; Goode, McCullough, & O'Hare, 2011; Markham, 1998; Turkle, 1996). Research can be situated offline, engaging with users and examining how online media fit into their lives generally or relate to specific aspects of it (boyd, 2007, 2008; Livingstone, 2002, 2008; Livingstone et al., 2007; Olsson, 2006). Another possibility spans these two approaches examining both online and offline spaces, examining users' activities online and connecting them with offline routines, exploring how these activities fit into their lives (Bakardjieva, 2005). The third approach is the path taken in this research[1]. Like any methodological approach this has an impact on the data gathered and the conclusions which can be drawn. This methodological decision complemented the aim of the research project which was to explore the use of online social media within the context of participants' everyday lives.

A multi-method approach was taken, encompassing a number of qualitative methods which would provide different insights into the role and use of online social media in the lives of the participants. The methods employed included a week long media diary, a semi-structured interview, a recorded online session, a period of online observation and an online survey. This chapter will report on findings relating to the use of online social media as discursive spaces by participants, drawing on data gathered in the interview and online session stages of the research.

---

1. This is by no means an exhaustive list of approaches to a qualitative study of internet use, it illustrates some of the decisions made over the course of this research project. This research project situates itself within the audience studies paradigm of research and draws on the ethnographically inspired empirical research carried out by authors such as Baym (2000, 2010), boyd (2007, 2008), Livingstone (2002), Livingstone et al. (2007), Markham (1998), Morley (1986), and Wellman and Haythornwaite (2002).

The recruitment of participants included people with varying levels of interest in political and public issues, from those who were members of political parties to those who expressed no interest in formal politics at all. To recruit the eleven participants I utilised a snowball approach, making contact with individuals in a number of different workplaces, political parties and civic groups. While eleven is a small number of participants and therefore results from this study are not generalisable to the population at large, the combination of methods utilised in this research leads to a set of descriptive data which sheds light on the ways online social media are embedded into everyday life for these individuals.

Table 1.   Summary table of Participants

Name	Gender	Age	Location	Education	Occupation	Civic Engagement (key below)
James	M	25	Rural	3rd Level Degree (Arts)	Unemployed	TP(MPP,M,V), CuC, P
Eoghan	M	26	City	Masters Degree (Arts/Business)	Project Manager	TP(MPP,M,V), P
David	M	27	City	Post Graduate Diploma (Arts)	Researcher	TP(L,M,V), CuC
Kevin	M	27	City	3rd Level Diploma (Business)	Public Sector	TP(M,V)
Michael	M	27	City	3rd Level Degree (Arts)	Marketing PLC	TP (M)
Patrick	M	28	Rural	3rd Level Degree (Business)	Air Steward	TP(V,M), CoC, P
Adam	M	29	Provincial Town	Apprenticeship	Mechanic	TP (V)
Joan	F	28	City	3rd Level Diploma (Hospitality)	Retail Manager	TP (M, V)
Cathy	F	28	City	3rd Level Degree (IT)	IT Analyst	TP (M, V)
Anne	F	29	Provincial Town	3rd Level Degree (Arts)	Public Councillor/ Carer	TP (MPP, M, V), P, CC
Joanne	F	29	Provincial Town	3rd Level Degree (Science)	Underwriter	TP (V, M, L), P

Key for Civic Engagement: TP: Traditional Political, MPP: Member Political Party, M: Media, V: Voting, CuC: Cultural Citizenship, P: Protest, L: Lobbying, CoC: Consumer Citizenship

For the participants, all in their late 20s, this stage of life is characterised by searching for jobs, building careers, purchasing houses, entering into married life and planning for or raising families. The increase in responsibilities associated with these aspects of life is reflected in some of the conceptions of citizenship which participants shared relating to their status as taxpayer, obeying the law and voting[1]. In terms of gender breakdown, the study included four female and seven male participants. Table 1 above provides an introduction to the participants including the predominant ways in which they engage with civic life in Ireland.

3.   Findings and discussion

The findings presented in this chapter relate to the use of online social media by participants, specifically examining the role of these sites in discursive practices of citizenship. Four areas are examined here; online social media sites used, attitudes towards posting and discussion, online social media as discursive spaces and the potential for the development of a public sphere through online social media. The findings presented in this chapter are drawn from interviews and online sessions with the eleven participants in the study.

3.1.   Online social media sites used

All eleven participants had multiple online social media profiles. These varied from social network sites such as *Facebook*, *Bebo* and *Twitter* to video sharing sites such as *YouTube*. A number of participants described how they had migrated from social networking site *Bebo* to *Facebook* in recent years, often retaining their *Bebo* account but rarely, if ever, accessing it.

---

1. When discussing their conceptions of citizenship all participants included ideas and activities associated with the sphere of public authority. This occurred in two modes. Firstly, for participants who were members of political parties or civic society groups, connection with this sphere was maintained on a regular basis through participation in collective forms of action both on and offline. For participants who were not involved in such groups, connection with this sphere was maintained through regular consumption of news and current affairs media. As for participants who were in employment, their conception of citizenship was bound up in their status as taxpayers and their interest in politics linked to this role. Community was a recurring and strong theme in participants' conceptions of what citizenship entailed, from those who worked on single issue campaigns in their community to those who felt respect and friendliness were duties to be carried out as citizens in their everyday lives. Ideas of community and the local were at the centre of tangible practices which they could engage in as citizens.

Facebook was the most popular online social media site used among participants; however the use of this site fluctuated between those who logged in daily to those who rarely logged into their profile at all. James, Eoghan, David, Thomas, Cathy, Anne and Joanne logged onto *Facebook* most days, had updated their profile information, posted photos and engaged in conversations on the site. While Joan, Kevin, Michael and Patrick all had profiles on *Facebook* with some personal information and profile pictures they used the site less frequently, sometimes less than once a week. For Joan and Kevin this was due to lack of access at work while Michael and Patrick had concerns about their privacy.

Facebook was viewed by participants as accessible and easy to use as well as being a space where the majority of their friends went online. This was in contrast to their views on *Twitter*, Cathy, Anne, Joanne, Eoghan and Michael, had accounts on *Twitter*. Of these participants Michael and Cathy could be classed as readers or 'listeners'[1] using this site to follow breaking news stories and celebrity life respectively. Anne, Joanne and Eoghan had created profiles but rarely, if ever, used them.

3.2. Attitudes towards posting and discussion

There were varying views towards posting among participants in this study. While all participants posted on social media sites there were divergent attitudes towards and practices of posting. All of the participants replied to friends' posts and had online conversations with them, however a number were reluctant to post, and on some occasions only posted if they felt they had something valuable to add. Attitudes towards posting varied depending on the type of site being used by participants from online social network sites, to forums and news media sites.

Cathy, Joan and Kevin, saw posting on social network sites such as *Facebook* as an activity reserved for interaction with friends and often those who they were in contact with offline on a regular basis.

---

1. 'Listener' describes *Twitter* users who do not send out tweets but follow others. In a survey conducted in 2011 40% of active *Twitter* accounts were found to be listeners (http://blog.Twitter.com/2011/09/one-hundred-million-voices.html?m=1).

"I wouldn't really post pictures of myself, I'd post up group photos... things that people can share or that other people can relate to" (Joan, 28, online session, January 2011).

"I wouldn't comment on public things. I'd comment on my friends things" (Cathy, 28, online session, January 2011).

"I have a lot of my own opinions but I don't go shouting them out to other people on social networking sites I just tend to keep to myself and if people do write up I'll study their opinions but I'd never really put up my own. I'm kind of reserved in that sense" (Kevin, 27, Interview, January 2011).

Anne who has two profiles on *Facebook* described the different uses she had for each of her profiles:

"On my private [profile], I post daft comments like, 'god I'm wrecked' or 'I'm starving' or 'I want a Mars bar'... you leave a comment and that's it and then you can go into your friends and talk about nothing, well not nothing but happier, everyday stuff about your lives and things that you have in common. So that's what I like about Facebook... on my [councillor profile] it's political issues or the photos on it would just be PC photos" (Anne, 29, online session, January 2011).

The images on Anne's councillor profile depict her raising money for local charities and participating in local campaigns and events.

Posts relating to everyday life were most frequently made by participants. This included text and photographs depicting events in their lives. On posting about everyday life Joanne considered why she posted these types of comments. Social media sites are often critiqued by the media in particular for the level of trivial or unimportant content. However, the insights given by participants here demonstrate that these sites and this type of content play an important role in connecting with friends, family and the wider community. The banalities of daily life and the phatic communication practices engaged in online can be viewed as a source of cohesion for these connections.

"I honestly couldn't tell you why. It's not like I want people to know what I'm up to but it's more like 'isn't this lovely, I want to say how lovely this is' that kind of thing. Like last night I was there on the couch watching that film [Forest Gump] and I was thinking about us going [on holiday] and I was just [thinking] isn't this brilliant so I just put it up" (Joanne, 29, online session, June 2011).

"You can just put your thoughts down, the other day I posted 'The painting and decorating of the house is complete roll on Thursday because my wooden floor is coming' because my house is just upside down and it's an absolute mess so it's kind of a way, because I'm so mad with the state of it. Someone else that you know has the same problem as you and feel a bit better and he feels a bit better and then you go your separate ways again" (Anne, 29, online session, January 2011).

Cathy and Adam expressed a reactive form of communication in so far as they tended to reply to comments made by others predominantly. Cathy only posted comments when she felt she had something of interest to say relating to an unusual event or if she was going on holidays.

"I would respond to things rather than leaving up comments and things like that. You know some people leave up messages four or five times a day and I'm not like that, I do it maybe once every two or three weeks. I do it when I have something to say basically" (Cathy, 28, online session, January 2011).

Adam also tended to reply to comments but when conducting online observation on his *Facebook* profile he did post a substantial amount of photos relating to his keen interest in motorbikes and cars, an area in which he had a considerable level of expertise. Relating to comments he said:

"I wouldn't put up any under my name. See the way [friend] there she wrote up a comment then I'd put something up under that" (Adam, 29, online session, June 2011).

For others such as Joan, content posted on *Facebook* was aimed at her friends and was intended to provide light relief for them.

"I'd post, funny videos from *YouTube* if I find something that makes me laugh, I'd post them for my friends... just silly little things that might amuse other people, that I kind of get a bit of fun out of" (Joan, 28, interview, January 2011).

The use of social networking sites by participants can be seen to reflect what boyd and Ellison (2007) describe as 'ego-centric' online spaces. They are used primarily to support offline social networks, to connect and maintain relationships with friends as opposed to meeting new people around shared interests; therefore they become closely linked with life and identity offline (boyd & Ellison, 2007). For participants, social networking sites and in particular *Facebook*, were the first and, for the heavier users, most frequently visited site when they went online. This framing of online interaction as predominantly 'ego-centric' can be seen to influence participants' conceptions and use of online social media more generally as discursive space. In the following sections this is addressed relating specifically to participants' attitudes towards online discussion of public issues.

3.3. Online social media sites as a discursive space

As with posting, there were varying attitudes towards discussions on online social media sites among participants. Those who entered into discussions about public issues on a regular basis tended to be those participants who were already active in spaces of discussion offline. Those who were members of political parties, Eoghan, Anne and James, regularly entered into discussions with people who shared their ideologies.

While Eoghan did display his political beliefs online and often entered into debates with friends through his *Facebook* profile he was critical of the medium, viewing face-to-face debate as a much better format. He felt that the nuances of political argument were lost in online discussion.

> "Political discussions I would tend to avoid having on *Facebook* because it's a crap form to do it… it's fine to put arguments forward but at the end of the day it doesn't really bring anything forward. All you get out of that is that other people that may not be in the party and aren't willing to read through everything, unless your argument is correct and hugely thought out… actual physical interaction you've body language, you've all those things which are taken away in the format of interaction online" (Eoghan, 26, Interview, January 2011).

James' profile contained many expressions of his political affiliations and beliefs, from status updates to his profile pictures, and the groups he joined displayed a sense of his party allegiance. He talked about using his profile picture as a canvassing tool during the election. Members of his party used the election poster of their local candidate for their profile picture. This practice was also demonstrated by Anne and Eoghan for their respective parties.

> "Well as you can see we're in election mode! Again especially in election mode including the last local election you tend to go a bit overboard on *Facebook*. As you can see people who have commented, likeminded people as you can see we all have the same profile picture" (James, 25, Online session, February 2011).

Anne talked about a change in her use of online social media since she joined her political party. She noticed a transformation in the way she talked about issues and the frequency of her posts. Since joining the party she tended to post more comments on political issues than she had before. She also noticed that the mode in which she addressed issues had changed from comments relating to her personal situation to comments which related to a wider societal concern.

"Before I was in [political party] I probably wouldn't have [posted] politically as in commenting on particular Fianna Fáil or Fine Gael or the state of the country. If there was a budget cut I would have said that is ridiculous, now I probably would put it up on *Facebook*" (Anne, 29, Interview, October 2010).

A second level of discussion became evident among a number of other participants who were not members of political parties or civic society groups: both Joanne and Michael talked about commenting on issues or events if they felt a sense of outrage about them. Michael talked in general terms saying that he entered into discussions very rarely but if he did it would be relating to

"something I'm very very bitter about or if something hilarious happens I'll jump on and do it. But it'd have to be one of those two things which are admittedly very rare occurrences" (Michael, 27, Interview, June 2011).

Joanne went into some detail about an event which caused her to post a news article and begin a discussion. This incited a discussion with a number of her friends on *Facebook*.

"One thing I remember lately, probably the last kind of current affairs topic, it was a while ago about a woman in Dublin and she was in council apartments and she froze to death[1]... I came across that somewhere on some news website and I posted it on *Facebook* because I was just disgusted, because I just couldn't believe that in this day and age that that kind of thing was happening and that actually caused a lot of people to comment on it... there was a lot of talk about the effectiveness of the country's politics and stuff like that" (Joanne, 29, Interview, June 2011).

A third level of discussion became apparent among another group of participants:

---

1. Joanne refers to the case of Rachel Peavoy a single mother who was found dead in her Dublin city flat on January 11th 2010 due to hypothermia. An inquest was held in Spring 2011 into her death. There was public concern that Dublin City Council's suspension of the centralised heating system in the area had contributed to her death (Newenham, 2011).

Joan, Cathy, Kevin and Patrick expressed no interest in entering discussions on *Facebook*. They viewed these sites as spaces for leisure and often expressed annoyance at people who used these sites to express opinions on public issues or politics.

> "I wouldn't feel the need to push it other people's faces all the time. It's something I'd discuss with friends, boyfriend or family but I wouldn't feel the need to push it out there... if you want to join a page fair enough but put your comments on that page keep each subject related to each subject" (Joan, 28, Interview, January 2011).

These attitudes towards online discussion of public issues revealed a sense that the online space is constructed in different ways for participants in relation to their offline civic practices. For participants who are engaged in civic practices offline, online social media profiles are utilised for the discussion of politics. While for those who are not engaged in these types of activity offline, online social media is a space in which the political should not be addressed. There is a sense here that boundaries are drawn around spaces where the discussion of public issues should take place and these should be adhered to. This provides an insight into the creation of 'public sphericules' (Gitlin, 1998) at a micro level, where participants can either participate in discussions or wish to ignore them completely.

3.4. Public sphere 2.0

Anne, James, David and Eoghan regularly engaged in online discussion of public issues on *Facebook*. James and David also utilised other more specialised sites to engage in more in-depth discussion. Anne's *Facebook* pages were the main site for discussion of public issues online. She found that discussions often involved people who were members of her political party and rarely friends from outside the party. She also browsed the *politics.ie* online political forum, reading different opinions and following threads using her partner's account. She had yet to set up her own account but felt she would get involved in debate on this site in the future.

"I'd probably see a discussion between my [political party] friends... there would be discussion, but my friends that would be outside of a political party, not really" (Anne, 29, Interview, October 2010).

James utilised his *Facebook* account to engage in discussion with a local radio current affairs programme. He also had an account on the more specialised *politics.ie* site where he engaged in more in depth debate of public issues and politics. He used these opportunities to discuss his party's policy and his views on history and political theory.

David also used his *Facebook* profile to discuss politics and public issues with friends. He described how discussion on *Facebook* was limited, often revolving around 'one-liners' and little in depth analysis.

"Usually there's one or two people who will comment on bigger political issues, they'll post a one liner usually, because of the nature of *Facebook* they are just one or two liner things. Because *Facebook* isn't conducive to discussion, [it's] sound bites. And equally if you are friends with somebody on it you are going to be preaching to the converted, everybody is going to be on the same wavelength anyway... in that sense *Facebook* can be a bit exclusive to some extent because inevitably you do focus in on people with similar interests. So in some cases it narrows your views or consolidates your point of view" (David, 27, Interview, February 2011).

While watching news and current affairs programming David often discussed both the production values and the issues being discussed with his friends. As well as these *Facebook* based discussions David also had an account on a specialist architectural site for discussion which often involved discussion of public issues.

Online discussion in these instances occurs between people of similar outlooks or political persuasion. The spaces for discussion on these sites can be seen to tie in with Gitlin's (1998) assertion that the development of ICTs could lead to the fragmentation of the public sphere into a collection of 'public sphericules' made up of a variety of interest groups.

In opposition to these uses of online social media as spaces where discursive practices can take place Joan, Kevin, Michael, Patrick, Thomas, Cathy and Joanne did not view online social media as a space for the discussion of politics and public issues. They felt that their profiles are not a space for the declaration of political beliefs; this division between the former group and the latter correlates with participants' modes of engagement with offline civic or political groups.

Kevin and Cathy's responses, reproduced here, demonstrate the sentiments expressed by these individuals in relation to the use of online social media for the expression of political opinions and discussion of public issues.

> "I'm not one for commenting to be honest I generally like to read other people's comments just read to see what other people's opinions are" (Kevin, 27, Online session, January 2011).

> "*Facebook* can be a way for people to vent their frustrations with politics, I'm not that type of person, I'll vent it but when you do that you're doing it very publically and I'm not like that I'd be more of a private person and I'd say it to the people that were amongst me but I wouldn't put it out there to the world" (Cathy, 28, Interview, January 2011).

Interviewees indicated a range of attitudes towards social media's potential as a site for a discursive space akin to Habermas's (1989) ideal public sphere. James, David, Anne and Eoghan saw these sites as a space for discussion of varying depth. The members of this group were already involved in offline citizenship activities where they participated in collective activism, political action and public discussion. Other participants, Kevin, Cathy and Joan viewed the discussion of politics as a more private pursuit happening offline among small groups of friends and family. Unlike the first group these participants were not involved in any community civic groups but did demonstrate an interest in keeping up to date with the news and current events.

Utopian perspectives view the internet as having the potential for the provision of a space where people can construct their identity independently of their demographic profile, providing a potential for debate to take place irrespective of the social situations of the individuals involved (Benkler, 2006; Negroponte, 1995) creating a space akin to Habermas's (1989) ideal public sphere. However this research revealed a sense that participation in online debate often correlates with offline collective civic activities. The idea that ICTs are playing a role in fragmenting the public sphere as per Gitlin (1998) is evident here. The online activity of participants who are involved in political parties and campaigning organisations illustrates this idea, through discussions which take place among people with similar outlooks and experiences. For those who do not participate in these types of collective civic activity this fragmentation manifests in the spatial divisions which they impose on their online social media use in relation to what types of content these sites should encompass.

4. Conclusions

This research illustrates that online social media sites in isolation will not create an online public sphere which is inclusive of a broader range of people. While the potential for the development of a public sphere exists in these spaces, through the technological affordances provided by online social media, this research finds that participation in these spaces by a broader public is contingent on individuals' offline civic activities. The empirical research points towards Gitlin's (1998) hypothesis that the impact of electronic media on the public sphere creates a landscape of 'public sphericules' consisting of disparate groups with little connection between them. Participation in these spaces is contingent on pre-established interests and orientations towards their content.

Online spaces where participants gathered around specialist interests can be seen to provide scope for the discussion of public issues. However it was those who were already engaged in the discussions of such issues offline that viewed these sites as having this potential. These sites were framed as hostile and confrontational spaces by participants who did not participate in discussion on them. These specialist sites also counter the discursive aims of Habermas's (1989) ideal public sphere as they tend to be populated by individuals who have well established ideological stances and views, visiting to relay their views and not necessarily enter into the reasoned debate which Habermas envisaged in the ideal public sphere.

The conceptualisation of the online space by participants also has an impact on the utilisation of these spaces for the discussion of public issues. Social networking sites such as *Facebook* were viewed by those who do not participate in collective civic activities as primarily a space for connecting with friends and relatives. Spaces were created where it is suitable to discuss certain topics and for some participants these lines were very firmly drawn. They shared activities and insights relating to the private sphere while the discussion of issues relating to the public sphere were cordoned off into specific spaces online. Discussions with participants who were involved in collective civic activities also pointed to this division of space. They moved to more specialised online social media spaces to discuss public issues as the structure of social networking sites was viewed as inconducive to in-depth discussions, reinforcing further the idea of fragmentation.

References

Anderson, B. (1991). *Imagined Communities: Reflections on the origin and spread of nationalism*. London: Verso.

Bakardjieva, M. (2005). *Internet Society: the Internet in everyday life*. London: Sage Publications.

Baym, N. K. (2000). *Tune in, log on: soaps, fandom, and online community*. London: Sage Publications.

Baym, N. K. (2010). *Personal Connections in the Digital Age*. Cambridge: Polity Press.

Benkler, Y. (2006). *The Wealth of Networks: How Social Production Transforms Markets and Freedom*. New Haven: Yale University Press.

boyd, d. m. (2007). Why youth (heart) social network sites: the role of networked publics in teenage social life. In D. Buckingham (Ed.), Y*outh, Identity and Digital Media* (pp. 119-142). Cambridge: MIT Press.

boyd, d. m. (2008). *Taken Out of Context: American Teen Sociality in Networked Publics.* PhD thesis. Berkeley: University of California. Retrieved from http://www.danah.org/papers/ TakenOutOfContext.pdf

boyd, d. m. & Ellison, N. B. (2007). Social Network Sites: Definition, History, and Scholarship. *Journal of Computer Mediated Communication, 13*(1), 210-230. doi: 10.1111/j.1083-6101.2007.00393.x

Calhoun, C. (Ed.). (1992). *Habermas and the Public Sphere.* Cambridge: The MIT Press.

Castells, M. (1996). *The Rise of the Network Society.* Malden Mass.: Blackwell.

Dahlgren, P. (2000). The Internet and the Democratisation of Civic Culture. *Political Communication, 17*(4), 335-340. doi: 10.1080/10584600050178933

Dahlgren, P. (2009). *Media and Political Engagement: Citizens, Communication and Democracy.* Cambridge: Cambridge University Press.

Dahlgren, P., & Gurevitch, M. (2005). Political Communication in a Changing World. In J. Curran & M. Gurevitch (Eds.), *Mass Media and Society* (4th ed.). London: Hodder Arnold.

Fraser, N. (1985). What's Critical About Critical Theory? The Case of Habermas and Gender. *New German Critique, 35*(Spring-Summer), 97-131. Retrieved from http://www.jstor.org/ stable/488202

Fraser, N. (1992). Rethinking the public sphere: A contribution to the critique of actually existing democracy. In C.Calhoun (Ed.), *Habermas and the Public Sphere.* Cambridge, MA: MIT Press.

Gitlin, T. (1998). Public Sphere or Public Sphericules. In T. Liebes & J. Curran (Eds.), *Media, Ritual and Identity* (pp. 168-174). London: Routledge.

Goode, L., McCullough, A., & O'Hare, G. (2011). Unruly publics and the fourth estate on YouTube. *Participations: Journal of Audience and Reception Studies, 8*(2), 594-615. Retrieved from http://www.participations.org/Volume%208/Issue%202/4b%20 Goode%20et%20al.pdf

Habermas, J. (1989). *The Structural Transformation of the Public Sphere: An Inquiry into a Category of Bourgeois Society* (originally published in German in 1962). Cambridge: Polity Press.

Hall, S., Hobson, D., Lowe, A., Willis, P. (Eds.). (1992). *Culture, media, language: working papers in cultural studies, 1972-79.* London: Routledge.

Hirzalla, F., & Van Zoonen, L. (2010). Beyond the Online/Offline Divide: How Youth's Online and Offline Civic Activities Converge. *Social Sciences Computer Review.* Retrieved from http://ssc.sagepub.com/content/early/2010/09/24/0894439310385538

Livingstone, S. (2002). *Young People and New Media: Childhood and the changing media environment*. London: Sage Publications.

Livingstone, S. (2008). Taking risky opportunities in youthful content creation: teenagers' use of social networking sites for intimacy, privacy and self-expression. *New Media & Society, 10*(3), 393-411. doi: 10.1177/1461444808089415

Livingstone, S., Couldry, N., & Markham, T. (2007). Youthful steps towards civic participation: Does the Internet help? In B. D. Loader (Ed.), *Young citizens in the digital age: Political engagement, young people and new media* (pp. 21-34). London: Routledge.

Markham, A. N. (1998). *Life Online: researching real experience in virtual space*. Walnut Creek CA: AltaMira Press.

McLuhan, M. (1964). *Understanding Media: the extensions of man*. London: Routledge.

Morley, D. (1986). *Family Television: Cultural Power and Domestic Leisure*. London: Comedia.

Morley, D. (1996). The Geography of Television: Ethnography, Communications, and Community. In L. Grossberg, J. Hay, & E. Wartella (Eds.), *The Audience and its Landscape*. Oxford: Westview Press.

Morley, D. (2007). *Media, Modernity and Technology: The Geography of the New*. Oxon: Routledge.

Negroponte, N. (1995). *Being Digital.* London: Hodder & Stoughton.

Newenham, P. (2011, April 7). Inquiry urged into death in cold flat. *The Irish Times*, 4. Retrieved from http://www.irishtimes.com/

Olsson, T. (2006). Active and calculated media use among young citizens: Empirical examples from a Swedish study. In D. Buckingham & R. Willett, *Digital Generations: Children, Young People and New Media*. New Jersey: Lawrence Erlbaum Associates Inc.

Papacharissi, Z. A. (2011). On convergent supersurfaces and public spheres online. *International Journal of Electronic Governance, 4*(1/2), 9-17. doi: 10.1504/IJEG.2011.041704

Rheingold, H. (2000). *The Virtual Community: Homesteading on the Virtual Frontier*. London: MIT Press.

Turkle, S. (1996). *Life on the Screen: Identity in the age of the Internet*. London: Weidenfeld & Nicolson.

Wellman, B., & Haythornwaite, C. (Eds.). (2002). *The Internet in Everyday Life*. Oxford: Blackwell Publishing.

9 Not Quite Kicking Off Everywhere: Feminist Notes on Digital Liberation

Angela Nagle[1]

Abstract

Increasingly, women's experience of online life seems to run counter to the optimistic expectations of the cyberfeminists of the 90s and the utopian fervour of the present. Female journalists and internet users find themselves at the receiving end of a level of verbal abuse online previously unthinkable in the public sphere. Women are showing greater signs of alienation from the online arena of political debate than in the culture of parliamentary politics and 'old media' institutions. In spite of the ever mounting evidence that digital liberation is not for all, the polemic of the universal emancipatory power of the internet continues to shape mainstream opinion and capture the political Left's imagination. While there have been sceptical female voices challenging these ideas since the early 90s, they have tended to be too rare, too marginal and too unwilling to make strident and fundamental challenges to the dominant cyberutopian narrative. This has meant that the women who speak out about the phenomenon of the remarkable prevalence of misogyny in online culture have been unable to link their experience to any wider politics and have been unable to articulate a coherent feminist critique to challenge the largely gender blind utopian orthodoxy. Focussing on one particular media moment sparked by the *New Statesman*, this chapter argues for the need to build such a discourse.

Keywords: women, cyberfeminism, cyberutopia, networked individualism, verbal abuse online.

1. Dublin City University, Dublin, Ireland; angelanagle@gmail.com

How to cite this chapter: Nagle, A. (2013). Not Quite Kicking Off Everywhere: Feminist Notes on Digital Liberation. In C. Fowley, C. English, & S. Thouësny (Eds.), *Internet Research, Theory, and Practice: Perspectives from Ireland* (pp. 157-175). Dublin: © Research-publishing.net.

1.   Introduction

Years after Haraway (1991) and later the Cyberfeminist Manifesto set the utopian tone of women's writing on the virtual world, Balka (1999) exclaimed "Where have all the feminist technology critics gone?" (title, emphasis removed). Today, I argue, feminist media critics remain critical of the power structures and the cultural politics of print, television, radio and film but the online world continues to get a curiously free pass, characterised in ways that echo the utopian fervour of the early cyberfeminists. So what happens when we are faced with information that suggests that the optimism of this school of thought might have been misplaced?

In November 2011 nine female journalists and bloggers went public, in the New Statesman, with their experience of verbal abuse online. This shocked many and set off a wave of women describing similar experiences in other newspapers and magazines, in opinion columns, blogs and on *Twitter*. These revelations appeared against a backdrop of the internet-centric Occupy movement, the rise of hacktivism as a form of protest, and prevailing cyberutopian fervour in the press and in academia[1]. Symbolism of the hacker group Anonymous who emerged from 4chan/b/[2] were to be seen at every demonstration and the publishing industry was churning out books celebrating the brave new egalitarian world that the internet would bring[3].

For a brief moment it seemed that the weight of damning evidence presented by these women would spark a new feminist critique of the cyberutopian fervour of the moment, arguing that the non-hierarchical, countercultural wave of digital liberation being trumpeted at the time in the media, in academia and among the political Left, was not gender blind and was not the egalitarian force it was often described as being. However, this moment never came. The story quickly petered out and no such critique emerged. The women were exposing evidence

---

1. See Castells (2011), Postills (2012) and Coleman (2012) for examples.

2. http://boards.4chan.org/b/

3. See Mason (2012), Shirky (2008) and Brooke (2011) for examples.

---

that ran counter to the dominant cyberutopian narrative that was sweeping the Left at that time, but no sure-footed articulation of that challenge emerged. This conspicuous absence is examined here.

2.   You should have your tongue ripped out

In her contribution to the *New Statesman* piece, feminist and trade union activist Cath Elliot wrote:

"If I'd been trying to keep a tally I would have lost count by now of the number of abusive comments I've received since I first started writing online back in 2007. And by abusive I don't mean comments that disagree with whatever I've written – I came up through the trade union movement don't forget, and I've worked in a men's prison, so I'm not some delicate flower who can't handle a bit of banter or heated debate – no, I'm talking about personal, usually sexualised abuse, the sort that on more than one occasion now has made me stop and wonder if what I'm doing is actually worth it. [...] I read about how I'm apparently too ugly for any man to want to rape, or I read graphic descriptions detailing precisely how certain implements should be shoved into one or more of my various orifices" (in Lewis, 2011a, Cath Elliot section, para. 1-2).

Feminist comedian Kate Smurthwaite added:

"The vast majority of the abuse is gender-related. There is a clear link to internet pornography. Much of the language used could have come straight from pornographic sites. For example, from this week: "IF THIS TRASH TALKING K*NT HAD HER F*CKNG, TONGUE RIPPED OUT OF HER SUCK-HOLE..."" (in Lewis, 2011a, Kate Smurthwaite section, para. 2, emphasis in original).

Blogger Dawn Foster wrote:

"The worst instance of online abuse I've encountered happened when I blogged about the Julian Assange extradition case. [...] Initially it was shocking: in the space of a week, I received a rabid email that included my home address, phone number and workplace address, included as a kind of threat. Then, after tweeting that I'd been waiting for a night bus for ages, someone replied that they hoped I'd get raped at the bus stop" (in Lewis, 2011a, Dawn Foster section, para. 1-2).

The piece quickly generated a lot of debate online and following on from this, the next day Penny (2011a) wrote on the subject in *The Independent*, saying:
"You come to expect it, as a woman writer, particularly if you're political. You come to expect the vitriol, the insults, the death threats. After a while, the emails and tweets and comments containing graphic fantasies of how and where and with what kitchen implements certain pseudonymous people would like to rape you cease to be shocking, and become merely a daily or weekly annoyance, something to phone your girlfriends about, seeking safety in hollow laughter. [...] Most mornings, when I go to check my email, Twitter and Facebook accounts, I have to sift through threats of violence, public speculations about my sexual preference and the odour and capacity of my genitals, and attempts to write off challenging ideas with the declaration that, since I and my friends are so very unattractive, anything we have to say must be irrelevant. [...] Efforts were made to track down and harass my family, including my two school-age sisters. After one particular round of rape threats, including the suggestion that, for criticising neoliberal economic policymaking, I should be made to fellate a row of bankers at knifepoint, I was informed that people were searching for my home address. I could go on" (Penny, 2011a, para. 1-7).

Lewis (2011a) who wrote the original piece for the *New Statesman* got such a strong reaction from women who had had similar experiences that she began collecting them and published some more shortly after.

Sex writer Petra Davis said that she wrote pseudonymously under male, female and gender neutral names and that it was only when she wrote as a female that she received regular misogynist abuse and threats. She wrote:
"When I started getting letters at my flat, I reported them to the police, but

they advised me to stop writing provocative material. Eventually, I was sent an email directing me to a website advertising my services as a sex worker, with my address on the front page under the legend 'fuck her till she screams, filth whore, rape me all night cut me open', and some images of sexually mutilated women. It was very strange, sitting quietly in front of my screen looking at those images, knowing that the violence done to these other women was intended as a lesson. [...] Of course, it didn't take long to take the site down, but by then I was thoroughly sick of the idea and more or less stopped writing about sex from any perspective" (in Lewis, 2011b, para. 10).

In response to a piece about police violence Nina Power found herself the topic of discussion on a blog popular with police, in which one commenter said, "Nina seems quite pretty. After we disband the Police, let's see pretty Nina walk through a sh1tty estate [...] and see how well her idea works out when the Gangstas decide they deserve to have her as a toy" (in Lewis, 2011b, para. 15).

Picking up on this, the American feminist writer Sady Doyle started a hashtag on *Twitter* called #mencallmethings which gathered thousands of tweets from women dealing with similar levels of abuse online from across English speaking cyberspace. Many men joined in expressing shock and male writers like Cohen (2011) wrote opinion pieces in solidarity with the women, criticising the willingness of editors to publish misogynist abuse of their female staff in comment threads.

The *New Satesman* story should not have come as a surprise. Women have recounted similar experiences for many years, although they are remarkably less theorised than acts of cyberfeminist subversion (Plant, 1998) or *Twitter* and *Facebook* revolutions. Internet fetishism and suspicion of feminism have been online bedfellows long before Julian Assange uttered the words "the Saudi Arabia of feminism" (cited in Colvin, 2011, para. 16). New Economy ideologue and futurologist Gilder (1994) quite comfortably married his ideas about the internet to his ultra-conservative ideas about women in the early 90s.

In 1994 internet culture magazine *Fringwear Review*'s edition on *chicks in psyberspace* gave female internet users the chance to describe their experiences of online life. What they described is remarkably similar to more mainstream online culture today, with the same ideas carrying over from geeky hacker subcultures to, almost two decades later, mainstream newspaper comment threads and global internet giants like *YouTube*. In a section called *How to pick up chicks on the internet* the final piece of sarcastically delivered advice reads:

> "If all else fails and she continues to bypass your brilliant email, rip her to shreds in public. Don't neglect to let your virtual friends know that she is one of the following: a dyke, a slut, virtually frigid or, better yet, that she's really a 14-year-old boy in Toronto. Send hatemail – women love to take abuse from men after all" (Whiteway & Brown, 1994, p. 44).

This is notably familiar to read today because it so perfectly characterises the online misogyny that women, from mainstream journalists to regular users of chat forums still repeatedly describe. Expressions like Tits or GTFO (get the fuck out) and memes like Idiot Nerd Girl and Annoying Facebook Girl are spread far beyond the confines of geek or gaming culture today and female bloggers and political commentators shock audiences when they reveal the extent of the threats and verbal abuse they receive from men online.

From conservative MP Louise Mensch receiving emails so threatening that she had to get a restraining order (Morris, 2012) to socialist feminists like Cath Elliot and Nina Power finding themselves the subject of descriptions of gang rape in online forums and comment threads, it seems women's experiences online are remarkably similar across the political spectrum.

So what was the outcome of the *New Statesman* furore and all the momentum built by these expressions of anger about women's treatment online? The media-dubbed 'stamp out misogynist trolling campaign' never became a real campaign. Some suggested greater comment thread moderation; others warned against allowing this to damage the greater project of online freedom, while others openly admitted that they simply did not know how to address the situation.

Beyond tacitly conceding the imperfection of the democratising medium, there were no clear or coherent challenges articulated to the cyberutopian orthodoxy of the day. Within days, the issue died down and went off the media radar again. It would prove not to be the first or last time.

Columns and blogs on this subject typically begin with outrage but end with bewilderment:

> "The fact of the matter is these kinds of pressuring tactics do work to silence women's voices, and that alone is reason enough to take them seriously. But how to do so without causing permanent shifts to your blood pressure? If anyone can figure out the strategy there, I'd love to hear it" (Marcotte, 2012, para. 3-4).

In the *New Statesman* piece Caroline Farrow concluded, "What can be done to reduce it? Nothing, nor would I support any moves to legislate for trolls" (in Lewis, 2011a, Caroline Farrow section, para. 7). Feminist blogger Natalie Dzerins wrote "As for a suggestion on how to make it stop? I'm afraid I have none. While we still live in a sexist society, any woman who sticks her head above the parapet will encounter misogynistic abuse" (in Lewis, 2011a, Natalie Dzerins section, para. 4). And Kate Smurthwaite concluded,

> "There is an underlying issue though the people who post these comments reveal a deep-seated hatred towards women. I find that unsurprising in our culture. Violent, extreme pornography is normal internet fare. Gang rape and prostitution are subjects for popular music. At least 95 per cent of actual rapists are still on the streets. That's the real problem. We need to address that" (in Lewis, 2011a, Kate Smurthwaite section, para. 6).

Despite the backdrop of a great deal of gender blind talk of digital revolution at that time, particularly in left-leaning media, none of the women saw their experience as grounds for questioning that tendency.

Morozov (2011) criticised the inherited cyberutopianism of American foreign policy thinking as a "voluntary intellectual handicap" (p. xvii). Perhaps contemporary mainstream discourse on online misogyny too is marked by the same kind of intellectual handicap because of how we, and the women who bring this issue to light, think about the internet. With experiences that run so counter to the dominant cyberutopian polemic of both the crypto-anarchist Left and the mainstream Silicon Valley free marketeers, the women who bring this subject to light seem unable or unwilling to use this information to directly challenge the inherited cyberutopian mythology that is all around us: that the network trumps the hierarchy, that hacker culture and amateurisation are radical challenges to power, and that the internet is a democratic, radicalising and liberating technology. To understand this we must first look at the language and ideas about the internet, which we have inherited.

3. The return of cyberutopia

Electronic Frontier Foundation cofounder Barlow (1995) told *New Perspectives Quarterly* that:

> "All the current power relationships on the planet are currently being disassembled, it's going to be up in the air. Ultimately, centralized anything is going to be greatly deemphasized and redistributed" (cited in Jacobs, 2001, p. 350).

Figures like Barlow within hacker culture and figures in more mainstream discourse like *Wired*'s Kelly (2010) made hubristic promises about the digital future, but their ideas were not unlike those that circulated in the academy. Many cyberfeminists have embraced these ideas too. While much of the more pessimistic analysis of the internet was based on the fear that it was a technology that would be impossible to regulate, Plant (1998) celebrated the anarchy of the internet because for her, the out of control technology signalled a break from male control.

In the years after the dot com bubble burst, visions like Negroponte's (1995) of a digital future in which the political effects of the internet would be so profound that "there will be no more room for nationalism than there is for smallpox" (p. 236) began to look absurd, and thinkers like Gilder (1994), Castells (1996) and Haraway (1991), once the cutting edge, soon began to look more like the false prophets of the so-called new economy years.

However, in 2009 when Iranian protesters poured onto the streets demanding the resignation of Ayatollah Khomeini, Western commentators soon dubbed it the 'Twitter Revolution' because of the role that social media played in organising and facilitating the uprising. Internet guru Shirky (2009) said, "This is it. The big one. This is the first revolution that has been catapulted onto the global stage and transmitted by social media" (para. 2). Blogger Malkin (2009) wrote "[i]n the hands of freedom-loving dissidents, the micro-blogging social network is a revolutionary samizdat – undermining the mullah-cracy's information blockades one tweet at a time" (excerpt, para. 5). As partially internet-facilitated uprisings spread across the Arab world, later dubbed "the Arab Spring", it seemed to many to be a confirmation of what thinkers like Negroponte (1995) had predicted long before.

While internet boosterism has been at different times the preserve of everyone from crypto-anarchist countercultures to Ronald Reagan to Silicon Valley free marketeers, the events of 2011 set off a seemingly unstoppable wave of cyberutopian fervour across a broad spectrum of the Left. Inspired by the Arab Spring, the indebted and underemployed youth of Spain and later America and the rest of the West, began to organise protests online, livestream events as they happened and build alternative online media and communities to resist government enforced austerity. The Spanish indignados and later the Occupy movement led the zeitgeist of the moment described by BBC journalist Mason (2012) "a hand brake turn for humanity" (p. 134).

These new internet-centric protest movements saw many aspects of 90s cyberutopianism becoming part of the organised Left, borrowing from the imagery, language and ideas of hacker culture, with the Guy Fawkes mask of the hacker collective Anonymous becoming a permanent fixture on demonstrations. Rheingold's (1993) vision of The Virtual Community represented an antidote to Putnam's (2000) less flattering vision of an atomised society and, for some on the Left, like Mason (2012), a digital formation of

Marx's *species being*. The hacker ethic, with its meritocracy of ideas and libertarian free speech advocacy is described in popular polemics as "the digital equivalent of Enlightenment coffee houses" (Brooke, 2011, p. xx) and we are told that "technology is breaking down traditional social barriers of status, class, power, wealth and geography, replacing them with an ethos of collaboration and transparency" (Brooke, 2011, p. ix).

A typical example of the kind of upbeat feminist perspective we have seen would be a TED talk called *Social media and the end of gender.* Blakley (2010) told an international web audience that "the social media applications that we all know and love, or love to hate, are actually going to free us from some of the absurd assumptions that we have as a society about gender. I think that social media is actually going to help us dismantle some of the silly and demeaning stereotypes that we see in media and advertising about gender. If you hadn't noticed, our media climate generally provides a very distorted mirror of our lives and of our gender and I think that's going to change" (video file - 00:30/01:03).

Whereas networked individualism was once the preserve of New Economy boosters and viewed with suspicion by some Marxist thinkers like Henwood (2003) and Barbrook (2007), since the events of 2009-2011 the Left has embraced the networked individualism of a younger generation of radicalised digital natives. Sceptics have, to varying degrees, always been marginal, but by the time women like those in the *New Statesman* came to experience and write about the dramatic backlash against women evident online, the cyberutopian vision of Silicon Valley that had at least taken some marginal criticism from the Left had now moved into the Left.

4.   Digital mythologies

Barthes (1972) wrote that "myth has the task of giving an historical intention a natural justification and making contingency appear eternal" (p. 142). To understand why women's experience of online life has not articulated itself as a challenge to the orthodoxy it runs counter to, we must look at the narratives, the language and the mythologies of cyberutopia. Making the case for the necessity of a critical feminist analysis, which can engage with the popular and the political requires a contrasting of these digital mythologies with the ever-expanding body of contradictory evidence of women's lived experience.

4.1.   The cyborg body is transcendent

In cyberpunk fiction, cyberspace was imagined as "a disembodied zone wilder than the wild west, racier than the space race, sexier than sex, even better than walking on the moon" (Plant, 1998, p. 180). Cyberfeminists were overwhelmingly optimistic about the potential that the virtual and new communications technologies held for women. In Gibson's (1984) Neuromancer, the natural human body was referred to as "meat" (p. 6). Cyberfeminists like Haraway (1991) thought women should embrace detachment from naturalistic notion about the body, saying she would rather be a cyborg than a goddess. For her, the cyborg held radical potential as a new way of thinking of the body; a mythology that would constitute a break from conceiving of the female body in terms the nature-culture dichotomy. The cyborg subject's ability to escape the biological body, which had been such a site of female oppression, was to be welcomed.

Wajcman (2004) for example, wrote that "[i]n cyberspace, all physical, bodily cues are removed from communication. As a result, our interactions are fundamentally different, because they are not subject to judgements based on sex, age, race, voice, accent or appearance but are based only on textual exchanges" (p. 66) but how many female internet users today can say their experience chimes with this description?

In 2007, tech writer, programming educator and blogger Kathy Sierra had been the keynote speaker at *South by Southwest Interactive* and a kind of mainstream tech guru when the personal backlash against her among anonymous commenters was so extreme that she had to close down her blog, withdraw from speaking engagements and public life and call the police. Personal details about her family and home address were posted among highly sexualised and threatening comments on various blogs and forums. Some of the posts included photoshopped images of her with a noose beside her head, a shooting target pointed at her face and of her being gagged with a thong. When she explained in her blog why she had to step back from public life, writing, "I have cancelled all speaking engagements. I am afraid to leave my yard. I will never feel the same" it sparked a whole new wave of hate online, with commenters saying she had taken things too personally and was making a fool of herself by overreacting (cited in Walsh, 2007, para. 9).

In this case the threat to her very real body was a sharp reminder that the theoretical work of the cyborg imaginary has some limitations. Playing a central role in the construction of identity and the policing of gender norms in online forums, the body has been aggressively, almost compulsively, reasserted online from the explosion of hardcore pornography through to the obsessive references to female anatomy and violence against women that characterises online countercultures such as the website 4chan/b/.

The very language of digital liberation is filled with depoliticised normative terms. Central to hacker culture, to *Wikileaks* and to the 'information revolution' has been the notion that there is a truth, which, if known, will liberate mankind. Julian Assange has earned the press title "Truth Warrior" in a "Truth Revolution", calling himself an "information activist" (Choney, 2010, para. 2).

But when we look at phenomena like 'pro-Ana'[1] online communities it hugely complicates the implied or explicit assumption that all communication is simply 'information' and that all 'information' is liberating. If we apply definitions used by Castells (2007) and popularised by *Wired magazine* here, the pro-Ana internet users must be doing something liberating by definition. They are pooling their resources, sharing information and asserting their autonomy through the internet, just as Iranian tweeters and Syrian bloggers have done.

---

1. Pro-Ana online communities are predominantly female pro-Anorexia internet users who use forums to spread information promoting anorexia and encouraging fellow anorexics to remain dangerously underweight.

4.2. The network trumps the hierarchy

In his study of Spanish internet users, Castells (2007) wrote:

"The more an individual has a project of autonomy (personal, professional, socio-political, communicative), the more she uses the Internet. And in a time sequence, the more he/she uses the Internet, the more autonomous she becomes vis-à-vis societal rules and institutions" (p. 244).

Central to the hacker and neo-left cyberutopian polemic about this new internet-led radicalism is the notion that the network trumps the hierarchy. Thinkers like Castells (1996) and Hardt and Negri (2004) created an intellectual framework for the multitude, the newly empowered networked individuals and what would later be called the smart swarm in tech start-up parlance. And yet we increasingly see distinctly hierarchical gendered patterns in online behaviour, often more rigidly policed along gender lines than those overtly hierarchical democratic institutions that are considered hopelessly stuffy and outdated by internet radicals.

Here in Ireland for example, the most popular political discussion forum Politics.ie (2010) surveyed their readers and found among respondents only 14% were female, making female participation on the website lower than it is in government. Feminists continue to criticise government and 'old media' institutions for their low female participation and their male dominated cultures but the same problems online are ignored and the mythology of the internet, that the network must trump the hierarchy, that decentralisation and democratisation of media are empowering us remain largely unchallenged by women. Even when, in the case of the writing sparked by the *New Statesman* piece, women are experiencing and describing evidence that might deeply problematise these notions, no such critique emerges.

The Irish example only reflects broader trends. A study by the University of Maryland's school of engineering showed that chatroom participants using female names were 25 times more likely to receive threatening and/or sexually explicit private messages than those with male or gender-neutral names

(Meyer & Cukier, 2006, p. 470). And for every feminist blog and celebrated act of countercultural transgression, there are also an abundance of explicitly misogynist memes, websites and cultures[1]. While mainstream forms of social media such as *Facebook* are used more by women, the untamed anonymous counterculture, which has been praised by many Left thinkers, appears to be extremely hostile to women. What if, counter to what Castells (1996) and internet boosters in big business and on the Left have been saying, the network does not trump the hierarchy? What if the tyranny of structurelessness at work in the more anarchic corners of the online world is actually worse for women than organised hierarchies found in 'old media'? What if the user-generated online world, without the influence of capital, without the big media institutions and without editorial judgement displays a greater hierarchy in practice?

4.3.   Hackers are the digital vanguard

The Guy Fawkes mask, symbol of the hacker collective Anonymous, has become the iconic image of the Occupy movement and associated campaigns for internet freedom, such as the anti-SOPA campaign. Countless newspaper articles and opinion columns on Occupy for many months used the image of the mask. Penny (2011b, 2011c), one of the most vocal bloggers against anonymous internet misogyny after the *New Statesman* piece was published, was among the many on the Left to praise the group and to cheer their actions against others. She tweeted "Anonymous have threatened the Tea Party. This makes my evening so much better" (Penny, 2011b, tweet). She also called DDoS hacking "the digital equivalent of a sit-in" (Penny, 2011c, para. 4).

Describing the pranking and attacks orchestrated by hacker collectives and trolls against others, Penny (2011c) wrote: "For cyberactivists, it has always been about poking fun: an anarchic collision of satire and direct action that makes a mockery of the powerful and self-satisfied. They do it "for the lulz," in cyberspeak" (para. 4).

---

1. These include viral pornographic material that has become a popular internet reference such as '2 girls 1 cup' and memes like Women Logic.

Penny's (2011c) depiction very much chimed with the largely unchallenged view on the Left and hacker culture's own flattering description of itself. Only a few years earlier, however, before hacktivism and 'lulz' had been embraced by many on the Left, feminist magazine *Bitchmedia* had a less flattering report on their experiences with the internet rebels. Friedman (2008) was blogging at Feministe.com when they came under attack from groups of commenters posting violent rape fantasies and threats about the writers and shutting down the site using DDoS attacks:

> "Then I got word that a loosely organized cybermob known as Anonymous was attempting to crash feminist sites, including Feministe, flooding comments sections with misogynist rants and threatening feminist bloggers with rape and other violence. This had happened before, but never with such organized force. No one was sure which systems would hold and which would fail; we didn't even know which site would be attacked next. Privately, we worried about our safety and strategized about how to defend our sites and ourselves. […] They zeroed in on one particular blogger, whose online name is Biting Beaver, posting her home address and calling for Anonymous members to kidnap her son and place damning phone calls to her neighbors and her local police" (Friedman, 2008, para. 3-10).

Quite contrary to Penny's (2011c) view, which became fashionable on the radical Left after the *Bitchmedia* piece, it described 'lulz' in less emancipatory tones: "While Anonymous's targets may be random, their methods are not. The culture of lulz is saturated with juvenile, racist, misogynist, and homophobic language and imagery" (Friedman, 2008, para. 7).

Praise for the radical hacktivist aspect this culture has come to almost completely drown out these unpleasant details. One is less likely to hear, for example, that hackers also attack feminist websites with some regularity, including the International Women's Day site (Sterling, 2011). In her essay *Anonymous: From the Lulz to Collective Action*, Coleman (2011) says that the prankster sensibility and anti-leader ethic that characterises the anarchic 4chan/b/ site contains a self-correcting democratising mechanism. And yet, it is hard to imagine a newspaper, a TV show, a film or an advertisement celebrating and organised around explicit misogyny to the extent that typifies much of 4chan/b/ the culture of 'lulz' and it is harder still to imagine such a cultural product being praised widely today in the academy and on the political Left.

5.   Conclusion

All of this suggests that a critical feminist analysis of cyberutopia and the online counterculture, were it to exist, would have to challenge several dominant ideas about the nature of online communication and the sexual politics of the online counterculture. It would have to start by considering the possibility that when we look at online cultures which are anarchic, decentralised, uncensored, unregulated and not organised by powerful institutions or market forces we do not necessarily find something that is better for women, we may even find that it is worse. Feminist media analysis, and in particular Marxist-feminist analysis, would therefore have something entirely counterintuitive to theorise, and it would have to do so against the dominant gender-blind academic and Left wing cheerleading of hacker culture, open source software, pirate culture and 'lulz' culture.

What we see in the *New Statesman* piece is the first step toward a recognition in public discourse that something does not add up about the dominant mythology of the internet-as-liberator. Perhaps the next step needs to involve a challenge to the flattering but constructed founding mythologies surrounding the user-generated, democratised, online world which have shaped our belief in its liberating potential.

Haraway's (1991) cyberfeminism was conceived as an ironic non-innocent creation myth to subvert all of those creation myths that had been woven into our language and our ways of thinking about womanhood. Over a quarter of a century later, it is the mythology of the virtual world, which Haraway (1991) helped to write, that needs to be deeply challenged and subverted, as the reality of women's experience throws up complications so profound that they simply cannot continue to be seen as mere exceptions to the rule.

References

Balka, E. (1999, November 11). *Where have all the feminist technology critics gone?* Retrieved from http://www.loka.org/alerts/loka.6.6.txt

Barbrook, R. (2007). *Imaginary futures: From thinking machines to the global village.* London: Pluto Press.

Barlow, J. P. (1995, March 22). Unmediated Man. *New Perspectives Quarterly.* Retrieved from http://business.highbeam.com/5175/article-1G1-16870315/unmediated-man

Barthes, R. (1972). *Mythologies.* New York: Farrar, Straus and Giroux.

Blakley, J. (2010, December). Social media and the end of gender [video]. *TED Blog.* Retrieved from http://blog.ted.com/2011/02/02/social-media-and-the-end-of-gender-johanna-blakley-on-ted-com/

Brooke, H. (2011). *The Revolution Will Be Digitised: Dispatches from the Information War.* New York: Random House.

Castells, M. (1996). *The Rise of the Network Society.* Oxford: Blackwell Publishers.

Castells, M. (2007). Communication, Power and Counter-power in the Network Society. *International Journal of Communication, 1,* 238-266. Retrieved from http://ijoc.org/ojs/index.php/ijoc/article/view/46/35

Castells, M. (2011, August 2). The Disgust Becomes a Network. *Adbusters.* Retrieved from http://www.adbusters.org/magazine/97/manuel-castells.html

Choney, S. (2010, July 26). Wikileaks founder sees himself as 'information activist'. *Msnbc. com.* Retrieved from http://www.msnbc.msn.com/id/38413617/ns/technology_and_science-security/t/wikileaks-founder-sees-himself-information-activist/#.T-AMd82Pc-U

Cohen, N. (2011, December 6). A regiment of women monsterers. *The Spectator.* Retrieved from http://blogs.spectator.co.uk/nick-cohen/2011/12/a-regiment-of-women-monsterers/

Coleman, E. G. (2011, April 6). Anonymous: From the Lulz to Collective Action. *Mediacommons.* Retrieved from http://mediacommons.futureofthebook.org/tne/pieces/anonymous-lulz-collective-action

Coleman, E. G. (2012). *Coding Freedom: The Ethics and Aesthetics of Hacking.* Princeton: Princeton University Press.

Colvin, M. (2011, December 27). WikiLeaks founder baffled by sex assault claims. *The Sunday Times*. Retrieved from http://www.theaustralian.com.au/in-depth/wikileaks/wikileaks-founder-baffled-by-sex-assault-claims/story-fn775xjq-1225976459286

Friedman, J. (2008). Wack Attack. Republished in *Bitchmedia*. Retrieved from http://bitchmagazine.org/article/from-the-archive-wack-attack

Gibson, W. (1984). *Neuromancer*. New York: Ace Books.

Gilder, G. (1994). Freedom From Welfare Dependency. *Religion & Liberty, 4*(2), n.p. Retrieved from http://www.acton.org/pub/religion-liberty/volume-4-number-2/freedom-welfare-dependency

Haraway, D. J. (1991). *Simians, Cyborgs, and Women: The Reinvention of Nature*. London: Free Association Books.

Hardt, M., & Negri, A. (2004). *Multitude: War and Democracy in the Age of Empire*. New York: The Penguin Press.

Henwood, D. (2003). *After the New Economy*. New York: The New Press.

Jacobs, K. (2001). Utopia Redux. In P. Ludlow (Ed.), *Crypto-Anarchy, Pirate States and Pirate Utopias* (pp. 349-352). Cambridge: The MIT Press.

Kelly, K. (2010). *What Technology Wants*. New York: Viking Press.

Lewis, H. (2011a, November 3). 'You should have your tongue ripped out': The reality of sexist abuse online. *New Statesman*. Retrieved from http://www.newstatesman.com/blogs/helen-lewis-hasteley/2011/11/comments-rape-abuse-women

Lewis H. (2011b, November 6). On rape threats an internet trolls. *New Statesman*. Retrieved from http://www.newstatesman.com/blogs/helen-lewis-hasteley/2011/11/rape-threats-abuse-sex-female

Malkin, M. (2009, June 18). *Iran, Twitter and Freedom* [blog]. Retrieved from http://michellemalkin.com/2009/06/18/iran-twitter-and-freedom/

Marcotte, A. (2012, June 13). Online misogyny: can't ignore it, can't not ignore it. *Slate*. Retrieved from http://www.slate.com/blogs/xx_factor/2012/06/13/online_misogyny_reflects_women_s_realities_though_in_a_cruder_way_than_is_customary_offline_.html

Mason, P. (2012). *Why It's Kicking Off Everywhere: The New Global Revolutions*. London: Verso.

Meyer, R., & Cukier, M. (2006). Assessing the Attack Threat due to IRC Channels. *Proceedings of the International Conference on Dependable Systems and Networks* (pp. 467-472). Retrieved from http://www.enre.umd.edu/content/rmeyer-assessing.pdf

Morozov, E. (2011). *The Net Delusion: How Not to Liberate the World*. London: Allen Lane.

Morris, S. (2012, June 11). Louise Mensch 'troll' sentenced over threatening email. *The Guardian*. Retrieved from http://www.guardian.co.uk/uk/2012/jun/11/louise-mensch-troll-sentenced-email

Negroponte, N. (1995). *Being Digital*. New York: Vintage Books.

Penny, L. (2011a, November 4). A woman's opinion is the mini-skirt of the internet. *The Independent*. Retrieved from http://www.independent.co.uk/opinion/commentators/laurie-penny-a-womans-opinion-is-the-miniskirt-of-the-internet-6256946.html

Penny, L. (2011b, May 5). Twitter @pennyred. Retrieved from http://twitter.com/PennyRed/status/66296171613786112

Penny, L. (2011c, October 31). Cyberactivism from Egypt to Occupy Wall Street. *The Nation*. Retrieved from http://www.thenation.com/article/163922/cyberactivism-egypt-occupy-wall-street#

Plant, S. (1998). *Zeroes and Ones: Digital Women and the New Technoculture*. London: Fourth Estate.

Politics.ie. (2010, July 26). *[P.ie survey] Over 86% of Politics.ie Readers are Male*. Retrieved from http://www.politics.ie/forum/media/134549-politics-ie-survey-over-86-politics-ie-readers-male.html

Postills, J. (2012, April 17). *Internet freedom and the new protest movements* [blog]. Retrieved from http://johnpostill.com/2012/04/17/internet-freedom-and-the-new-protest-movements/

Putnam, R. D. (2000). *Bowling Alone: The Collapse and Revival of American Community*. New York: Simon and Schuster.

Rheingold, H. (1993). *The Virtual Community: Homesteading on the electronic frontier*. New York: Addison Wesley.

Shirky, C. (2008). *Here Comes Everybody: How Change Happens When People Come Together*. London: Penguin Books.

Shirky, C. (2009). Q&A with Clay Shirky on Twitter and Iran. *TED blog*. Retrieved from http://blog.ted.com/2009/06/16/qa_with_clay_sh/

Sterling, B. (2011, March 8). DDOS hacker keen to beat up girls. *Wired*. Retrieved from http://www.wired.com/beyond_the_beyond/2011/03/ddos-hackers-keen-to-beat-up-girls/

Wajcman, J. (2004). *Techno Feminism*. Cambride: Polity Press.

Walsh, J. (2007, March 31). *Men who hate women on the web*. *Salon*. Retrieved from http://www.salon.com/2007/03/31/sierra/

Whiteway, E., & Brown, T. (1994). *How to pick up chicks on the internet*. Austin, Texas: Fringeware Review.

10 We are All Friends Nowadays: But What is the Outcome of Online Friendship for Young People in Terms of Individual Social Capital?

Anne Rice[1]

Abstract

For contemporary young people friendship has changed considerably from previous generations and nowadays weak ties represent the bulk of youth online friendships. These acquaintances do not provide quality relationships as young people do not seek to gain anything from such friends nor do they expect to help them out. Nevertheless weak ties have an indirect benefit to social capital and are extremely important in demonstrating popularity and status. Other online friends directly benefit from the individual's social capital. Firstly, social networking provides a unique extra dimension to bonding friendship and unlike previous generations online friends benefit from instantaneous textual therapy, which promotes good health and well-being. Secondly, social networking has opened up the channels of sociability between young people and a diverse range of others. Thus linking social capital is increased and the traditional concept of youth-youth friendship has been joined by youth-professional and youth-business friendships. Young people essentially view these friends as 'in between' or 'just in case' friends who are instrumental in terms of sourcing new information while businesses and organisations welcome online friendship as a new marketing tool. As such, some online friends represent a desire to 'get ahead' rather than 'get along'.

Keywords: social networking, friendship, social capital, young people.

1. Queen's University Belfast, Belfast, Northern Ireland; michael.rice16@btinternet.com

How to cite this chapter: Rice, A. (2013). We are All Friends Nowadays: But What is the Outcome of Online Friendship for Young People in Terms of Individual Social Capital? In C. Fowley, C. English, & S. Thouësny (Eds.), *Internet Research, Theory, and Practice: Perspectives from Ireland* (pp. 177-197). Dublin: © Research-publishing.net.

1.   Introduction

Contemporary society has experienced large scale technological change with widespread use of new technologies including the internet and associated social networking websites such as *Facebook*. This has been accompanied by, while also contributing to, significant shifts in social interaction. In this contemporary social networking era almost everyone appears to be friends online but it remains unclear what actual resources are gained by the individual through the online network. In other words what is the social capital outcome of online friendship for young people?

This research[1] was carried out between 2010 and 2011 in a rural area in Northern Ireland and involved eleven youth focus groups (including five pilot focus groups) and thirty six in-depth interviews (carried out in pairs of parent-youth combinations)[2]. The sample population were young people in full-time education and their parents. The selection criteria for the young people was that they were in the 16-18 age range and lived at home with at least one parent or guardian.

The overall aim of the research was to investigate the impact of social networking on individual, community and family social capital. Based on findings from this investigation this chapter specifically examines the outcome of online friendship for young people's individual social capital. As such, it focuses specifically on youth, as opposed to parental accounts, of young people's social networking activity.

This chapter begins by presenting a brief overview of social capital and its relevance to online friendship. Having discussed why social capital is an important concept for understanding online friendship, the chapter then progresses to critically assess the social capital outcome of social networking.

---

1. This chapter is based on findings from the author's PhD research undertaken in the School of Planning, Architecture and Civil Engineering, Queen's University Belfast under the supervision of Dr. Ruth McAreavey and Prof. Aileen Stockdale.

2. The following abbreviations indicate the source of data. MFG = mixed gender focus group, BFG = all boys focus group, GFG = all girls focus group, PCI = parent child interview, POI = parent only interview, COI = child only interview.

This reveals that for the individual online friendships are direct, indirect and often unused sources of social capital. The chapter concludes with a discussion of contemporary online friendship and how it has increased the young person's ability to nurture their own stock of social capital.

2. Social capital and online friendship

Social capital is, broadly speaking, the resources people gather through their relationships. Explained in basic terms, social relations matter and people working together are able to tap into resources that otherwise would not be available to them on their own. Social capital is largely upheld as a positive resource and is linked to an array of social benefits, from better health to good educational achievement. However, social capital is not always a benefit for everyone and can produce a number of negative outcomes. For example, for those outside the network it can signify exclusion (Field, 2008; Portes, 1998). Nevertheless, as for the young people in this study the online network is an inclusive space, where friends are added quite randomly, this chapter focuses on the positive benefits of social networking to the individual.

Social capital has been valuable in the analysis of youth social relations (Raffo & Reeves, 2000; Seaman & Sweeting, 2004). Similarly in terms of advancing knowledge about online relationships formed through social networking, social capital is frequently the lens of inquiry. This inquiry has largely focused on the bridging/bonding distinction of social capital. This differentiation splits social capital into two groups; bridging, i.e., information produced from weak ties, or bonding, i.e., emotional support produced from close bonds (Putnam, 2000). Bonding social capital stems from emotionally deep relationships such as family, close friends and relatives. This is an inward looking form of social capital that facilitates exclusive identities, reinforces homogenous groups and acts as the "sociological superglue" (Putnam, 2000, p. 22). Bridging social capital is found in connections between people which assist with information seeking but do not offer deep emotional support. Unlike bonding social capital it is outward looking, facilitates inclusive identities, is accessed by individuals outside of their usual social circle and acts as the "sociological WD-40[1]" (Putnam, 2000, p. 22).

Early indications point to social networking mainly assisting with the development of bridging social capital, in other words the formation of weak ties (Donath & boyd, 2004; Ellison, Steinfield, & Lampe, 2007). For example, a study by Ellison et al. (2007) consisted of an online survey of 286 undergraduate students and concluded that the social networking website, *Facebook*, encouraged bridging social capital among the students. However, as the authors point out the positive correlations with social networking and bridging social capital may have much to do with a focus on the university and the undergraduate experience.

For the young people in this study the school environment also produces an extensive amount of bridging ties (and a small subset of close bonding friends) but the majority of these ties collectively produce side benefits of belonging to a large network. They are not directly utilised in terms of social capital. Therefore it becomes useful to think of social capital and its associated benefits not simply in terms of a distinction between bridging and bonding but also in terms of direct and indirect social capital. Focusing on the direct/indirect social capital benefits of online friendship, the following section shows that young people benefit directly from small subsets of close and linking friends while the remaining large body of weak ties generates indirect and unused benefits.

3. The direct benefit of social networking to young people's social capital

For the most part young people are drawn to *Facebook* because it is a multi-purpose website where they share and receive photos, comments and status

---

1. WD 40 is "the trademark name of a penetrating oil and water-displacing spray [...] originally designed to repel water and prevent corrosion" (http://en.wikipedia.org/wiki/WD-40).

updates between a large number of online friends, while at the same time view which of their friends are online and available for private (textual) chat. Chloe explains that *Facebook* appeals because:

> **Chloe**: There are always friends online and you will always be able to talk to someone. You can see who's on private chat and that's handy if you want to have a private conversation with your close mates. For the rest of them, you get to see what they are saying, through their status updates and their comments on people's walls[1]. (COI)

Thus social networking incorporates two spaces, occupied by two types of friends. On private chat, close friends communicate privately from the rest of the online network. This one to one textual communication cements bonds between close friends.

The public space is home to the rest of the online network, individuals who are added as friends but only share loose connections with each other. While this loosely connected network has a lack of relevance to their own lives, young people continue to view details about a wide range of others. For example, Olive refers to *Facebook* as:

> **Olive**: A place to find out about people and somewhere you see what others are up to. (PCI)

In terms of social capital, it is private chat that generates a direct benefit for young people. For the young people in the study, school is the main source of close friendships. Outside of school these friendships are supplemented with online communication. While this is often mainly a mundane recap of the school day, this virtual after school club also serves as a vital support in more stressful times. Janet and her friends outline the therapeutic value of social networking during examinations:

---

1. In order to preserve the anonymity of the participants all of the data contains fictional names. The researcher is referred to as Anne in the in-depth interviews and focus groups.

Janet: Especially round exam time and you're revising, or suppose to, you get a sort of comfort that someone is as bogged off as you.

Paula: Yep when you're cracking up in your room you get relief from the fact that you're not the only one doing nothing or feeling the way you do.

Janet: When you *Facebook* it's all written and it's totally out of your system. Then you can see what's happening more clearly cus you can read what you're saying and when you've so much in your head there's no other way you can deal with it.

Amanda: Yeah you can't tell your family cus they don't really get it like and so *Facebook* is the best way you can cope like. (GFG)

Two interrelated features of online friendship are thus shown to directly benefit the individual. Firstly, it promotes communication between intimate friends and this is therapeutic as friends play a vital role in mental health and well-being (Brown & Harris, 1978; Sherbourne, Hays, & Wells, 1995). For the young people in this study, this is especially the case during examinations, when online communication through social networking functions as a wider counselling forum for close friends as opposed to providing support with subject-specific revision.

Secondly, writing is an activity that has a longstanding recognition in psychology for its potential to reorganise thoughts and feelings (Bucci, 1995). Social networking is well placed within this psychological tradition, as with the exception of its visual dimension (the sharing of photographs and the creation of ones profile picture) it is essentially a textual mode of communication through comments, status updates and private online chat. As the therapeutic power of writing is especially beneficial following a traumatic experience (cognitive change theory) or for those who do not openly talk about their emotions (inhibition theory) (Graybeal, Sexton, & Pennebaker, 2002) online chat is therefore, in some instances, more valuable than face-to-face communication between friends. This is because online chat, due to its textual nature, helps to clarify thinking, especially in the face of trauma, and brings extra benefit to those who typically do not engage with others about their problems.

In this study, as is typical of qualitative research in general, "snippets" of other people's experiences and lives emerged (Holland, 2007, p. 18). In the focus group environment, these fragments of others lives were often discussed in a more forthcoming manner than the details discussed about their own lives. For example, Amanda and her friends speak openly about a close friend (who is not present) and the online support they give her following the death of her mother.

> **Amanda**: A girl in our school's mum passed away recently and the chat between her and us on *Facebook* was really deep and we were consoling her through it and she was devastated. I think it really helped her cope, I do. And it was comforting for her to let it all out without actually seeing everyone in person.

> **Paula**: If you had to go and knock on her door you would kind of not know if she was up for people calling and then there'd be the thing with not knowing what to say to the rest of the ones in her house. But *Facebook* was good and she was able to like draw on support from us at a time when she really needed her friends. (GFG)

For Amanda and friends social networking provides support that would be more difficult through physical contact. While the awkwardness these young people demonstrate may be linked to puberty and growing up, not necessarily a response to death, it nevertheless makes the benefit of a visit and the value of physical support interaction debatable. They choose *Facebook* as the space to discuss grief and offer support while remaining at a distance and avoiding the uncertainty of a face-to-face encounter. This type of 'intimacy at a distance' cannot be underrated as the quality of online peer support has recently been described as equal to the more formal web or telephone-based sessions offered by fully trained counsellors (Fukkink, 2011).

In addition to improving well-being during times of sadness, social networking has a positive impact on a variety of other sensitive teenage issues, such as those related to sex and relationships, depression, eating disorders or drug and alcohol use (Gould, Munfakh, Lubell, Kleinman, & Parker, 2002; Leung, 2007). However, support during the sadness connected to death is highly significant compared to sadness induced by other experiences. Death, along with divorce and moving house, is a 'critical moment' when the individual's experience is different from their everyday routines and that of those around them (Giddens, 1991). Therefore the direct benefit of online friendship to well-being does have wider applicability, not just in terms of examinations and typical collective situations, but to a range of life experiences at an individual level. These include not only 'typical and passing' teenage issues but also the more critical and acute ones such as the death of a parent.

Despite online friendship's wider remit to help young people cope with a number of sensitive teenage issues, in the focus group environment, only the value of online friendships to cope with examination stress was divulged. This reluctance to discuss other more sensitive issues is not surprising and relates to the peer setting of the focus group and the way the 'group effect' influences the group discussion. The group effect causes participants not to give their own opinions but rather reflect those of other group members (Hesse-Biber & Leavy, 2006).

In contrast, in-depth interviews with young people reveal that online friends support each other on a much wider range of issues than examinations, including those which concern them directly, such as teenage pregnancy, and those connected to family members such as divorce and illness. For example, Emma reveals how social networking helped her cope with her younger sister's illness:

> **Emma**: Like the whole family were really worried because my sister was going through tests...

> **Anne**: Did you speak with your friends about it?

Emma: Yeah but only two of my closest friends but not much in school like in front of the others, more at home using private chat. We never actually talked about why that was but I think they knew I'd have burst into tears thinking or talking about it in school. They were always kind to me and tried to cheer me up. (COI)

The unspoken rule not to discuss the illness in school is similar to the awkwardness Amanda and Paula display in response to the death of their friend's mother. Emma's friends, while sensitive to the situation, are unsure how to cope with her emotional state. Consequently, like Paula and Amanda, they resort to only discussing it online rather than in person. In both instances peer support is not public, either in the school setting (in Emma's case) or in the home of the bereaved girl, but is facilitated by private chat on *Facebook*. Thus in the two situations the social awkwardness of face-to-face and place-based contact and support is circumvented and the quality of the communication is enhanced through social networking.

4.   Exploiting vertical links to 'get ahead' rather than 'get along': the direct but short term social capital benefit of linking with those outside the peer group

While bonding friends avail of a direct social capital benefit through active textual communication (from peer group friends), young people also receive direct social capital benefits from linking online with those outside the peer group. Unlike bonding friends, who serve as confidants, these linking friends do not maintain an actual friendship. They are 'informational friends', and reflect an instrumental and exploitive dimension to contemporary friendship. While these easily created links do provide direct social capital benefits to the individual, these are only short-term.

The transient nature of such links, and the way they are frequently and effortlessly dissolved is explained by Sean:

Sean: I actually plan to get rid of her (delete his female politician friend) cus I don't need her now. I only added her for my cousin. He was having no joy getting a new wheelchair but only for her she got the ball rolling. I get updates from her but I don't really even read them now. I am actually going to delete her when I get round to it. (PCI)

Sean's friendship with this politician has served its purpose and he now ignores the *Facebook* updates and information he receives from her. Unlike the early days, when he was trying to help his younger cousin obtain a new outdoor powered wheelchair, the friendship is irrelevant and he has no qualms about deleting her altogether.

In contrast to Sean, who has no offline connection with this politician, other young people reveal that an offline connection with linking friends, such as teachers, sometimes brings asymmetrical power relations into play. For example, the inclusion of a teacher as a linking friend, presents a unique dilemma.

Anne: Would you ever add teachers?

Michaela: Yes we have added certain teachers that we are not going to name, not a good idea.

Carroll: It's so easy to go on *Facebook* and rant about a teacher and say things like I so hate her or whatever but then even if you haven't them added but you have other teachers added they will tell them. It has happened and people end up getting shouted at and stuff… (MFG)

Teachers, unlike other linking friends, have a daily offline connection with young people and are often referred to negatively in the daily chat sessions that recap the school day. Consequently, schools are beginning to formalise policies on teacher-pupil online friendships as Sheila, a parent and school secretary, highlights:

Sheila: Before the end of term the principal asked all staff and teachers to delete anyone under eighteen off their friend list as a way of obviously protecting children and us as staff also. (POI)

While current pupils and teachers tend not to be *Facebook* friends, a small minority of teachers have online contact with some past pupils. After their daily offline encounters have ceased (due to pupils moving to another school to complete A Levels or progress to further/higher education or employment), these past pupils enrich their social capital by linking online with teachers. For the teachers the decision to accept past pupils' requests is based on the recognition that the young person is genuinely motivated by positive reasons stay in contact, such as wanting to further their education or career.

Rosie provides an insight into how such a friendship comes about. She requests a former male teacher as an online friend in order to obtain help with their future studies. His friendship is a resource she plans to use in the transition from school to university. This is explained by Rosie, who says:

> **Rosie**: Well I actually requested my biology teacher before school broke up.
>
> **Anne**: Why?
>
> **Rosie**: I want to do Bio chemistry at Queens [a local university], if I get in, he [her biology teacher] has told us to stay in touch and he is the sort of person that would help you. It's like he has such a broad knowledge about everything so I suppose it's for security. Two of my friends have applied for the same course and they have added him too. He's big into *Facebook* but he doesn't request people. But if you request him he will add you ok. We are all really good friends with him. That's what happens when you do A-levels your teachers talk to you differently than if you were in year 8 or 9 and they become more like a friend. (COI)

From this excerpt, it is clear that the girls perceive their former teacher as a 'just in case friend,' used, as Rosie puts it as 'security', to branch out from the smaller teacher-led surroundings of school into the larger and more independent university environment. Close friends often share mutual goals (Salmela-Aro, 2007) and for these girls it is to settle into their university course and so they collectively decide to add this teacher as a friend. As this study is a snap shot of young people's lives as opposed to a life-span or developmental analysis the exact way this connection will endure is unclear. Nevertheless, it is possible to predict, based on Sean's example of the short shelf life of some online links, that when it has served its purpose and their goal is achieved, the online friendship will probably end accordingly.

In contrast to the short term benefit of linking with certain people from outside the peer group, 'business type' friends produce a more enduring benefit in terms of individual social capital. Urshla has strategically added linking friends whom she refers to as 'business type' friends, and they account for 19 of her total 480 friends. The local dress hire shop is one example of Urshla's linking friends.

> **Anne**: Why did you add the lady from the hire shop?

> **Urshla**: Well round the time of the formal last year I added her because I wanted to see her updates. It was things like special offers or things like what evenings she would have free appointments. Now I'm not interested in that as much but I still love to see what new dresses she has in.

> **Anne**: Do you consider yourself to be a friend of the business or the lady?

> **Urshla**: Neither they are not your friend but you are connected with them. People link to loads of 'businesses type' friends because they all have a *Facebook* account now, football clubs, garden centres, toy stores, night clubs.

> **Anne**: How do you feel about businesses knowing what you have on *Facebook*?

> **Urshla**: It is not a worry because they have so many people added and they are not going to really focus on what one person is getting up to. You

don't mean anything to them apart from the fact that they want to get their message out to you in order to get your custom. (COI)

This extract underscores two important points. Firstly, young people are not concerned that these 'business type' links will want to focus on them as individuals. In contrast, young people do not perceive such friendships as opening windows into their social lives, but simply as reflecting a business-customer relationship. Secondly, in contrast to the 'people type' friends such as politicians or teachers, young people do not contact 'business type' friends to request specific information; instead the flow of information is one directional, from the business to the young person and contains notification of promotional offers and events. For example, Chloe explains:

> **Chloe**: I have loads of friends added that aren't people, like I have nightclubs added... and that way I know who is going to be playing in them and what type of drink promotions they will have on. (COI)

Contemporary friendship no longer encompasses personal relations but is a mixture of various connections, some of which are purely informational.

While Urshla feels no strong connection with the dress hire shop or the lady that owns it, young people do tend to view 'business type' linking friends as actual friends when they are more closely connected to them offline. For example, Olive spends a lot of time at her local sports club and works on a voluntary basis to fundraise for it through sponsored walks and helping out at events. She explains:

> **Olive**: I have the camogie[1] club added as a friend and then I get to see all the things happening and it helps me plan out what is coming up. When they update it comes up as a newsfeed. If you missed training all you have to do is log on and usually that night Gillian [her sports coach] will have it updated.

---

1. Camogie is a female sport played in Ireland that is similar to hockey.

Anne: Do you consider the club as a friend?

Olive: Yeah if you have a hundred friends and you add it then it becomes that you have 101 friends so yeah they are a friend. I suppose they are more of a proper friend than the hairdresser, she's just a business I added. (COI)

Like many others in the study, she associates the club as a 'proper' online friend whereas she sees her other linking friends such as a local hairdresser not as a social friend but 'just a business I added'. Therefore, linking friends range in quality from those with a very short life-span, to those which are more long term, such as organisations like the camogie club where there are actual offline friendships.

5.   Social networking: the indirect benefit of inactive online friends

Linking friends and bonding friends apart, the net social capital value of the large online network is an indirect one. However, these fringe or indirect benefits are perceived as valuable to young people. Indeed they are the part and parcel of the desire to go online. For example, while it is non-obligatory for young people to set up an online account, compared to going to school or doing homework, it is however almost compulsory to have an online presence in terms of peer pressure. This is summed up when Emma says that:

Emma: You're under so much pressure at school to have the right things, the right phone, the right shoes and all. Having a profile and being online is one of them. Because everyone strives to have these things they become almost the norm and you stand out as unpopular or weird if you don't have them. (PCI)

Thus social networking is much more than a means of communicating, it is a desirable product in youth consumer culture which is used to ensure acceptance and popularity among the peer group.

While peer acceptance and being popular has always been important to young people (Coleman, 1988), it has taken on a new public dimension in the social networking era. This is because online friend lists display the precise number of friends each individual has and also because this calculation reaches a wider audience than would be possible offline. Popularity is no longer only visible to those physically present, such as the school yard or the youth club, but has a more permanent existence which transcends physical space and time.

For young people, the world of social networking offers the promise that their popularity can be showcased through the size of their friend list. This list expands rapidly during the initial weeks and months of having an account, with frequent requests to become friends and the accumulation of new friends gaining pace. Subsequently, the rate of accumulation of new friends reduces. This pattern is highlighted in the discussion below:

> **Janet**: Yeah when you're up and running you only add about one maybe two proper requests every couple of months and like you can't count the usual crap you get from other countries like. If I was only going on it now instead of about two years ago like then it'd be different cus all my friends they'd all want me to be adding them like all at the one time you know but it's different now cus they're all on it.

> **Anne**: Is this the same for everybody?

> **William**: Yeah pretty much everyone has a massive amount of requests but then that falls after the... what would you call it? The honeymoon period (laughter)... (MFG)

The post 'honeymoon period' is one in which requests dwindle and numbers of online friends level off. Nevertheless, young people by this point commonly have several hundred online friends and are satisfied that their friend list has a high impact in terms of demonstrating popularity.

6.   The bulk of online friends are an unused social capital resource

Despite these fringe benefits, such as demonstrating popularity, the bulk of young peoples' online friends represent an unused social capital resource. In many ways this is contrary to what might be expected considering that, in comparison to close friends, weak ties have their own particular value in that they generate additional information (Granovetter, 1973). It would therefore appear that social networking is a valuable information resource and a favourable location for young people to develop and nurture their own stock of bridging social capital. Social capital can be, as shown earlier, either bridging or bonding. As young people share ongoing information among extensive numbers of weak ties it appears that social networking has the potential to increase bridging social capital to almost endless possibilities.

Yet in reality these many inactive online connections only provide tenuous links, as social networking essentially concerns split-level communication. Private chat is home to communication between close friends. The remaining body of weaker ties generally inhabit the more public space where comments are posted, statuses updated and photos uploaded. These weaker ties share information which is ongoing and easily accessible but often irrelevant and meaningless. For example, during Malachy's interview, (when asked to scroll down his friend list and pick a friend who he feels he has added but knows very little about) he reads aloud a status update which announces:

> **Malachy**: I definitely caught something... mouth tastes like crap, headache, burning stomach, double vision... Must be the new Wine Flu.

Malachy is unsure if she is joking, making a joke at someone else's expense, or if she actually is feeling unwell and he comments quite dismissively:

Malachy: It probably means something to some of her friends. (COI)

This abstract shows that communication with weak online friends, unlike close friends, is detached from physical place, with no tone and body language[1] to rely on. The absence of a physical dimension to their friendship often results in misinterpretation as opposed to enriched social capital. This is reiterated many times throughout the study. For example, Richard explains:

> **Richard**: Like your status its written so people who maybe don't really know the way you go on might think you are being serious when you are not. Or think you are joking when you are serious. Things like lol [laugh out loud] after a comment doesn't really do it cus people now just put lol at the end of every message. If you say something in the café or the chippy people get your meaning cus they see you and can hear the way you are saying it. Yeah I think there is a big potential for people who don't really know you to get the wrong end of the stick on *Facebook* like. (MFG)

Therefore, although young people are really well connected virtually, this does not compensate for place-based connections which yield a richer social capital outcome and a better understanding of others.

7. Conclusion

The bridging/bonding distinction of social capital still has relevance in understanding how individuals nurture their own stock of social capital in the social networking era. However, a fuller understanding can be obtained by examining the distinct social capital benefits of social networking. These benefits are best understood as a continuum that ranges from direct (maximum benefit), to indirect (mid range benefit) and unused benefits (low benefit). This chapter reveals that the maximum benefits are directly sourced by individuals (bonding

---

1. This is not something that is exclusively problematic to social networking but something that has been found to also limit email communication and internet communication in general (Ryen, 2004; Silverman, 2007).

and linking social capital). These direct benefits are consciously recognised by the individuals as improving their lives. Mid way on the continuum is bridging social capital, which is found in the indirect or fringe benefits of belonging to the large online network. These benefits are often taken for granted and less obvious to the individual. Finally, the lowest benefits are those which are unused and often remain an untapped social capital resource.

From exploring the social capital benefits of social networking it becomes clear that the principal transformation that social networking has brought to contemporary friendship is the individual's capacity to directly nurture their own stock of social capital. For example, close friendship yields a direct social capital benefit to the individual. While close friends may have always been a direct source of social capital for the young person, social networking provides 'textual therapy', a resource that was unavailable to bonding friends in the pre internet era. This has a positive impact on health and well-being and it would appear that it has replaced 'talking therapy' as a social capital resource previously provided by the telephone.

On the surface this shift from 'talking' to 'textual' therapy appears to be a symptom of a depersonalised modern society, however bonding friendship and the textual therapy it offers is heavily reliant on regular face-to-face encounters. Therefore, in order to avail of the textual benefit of social networking, contemporary youth must first invest in and sustain personal relations. Hence social networking, at least in terms of bonding friends, does not contribute to a depersonalised society; instead it emphasises that despite the many ways young people can connect with each other, social relations in a physical place remain of critical importance for the individual to directly nurture their social capital.

Links with others outside the peer group also directly enhance the individual's social capital, something that was less possible for the youth of previous generations. Unlike the small subset of bonding friends, these links have endless possibilities and can potentially develop social capital across a wider scale, as such online friendships do not require in-person contact, and function better when dislocated from physical hubs of interaction, such as school. Unlike bonding friendship, these links open up and strengthen connections with young people and professionals, businesses and organisations. Consequently youth friendship is stretched from horizontal links between young people themselves to include vertical links with a range of others outside the peer group.

However, this benefit is short lived as it is based on the desire to source information rather than to nurture an actual friendship. These fragile and easily terminated links with those outside the peer group are often perceived by young people as nothing more than a *Google* search for information. While acquaintances in the past may have been treated the same way, previous generations did not have access to the wide range of linking friends that social networking grants access to. As such, contemporary online friendship appears to be more about self-interest, exploitation and ambition than that of previous generations.

However, when a youth-organisation link is strong in an offline sense, the online link represents less of an individualistic pursuit. Links between organisations and young people provide mutual social capital benefits to the organisation as well as the individual. Indeed organisations have never been in a better position to consolidate their presence in the lives of young people, at least those who are already involved with them. The fact that online links can strengthen existing social capital is welcome news given the reported decline in organisational vibrancy (Putnam, 2000).

The information shared between online linking and bonding friends sits in sharp contrast to that generated by the remaining online friends who make up the young person's friend list. This large body of inactive friends often share information which is not useful or specific. As such, young peoples' relationship with the large network is one of 'information gazing' and not 'information seeking'. Subsequently, information from inactive friends does nothing to enhance the quality of these weak ties and so the social capital outcome is – while not entirely non-productive in that young people are kept informed, enjoy finding out about others and can showcase their popularity – often at best an indirect and at worst an unused benefit.

References

Brown, G. W., & Harris, T (Eds.). (1978). *Social Origins of Depression: A Study of Psychiatric Disorder in Women*. Abingdon, Oxfordshire: Travistock Publications Limited.

Bucci, W. (1995). The power of the narrative: a multiple code account. In J. W. Pennebaker (Ed.), *Emotion, Disclosure, and Health* (pp. 93-124). American Psychological Association, Washington, DC.

Coleman, J. S. (1988). Social Capital in the Creation of Human Capital. *American Journal of Sociology, 94*(Supplement), S95-S120. Retrieved from http://www.jstor.org/stable/2780243

Donath, J., & boyd, d. m. (2004). Public Displays of Connection. *BT Technology Journal, 22*(4), 71-82. doi: 10.1023/B:BTTJ.0000047585.06264.cc

Ellison, N. B, Steinfield, C., & Lampe, C. (2007). The benefits of Facebook "Friends:" Social capital and college students' use of online social network sites. *Journal of Computer-Mediated Communication, 12*(4), 1143-1168. doi: 10.1111/j.1083-6101.2007.00367.x

Field, J. (2008). *Social Capital* (2nd ed.). Oxon: Routledge.

Fukkink, R. (2011). Peer counselling in an online chat service: a content analysis of social support. *Cyberpsychology, Behavior, and Social Networking, 14*(4), 247-251. doi: 10.1089/cyber.2010.0163

Giddens, A. (1991). *Modernity and Self-Identity: Self and Society in the Late Modern Age*. Cambridge: Polity Press.

Gould, M. S, Munfakh, J. L. H., Lubell, K, Kleinman, M, & Parker, S. (2002). Seeking help from the internet during adolescence. *Journal of the Academy of Child & Adolescent Psychiatry, 41*(10), 1182-1189. doi: 10.1097/00004583-200210000-00007

Granovetter, M. S. (1973). The strength of weak ties. *American Journal of Sociology, 78*(6), 1360-1380. Retrieved from http://www.jstor.org/stable/2776392

Graybeal, A., Sexton, J. D., & Pennebaker, J. W. (2002). The Role of Story-Making in Disclosure Writing: The Psychometrics of Narrative. *Psychology & Health, 17*(5), 571-581. doi: 10.1080/08870440290025786

Hesse-Biber, S. N., & Leavy, P. (2006). *The Practice of Qualitative Research*. London: Sage Publications.

Holland, J. (2007). Inventing adulthoods: Making the most of what you have. In H. Helve & J. Bynner (Eds.), *Youth and Social Capital* (pp. 11-28). London: The Tufnell Press.

Leung, L. (2007). Stressful life events , motives for internet use, and social support among digital kids. *Cyberpsychology, Behavior, and Social Networking, 10*(2), 204-214. doi: 10.1089/cpb.2006.9967

Portes, A. (1998). Social capital: Its origins and applications in modern sociology. *Annual Review of Sociology, 24*, 1-24. Retrieved from http://www.annualreviews.org/doi/pdf/10.1146/annurev.soc.24.1.1

Putnam , R. D. (2000). *Bowling Alone: The Collapse and Revival of American Community.* New York: Simon & Schuster.

Raffo, C., & Reeves, M. (2000). Youth transitions and social exclusion: developments in social capital theory. *Journal of Youth Studies, 3*(2), 147-166. doi: 10.1080/713684372

Ryen, A. (2004). Ethical Issues. In C. Seale, G. Gobo, J. Gubrium & D. Silverman (Eds.), *Qualitative Research Practice* (pp. 217-29). London: Sage Publications.

Salmela-Aro, K. (2007). Adolescent's and young adults goal related ties. In H. Helve & J. Bynner (Eds.), *Youth and Social Capital* (pp. 127-135). London: The Tufnell Press.

Seaman, P., & Sweeting, H. (2004). Assisting young people's access to social capital in contemporary families: a qualitative study. *Journal of Youth Studies, 7*(2), 173-190. doi: 10.1080/1367626042000238703

Sherbourne, C. D, Hays, R. D, & Wells, K. B. (1995). Personal and psychosocial risk factors for physical and mental health outcomes and course of depression among depressed patients. *Journal of Consulting and Clinical Psychology, 63*(3), 345-355. doi: 10.1037/0022-006X.63.3.345

Silverman, D. (2007). *Interpreting Qualitative Data.* London: Sage Publications.

11 Romanian Diaspora in the Making? An Online Ethnography of Romaniancommunity.net

Gloria Macri[1]

Abstract

This chapter presents a case study of an online ethnography which examines the Romanian Community of Ireland forum. Apart from highlighting the main challenges and advantages of engaging with an ethnographic methodology online, this chapter also showcases the key findings emerging in relation to the meanings which members of this community associate with the internet. The chapter also reflects critically on the type of community which takes shape on this online forum and, more importantly, its relation to a presumed 'offline' Romanian diaspora. Is the 'virtual' community an exact replica of the entire Romanian community in Ireland? Does it represent the online dimension of an alleged Romanian diaspora in Ireland, or does it represent a community in its own right, overlapping only partly with any offline counterpart? Findings reveal that the internet, and in particular this discussion forum, tends to occupy an important role in the life of online Romanians by acting as more than a tool for seeking information and advice, but also as the 'glue' that enhances the bonding of the diaspora members and as an essential space for debate, a 'round table' where Romanians discuss their lives in Ireland and the 'fate' of the motherland.

Keywords: diaspora, media, identity, the internet, online ethnography.

1. School of Communications, Dublin City University, Dublin, Ireland; gloria.macri2@mail.dcu.ie

How to cite this chapter: Macri, G. (2013). Romanian Diaspora in the Making? An Online Ethnography of Romaniancommunity. net. In C. Fowley, C. English, & S. Thouësny (Eds.), *Internet Research, Theory, and Practice: Perspectives from Ireland* (pp. 199-223). Dublin: © Research-publishing.net.

1. Introduction

This chapter critically explores the key role of the internet as a medium through which Romanians in Ireland communicate and interact with each other. At the same time, it discusses in detail the methodological implications of choosing an online fieldwork location. Findings presented in this chapter are part of my wider doctoral research which highlights the online construction of diasporic discourses of identity among Romanians in Ireland. The chapter thus aims to cast some light on the main challenges and advantages of doing ethnographies online, but also to reflect on the types of communities that take shape online: are such communities different from their offline counterparts? This aspect is particularly important from the diasporic perspective. By choosing to showcase the engagement of Romanians in Ireland with the virtual space, important findings emerge as to whether this 'virtual' group is representative of *all* Romanians in Ireland or at the least of those who have developed awareness around their diasporic belonging.

In order to unravel these aspects, the present chapter is structured as follows: the first section provides a background to the case study in order to bring to the fore some of the key aspects that characterise Romanians in Ireland from a statistical point of view (based on available Census data) but also in relation to their associational life and their diasporic media production. The latter aspects will help contextualise the relevance of the internet, and of the forum in particular, for this community. Following this succinct description of Romanians in Ireland, the chapter then discusses some of the main points emerging from literature on the role of the internet for migrant and diasporic communities. This section also includes a brief discussion in relation to the sometimes interchangeable (hence problematic) use of the two above-mentioned concepts in existing scholarship. The next section presents a critical assessment of the methodology used. This part of the chapter reflects on the theoretical grounding of the research method employed, namely virtual ethnography, but also on the key differences between 'traditional' and online ethnographies. The ethical implications of a study of virtual communities are also discussed in detail. Finally, the last section of the chapter discusses the main findings of the research as it strives to uncover who are Romanians online and how they understand their online involvement.

2.   Background to the case study

Ireland has never been one of the main migration destinations for Romanians, as was the case of Italy and Spain. At the surface level this may be explained by Ireland's remote location as well as the possible language difficulties, in comparison with the easiness Romanians have in comprehending Italian or Spanish due to the common Latin origin of the two languages. Another and perhaps more important aspect is the fact that by the time the Celtic Tiger was well underway, Italy and Spain were already becoming popular destinations for Romanians. Moreover, the strong networked character of Romanian migration can explain why Romanians have oriented themselves predominantly to these two countries.

Very little information is available statistically about the Romanian population living in Ireland. To a great extent all existing information is sourced from the last two Censuses[1] recorded in 2006 and 2011. The 2006 Census mentioned a figure of 8,492 Romanian-born residents[2]. This figure has been subject to change in recent years given the fact that in January 2007 Romania joined the European Union. The latest Census data indicates a figure of 17,995 Romanians in Ireland, the sharpest increase of all non-Irish residents, nearly 112 per cent increase.

The Census also indicates that Romanians tend to be heavily concentrated in Dublin, with around 35 per cent (2006) and respectively 32 per cent (2011) living in the city. The rest, according to the same data set, are spread in small communities throughout the country.

From the gender ratio perspective, Census data show that men constitute only

---

1. Census, Central Statistics Office Ireland. Retrieved from http://www.cso.ie/en/census/

2. Persons that are usually resident in the state and that were present in their usual residence on Census night.

slightly more than half of the number of Romanian migrants (54 per cent in 2006 and 51 per cent in 2011). Furthermore, the Census states that most of the Romanian migrants can be found in the 25 to 44 age bracket (about 62 per cent of the total) and this seems to fit the pattern of most other Eastern European migrants. This confirms that the Romanian community in Ireland is largely constituted by a labour active population. According to the 2006 Census, 70 per cent of males and 42 per cent of females were employed. This aspect also highlights the fact that the Romanian community in Ireland is a relatively new community.

In relation to associational life, face-to-face conversations with key informants in the Romanian community in Ireland (as well as several posts archived on the forum) have revealed that the first voluntary community organisations were formed around the Orthodox core of the community in the early years (1978-1981). It was only later (1998-2004) that more Romanian organisations and associations emerged, mostly on the basis of existing social ties and connections between their members. These organisations were mainly concerned with providing assistance with regard to some of the problems that Romanians in Ireland were facing at the time: asylum seeking, deportations, IBC and work permit applications just to name a few. Following Romania's entry into the European Union the activities of these organisations shifted towards the organisation of language courses, and celebration of particular events, e.g., Romania's National Day, International Children's Day, Women's day, etc.

In light of existing literature (Cavanagh, 2007; Georgiou, 2006) which invariably recognises the vital role of the public sphere in the process of shaping and 'baptising' (diasporic) identity discourses, it was interesting to note that the above-mentioned Romanian organisations in Ireland did not seem to contribute much in this respect. Furthermore, Romanian migrants, unlike some of the other migrant communities living in Ireland, did not have a distinct 'physical' place (such as a community centre or a favourite pub, etc.) where they gathered up and chatted freely about, among many other aspects, their identities. It was from this perspective that the internet community began to reveal its research potential.

Moreover, traditional forms of Romanian diasporic media production (e.g., newspapers, radio shows/stations, etc.) were rather modest and focused mainly on reproducing news from the homeland and the host society's mainstream media, thus having a minimal impact on the process of negotiation of diasporic identities. Furthermore, most of these media productions initiatives could not overcome some of the main challenges that diasporic media generally have to face, namely shortages of human and financial resources. Last but not least, forum conversations point towards numerous concerns of community members in relation to the poor quality of the material published, issues of ownership (private vs. community owned) and representation, as questions emerge about whether the so-called 'diasporic newspaper' actually represent the entire community or rather the voice of its individual editors.

The forum emerged in 2004 when the website http://www.romaniancommunity. net[1] was taken over by the members of the umbrella community Romanian Community of Ireland. Before 2004, the above-mentioned website served only as a portal of news pertaining to the community, the homeland or the host society. The forum represents the most dynamic part of the website and even during the times when the website was down due to several technical problems, the forum was always 'kept alive' through a direct link to the database of messages. It thus seems as if the forum acts as the 'heart of the community'.

The look of the forum is rather plain and functional, containing very few visual elements besides the logo and the stylised name of the community. Both logo and the website have been revamped several times throughout the years. The forum is structured around fifteen sections[2], each containing two to eight sub-sections. Furthermore, each subsection is split into threads of discussion which contain the posts made by users and the moderators on each particular topic. A brief look at the forum statistics highlights the fact that the most prolific sub-section is the

---

1. In spite of the English name of the internet domain, the 'official' language of the forum is Romanian. However in some occasions a mix of the two languages is used, both in the titles of some of the sections as well as in the messages posted.

2. The sections are entitled: 1. Upgrade Issues; 2. Welcome; 3. General; 4. The Romanian Community of Ireland; 5. Romanian Embassy; 6. Offtopic; 7. Emigration (Immigration); 8. Section dedicated to the gender 'conflicts'; 9. Culture and innovation; 10. Family; 11. Advertising; 12. Medical Forum; 13. Education; 14. Entertainment; 15. For specialists.

'General Matters' category, with 512 discussion threads and 8,462 posts[1]. While the structure of the forum seems quite complex and clear cut, it needs to be noted that discussion threads are not as neatly categorised on the forum. Thus, when a new topic of discussion emerges, the thread seems to get created mainly in the 'General Matters' category, which could explain its significant size. Hence, this sub-section includes numerous messages on a great variety of topics.

In relation to the patterns of posting, it can be easily observed that while some discussion threads get no (or at best a few) responses, others stimulate a good number of posts. On the other hand, while some of the discussions may become 'abandoned' (as no users will make any posts in the thread for months and even years), these threads may be reopened at a later time, triggered by certain new events. It is also important to note that while some topics are 'kept alive' by the users through continuous posting, others are maintained on top by forum administrators and moderators by making them 'sticky' (i.e., sticking them on top of the other threads which are chronologically sorted).

Forum statistics indicate that at the time when data collection was completed[2] there were 883 members registered on the forum, but as the information can be accessed even without registration, the 'readership' of the forum may have been even higher. Out of the total number of registered users, about 100 members are also categorised as active. The degree of interaction between users as well as the number of posts is significant, taking into account, of course, the rather small size of the Romanian community in Ireland.

Hence, having started in 2004 as a coordinated effort of a very small group of volunteers to help facilitate access to information for those Romanian migrants who were struggling to regulate their stay in Ireland (asylum seekers, IBC applicants, work permit renewals, etc.), by 2010 (when data collection for this study finished) the forum had already become a lively arena, Romanians of various educational and occupational backgrounds meet there everyday and

---

1. As of December 6th 2011.

2. May 31st 2010.

approach a great variety of topics, from sharing information about life in Ireland to commenting on news stories from various sources, from complaining about daily problems to discussing complex issues such as identity and belonging. Since October 2011, the forum has been integrated with a new online platform, i.e., the *Facebook* page of the Romanian Community of Ireland. This strategy allows forum threads to be simultaneously posted on *Facebook* and the users' *Facebook* posts to be fed back into the forum as comments.

3.   Old wine, in new bottles?
The roles of the internet in diasporic life

Before examining the role played by the internet in the lives of migrants and diasporeans, a few considerations need to be made in relation to these two concepts which often seem to overlap in existing literature (see Hiller & Franz, 2004; Shi, 2005). Particularly in empirical studies, groups of immigrants of an alleged common ancestry have been described interchangeably as 'migrants', 'diasporas' (and sometimes 'ethnics') without building a strong rationale for doing so and also without questioning whether these labels attached to a particular group correspond to the groups' own feelings about their belonging. Clarifying to a certain extent the similarities and differences between these concepts allows us to understand the meanings that online Romanians associate to their forum participation and to their belonging to a 'virtual' community.

The concept of 'diaspora' is, according to Sreberny (2000) a key term in the contemporary debates about immigration and identity. Safran (1991) gives probably the most well-known account of what classic diaspora is. The author points out that these diasporas: involve dispersal from an original place; have a collective memory and a vision of their homeland; feel that perfect acceptance and integration into the host society is not attainable; contemplate the return to the homeland; are committed to maintain and restore the original homeland, and feel a strong ethnic group consciousness based on a sense of distinctiveness, a common history, and a belief in a common fate (pp. 83-84).

Many authors feel that the classic meaning of diaspora, as defined by Safran (1991), tends to be rather restrictive, referring only to very few groups, in particular Jewish or ancient Greek. The modern understanding of diasporas includes a great variety of groups whose circumstances are quite different (Reis, 2004) and, according to Clifford (1994), these groups tend to experience 'inbetweenness', a lived tension generated by experiencing "separation and entanglement, of living here and remembering/desiring another place" (p. 311). Hence, the meaning of diasporas has changed considerably since the first diasporas were documented and, as Wieviorka (2007) concludes, there is an ongoing process of creating new forms of diasporas which co-exist with old ones. We should then re-conceptualise 'diaspora' in terms of its multiple connections and links (Tsagarousianou, 2004) with home and the host society as well as multiple 'Others'.

In spite of its limitations, Safran's (1991) definition however clearly denotes the line of difference between a diasporic and a migrant community. Hence, while the term 'migrant' generally refers to a very broad category and is applied to persons who leave their usual place of residence in order to settle in a different place, diasporas are not to be reduced to immigrant communities which tend to be rather temporary and lack a particular group consciousness. Furthermore, while migrants may form a diaspora, the latter is not necessarily made up of people who have geographically re-settled, nor is it equivalent to a group of people of the same nationality. These aspects become even more important when referring to the online involvement of these communities. For example, many studies (Hiller & Franz, 2004; Miller & Slater, 2000) signal the emphasis which migrants place on the internet as a tool for searching for information and enhancing the social networks needed in their process of relocation, both before and after their departure from the homeland.

However, from a diasporic perspective, the internet represents much more than a source of information and social contacts. A few studies in the field of media and (diasporic) identities have given prominence to the internet as the favourite medium mobilised by these communities in order to construct and articulate their identity discourses. The main reason appears to be linked to the fact that new media technologies enable almost instantaneous sharing, identity formation, communication and publicisation (Srinivasan, 2006, p. 504). Thus, the internet undeniably enables its users to become active cultural producers and explore significant questions about their identities, often in ways which may not otherwise be possible in 'offline' life (Cheung, 2004, p. 55).

Apart from Cheung (2004), many other scholars also argue that the internet has contributed greatly to the re-invention of diasporic connections and therefore leads to new forms of identification (Nedelcu, 2000; Parker & Song, 2006). Other scholars caution against the assumption that a change of medium necessarily needs to be equated with a change in what is actually transmitted or in the types of communities that it produces (Mandaville, 2001). Thus, while diasporic groups may use the internet in the process of imagining themselves as a community and acquiring a sense of belonging to this community, this medium may facilitate and enhance but not necessarily radically transform the types of interactions which exist among members of a community offline.

Gauntlett (2004) sees the internet as key for the study of identity and argues that this is mainly because the web enhances the public sphere, it gives anonymity and also allows room for identity play in cyberspace. Foster (1996) supports this view and argues that the internet "allows each individual user an equal voice, or at the least an equal opportunity to speak" (p. 23). There are also scholars who are critical about internet's capacity to act as a public sphere. Sparks (1998, cited in Cavanagh, 2007) for example mentions that we should ask ourselves the question of whether the internet guarantees access to all and whether the citizens have the right to exchange opinions in an unrestricted manner as Habermas (1974) asserted. DiMaggio, Hargittai, Neuman, and Robinson (2001) also question the power of the internet, and in particular the discussion boards, to allow for a rational consensus to occur over a particular matter of interest. However, they feel that the internet definitely constitutes a step in the direction of becoming a renewed public sphere.

In a similar vein, Papacharissi (2002) argues that the internet, as a public space, has indeed the power to facilitate, but not necessarily ensure, the restoration of the public sphere. She goes on to further argue that the internet facilitates very diverse people to come together and to expand on each other's horizons with culturally diverse viewpoints (p. 23). Similarly, Cavanagh (2007) asserts that the internet is important because it constitutes a space of cohesion and sociality (p. 97). In relation to the particular case of diasporas, Georgiou (2006) argues that electronic media are more compatible with the transnational nature of a diaspora. These media "saturate the diasporic space" (Georgiou, 2006, p. 12) therefore playing an increasing role in the construction of meanings and negotiating identities. Triandafyllidou and Wodak (2003) also insist on the fact that new media technologies tend to create "a sense of immediacy and closeness among people who are physically very far and who may even not know each other" (p. 207). Its volatility and degree of deterritorialisation, in Hepp's (2004) view, favour the articulation of hybrid and transnational cultures and identities.

4. Engaging with an online community – methodological challenges and solutions

A brief look at scholarship aimed at capturing diasporic identity narratives indicates that the great majority of these studies have favoured the interview technique in order to gather data about diasporeans' feelings of belonging (Ogan, 2001; Popov, 2010; Ryan, 2007). Interviews can be ideal research methods for topics as intricate as the study of identity as they allow the researcher to reach a deeper understanding of the meanings that people assign to their everyday experiences which contribute to the shaping of their identity. However the main weakness of the interview from this point of view is that it does not allow for identities to be studied in interaction. The missing link between the individual narrative and the collective discourse rarely emerges from a methodology based entirely on this research technique.

Engaging in an ethnographic study of online diasporic communities presents certain advantages when compared with the already established tradition of face-to-face interview-based identity research. By focusing on an interactive form of new media (as is the case of the discussion forum) one is able to experience a dynamic understanding of how collective identities take shape in interaction.

There is still a significant debate in relation to the online-offline approaches to identity, both at theoretical as well as methodological level. On the one side it is argued that there is no ground for the formation or articulation of a coherent identity discourse online (Lockard, 1996; Mitra, 1997; Turkle, 1995). It is argued that identities online tend to suffer from some kind of volatility, thus rendering them as transient phenomena. Similarly, the 'online' focus is also deemed to bear negative (even perilous) consequences for the methodological framework of the research. Authenticity online, i.e., the certitude that you are who you say you are, has come into question at times (Turkle, 1995). However, as more and more researchers acknowledge, it appears that virtual interactions are not necessarily 'unreal' and not so different from the face-to-face interactions (Hine, 2008). Kozinets (2010) furthermore suggests that it is impossible to ignore new media and the internet precisely because our social worlds are increasingly going digital.

While the virtual world is important in today's societies, this does not imply that online social research will simply replace face-to-face research. However, as Kozinets (2010) asserts, when particular phenomena appear solely online or when the lives of certain communities only acquire a virtual dimension, it is absolutely acceptable for research methodologies to focus exclusively on the online aspects and manifestations. Thus, the choice between online and offline does not refer simply to methodological practicalities (e.g., financial costs, accessibility, and the amount of effort involved). The decision is informed by the specificities and manifestations of the phenomena to be studied. There are only a few studies which credit the internet with a significant role in the shaping of identitarian discourses and in most cases the accent has fallen on the static content of personal pages and diasporic websites (Parker & Song, 2006; Thompson, 2002) rather the dynamic interactions which take place on the online discussion fora (Chan, 2005; Elias, Lemish, & Khvorostianov, 2007). Even fewer of these studies adopt an ethnographic approach to these online community formations (e.g., Ignacio, 2005; Miller & Slater, 2000).

It is important to note that forum data cannot simply be conceived of as plain text. Besides its rich archived content, the forum also represents a community with its own culture and norms, a community of members that are interacting on a daily basis, exchanging messages and negotiating meanings. Hence, an immersion into the collective identity discourses constructed on a diasporic forum requires a methodological frame that is sensitive to such intricate aspects which often go beyond the textual level. For this particular purpose, this study engages with a qualitative methodology, a virtual ethnography (Hine, 2001) of the online discussion forum of Romanians in Ireland in an effort to achieve a deeper understanding of the formation of this community, and to answer the question of whether this aggregation of Romanians around the virtual space constitutes (or has the premises to constitute) a diasporic community.

Moreover, in comparison to the small number of similar studies, the methodology employed by this research takes advantage of the tremendous amount of information contained in the archives of the forum by including all this material in the analysis[1] rather than selecting only some threads of discussion deemed relevant to the topic of diasporic identity. The result is a study that reveals an image of the online community as a whole, pointing towards more than just a few salient identity-related aspects emerging from several discussion threads, but rather to a deeper understanding of the community with all its relevant moments. This approach allows the researcher to take more than a snapshot of how members of a community define their cultural identities (as tends to be the case of many studies focusing exclusively on interview-centred methodologies), but rather to capture 'the motion' as well, namely the process of negotiation and collective construction of identities. It is a matter of following in the path of the 'offline' ethnographer and becoming deeply immersed in the studied community, even if in this case that is to be achieved by innovatively adapting the traditional ethnographic methods.

---

1. Data presented in this chapter runs over a period of more than six years (2004-2010), totalling a number of 2,227 discussion threads and 25,151 posts. This is particularly useful for the analysis as it includes many key moments in the life of the Romanian community in Ireland (RCI), such as Romanians becoming EU citizens (January 1st 2007) etc. and the implications that these contexts have had on the pattern of settlement, integration and identity strategies.

From its origins in nineteenth-century Western anthropology, when the term was associated with the study of 'the distant', a descriptive account of a community or culture (Atkinson & Hammersley, 2007; Oberhuber & Krzyzanowski, 2008), ethnographic research has grown to be increasingly applied to contemporary communities or societies and the definition of this method is generally flexible. There is often little consideration for the differences between online and offline ethnographic research. To a great extent, these discussions overlap with the conundrum of studying 'virtual' vs. 'real' communities, online vs. offline identities. Hine (2001) notes that while a 'traditional' ethnographer is generally with a particular community in the long term, in the case of online ethnographies this aspect is rather difficult to uncover. In other words, how could long-term involvement be 'quantified' in an online research? Hine (2001) seems to argue however that even in the case of 'traditional' ethnographies, the researcher could not be involved in absolutely all aspects of the community's life. Thus, the ethnographer's notes could only capture snapshots in the life of that community rather than pay a holistic attention to all practices as constitutive of a distinctive culture (p. 20). If anything, the online researcher is more fortunate due to the archival facilities that the internet allows. Hine (2001) concludes that online ethnographies have so far contributed significantly to a changing relationship between the ethnographer and participants as they "no longer need to share the same time frame" (p. 23). Moreover, she argues that 'traditional' ethnographies have become a rarity today due to the manifold time and budget limitations.

Ethical considerations in relation to the process of data collection and analysis have also been comparatively discussed. While in the case of 'traditional' ethnographies the researcher was physically present among a community whose members accepted his presence, the internet has often been considered the perfect research environment because it allows the researcher a privileged position, i.e., according to Paccagnella (1997) "to become a *lurker*, an unseen, silent witness to the meetings of the community" (cited in Senjković & Dukić, 2005, p. 46). He feels that lurking tends to "reduce the deformation of the veracity" produced by the researcher's presence during face-to-face interaction (Paccagnella, 1997, cited in Senjković & Dukić, 2005, p. 46). Other scholars have also suggested that since the internet sites are free to read (thus not requiring a username or password in order to log in) their content is safely regarded as a public domain (Parker & Song, 2006, p. 183).

There are authors however who insist on the need to ensure anonymity of the online subjects and to obtain the informed consent prior to engaging with the data in our research (Hine, 2001). Several scholars however assert that this is difficult and not always possible online (Eynon, Fry, & Schroeder, 2008) mainly because it is difficult to assess whether online users have actually understood the context of the research. Thus, while the presence of the ethnographer needs to be accepted by those who inhabit the setting (Hine, 2008, p. 259), many questions still emerge: how to gain the consent of the members, who owns the data, how do we handle the information, and how do we address the members' vulnerability (due to exposing their opinions) (Kozinets, 2010)?

Eynon et al. (2008) argue that online research is, from an ethical perspective, not that much different from offline research in that a balance always needs to be achieved "between the potential and significance of harm to the participants and the benefits of the research to the individual and society more generally" (p. 27). In relation to the present study, great consideration has been given to the recommendations made in the report prepared by Ess and the AoIR ethics working committee (2002). The authors of the above-mentioned report draw attention to several important aspects which need to be considered when making ethical decisions about internet research. Firstly, Ess and his colleagues (2002) point out that an assessment needs to be carried out in order to reveal any website privacy policy or statement related to privacy of the information stored. In the case of the website (and forum) of the Romanian Community of Ireland, no such document was identified.

Furthermore, according to Ess and the AoIR ethics working committee (2002) attention needs to be paid to the research participants' awareness and expectations of privacy online. On the one hand this implies that if a research project involves the online participation of children, minors or any vulnerable individuals, the researcher's obligation to protect their subjects is heightened. On the other hand, the researcher also needs to assess users' expectations and awareness of the private/public character of the online content. According to Ess and colleagues (2002), if the assumption of participants in an online environment is that their communication is private, then there is a greater obligation on the part of the researcher to protect the identities of the subjects (p. 7) and also to clearly inform them about the nature of the research.

A long term observation of the profile of the users, their interactions and the conversations taking place on the Romanian Community of Ireland forum revealed that no participants to the discussion were under-age or vulnerable adults. Furthermore, on numerous occasions, users of the forum indicated that they were well aware of the public content of their conversations: a first clue in support of this statement is the fact that during the registration on the forum a great majority of users do not give any indication in relation to their name, address or any other personal details (some exceptions refer to gender and age); secondly, on many occasions direct references were clearly made by participants on the forum in connection with the public character of their posts online. Even under these circumstances, the internet researcher still holds a tremendous responsibility to ensure that the use of the online material does not imply any risks for the authors of the posts or for the online community (in this case the Romanian Community of Ireland forum).

Thus, several measures were implemented in order to ensure that the anonymity of the forum users is at all times protected during the data analysis and reporting on the findings. While the publication of findings of this study frequently involved making references, paraphrasing and direct citation from the forum material, the names, usernames and/or nicknames of the subjects were never used in any reporting or publication. Instead, a unique code containing the gender and a random two digit number was attached to each user in order to correlate the posts of a person throughout the report. It is also worth adding that, due to the significant number of posts on the forum as well as the fact that the original language of posts is Romanian (which implies translation into English when used in any publication), it means that the chances of recognising users are slim.

The issue of obtaining the informed consent from the forum users was deemed as unattainable in this particular situation. This is purely because, by accessing information from the last six years, many of the forum users whose posts I have read no longer contribute to the forum. Thus, I have opted for informing the forum owner and administrator about my intentions to study the group. Only following his permission to access forum data did I engage in any form of data collection and analysis.

Apart from the important decisions related to the ethics of internet research, several key aspects also need to be discussed in relation to the insider-outsider dilemma. The 'dangers' of engaging with research on people with a similar background or which are part of the same group is, according to Turnbull (2000 cited in Ryan, 2007) mainly related to a sort of superficiality, i.e., skimming over things which we all assume to be shared and which are 'taken for granted'. However in relation to my own position in this research process it needs to be stated that while I am clearly a cultural insider (I too am a Romanian migrant in Ireland), this aspect was also key to decoding part of the cultural context which might otherwise lie hidden. This also reflected in the ability to translate the forum material as closely as possible to the original meaning. This was particularly the case of translating traditional sayings or Romanian idioms whose meanings would otherwise be inaccessible to non-native or computer-generated translators.

Moreover, it also needs to be noted that while I am a cultural insider based on my nationality and ethnicity, the same cannot be said about my belonging to the forum community. Before starting out on this research journey I was not a member of the forum, thus, in this respect, I was still 'an outsider' just like almost all ethnographers at the onset of their fieldwork research. This mix of being both an insider and an outsider brings multiple advantages as it allows me to be at the same time sensitive to the hidden meanings in the members' discourse and to the cultural context from which their discourses originate, while at the same time keeping a certain distance between myself and the members of the group, a particular detachment which allowed me to maintain the neutral attitude which a researcher is supposed to hold.

5. Discussion of the findings

The internet, and in particular this discussion forum, tends to occupy an important role in the life of online Romanians, given the relative absence of other means of diasporic participation. Hence, the forum emerges as the main platform for community interaction and the collective negotiation of identities. Findings emerging from the users' postings indicate that the forum acts as an important tool for information, advice and support for the community. However, the 'newcomers' and the prospective members of this online community often have their limits tested by the more senior and established members. It emerges that through information and advice given, the forum sometimes acts as a symbolic Ellis Island, where migrants are tested and filtered before they are finally given the 'go ahead' into Ireland.

> If you went to the university just to have an engineer degree, then you are not needed here in Ireland. They have enough engineers with degrees. What they need are people able to do the jobs. If you are good you can own the market. [...] nobody gives you anything for free. You have to work and make compromises. So you need to re-analyse yourself. I know that my words may be tough, but this is reality [...] Wake up! (2006 - M03).

At the same time the forum emerges as 'the glue' that enhances the bonding of the diaspora members, thus impacting positively on the process of collective identification and community construction. The stories of love (and hate) for the motherland and the rich descriptions of challenges as well as benefits associated with their new lives in the host community act as common points of identification in the diasporic discourse and they bring the forum members closer together[1]. For example, almost all Romanians on the forum seem to have an intricate relation with their country and their co-citizens. At times they lament their homeland's slow progress and they describe its economic and political situation as extremely sad, calling their ancestral home 'the

---

1. For a detailed account of these aspects see also Macri (2010, 2011a, 2011b).

Valley of Sorrows'[1]. However, on other occasions forum members argue that an important distinction needs to be made between Romania as a country that needs to be loved and the people that live in it. This resonates with one of the most popular sayings in Romania: 'Romania is a beautiful country, too bad it is inhabited'. Hence, this complex bond with their homeland unravels continuously through their discourse and it seems to resemble a puzzle with many different facets, some good (which make them proud), and some bad (which bring stigma and shame):

> For me there are two Romanias. One is written with capital 'R' and the other one is written with small caps 'r'. In the (R)omania (with capital letter) I include the Romanian university graduates, those people that work hard and are very appreciated in their workplaces and the communities they are part of. On the other hand we have the (r)omania (with no capital letter) that includes those that steal from ATMs and shops, those that beg on the streets, the bureaucracy that makes one waste their time [...] and those Romanians that are not open to other opinions than their own (2007 – F07).

This double-voiced discourse integrates most of the definitions and perceptions of 'home' expressed by online Romanians and it contains the key to understanding the interplay between stigma and pride in relation to their country of origin. Their experiences and opinions of 'home' act as common points of identification in their diasporic discourse, but so do their narrations of their process of integration in Ireland. For some subjects integration was achieved with significant sacrifices, for others with relative ease, yet almost all online participants to the forum revealed similar experiences with the Irish society and comparable frustrations inherent to the integration process into the host country.

These stories of love and hate for the country of origin and the one of destination seem to create the premises for bringing forum members closer together in a

---

1. The 'valley of sorrows' is a reference to one of the most popular Romanian children stories by Petre Ispirescu and entitled '*Tinerețe fără bătrânețe, și viață fără de moarte*' [Youth without old age and life without death]. In the story, the 'valley of sorrows' represents the liminal space between two different worlds: the world of the living and the world of the immortals. It symbolises the trials and tribulations that one needs to surpass before achieving a superior state) in this case, immortality.

shared exercise of imagining 'the home' and 'the host'. For many participants, the forum also constitutes a source of Romanianness. For some, this aspect is strictly language-related as the forum allows them to 'practice' the language everyday. For others however, the forum constitutes a 'sacred' space where respect for Romanians and Romanianness is of key importance. For them, this online space seems to help the participants to create a sense of unity of Romanians as a group in spite of its heterogeneity

> [...] we are here firstly because we are Romanians and that should be the most important thing. Each of us is different, we have different opinions to each other and maybe this is what makes dialogue possible. If we would all be the same then maybe we would have nothing to talk about (2006 – M01).

References to the host society are also manifold. Thus, the majority of forum participants also highlighted the role that this online medium played in constituting a space where collective feelings of revolt, embarrassment and stigmatised identities are expressed. It is a space that allows its participants to relieve some of the tensions and frustrations experienced in the process of integration in the new country. In this space, diaspora struggles to mobilise their efforts to change the image of the Romanian community and 'liberate' the Romanian identity from the perceived stigma attached to it. These alternations of references to 'the home' and 'the host' in their online discourses also constitute important clues to their transnational belonging. Online Romanians are neither fully 'here' or 'there', experiencing at times a connection to both the homeland and the host community, while at other times feeling rejected by both.

Summarising the arguments presented so far, the forum is perceived by many of its users as an essential space for debate, a 'round table' where Romanians discuss their lives in Ireland and the 'fate' of the motherland. But does the forum reflect a diasporic 'offline' community or are they simply migrants in search for information who are brought together on this forum solely by their shared nationality/country of birth? Is the forum conducive to the formation of a diasporic community or not? In order to establish the answer such questions we need to understand who Romanians online are.

Statistically speaking, online Romanians are a minority compared to the total number of Romanians in Ireland. One of the main challenges is that there is insufficient information emerging from the forum in relation to the profile of its users (i.e., their gender, age, occupation, etc.). However, their demographic characteristics are in most cases revealed through their posts on the forum. Thus, by parsing through all messages on the forum, several general insights could be drawn: the forum tends to be populated mainly by a male audience and their age seems to reflect the 2006 Census profile of the Romanian community in Ireland, with most people found in the 25 to 44 age bracket. While most of the forum users live in Ireland, there are also those that visit the forum from their locations in Romania (mostly in search of information about their imminent trip to Ireland) or from other countries such as Italy, Spain, UK, etc. Amongst those that connect to the forum from Ireland, a great majority seem to live in Dublin, thus in accordance with the findings of the Census (2006, 2011).

Nevertheless there are categories of Romanians in Ireland who are significantly underrepresented among active members (as is the case of women) or entirely absent from the forum (as is the case of Romanian gypsies). Hence, the forum is not statistically representative of *all* Romanians in Ireland. Besides these demographic characteristics that build the profile of the forum users, there were also multiple instances on the forum when members talked about themselves in a collective manner, by evaluating their identity in opposition with their 'offline' counterparts. On these occasions, it became evident that forum participants perceive themselves as an elite: a group of well-behaved, intelligent, informed and well-educated people. Furthermore they are the ones who succeeded in their goals and are 'still there' [i.e., on the forum and in Ireland] after recession hit the country. According to the exact words of one of the forum users, they see themselves as the 'upper class' among Romanians in Ireland.

It is interesting to note that some users perceive the forum as a close-knit community, or even a family. The high degree of familiarity between members can be explained by the long time they have spent together on the forum which has allowed them to get to know each other gradually, just like in everyday life. Moreover, forum users tend to meet each other offline, however this happens only in very small groups and at family level. As previously mentioned, forum postings reveal that many online participants to the forum articulate complex feelings of belonging in relation to the home and the host community. Benchmarking this online community against Safran's (1991) discussion of the defining elements of a diaspora clearly shows that, even if it does not represent the mirror image of all Romanians in Ireland, this online community nevertheless represents a diasporic community. Online Romanians underwent dispersal from the homeland, even though it was not experienced at the same traumatic level as the 'classic' diasporas. Furthermore, they showed evidence of a collective memory and vision of their homeland as they tried to propose solutions for improving the Romanian image abroad. Last but not least, online Romanians developed consciousness surrounding their group as a (diasporic) community. In addition to these aspects, transnational belonging, an element which was rather ignored in Safran's (1991) account of the features that define a diaspora, emerged as an essential characteristic of Romanians online.

6. Conclusions

Taking all these aspects into consideration, it can be noted that the forum of the Romanian Community of Ireland acts as a public sphere, understood in a broader sense than Habermas's (1974) rather strict definition. It represents a space that allows Romanians to come together and discuss the matters that they consider of utmost importance and to attempt to correct some of the problematic issues. Furthermore, by facilitating the participation of Romanians from various locations in this virtual space, the forum has the potential to enhance the transnational dimension of the Romanian diaspora.

Last but not least, it represents a lively arena for the circulation of information and collective negotiation of cultural meanings and identities of the Romanian diaspora in Ireland. These findings are consistent with data from similar research (Chan, 2005; Elias et al., 2007; Miller & Slater, 2000) arguing that the internet and in particular discussion forums play a complex role in articulating diasporic identifications and feelings of belonging. In the effort to determine the position of this online community in relation to the wider community of Romanians in Ireland, I took note of the forum members' very own definitions of themselves. It emerged that they imagined themselves as rather different from the 'offline' side of the Romanian community in Ireland. Social class emerged as a key identity marker from this perspective as forum members often portrayed themselves as the elite part of the community: they saw themselves as more educated, more in control of their destiny and of the 'Romanian project', namely the restoration of their homeland and the reconstruction of the image of Romanianness on more positive values.

References

Atkinson, P., & Hammersley, M. (2007). *Ethnography. Principles in practice* (3rd ed.). London: Routledge.

Cavanagh, A. (2007). *Sociology in the Age of the Internet*. Berkshire, UK: Open University Press.

Chan, B. (2005). Imagining the Homeland: The Internet and Diasporic Discourse of Nationalism. *Journal of Communication Inquiry, 29*(4), 336-368. doi: 10.1177/0196859905278499

Cheung, C. (2004). Identity Construction and Self-Presentation on Personal Homepages: Emancipatory Potentials and Reality Constraints. In D. Gauntlett & R. Horsley (Eds.), *Web.Studies* (pp. 53-68) (2nd ed.). London: Arnold.

Clifford, J. (1994). Diasporas. *Cultural Anthropology, 9*(3), 302-338. doi: 10.1525/can.1994.9.3.02a00040

DiMaggio, P., Hargittai, E., Neuman, W. R., & Robinson, J. P. (2001). Social Implications of the Internet. *Annual Review of Sociology, 27*, 307-336. doi: 10.1146/annurev.soc.27.1.307

Elias, N., Lemish, D., & Khvorostianov, N. (2007). *Homeland Identities - The Internet in the Lives of Immigrant Adolescents from the Former Soviet Union in Israel*. Retrieved from http://cmsprod.bgu.ac.il/NR/rdonlyres/34396BDB-6C0E-4931-A077-697451885123/34392/EliasLemishedited.pdf

Ess, C., & AoIR ethics research committee. (2002). *Ethical decision-making and Internet research: Recommendations from the AoIR ethics working committee.* Charles Ess and the Association of Internet Researchers. Retrieved from www.aoir.org/reports/ethics.pdf

Eynon, R., Fry, J., & Schroeder, R. (2008). The ethics of Internet research. In N. G. Fielding, R. M. Lee, & G. Blank (Eds.), *The SAGE Handbook of online research methods* (pp. 23-41). London: Sage Publications.

Foster, D. (1996). Community and Identity in the Electronic Village. In D. Porter (Ed.), *Internet Culture* (pp. 23-37). London: Routledge.

Gauntlett, D. (2004). Web Studies: What's New. In D. Gauntlett & R. Horsley (Eds.), *Web Studies* (pp. 3-23) (2nd ed.). London: Arnold.

Georgiou, M. (2006). *Diaspora, Identity and the Media: Diasporic Transnationalism and Mediated Spatialities.* Cresskill, New Jersey: Hampton Pres inc.

Habermas, J. (1974). The Public Sphere: An Encyclopedia Article (1964). *New German Critique, 3*(3), 49-55. Retrieved from http://www.jstor.org/stable/487737

Hepp, A. (2004). Media Connectivity: a New World of Mobility? The Internet, Identity and Deterritorialization in Europe. *Paper given at the Internet Identities in Europe, international conference organised by the European Centre for Gender Studies and ESCUS, University of Sheffield.* Retrieved from www.shef.ac.uk/content/1/c6/04/88/28/Hepp.pdf

Hiller, H. H., & Franz, T. M. (2004). New Ties, Old Ties and Lost Ties: The Use of the Internet in Diaspora. *New Media & Society, 6*(6), 731-752. doi: 10.1177/146144804044327

Hine, C. (2001). *Virtual Ethnography.* London: Sage Publications.

Hine, C. (2008). Virtual ethnography: modes, varieties, affordancies. In N. G. Fielding, R. M. Lee, & G. Blank (Eds.), *The SAGE Handbook of online research methods* (pp. 257-270). London: Sage Publications.

Ignacio, E. N. (2005). *Building diaspora: Filipino community formation on the Internet.* Piscataway, NJ: Rutgers University Press.

Kozinets, R. V. (2010). *Netnography: doing ethnographic research online.* London: SAGE Publications Ltd.

Lockard, J. (1996). Progressive Politics, Electronic Individualism and the Myth of Virtual Community. In D. Porter (Ed.), *Internet Culture* (pp. 219-231). London: Routledge.

Macri, G. (2010). Who do they think they are? Online Narratives among the Romanian minority in Ireland. In L. De Pretto, G. Macri, & C. Wong (Eds.), *Diasporas: revisiting and discovering* (pp. 205-213). Oxford: Inter-disciplinary Press. Retrieved from http://www.inter-disciplinary.net/wp-content/uploads/2010/04/dias2ever3090410.pdf

Macri, G. (2011a). Logging into Diaspora – Media and Online Identity Narratives among Romanians in Ireland. *Observatorio (OBS*) Journal, 5*(2), 41-52. Retrieved from http://obs.obercom.pt/index.php/obs/article/view/443/428

Macri, G. (2011b). Stories of Love and Hate. Images of 'Homeland' in the Identity Narratives of Romanians in Ireland. *International Review of Social Research, 1*(2), 125-143.

Mandaville, P. (2001). Reimagining Islam in Diaspora: The Politics of Mediated Community. Gazette, 63(2-3), 169-186. Retrieved from http://goo.gl/HAQYU

Miller, D., & Slater, D. (2000). *The Internet. An Etnographic Approach*. Oxford: Berg Publishers.

Mitra, A. (1997). Virtual commonality: looking for India on the Internet. In S. Jones (Ed.), *Virtual cultures*. Newbury Park: Sage Publications.

Nedelcu, M. F. (2000). Instrumentalizarea Spaţiilor Virtuale. Noi Strategii de Reproducere Şi Conversie a Capitalurilor În Situaţia Migratorie [The Instrumentalisation of Virtual Spaces. New Strategies for the Reproduction and Conversion of the Capitals [assets] in the Migratory Context. *Sociologie Românească [Romanian Sociology], 2*, 80-96.

Oberhuber, F., & Krzyzanowski, M. (2008). Discourse analysis and ethnography. In R. Wodak & M. Krzyzanowski (Eds.), *Qualitative discourse analysis in the social sciences*. Basingstoke: Palgrave Macmillan.

Ogan, C. (2001). *Communication and identity in the diaspora: Turkish migrants in Amsterdam and their use of media*. New York: Lexington Books.

Paccagnella, L. (1997). Getting the seats of your pants dirty: strategies for ethnographic research on virtual communities. *Journal of computer-mediated education, 3*(1). Retrieved from http://jcmc.indiana.edu/vol3/issue1/paccagnella.html

Papacharissi, Z. A. (2002). The virtual sphere: The internet as a public sphere. *New Media & Society, 4*(1), 9-27. doi: 10.1177/14614440222226244

Parker, D., & Song, M. (2006). Ethnicity, Social Capital and the Internet: British Chinese websites. *Ethnicities, 6*(2), 178-202. doi: 10.1177/1468796806063751

Popov, A. (2010). Making Sense of Home and Homeland: Former-Soviet Greeks' Motivations and Strategies for a Transnational Migrant Circuit. *Journal of Ethnic and Migration Studies, 36*(1), 67-85. doi: 10.1080/13691830903123211

Reis, M. (2004). Theorizing Diaspora: Perspectives on "Classical" and "Contemporary" Diaspora. *International Migration, 42*(2), 41-60. doi: 10.1111/j.0020-7985.2004.00280.x

Ryan, L. (2007). Who Do You Think You Are? Irish Nurses Encountering Ethnicity And Constructing Identity In Britain. *Ethnic and Racial Studies, 30*(3), 416-438. doi: 10.1080/01419870701217498

Safran, W. (1991). Diasporas in Modern Societies: Myths of Homeland and Return. *Diaspora, 1*(1), 83-99. doi: 10.1353/dsp.1991.0004

Senjković, R., & Dukić, D. (2005). Virtual Homeland? Reading the music on offer on a particular web page. *International Journal of Cultural Studies, 8*(1), 44-62. doi: 10.1177/1367877905050162

Shi, Y. (2005). Identity Construction of the Chinese Diaspora, Ethnic Media Use, Community Formation, and the Possibility of Social Activism. *Continuum: Journal of Media and Cultural Studies, 19*(1), 55-72.

Sparks. C. (1998). Is there a global public sphere. In D. Thussu (ed.), *Electronic Empires: Global Media and Local Resistance*. New York: Arnold.

Sreberny, A. (2000). Media and Diasporic Consciousness: An Exploration among Iranians in London. In S. Cottle (Ed.), *Ethnic Minorities and the Media: Changing Cultural Boundaries* (pp. 179-196). Buckingham: Open University Press.

Srinivasan, R. (2006). Indigenous, Ethnic and Cultural Articulations of New Media. *International Journal of Cultural Studies, 9*(4), 497-518. doi: 10.1177/1367877906069899

Thompson, K. (2002). Border Crossings and Diasporic Identities: Media Use and Leisure Practices of an Ethnic Minority. *Qualitative Sociology, 25*(3), 409-418.

Triandafyllidou, A., & Wodak, R. (2003). Conceptual and methodological questions in the study of collective identities. *Journal of Language and Politics, 2*(2), 205-223. doi: 10.1075/jlp.2.2.02tri

Tsagarousianou, R. (2004). Rethinking the Concept of Diaspora: Mobility, Connectivity and Communication in a Globalised World. *Westminster Papers in Communication and Culture, 1*(1), 52-66. Retrieved from http://www.westminster.ac.uk/__data/assets/pdf_file/0014/20219/005WPCC-Vol1-No1-Roza_Tsagarousianou.pdf

Turnbull. A. (2000). Collaboration and Censorship in the Oral History Interview. *International Journal of Social Research Methodology, 3*(1), 15-34. doi: 10.1080/136455700294905

Turkle, S. (1995). *Life on the screen: identity in the age of the Internet*. New York: Simon & Schuster.

Wieviorka, M. (2007). The Construction of What? In G. G. Raymond & T. Modood (Eds.), *The Construction of Minority Identities in France and Britain* (pp. 33-47). Basingstoke: Palgrave Macmillan.

12 What's 'Smart' About Working from Home: Telework and the Sustainable Consumption of Distance in Ireland?

Michael Hynes[1]

Abstract

The use of technology is pervasive in contemporary society, transforming lives and work environments. The internet and the availability of portable personal communication devices have resulted in immense societal change. Frequently held views of the relationship between individuals and technology are dominated by a production-centric perspective, with limited attention being paid to the social and environmental impacts of consumption. Elevated by improvements in information communication technologies and infrastructure, telework was heralded as an innovative way of working with the added potential of reducing travel demand. But early optimistic expectations failed to materialise, largely due to a poor understanding of social, political, and personal issues involved. This chapter presents an examination of telework in Ireland and argues for a more holistic approach to investigation. Before telework can be accepted as a potential benefit to the sustainable consumption of distance, the environmental consequences of changes in working practices must be understood. Researching an organisation with a telework culture, this paper investigated the environmental impacts of individuals working from home. Teleworkers reported no increase in water and other goods consumption, and no additional travel needs. However, they felt they increased their domestic food and energy consumption, and produced more waste working from home.

Keywords: telework, sustainability, consumption, ecological footprinting, mobility.

1. School of Political Science & Sociology, National University of Ireland, Galway, Ireland; m.hynes5@nuigalway.ie

How to cite this chapter: Hynes, M. (2013). What's 'Smart' About Working from Home: Telework and the Sustainable Consumption of Distance in Ireland? In C. Fowley, C. English, & S. Thouësny (Eds.), *Internet Research, Theory, and Practice: Perspectives from Ireland* (pp. 225-243). Dublin: © Research-publishing.net.

1. Introduction

The information communication technologies revolution of the last few decades has brought with it requirements for a new type of work, one that depends more on intellectual processing of information than on the physical labour of the past. People who perform and engage in this type of labour are frequently described as 'knowledge workers' (Drucker, 2000; Kling & Scacchi, 1982). Knowledge workers generally do not require access to industrial equipment or raw materials to carry out their tasks, but they do need access to the continuous flow of data to create information. Once they have access to data, and the necessary technology infrastructure and competencies, they may not be required to be present at any given physical worksite or location to accomplish their tasks. Telework occurs when information communication technologies are applied to enable work be performed at a distance from the location where the results are needed, or where that work would traditionally have been accomplished in the past.

The practice of telework has been highlighted as a cure for a variety of organisational and social problems in much of the recent research literature. It has been suggested as a strategy to help organisations reduce their infrastructural and on-going utilities costs (Egan, 1997; Van Horn & Storen, 2000), respond to employees' need for a more enhanced work-life balance (Hilbrecht, Shaw, Johnson, & Andrey, 2008; Shamir & Salomon, 1985), and as a way of promoting better social inclusion for people with disabilities, or who have been previously excluded from the traditional workplace for a variety of reasons such as locality, social class, or educational status (Anderson, Bricout, & West, 2001; Hesse, 1995; Kenyon, Lyons, & Rafferty, 2002). Telework has also been suggested as a means of reducing air and noise pollution, and traffic congestion in and around urban areas (Dwelly & Lake, 2008; Irwin, 2004). However, information communication technologies utilised for telework do not in themselves lead to overall travel suppression (Mokhtarian, 1990, 1991, 2002) and there are additional environmental consequences arising from the need to change or update technological equipment, infrastructure, living space, and other such lifestyle transformations (Arnfalk, 2002). It is claimed that telework and other forms of distributed work collaboration are on the increase (Andriessen & Vartiainen, 2006; Brodt & Verburg, 2007) and efforts to limit climate change may accelerate this trend towards more flexible distributed organisations in the future (WWF, 2009). Yet, it is clear telework has failed to live up to its initial promise and early predictions (see Huws, 1991, for an overview of early telework forecasts) and although statistics suggest telework has increased, "the reality remains far removed from the early forecasts in the late 1970s and early 1980s" (Pyöriä, 2011, p. 2) and the actual global extent of telework may be much smaller than often imagined (White et al., 2010).

Sociology is often criticised for not discussing technology in a manner that has influence over its direction and development, and this work serves as a call for the discipline to become more involved at all stages of technology development, implementation, and adoption. Society is vulnerable to what Winner (1997) described as "technological somnambulism" (p. 57), which is our semi-conscious, sleepwalking attitude towards technology. He believed we often release technology into society and quickly abdicate responsibility toward it, and maintained we should manage and debate the terms of our relationships with technologies long before they become embedded into our daily and working lives. It also echoes a call from Law and Urry (2004) for social science to "interfere in the realities, to make a difference, to engage in an ontological politics, and to help shape new realities" (p. 404). Consequently, we should no longer simply view technology as a *black box* shaping the trajectory of society but rather a component having varying degrees of influence, or not, in time and space. It is imperative that we no longer relinquish this important research space to developers and engineers but seek to engage with these other disciplines to find a healthy and accommodating fit and understanding for technology within society.

Significant initial efforts to promote telework in Ireland at the beginning of the century ended abruptly and, as this author maintains, proved to be ineffectual in the long run. Some of the blame for the lack of success in implementation can be placed on the lack of adequate research into significant social components that make up the practice of telework, including Irish employers unwillingness to support this technology-aided way of working (Hynes, forthcoming). Whilst significant importance was placed on economic issues and the consequence of telework for the development of a 'smart economy', little in the way of the social and domestic issues involved were discussed or considered. Indeed, national and regional telework policy resided firmly within a sphere of a laissez-faire attitude among government and other decision-makers, effectively giving employers' undisputed power when it came to the introduction and recognition of such work practices. As many were unaware, or indeed unconvinced, of the benefits that can accrue from telework the practice principally became the providence of a handful of organisations, generally within the Civil Service and technology industries.

2. Telework in Ireland

Much of the initial pioneering work in developing telework frameworks and schemes within the European Community took place in the peripheral countries and regions of Europe, including Ireland. The expectation was that more dispersed populations with significant distance and location barriers to overcome would benefit most from individuals working from home. Results from early research were largely mixed and inconclusive (see ECaTT, 2000; SusTel, 2003) and point to inconsistencies particularly in the Irish case:

> "While there has been stronger growth in Scandinavian countries, further west development has been slow by European standards. Ireland has been to some extent a puzzle. Despite energetic early work by telework pioneers, and Ireland's developing reputation as a place for high-tech investment, progress has been below the European average" (Lake, 2009, p. 1).

Similar results were found in the standard Eurobarometer survey (European Commission, 2001). This showed regular telework in Ireland at just 2.4 per cent of the adult workforce, and occasional teleworkers at 6.1 per cent. European averages, by contrast, were 5 per cent for regular and 6.6 per cent for occasional teleworkers. More recent data on telework in Ireland was published in February 2003 by the Central Statistics Office in Cork (CSO, 2003). Detailed questions were added to the Quarterly National Household Survey (QNHS) to determine levels of home-based workers outside of the large agricultural sector, teleworkers being the most significant constituent. The summarised data confirmed there were 59,200 teleworkers in Ireland, representing just 3.5 per cent of the workforce, with approximately 38 per cent of these workers residing in the Dublin region. This raises interesting questions about the difficulty with developing and implementing telework in Ireland.

There is no employment (or other) legislation dealing specifically with the subject of telework or the status of teleworkers at present on the statute books in Ireland. When the European Framework Agreement on Telework (Europa, 2002) was concluded, the majority of countries elected to implement the agreement through bipartite collective agreements. Ireland, however, elected implementation through soft law[1] mechanisms giving employers an effective veto over any telework proposal or request. Adam and Crossan (2001) maintained that where telework existed it had been implemented in an ad-hoc manner and was largely employee-driven. Telework was not actively encouraged and management commitment was virtually non-existent. As a result, the necessary support was not forthcoming and the practice of telework was not seen as a priority within the organisations sampled. It appeared Irish managers were not yet convinced of the benefits inherent in the concept of telework, or they were uncertain whether the benefits were worth the risks resulting from the introduction of this new method of (re)organising work.

The efforts, in respect of telework, by policy and decision-makers in Ireland can largely be characterised as bridging an informational gap which existed at the turn of the century. While some clarification in respect of the tax implications was provided by the Revenue Commissioners (Revenue, 2001), overall strategies and policy to promote and develop telework in the country could be described as improvised. No evidence is available that would indicate a willingness to

---

1. Soft law is the term applied to measures such as guidelines, declarations and opinions, which, in contrast to directives, regulations and decisions, are not binding on those to whom they are addressed.

research or better understand the often complex social, personal, and political issues involved when adopting this way of working. Even today, telework remains largely unexplored as a tool for economic and social development, and environmental protection. Indeed, much of the early enthusiasm shown at governmental level has long since faded in an atmosphere of ambiguity and uncertainty, along with outdated or shut-down web portals, action groups, and reports[1]. Consequently, a considerable gap in knowledge currently exists that needs to be bridged.

Given the plethora of technological developments since many of these original studies and reports were commissioned, a fresh approach to the subject of telework is essential. However, before any strategy for promotion and implementation can be developed it is imperative to define and critically test the credentials of telework as a virtual mobility tool that has the potential to reduce the consumption of distance. Telework promises some direct savings by eliminating the daily commute and various auxiliary savings in utilities and building expenditure. But does working from home actually reduce or increase a person's carbon footprint? Whilst it has been strongly promoted in Ireland as an economic instrument and given little attention as a virtual mobility tool (Callanan, 1999; e-Work Action Forum, 2003; Irish DoETE, 2001), is telework an effective tool for reducing environmentally harmful work-related mobility or does it simply shift any environmental impacts (and their costs) from the worksite to home?

Our understanding of the overall implications of telework in terms of consumption is limited. Telework is frequently promoted on environmental grounds because of its potential to suppress or eliminate certain mobility, but many studies have this single issue focus (Andrey, Burns, & Doherty, 2004; Atkyns, Blazek, & Roitz, 2002; Nelson, Safirova, & Walls, 2007) and there is no universally accepted method for assessing the implications for sustainability of individuals teleworking (Devuyst & Van Volsems, 2001). Much of what

---

1. It is difficult to get current information on telework in Ireland as many of the associated research websites and information portals have been closed since the early part of the decade. In addition, much of the early research relied heavily on EU funding, which was short-term in nature. There are currently no longitudinal studies or on-going research in this area, to this author's knowledge.

exists on the issue at present is excessively optimistic, lacking any real critical investigation or analysis of the practice. Although of an often complex nature, telework needs a wider framework to provide a clearer understanding of the broader implications of its sustainability merits. A teleworker, for instance, may need to consume more heat and energy at home if their house would otherwise have been unoccupied when they were at work, though the extent to which home energy use is offset by decreased workplace energy consumption has also not been sufficiently determined (Hopkinson & James, 2003; Kitou & Horvath, 2003). Many family homes may still have occupants whilst one or more adults go out to work, so the change to telework may not be so noticeable with regards to energy consumption. More importantly, the consequences of telework for general consumption behaviour and waste generation have not, to-date, been comprehensively accounted for. Moos, Andrey, and Johnson (2006) used an ecological-footprint approach to assessing the overall sustainability of telework, and their research moved beyond single-issue studies and single-data analysis. They provided an exploratory investigation and suggested the assumed benefits of telework for society at large must be more carefully examined to "avoid promoting telework's ostensible tendency to reduce air pollution only to find that other harmful effects offset these gains" (Moos et al., 2006, p. 12). This research will complement this particular body of knowledge by using a self-assessment approach to measure impacts using *Ecological Footprinting* to ascertain the environmental impact of telework in Ireland.

What is ecological footprinting and could it be useful in assessing the environmental impacts of telework? Wackernagel and Rees (1996) describe ecological footprinting analysis as an accounting tool that enables us "to estimate the resource consumption and waste assimilation requirements of a defined human population or economy in terms of a corresponding productive land area" (p. 9). It has been widely acclaimed for presenting current total human resource use in a manner that communicates easily to most people, but there is some concern when these calculations are used in interpreting it as an indicator of something else. While some argue in favour of its use for policy decision-making in the context of sustainability (Collins, Flynn, Wiedmann, &

Barrett, 2006; Wackernagel & Silemtein, 2000) others see a much more limited role for ecological footprinting (Ayres, 2000; Fiala, 2008). Although research using the application of ecological footprinting on its utility as a policy tool is largely applied at a national level with some success (Monfreda, Wackernagel, & Deumling, 2004; Wackernagel et al., 1999), some research has applied it at a regional and city level (Barrett, 2001; Rees & Wackernagel, 1996). In the context of this particular research we will consider a meso-level investigation using ecological footprinting analysis at an organisational level.

3.   The case study

The purpose of this case study, which took place in March 2012, was to examine the assumed environmental impacts of a person's decision to telework. The empirical evidence was gathered from a multinational company which operates from eight separate locations across Ireland, and which embraced a flexible working culture as an affirmative option for organisational change over the past number of years[1]. The organisation has a diverse workforce of management, sales, administration, technology personnel, and manufacturing workers, and their headquarters in Ireland is located in the Dublin West region. Many of the worksites across the country focus principally on manufacturing and would have difficulty implementing telework on a large scale, but the Dublin headquarters actively promotes and encourages the practice as a legitimate and progressive method of working.

As one of the foremost companies in the country with an established flexible working and telework program, the organisation was deemed the most appropriate for this particular research. The number of potential teleworkers at the Dublin site was calculated at 114[2] and a personalised email was send to each of these employees and managers inviting them to participate in the research, beginning with answering a carefully structured online questionnaire

---

1. The organisation involved requested to remain anonymous for this particular study.

2. This figure of potential teleworkers was provided by the Human Resources Manager.

using the Limesurvey software. 53 individuals took part, a response rate of just over 46 per cent. The research relied on self-reflection and self-assessment to estimate the impact of telework on a person's carbon footprint when they worked from home, focussing on six key areas of household consumption: food, energy, travel, goods[1] water and waste. This data constitutes a discursive framework of the assumed environmental impact of teleworkers rather than actual measurement, and thus has obvious limitations in the context of comprehensive assertions and conclusions. The respondents were asked to consider their consumption requirements on days they teleworked, and contrast these needs with days where they commuted to their centrally-located office. In addition, five[2] respondents were selected at random and interviewed to allow for more in-depth analysis of telework in general, and issues of sustainability and environmental concerns interconnected with this method of working.

4.   Results

Figure 1.   Food and energy consumption

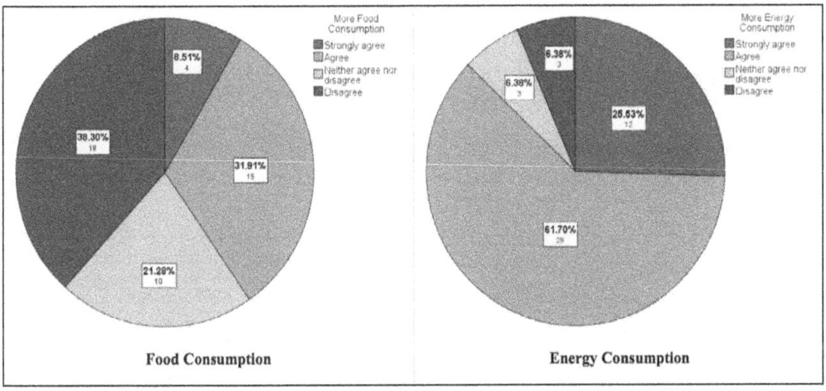

1. Goods, in this instance, refer to new equipment, furniture, clothing or other items that may need to be purchased by teleworkers other than foodstuffs.

2. The number of interviewees was agreed with the organisation beforehand in an attempt to minimise disruption as the company was actively involved in other areas of research. The interviews were carried out over distance with the individuals from their homes in an informal manner using a teleconferencing facility, and all interviews were recorded and consent obtained.

Figure 2. Travel and goods/item consumption

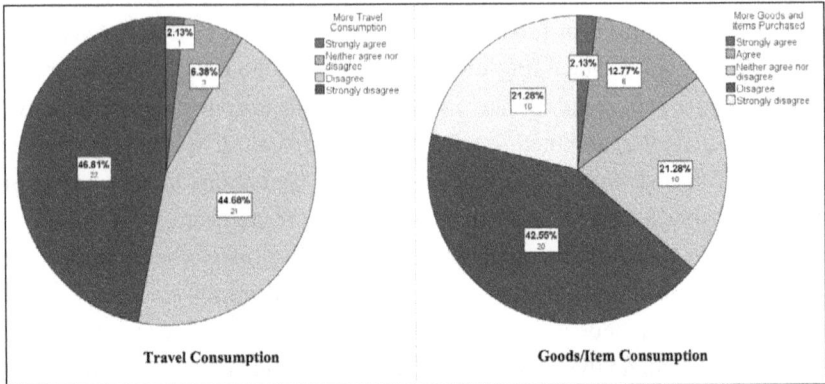

Figure 3. Water consumption and waste production

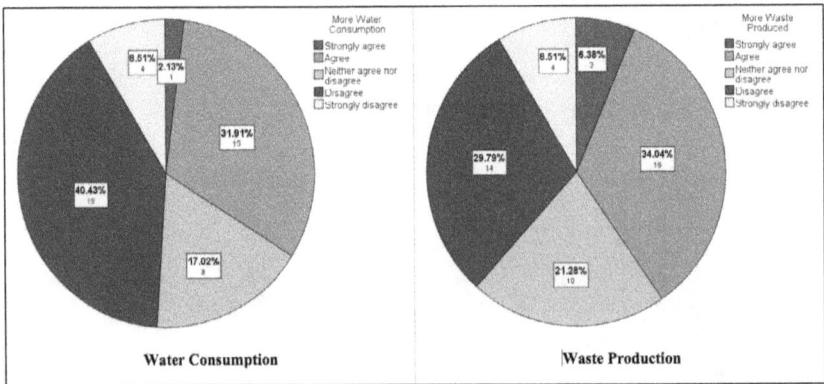

As illustrated in the graphs above (Figure 1, Figure 2, and Figure 3), 40 per cent ($N = 22$) agreed or strongly agreed that their food consumption in the home increased when teleworking, with 21 per cent ($N = 10$) undecided on this issue. Over 87 per cent ($N = 41$) of the respondents either agreed or strongly agreed that their domestic energy consumption increased, whilst the majority of respondents, over 91 per cent ($N = 43$), felt that their consumption of distance did not increase during episodes of telework. Similarly, most of the respondents felt their purchase of goods and other items was unaffected by their telework practices. Figures were somewhat mixed on additional water consumption and waste produced when working from home.

Contrasting the figures for respondents who agreed and strongly agreed with those who disagreed and strongly disagreed, and eliminating the undecided, the reported changes in impact are listed in Table 1 below.

Table 1.   Self-reported changes in environmental impact due to telework

Category of Domestic Consumption	Reported Increase
Food Consumption	Yes
Energy Consumption	Yes
Travel Consumption	No
Goods & Items Purchased	No
Water Consumption	No
Waste Produced	Yes

The issue of overall environmental concern and the need to reduce the consequence of transport's negative impact on the environment was explored with the five interviewees. This concern was often an incidental consideration in their choice to telework, but many felt satisfied that such a decision reduced their overall commuting impact:

> **Teleworker A1:** [Environmental concerns] wouldn't have been the biggest reason but it would have been a concern yes, and because we have the one car it is great that it cuts down our commute - (female, employee, aged 30-35).

> **Teleworker A2:** I live about thirty minutes away but I do car share anyway so between the two of us we usually sort of agree, and particularly these days [reference to the current economic situation in the country], the other thing is it's half an hour or an hour depending on the traffic out of your day at both ends so from that point of view it's a sort of double bonus - (male, management, aged 55-60).

Teleworker A3: It's probably not so much environmental it's probably more personal from the point of view of getting a bit more time back at home because I spend so much time on the road... I was involved in a big project with one of my colleagues over in Sligo and we had been meeting up halfway so I'd drive an hour each way but because of the snows [last year] we couldn't do that so we sat down and we called up each other and sat down with our laptops and our docking stations and in our various offices on either side of the country and we both said at the end of that we got more done that day working over the telephone and on our laptops you know spatially separated than we had done anywhere because straight away we were saving ourselves two hours travelling time and we were in environments that were a lot more conducive to work rather than sitting in a pub and obviously it's a lot more private as well and we found there were no issues at all so that worked out really really well - (male, employee, aged 35-40).

Teleworker A5: ...not really no it's more social kind of reasons in terms of, what would you say, its more work/life balance - (female, employee, aged 35-40).

When asked if they considered telework had increased their overall expenditure at home, such as electricity, heating, and energy costs, the responses were largely similar, with most respondents attributing any increase in their bills to other issues such as the economic downturn in the country, or exceptional weather events:

Teleworker A1: I mean our bills haven't gone up dramatically or anything like that, I did ask my husband about it and I tend not to turn on the lights so there's not much electricity being used, you know the kettle does go on for a cup of tea now and again that's about it but the heating bill probably did go up but ever so slightly nothing that my husband told me he could notice - (female, employee, aged 30-35).

Teleworker A2: I would say anything that I have noticed would be offset by the fact that I'm not having to take an hour's car journey which probably costs a good couple of litres [of petrol] anyway - (male, management, aged 55-60).

Teleworker A4: I'm not sure what I save on petrol costs verses the additional power requirements in the house but it's probably not much but yea it's a contribution towards not being part of the drain on the environment as well I guess - (male, aged 30-35).

Teleworker A5: When you just telework infrequently I think the benefits cover the costs - (female, employee, aged 35-40).

5. Discussion and conclusions

Before the practice of telework can be endorsed as an instrument for encouraging a positive approach to the sustainable consumption of distance, it is crucial that we have a more robust understanding of the true social and environmental implications of individuals working from home. This particular body of research is a movement towards a better understanding of how teleworkers evaluate themselves and their impact on the environment overall and is not simply confined to the context of travel and their daily commute. Whilst it can be argued that the findings presented here are merely suggestive, given the size of the sample, it is nevertheless an important initial step in a necessary investigation process.

The single-focused nature of many previous studies of telework has led to a frequently simplistic consideration of complex social and environmental interactions, and this particular study widens the boundaries of investigation of telework to provide a more representative and realistic conception of working from home. But this is a tentative preliminary step in any such research and there are limitations to this particular body of research. The possibility of a value-action gap in individual's self-reporting their consumption patterns is ever present, and this study is confined to a single employer who have adopted a philosophy of supporting flexible working arrangements. This particular organisation may not be representative of employers in general in Ireland, and the low number of participants may not be reflective of teleworkers overall.

With the limited number of teleworkers currently operating in Ireland and the complexity involved in getting these often mobile workers to engage with researchers there is a need for better approaches to future research on the subject. It is also paramount for future research to continue to focus on managers' and employers' views of teleworking. Notwithstanding this, the concept employed in this study sets about broadening the investigation framework into telework and seeks to provide a platform for further studies in this area and should be viewed thus.

Finally, there is a need to develop enriched methodologies and indicators that can better capture the complex nature of telework, including its impact on the environment. Longitudinal research work combining time-use of material consumption data would be particularly useful in this respect. Notwithstanding some of its obvious limitations, research presented in this chapter offers a preliminary step towards understanding the multifaceted social, political, economic, and environmental issues surrounding the practice of telework in Ireland. Further sociological perspectives will be critical in re-visiting many of the social issues involved, and exploring telework for its potential as a tool for greater sustainability and enhanced resource-efficiency.

Acknowledgement. This research was undertaken as part of the ConsEnSus Project (www.consensus.ie), a four year interdisciplinary cross-border household analysis of consumption, environment, and sustainability in Ireland. The project was funded by the Science, Technology, Research and Innovation for the Environment (STRIVE) Programme 2007-2013, financed by the Irish Government under the National Development Plan 2007-2013, and administered on behalf of the Department of the Environment, Heritage and Local Government by the Environmental Protection Agency (EPA). The Consensus Project involves collaboration between the National University of Ireland Galway and Trinity College Dublin.

References

Adam, F., & Crossan, G. (2001). Teleworking in Ireland: Issues and Perspectives. In N. Johnson (Ed.), *Telecommuting and Virtual Offices: Issues and Opportunities* (pp. 28-49). Hershey, PA: Idea Group Publishing.

Anderson, J., Bricout, J. C., & West, M. D. (2001). Telecommuting: Meeting the Needs of Businesses and Employees with Disabilities. *Journal of Vocational Rehabilitation, 16*(2), 97-104.

Andrey, J., Burns, K. R., & Doherty, S. T. (2004). Toward Sustainable Transportation: Exploring Transportation Decision Making in Teleworking Households in a Mid-Sized Canadian City. *Canadian Journal of Urban Research, 13*(2), 257-277.

Andriessen, J. H. E., & Vartiainen, M. (2006). *Mobile Virtual Work: A New Paradigm?* Berlin: Springer Verlag.

Arnfalk, P. (2002). *Virtual Mobility and Pollution Prevention - The Emerging Role of ICT Based Communication in Organisations and its Impact on Travel*. Library at the IIIEE: Lund.

Atkyns, R., Blazek, M., & Roitz, J. (2002). Measurement of Environmental Impacts of Telework Adoption Amidst Change in Complex Organizations: AT&T Survey Methodology and Results. Resources, Conservation and Recycling, 36(3), 267-285. doi: 10.1016/S0921-3449(02)00082-4

Ayres, R. U. (2000). Commentary on the Utility of the Ecological Footprint Concept. *Ecological Economics, 32*(3), 347-349. doi: 10.1016/S0921-8009(99)00151-2

Barrett, J. (2001). Component Ecological Footprint: Developing Sustainable Scenarios. *Impact Assessment and Project Appraisal, 19*(2), 107-118. doi: 10.3152/147154601781767069

Brodt, T. L., & Verburg, R. M. (2007). Managing Mobile Work - Insights from European Practice. New Technology, Work and Employment, 22(1), 52-65. doi: 10.1111/j.1468-005X.2007.00183.x

Callanan, T. A. (1999). *New Ways of Living and Working: Teleworking in Ireland*. For: Department of Enterprise Trade and Employment, Report of the National Advisory Council on Teleworking. Dublin 2. Retrieved from http://www.djei.ie/publications/trade/2003/teleworking.pdf

Collins, A., Flynn, A., Wiedmann, T., & Barrett, J. (2006). The Environmental Impacts of Consumption at a Subnational Level: The Ecological Footprint of Cardiff. *Journal of Industrial Ecology, 10*(3), 9-24. doi: 10.1162/jiec.2006.10.3.9

CSO. (2003). *Quarterly National Household Survey: Module on Teleworking*. For: Central Statistics Office. Cork. Retrieved from http://www.stile.be/wp5/QNHS%20release%20 module%20on%20Teleworking.pdf

Devuyst, D., & Van Volsems, S. (2001). Sustainable Lifestyle Assessment. In D. Devuyst, L. Hens, & W. d. Lannoy (Eds.), *How Green is the City?: Sustainability Assessment and the Management of Urban Environments* (pp. 393-418). New York: Columbia University Press.

Drucker, P. F. (2000). Implementing the Effective Management of Knowledge Knowledge Worker Productivity: The Biggest Challenge. In J. W. Cortada & J. A. Woods (Eds.), *The Knowledge Management Yearbook 2000-2001* (pp. 267-283). Woburn: Butterworth-Heinemann.

Dwelly, T., & Lake, A. (2008). *Can Homeworking Save the Planet? How Homes can become Workspaces in a Low Carbon Economy*. London: The Smith Institute. Retrieved from http://www.flexibility.co.uk/downloads/Canhomeworkingsavetheplanet.pdf

e-Work Action Forum. (2003). *Report of the e-Work Action Forum 2002*. Dublin 2: Department of Enterprise Trade and Employment. Retrieved from http://www.djei.ie/publications/ enterprise/2000/e-work/index.htm

ECaTT. (2000). The ECaTT Project. Website: *Empirica*. Retrieved from http://www.ecatt.com/

Egan, B. (1997). *Feasibility and Cost Benefit Analysis*. Paper presented at the International Telework Association Annual International Conference, Crystal City, VA.

Europa. (2002). Teleworking. *Website: Summaries of EU legislation*. Retrieved from http:// europa.eu/legislation_summaries/employment_and_social_policy/employment_rights_ and_work_organisation/c10131_en.htm

European Commission. (2001). *Benchmarking Report Following-up the Strategies for Jobs in the Information Society*. Brussels: Commission of the European Communities. Retrieved from http://csdle.lex.unict.it/docs/labourweb/Benchmarking-Report-following-up-the-Strategies-for-jobs-in-the-Information-Society-/1541.aspx

Fiala, N. (2008). Measuring Sustainability: Why the Ecological Footprint is Bad Economics and Bad Environmental Science. *Ecological Economics, 67*(4), 519-525. doi: 10.1016/j. ecolecon.2008.07.023

Hesse, B. W. (1995). Curb Cuts in the Virtual Community: Telework and Persons with Disabilities. *Proceedings of the 28th Annual Hawaii International Conference on System Sciences, Hawaii* (pp. 418-425).

Hilbrecht, M., Shaw, S. M., Johnson, L. C., & Andrey, J. (2008). 'I'm Home for the Kids': Contradictory Implications for Work–Life Balance of Teleworking Mothers. *Gender, Work & Organization, 15*(5), 454-476. doi: 10.1111/j.1468-0432.2008.00413.x

Hopkinson, P., & James, P. (2003). *UK Report on National SUSTEL Fieldwork*. Bradford: Sustainable Telework.

Huws, U. (1991). Telework: Projections. *Futures, 23*(1), 19-31. doi: 10.1016/0016-3287(91)90003-K

Hynes, M. (forthcoming). *Telework Policy in Ireland* [Draft]. Forthcoming 2013.

Irish DoETE. (2001). *Address by Mr. Noel Treacy T.D.*, Minister for Science, Technology and Commerce at the Launch of Telework Ireland's Teleworking Manuals and the Relaunch of their Website in Buswell's Hotel on 25th May, 2000 at 12 p.m [Website]. Retrieved from http://www.djei.ie/press/2000/250500.htm

Irwin, F. (2004). *Gaining the Air Quality and Climate Benefit for Telework*. World Resources Institute. Retrieved from http://goo.gl/IvdkU

Kenyon, S., Lyons, G., & Rafferty, J. (2002). Transport and Social Exclusion: Investigating the Possibility of Promoting Inclusion through Virtual Mobility. *Journal of Transport Geography, 10*(3), 207-219. doi: 10.1016/S0966-6923(02)00012-1

Kitou, E., & Horvath, A. (2003). Energy-Related Emissions from Telework. *Environment Science Technology, 37*(16), 3467-3475. doi: 10.1021/es025849p

Kling, R., & Scacchi, W. (1982). The Web of Computing: Computer Technology as Social Organization. *Advances in Computers, 21*, 1-90. doi: 10.1016/S0065-2458(08)60567-7

Lake, A. (2009). Teleworking in Ireland; Slow but Typical Growth Patterns on the Edge of Europe. Blog Title: *Flexibility*. Retrieved from http://www.flexibility.co.uk/flexwork/location/Teleworking-Ireland.htm

Law, J., & Urry, J. (2004). Enacting the Social. *Economy and Society, 33*(3), 390-410. doi: 10.1080/0308514042000225716

Mokhtarian, P. L. (1990). A Typology of Relationships Between Telecommunications and Transportation. *Transportation Research Part A: General, 24*(3), 231-242. doi: 10.1016/0191-2607(90)90060-J

Mokhtarian, P. L. (1991). Telecommuting and Travel: State of the Practice, State of the Art. *Transportation, 18*(4), 319-342. Retrieved from http://link.springer.com/article/10.1007/BF00186563

Mokhtarian, P. L. (2002). Telecommunications and Travel: The Case for Complementarity. *Journal of Industrial Ecology, 6*(2), 43-57. doi: 10.1162/108819802763471771

Monfreda, C., Wackernagel, M., & Deumling, D. (2004). Establishing National Natural Capital Accounts Based on Detailed Ecological Footprint and Biological Capacity Assessments. *Land Use Policy, 21*(3), 231-246. doi: 10.1016/j.landusepol.2003.10.009

Moos, M., Andrey, J., & Johnson, L. C. (2006). The Sustainability of Telework: An Ecological-Footprinting Approach. *Sustainability: Science Practice and Policy, 2*(1), 3-14. Retrieved from http://sspp.proquest.com/static_content/vol2iss1/0511-020.moos.pdf

Nelson, P., Safirova, E., & Walls, M. (2007). Telecommuting and Environmental Policy: Lessons from the eCommute Program. *Transportation Research Part D: Transport and Environment, 12*(3), 195-207. doi: 10.1016/j.trd.2007.01.011

Pyöriä, P. (2011). Managing Telework: Risks, Fears and Rules. *Management Research News, 34*(4), 386-399. doi: 10.1108/01409171111117843

Rees, W. E., & Wackernagel, M. (1996). Urban Ecological Footprints: Why Cities Cannot be Sustainable – And Why They are a Key to Sustainability. Environmental Impact *Assessment Review, 16*(4-6), 223-248. doi: 10.1016/S0195-9255(96)00022-4

Revenue. (2001). eWorking and Tax - IT69. *Website: Revenue.* Retrieved from http://www.revenue.ie/en/tax/it/leaflets/it69.html

Shamir, B., & Salomon, I. (1985). Work-at-Home and the Quality of Working Life. *Academy of Management Review, 10*(3), 455-464.

SusTel. (2003). SUStainable TELework - Assessing and Optimising the Ecological and Social Benefits of Teleworking. *Website: SusTel.* Retrieved from http://www.ist-world.org/ProjectDetails.aspx?ProjectId=7bd1d8d1af094dcdb0573f9570fee636

Van Horn, C., & Storen, D. (2000). *Telework: Coming of age? Evaluating the Potential Benefits of Telework* (pp. 3-32). Washington, DC: US Department of Labor.

Wackernagel, M., Onisto, L., Bello, P., Callejas Linares, A., López Falfán, I. S., Méndez García, J., Suárez Guerrero, A. I., & Suárez Guerrero, M. G. (1999). National Natural Capital Accounting with the Ecological Footprint Concept. *Ecological Economics, 29*(3), 375-390.

Wackernagel, M., & Rees, W. E. (1996). *Our Ecological Footprint: Reducing Human Impact on the Earth.* Gabriola Island, BC: New Society Publishers.

Wackernagel, M., & Silemtein, J. (2000). Big Things First: Focusing on the Scale Imperative with the Ecological Footprint. *Ecological Economics, 32*(3), 391-394. doi: 10.1016/S0921-8009(99)00161-5

White, P., Christodoulou, G., Mackett, R., Titheridge, H., Thoreau, R., & Polak, J. (2010). The Impacts of Teleworking on Sustainability and Travel. In T. Manzi, K. Lucas, T. L. Jones, & J. Allen (Eds.), *Social Sustainability in Urban Areas: Communities, Connectivity and the Urban Fabric* (pp. 141-154). London: Earthscan Publications Ltd.

Winner, L. (1997). Technologies as Forms of Life. In K. Shrader-Frechette & L. Westra (Eds.), *Technology and Values* (pp. 55-70). Lanham, MD: Rowman & Littlefield Publishers, Inc.

WWF. (2009). *From Workplace to Anywhere: Assessing the Global Opportunities to Reduce Greenhouse Emmissions with Virtual Meetings and Telecommuting.* WWF Sweden: World Wildlife Fund. Retrieved from http://www.worldwildlife.org/who/media/press/2009/ WWFBinaryitem11939.pdf

13 Surveillance Privacy and Technology: Contemporary Irish Perspectives

Kenny Doyle[1]

Abstract

S urveillance is typically envisaged as the act of a person being physically watched, their movements and behaviour monitored in a given space and time. While this type of watching undoubtedly takes place, there is also the more subtle and pervasive monitoring of people through the data they accumulate in their daily lives. Contemporary Irish society is mediated by digital technology; the daily life of the typical person creates a mass of data which can offer many telling clues as to the type of life they lead. This form of surveillance is called dataveillance (Clarke, 1988). It is unclear however exactly how much citizens know about these practices and how they negotiate with and respond to surveillance systems. This study aimed -by conducting focused interviews with Irish citizens – to explore the levels of knowledge regarding surveillance and privacy and to ascertain the importance placed on these concepts. Using Harper's (2011) typology of subject positions, a further aim was to uncover any discursive repertoires used when defining or speaking about these concepts. It was found that widely used conceptions of privacy and surveillance are inadequate to describe contemporary reality; and that forms of sociality have changed with the widespread use of information and communication technologies (ICT).

Keywords: surveillance, technology, privacy, Ireland, dataveillance the internet, social networking, ICT.

---

1. Waterford Institute of Technology, Waterford, Ireland; kdoyle@wit.ie

How to cite this chapter: Doyle, K. (2013). Surveillance Privacy and Technology: Contemporary Irish Perspectives. In C. Fowley, C. English, & S. Thouësny (Eds.), *Internet Research, Theory, and Practice: Perspectives from Ireland* (pp. 245-273). Dublin: © Research-publishing.net.

1.   Introduction

The last three decades have been defined by technological change, particularly that of information and communications technology. In particular the advent of personal computing and the internet has freed up information and communications capabilities between most people of the developed world: "[w]ith little exaggeration, we may call the 21st century the age of networks" (Van Dijk, 2006, p. 2). Technologically enabled global networks have profoundly altered our lives in almost all areas including work, consumption, entertainment and learning. Zimmer (2008) tells us however that "the true relationship between a society and its technology is often not purely benevolent, but instead may require a sacrifice for society to enjoy its benefits" (p. 111). The sacrifice of the information age is most commonly held to be personal privacy; Scott McNealy, chairman of Sun Microsystems, famously stated in 1999 "you have zero privacy anyway, get over it" (cited in Manes, 2000, p. 312).

Since then the technologies and services of Web 2.0 such as social networking sites (SNS), enhanced search engine capabilities and the personalised internet have shown both Zimmer (2008) and McNealy (1999) to be correct. The question to be asked however is why is it that conceptions of privacy have changed so much within such a short space of time. Academic discussions of privacy have abounded since Warren and Brandeis (1890) wrote about the threat posed to privacy by the burgeoning newspaper industry. Yet the reality is that despite academic findings which consistently report that people are worried about losing privacy, technologies that arguably compromise it are increasingly popular. It is not just internet based technologies which can be seen to threaten privacy; as computing technology gets smaller and cheaper it becomes ubiquitous. A key element of this is the increase of digital technologies which are characterised by the fact that they leave information in their wake. In the workplace for example, electronic key cards can be configured so that each one has a unique signature, making it possible to know exactly when each person arrives to work, how often they pass through different doors, and even how much time they spend in the bathroom. This is but one example of data generating technologies which have become unremarkable aspects of contemporary life, yet allow for the constant surveillance of people as they go about their daily routine. This chapter aims to explore some of the reasons for the seemingly contradictory positions relating to surveillance privacy and technology by examining the discursive repertoires used to describe them.

1.1. Surveillance

Surveillance is defined in the Oxford English Dictionary (2012) as "close observation, especially of a suspected spy or criminal" (p. 734). This definition is typical of the embodied and ocular definition of surveillance; it describes the physical act of a person or group of people being watched by another person or group of people. A further element of note in this definition is the example of who would most likely be the focus of surveillance: 'a suspected spy or criminal'. In common parlance, surveillance is a value laden term with which there is an implicit association of wrongdoing. A person who is under surveillance is a person of interest to law enforcement, a person who is suspected of committing a crime in the past or future and is therefore a legitimate target to be watched. While this definition no doubt describes relatively common social practices, it is too narrow and only describes negative aspects. A mother watching her child at play, a lifeguard scanning the shoreline, a doctor monitoring a patient's heart rate or blood pressure are all further examples of surveillance which infer no element of wrongdoing, and instead would describe acts of caring. Yet even with these examples, a vast and ever increasing field of surveillance is still excluded; that of the monitoring of digital traces.

Contemporary Irish society is one which is increasingly mediated by digital technologies; for example in December 2011 the Central Statistics Office (CSO) reported that 78% of all Irish households had access to the internet, up from 57% in 2007 (CSO, 2011, p. 5). The take up of internet enabled smart phones is predicted to increase (Amárach Research, 2011) and the use of social networking is estimated at around 68% of the population (Comscore, 2011; Ipsos Mrbi, 2012). As well as telecommunications and the internet, there are also a number of other processes which are prevalent, such as loyalty points cards for shops and supermarkets, and credit and debit cards for undertaking financial transactions. The point of note with all of the above mentioned items is that they all generate data trails which can offer telling clues as to the kind of lives being lived by data subjects. This form of monitoring of digital remnants is referred to as dataveillance by Clarke (1988). Dataveillance – which is shorthand for data surveillance – is described as the "systematic monitoring of people's actions or communications through the application of information technology" (Clarke, 1988, p. 499).

While commonly held conceptions of surveillance most often relate to the physical watching of embodied individuals in space and time, dataveillance is concerned with recording the traces people leave behind as they go about their daily lives. The permeation of information and communications technology into almost all spheres of contemporary life means that people are constantly and unwittingly leaving digital markers in their wake. Whether it's through the use of mobile telephones, the internet, credit or debit cards, customer loyalty cards, or even simply driving on a public road past speed cameras, data is constantly being generated. This data is used by an array of state, corporate and commercial actors to identify, profile and classify whole populations. The reasons for doing this range from customer relations management, law enforcement, to consumer profiling for the purpose of direct marketing.

Bearing in mind the extension of meaning of the word surveillance to include actions of caring, and to include the process of dataveillance, a more apt definition would be that devised by Lyon (2007). He defines surveillance as "the focused systematic and routine attention to personal details for purposes of influence, management, protection or direction" (Lyon, 2007, p. 14) In this definition, 'personal details' refer to the observable actions just as much as the digital traces left behind, as well as the extension of the reasons for surveillance beyond the implicit suspicion definition offered above.

1.2.   The Panopticon

While the most common metaphor used in common parlance when talking about surveillance is Orwell's (1948) *Big Brother*; the ubiquitous metaphor in surveillance studies literature is the Panopticon. This was a model for a prison originally envisaged by Utilitarian philosopher Bentham (1787/1995) who saw his design as being not just a prison but an 'inspection house' which was

"applicable to any sort of establishment, in which persons of any description are to be kept under inspection; and in particular to penitentiary houses, prisons, houses of industry work houses, poor houses, lazerettos, manufactories, hospitals, mad houses and schools" (p. 29).

The idea for the Panopticon was elaborated in a series of letters written by Bentham in 1787. He saw it as being more than an efficient means of operating institutions and claimed that it could be used as part of a viable plan for widespread social and disciplinary reform. The defining aspect of the Panopticon is that of visibility; the circular building is designed with a central observation tower which every cell faces. The cells are backlit, which makes them and their occupants constantly visible to the inhabitant of the inspection tower. The key however is that the inspector is invisible to those in the cells and thus power is tied in with visibility. The gaze from the inspection tower is unverifiable and so the inmates must assume that they are under constant observation and behave according to the prescribed norms of the institution. Bentham (1787/1995) did not see this as being just a means of controlling inmates or maintaining order inside institutions. He saw it as being a "new mode of obtaining power over mind, in a quantity hitherto without example" (Bentham, 1787/1995, p. 30). This 'power over mind' would allow for effective rehabilitation of inmates and would act as a mode of re-socialisation, where errant ways of being could be corrected through constant surveillance, with the aim of keeping inmates close to prescribed norms of behaviour. The utility of the Panopticon design is that it takes into account the fact that it is impossible to constantly inspect all inmates, and in practice does not try to do so. Instead the purpose of the design is to make the inmates believe that they are under constant inspection and compel them to behave accordingly. The Panopticon is thus a machinery of power; in practice it is irrelevant whether or not the observation tower is occupied; what matters is that the inmates believe that it is occupied and behave accordingly.

"Hence the major effect of the Panopticon: to induce in the inmate a state of conscious and permanent visibility that assures the automatic functioning of power. So to arrange things that the surveillance is permanent in its effects, even if it is discontinuous in its action; that the perfection of power should tend to render its actual exercise unnecessary; [...] in short, that the inmates should be caught up in a power situation of which they are themselves the bearers" (Foucault, 1977, p. 201).

Foucault (1977) used the idea of the Panopticon to underpin his schematisation of the Disciplinary Society. Foucault (1977) saw the Panopticon as being emblematic of a new form of discipline, a new mode of exercising power which was productive rather than destructive. This new form of power created obedient subjects rather than simply obliterating the disobedient. Whereas older forms of discipline physically and brutally punished deviations from the rule in the form of public spectacles of power and violence, the aim of disciplinary power is to inculcate and to teach, so that the norms and rules become internalised thus creating useful, productive and law abiding citizens.

The Panopticon is a central metaphor in surveillance studies; technologies such as the video camera may have rendered the architectural design redundant; yet the underlying idea of imposing discipline through potentially constant yet unverifiable monitoring has endured. Poster (1996) extended the panoptic metaphor to include the capability of technology to facilitate the digital 'super-panopticon' and Lyon (1994) has described the 'electronic Panopticon'. The technological removal of spatial and temporal limitations allows for the spread of panopticism beyond the bricks and mortar of the inspection tower envisaged by Bentham (1787/1995). In its original guise, panoptic power was exercised by a central authority as a means of enforcing institutional norms. The main argument against the different forms of digital Panopticon is that there is no central authority which has the requisite power to rule over a dispersed, decentred and supra-national network such as the internet.

Mathieson (1997) noted the operation in concert with panoptic methods and practices of what he termed the Synopticon which he describes as
"a unique and enormously extensive system enabling the many to see and

contemplate the few so that the tendency for the few to see and supervise the many is contextualised by a highly significant counterpart" (p. 219).

It is through the contemplation of the many that the core processes of synopticism operate. Through the mass media it is possible to see the powerful, wealthy and successful few, whose stories and images are displayed as examples to be followed by the many. It is thus at the level of culture that success stories are disseminated; stars of entertainment, sport or any other form of public life are players in this form of display. The examples set by them, whether through following their success or mimicking their patterns of consumption, create another set of norms which operate in tandem with those set through panoptic methods. Whereas panoptic power is that which is hidden and unknowable, synopticism operates through displays which are offered as examples to be followed or avoided depending on the context. Where panopticism operates through coercion, or at least the threat of coercion, synopticism operates through seduction or inducement towards particular culturally desirable behaviour. In the panoptic sense the few watch the many in order to ensure compliance with, and to root out deviations from the norm. In the synoptic sense, the many watch the few in order to be acculturated and taught what the norms are. If the Panopticon relates to the invisible watching of power, then the Synopticon relates to the broadcasting of power. Through the mass media synoptic messages are displayed which show the viewers how they are expected to live, the norms they are expected to uphold, the goals they should aim for and the legitimate means available to them to achieve these goals.

By way of example, Andrejevic (2004) claimed that reality television programs acted "neatly as an advertisement for the benefits of submission to comprehensive surveillance" (p. 2). Reality Television shows such as *Big Brother* or *Survivor* operated according to two main principles: firstly that contestants were drawn from the public at large and secondly that fame and fortune were possible through the process of opening oneself up completely by being constantly on display. Surveillance is thus seen as a key facilitator of reality as it forces participants to be their true selves by making it difficult to maintain a false front. At the same time, such shows valued self disclosure and self expression above all else. Reality television programs synoptically normalised such a culture of self display as a means of attaining wealth and status, and in the process normalised systems of surveillance:

> "Pervasive surveillance is presented as one of the hip attributes of the contemporary world [...]. In this respect the reality trend aligns itself with the efforts of the proponents of the new economy to destigmatize surveillance and reposition it as a form of convenience" (Andrejevic, 2004, p. 105).

This repositioning of surveillance ties in with the advent of a widespread culture of display. The motivations and attitudes identified by Andrejevic (2004) while describing reality television have since diffused across society via social networking and other forms of networked communications. These motivations include the wish for users to be visible and available which may seem at first glance to be anathema to commonly held and traditional conceptions of privacy.

1.3. Privacy

To define privacy is a notoriously difficult task; the Oxford English Dictionary (2012) describes it as "a state in which one is not observed or disturbed by other people, the state of being free from public attention" (p. 572). This definition is overly individualistic and describes just one aspect of privacy, namely seclusion. In these terms privacy is essentially formulated as Warren and Brandeis's (1890) "right to be left alone" (p. 194). In this sense privacy can be seen in terms of opposition: it is a zero sum game where the individual is pitted against society at large and any claim to individual privacy is made against the claims of society such as security or efficiency. Here privacy would be lost as soon as one enters social relations, as the perfect state of privacy is isolation. In this sense privacy is also commonly described in terms of a spatial metaphor, where its violation is spoken of as an invasion. A more complete definition would include reference to privacy involving the ability to control to some degree the dissemination of information regarding one self. This element can be found in the definition of Westin (1967) who states that privacy is "the claim of individuals, groups, or institutions to determine for themselves when, how, and to what extent information about them is communicated to others" (p. 7).

In his study of the interaction order of social life, Goffman (1959) devised a scheme based around the dramaturgical metaphor. This scheme viewed social life in terms of performances, where people present themselves in particular ways depending on the situation. The dramaturgical metaphor was utilised when describing front and back areas. Front areas are those where a performance must be maintained such as in a restaurant: when waiting staff are in view of customers they must maintain the decorum, the manners and any other relevant behaviours associated with the performance of being a waiter. Back areas then describe the places where the staff are out of sight of the customers and so can drop the behaviours associated with the performance. In a wider sense, if social life is divided up into front and back areas, then to some degree almost all areas involve some element of performance which is determined by the situation and the roles associated with it. A Goffmanian perspective on privacy would determine the home as being an inviolable space where the performances of social life at large can be dropped, and the essential or true self can be revealed. Jenkins (2004) describes back areas as places where people can "be free of the anxieties of presentation, it is the domain of self image rather than public image" (p. 71). Privacy is the domain of self development, a place free from the necessities of maintaining public performances or faces, a place where one can be their true self. At the level of the individual, Westin (1967) claims that this ability to withdraw to the realm of the private facilitates reflective solitude, allowing for an organisation of the self which enables the individual to "integrate his experiences into a meaningful pattern and to exert his individuality on events" (cited in Steeves 2009, p. 198). This reflective solitude also allows for intellectual development and for the undertaking of complex tasks, free from the interruption of others, which benefits both the individual and society.

These definitions of privacy are focussed on how it affects individuals; a further strand of the concept is to be found if one looks at the social values and benefits of privacy. The need for a social perspective on privacy is succinctly stated by

Moore (1984) who claims that "the need for privacy is a socially created need, without society there would be no need for privacy" (p. 73). In the back areas mentioned above, not only is there a benefit accrued to individuals, but for similar reasons there are benefits for society as a whole. If individuals are given the space and time for personal development and self reflexivity, then society will benefit from being constituted by more rounded individuals. While Westin (1967) defined the fullest state of privacy in terms of withdrawal from sociality; Altman (1975) defined privacy as "a dynamic process involving selective control over a self-boundary" (p. 6). It is through the continued process of engagement and withdrawal from sociality that boundaries between people are maintained and social identities are created based on these boundaries and markers of difference. As well as privacy being a space for self creation and development which benefits society at large, it is also a space which fosters group solidarity. In the back areas mentioned above, there was mention of a true self free from the necessity of masks which are dictated by social roles. In this back space strong ties are formed and maintained, such as in the family unit where inhibitions can be lowered and confidences and intimacies earned and maintained.

Despite the benefits granted by privacy to individuals and society, there is growing credence given to the idea that increased transparency is both desirable and necessary. As we have seen above, the desirability of transparency has been strengthened by norms set synoptically by reality television and celebrity culture. The necessity for transparency however is often couched in terms of security, where the rationale for any new surveillance measure is most often to prevent crime: criminal 'others' commit crimes and so these people that are the intended targets of surveillance measures. Such measures should thus not concern those who abide by the law and have nothing to hide.

1.4.   Nothing to hide?

A recurring rebuttal to questions asked about surveillance is some variation of 'I've nothing to hide and therefore nothing to fear'. This rationale recurs across many strands of international research into surveillance (O'Hara & Shadbolt,

2008; Schneier, 2008; Solove, 2011). Schneier (2008) claims that this phrase is inaccurate because it fails to adequately account for the full definition of privacy, and sees it just as being about 'hiding a wrong' (p. 79). Privacy in these terms is seen as a screen behind which illegal or immoral deeds can be obscured. As we have seen above, privacy is much more nuanced and complicated and is irreducible to such narrow conceptualisation. Privacy is a socially constant yet culturally determined value; almost all cultures have some degree of privacy relating to the body which can differ significantly according to cultural or religious values. Nissenbaum (2010) and Zimmer (2008) describe privacy in terms of contextual integrity which claims that information is never reducible to a simple either/or public or private schema which is universally applicable. There are implicit and explicit norms associated with almost every social situation which "explain the boundaries of our underlying entitlements regarding personal information, [...] our privacy is invaded when these informational norms are contravened" (Zimmer, 2008, p. 115). Thus instead of keeping to a simplistic dyad of public/private, contextual integrity looks to the social context in which the information is requested and looks to see whether the request is appropriate for the situation.

Solove (2011) makes three points of reference in response to the "nothing to hide" argument: these are aggregation, exclusion and distortion. Aggregation describes how while one piece of innocuous data might be harmless and therefore not valued as private, an amalgamation of a multitude of these innocuous pieces of data can have a mosaic effect of creating a larger and more revealing picture of the person and their behaviour. With this in mind, it is conceivable that there is not really such a thing as innocuous or harmless data and it becomes harder to determine what information about oneself should be valued as private. Exclusion describes when the data controller excludes the data subject from accessing or challenging any data held about them. Distortion refers more generally to the images created in a mosaic fashion through aggregation of data and how such images will never be fully accurate and will only describe the elements of a personality that happen to be amenable to capture by these methods. These pieces of data are rarely contextualised and give a bald, one dimensional version of selfhood which is rarely accurate.

Aside from these concerns is the simpler questioning of institutions themselves. While institutions or organisations may be trustworthy and have strict data handling procedures, the institutions are comprised of people who may be dishonest, curious, unmotivated, corrupt or even simply inept. It is best summarised by O'Hara and Stevens (2006) who said in response to the 'nothing to hide nothing to fear' argument:

> "if you keep within the law, and the government keeps within the law, and its employees keep within the law, and the computer holding the database doesn't screw up, and the system is designed according to well-understood software engineering principles and maintained properly, [...] and all the data are entered carefully, and the police are adequately trained to use the system, and the system isn't hacked into, [... then] you have nothing to fear" (pp. 251-252).

The view that only people with something to hide should value privacy is one which is overly simplistic. As we have seen it is almost impossible to know which information should be classed as private without having it contextualised; in the days of pervasive data gathering, the mosaic effect as described by Solove (2011) shows how any piece of information can be potentially sensitive when it is combined with others. Moreover, for the reasons outlined above by O'Hara and Shadbolt (2008), institutions cannot always be trusted as they can be prone to leaking information. These facts render commonly held ideas about surveillance and privacy problematic; therefore, there is a need to explore the manner in which these concepts are understood and valued.

2.   Methods

Surveillance and privacy are topics that have been and will continue to be widely researched across a range of disciplines. The most wide reaching research is the Globalisation of Personal Data (GPD) Project International Survey on Privacy and Surveillance[1] conducted in 2006/2007 at Queens

---

1. Retrieved from https://qspace.library.queensu.ca/bitstream/1974/7659/23/GPD_Survey_Methdology_2011-11-13.pdf

University Toronto. In the European context, Eurobarometer polls are conducted across the member states of the European Union every 5 years with a sample of 27,000 respondents; these polls include questions on privacy, data protection and surveillance. Both the GPD survey and the Eurobarometer polls are conducted via the telephone, using quantitative methodologies. As these polls provide ready made and extensive data sets, there was little reason to conduct further quantitative research in this area. The knowledge gap instead pointed to the need for qualitative research that would explore the reasons behind the trends identified in both data sets. With this in mind, the interview topic guide was drawn up with close reference to the questions asked in both the GPD and Eurobarometer surveys.

2.1. Context and participants

This study was conducted between September 2010 and April 2011. The aim of the study was to ascertain the knowledge levels of Irish citizens with regard to digital surveillance and its effect on privacy, to understand how these concepts are defined, and how people interact with these systems by aiming to uncover any discursive repertoires used. A further aim was to explore how practices of surveillance are instituted in differing social situations such as contemporary work, consumption and law enforcement. The study aimed to get a bottom up view of surveillance by investigating the lived experience of those who are subjected to it. In order to get such data from interview subjects, it is preferable to allow them to speak in their own words. The information garnered from quantitative research projects, while useful, is not capable of capturing the requisite nuances, subtleties of meaning and underlying motivations. Therefore, the qualitative interview was the method employed in this study. The open ended nature of qualitative questioning allows for the expression of the participants' understanding, knowledge, experience and values in a meaningful way. Bryman (2008) notes how semi-structured or flexible interview techniques are effective in comparison to structured interviews:

> "after all, if a structured method of data collection is employed, since this is bound to be the product of an investigator's ruminations about the object of enquiry, certain decisions must have been made about what he

or she expects to find and about the nature of the social reality that would be encountered" (p. 389).

It was hoped that the flexible semi-structured format would open up the field of enquiry beyond the research design envisaged. In this format, participants generated areas of interest not foreseen by the researcher and were able to express the elements of the field which were of importance to them and thus worthy of further questioning. With each participant, the location of the interview was designated as a place of their choosing, either in the participants' home or in a neutral location such as a hotel, coffee shop or pub. The only stipulation was that the location be quiet enough to allow for the recording of decipherable audio. The style of the interview was determinedly informal, every effort being made to make the subjects at ease and comfortable. The interview followed a semi-structured template, with a list of topics and questions to be covered but the order in which they were discussed determined by the flow of the conversation. While this structure allowed for a conversational style which put respondents at ease, having a set list of themes, topics and questions made it easier to compare the answers of different respondents and to thematically categorise and analyse them at a later stage.

The sample consisted of fifteen people, each of whom took part in an interview which lasted between sixty and ninety minutes. Of the fifteen people interviewed, seven were male and eight were female, with a mean age of thirty. The youngest respondent was nineteen years old, and the oldest was forty-six. As per the instructions of the ethics committee of Waterford Institute of Technology, there were no respondents under the age of eighteen. There were varied methods of recruitment; the first phase involved simple word of mouth where acquaintances and friends were asked to nominate people known to them but not to the researcher, this yielded a total of five interviews. At each interview respondents were asked if they would nominate any other people, this method of snowballing yielded a further four interviews. At this point the age profile was in the high thirties and a concerted effort was made to find participants between the ages of eighteen and twenty-five. The remaining six respondents were recruited through a group page set up on *Facebook* which outlined the details of the project and asked for interested people to get in touch. This method allowed for a greater geographical spread with interviewees from a broader range of locations in Ireland. The use of social networking as a tool of recruitment allowed for the targeting of people within a specific age range; however, it only allowed for people who used social networking sites to take part, which meant that the eighteen to twenty-five year old demographic who do not use social networking sites was not represented.

2.2. Vignettes

There can be a problem of definition when asking questions about topics such as surveillance and privacy. Surveillance and privacy are both value laden terms which have an inbuilt set of assumptions; these include the assumption that surveillance is bad, authoritarian and intrusive and the assumption that privacy is good and must always be protected at all costs. Such variance of meaning does not always allow to determine which sense of the word the interviewee is using. A means of addressing these problems was through the use of content specific vignettes: this method involved the construction of brief third person narratives as examples of the concepts in question. In drawing up the vignettes to be used, a number of factors had to be considered. Stories must be believable, describe everyday situations, and avoid exceptional situations, circumstances or characters. In using content specific vignettes, the aim was to describe mundane, believable and relatable situations and characters (Barter & Renold, 1999; Finch, 1987; Veal, 2002). A further element of consideration was the length and complexity of the vignette; Finch (1987) claims that more than three changes to a storyline in a vignette will render it too complex and difficult for respondents to remember (p. 107). The vignettes used were thus short, concise and to the point: there were scarce details given which would influence or lead the respondent. An example of one vignette was:

> *Ann shops regularly in the same supermarket, she recently accepted a loyalty points card which she presents at the till each time she is shopping. By using the card she gets a discount on her purchases, in return for this the supermarket gets a detailed list of her preferences*

and they can compile a profile of their customers. This information is used by the supermarket to tailor special offers and discounts to Ann.

After the vignette was read, the respondents' opinion was sought about potential issues raised by asking an open question such as "what do you think about this?" Thus vignettes offered an applied real world example of the concept in question, while the use of a third person narrative gave the respondents a level of distance which could potentially allow for more honest answers. At the point of analysis, the vignettes also offered an opportunity to explore the differences between self declaration and third person declaration.

3.   Results and discussion

3.1.   Defining terms

During the interviews respondents were asked early on to define both surveillance and privacy. Overall the definitions of surveillance matched the embodied ocular definition as typified by the dictionary definition given above. The most commonly mentioned form of surveillance was CCTV; yet when they were gently pushed towards talking about data trails, all respondents knew something and were able to speak at length. Most respondents also defined surveillance in negative terms, as being the exercise of malevolent power which was imposed on people, yet others mentioned situations where surveillance operated in their favour. One person noted how financial institutions monitor transactions so as to minimise the occurrence of fraud:

> **Mark:** I know like that the bank like would kinda use transaction history... I mean I was on holiday before and they'd actually like you'd get a phone call because you're in a foreign country spending... because they don't know whether it's you or not and the history might suggest that you're not going to be abroad spending that kind of money... so they are kind of I suppose they are keeping an eye on you really.

An addition to Lyon's (2007) definition of surveillance was given by Peter, aged 45, who was quite knowledgeable about elements of internet monitoring yet weighed these factors up against the convenience offered by the technology, "at the end of the day it makes life easier". This same logic of convenience was also applied to internet shopping for groceries,

> **Peter:** I know they keep all of your details like a record of what you eat and stuff but ya know like it's better than being stuck in a supermarket on your day off with lots of screaming kids.

So despite Peter being quite knowledgeable about consumer profiling, the short term benefit of convenience outweighed the more abstract and merely potential costs of surveillance and profiling. Lester (2001) talks about the "tyranny of convenience" which describes how "consumers are compelled to go online for an increasing array of transactions" (p. 28, cited in Andrejevic, 2002, p. 238). The methods of compelling consumers online are usually based on considerations of cost efficiency or convenience, so in Peter's case it was the convenience of being able to shop quickly from home that informed his choice. A further example of incentivised migration to online service can be seen in banking, where customers are offered reduced transaction fees on the condition that they activate and use an internet banking service. A further question asked if respondents would be happy to give up personal details or elements of their privacy for financial gain and almost all replied in the negative. Interestingly however, one of the vignettes described a situation involving a supermarket customer loyalty card and many of those who answered in the negative actually used these cards.

In defining privacy the majority of respondents mentioned both the spatial metaphor and Westin's (1967) notion of controlling information flows regarding themselves (p. 7). In discussing the control of personal data flows, there were common references made to particular privileged data such as financial details and health records. Privacy was thus described as a bulwark against identity theft which is believed to be prevalent although no respondent knew personally of any instances of its occurrence. The spatial metaphor was commonly described in terms of the home being a privileged space which falls under the control of its occupants. The socially contextual nature of privacy was also often mentioned:

> **Hannah:** I think people have different levels of privacy, some people find stuff that maybe that I would have no bother sharing with people.

This quote illustrates the variation of privacy expectations; as noted above, the popular distinction between private and public is oversimplified. What is seen as private will depend upon a multitude of factors such as culture, personal opinion or social context. The contextual nature of privacy as previously described by Nissenbaum (2010) and Zimmer (2008) is not just dependent on the situation; Hannah defines privacy as a subjective value which also differs according to who is making the claim.

All respondents believed that we now have less privacy than we did in the past, and all bar one blamed technologically mediated communication for this.

> **Sean:** It's very obvious that we have less because we're depending on much more artificial means of communication as well, we're not communicating as much face to face as we were you know.

Only one respondent spoke of privacy as being socially beneficial, all other definitions spoke of it in terms of an individual good. The social benefit mentioned was that privacy allowed for and even fostered creativity, in response to the question what would you think would happen if privacy was completely lost this interviewee said:

> **Rory:** Em I think you would get a society that would totally lack creativity, it would totally lack any form of innovation in themselves because I think that no matter what they do, what they create any idea they have is gonna be taken, taken from them, ...I think it comes down to every sort of innovation or any sort of creativity that people have or any sort of idea it would just totally stifle creativity and progress.

Rory equates privacy with creativity which is a sentiment seen above in Westin's (1967) concept of reflective solitude, which allows people the space to experiment and try new ways of doing things free from the view of others. Reflective solitude allows for intellectual development and for the undertaking of complex tasks free from interruption. Innovation and creativity are thus coupled with privacy in the form of reflective solitude. The strict monitoring of tasks leads to employees matching their work to the standards they believe to be expected of them in what Zuboff (1988) calls 'anticipatory conformity'. This is similar to the exercise of panoptic supervision, where workers act as if the eyes of their supervisors are on them at all times and behave in a manner which they anticipate will conform to their expectations. This leads to risk averse behaviour where employees will not act outside of given guidelines and this "would severely curtail creative thinking, as employees would begin to act and then think in response to an unseen observer" (Martin & Freeman, 2003, p. 356).

3.2. Discursive repertoires

Harper (2011) denotes three broad subject positions when speaking about surveillance: the suspicious position, the indifferent position, and the position of balancing (p. 2). All three of these repertoires among others were evident during the interviews. The suspicious subject position is often correlated to discourses of paranoia, "this term appears to be deployed to undermine the legitimacy of a suspicious position as we see when more suspicious narratives are denoted as conspiracy theories" (Harper, 2011, p. 2). Thus when respondents characterised themselves as suspicious of surveillance they often felt the need to distance themselves from being perceived as being paranoid or from being believers of conspiracy theories. This was evident for example when Anna a 27 year old said:

> **Anna:** We are a technological society, all that information, I don't think you're even aware of how much your information goes you know you join all these different sites and God knows who knows what, and there could be some big guy in this big building just you know accumulating it all into graphs, to make a few bob you know, although that's a bit of a conspiracy theory I try not to go there (laughs).

There are a number of interesting points in this section; firstly Anna is describing the process of information capitalism (Wall, 2006, p. 340), where personal data is garnered, warehoused, interrogated and ultimately mined for the purposes of extracting useful information for sales and marketing. The internet adage originally espoused by the blogger Andrew Lewis (2010): "if something is for free then you are the product" applies here; many free services online require some level of registration. As the registered service is used, it generates saleable data pertaining to the user. In social media for example, a user is required to register. As the site is used, all information is stored, aggregated and offered in some form to sales and marketing professionals. And yet, describing the process makes Anna feel overly paranoid, and makes her partially recant by saying "that's a bit of a conspiracy theory I try not to go there". Harper (2011) refers to this type of action as 'rhetorical inoculation' where the expression of views which could be labelled as paranoid is followed by laughter, joking or some method of semantic distantiation (p. 11). Another interesting point here is the anthropomorphosis of the process; in this description, it is not a computer program but "a big guy in a big building". In the same interview, Anna talks about shopping on line and mentions how she particularly loves Amazon because "they get me". This humanising of technology also came up in other interviews, in particular when talking about privacy. A number of interviewees only had a problem with dataveillance if they thought that a person at the other end was reading the content, and had no problem with the process when it was carried out automatically by a computer program or algorithm.

A further position which is related to suspicion is function creep or the slippery slope argument; this subject position states that if we allow surveillance for one reason, it will inevitably be used for many others and so the allowances made for what Agamben (2005) calls 'the state of exception' should be minimal. A central point is an ingrained cynicism, a belief that governments and state actors will opportunistically prey on public fears such as terrorism or organised crime and use them to institute surveillance measures which will increase their power at the cost of the citizenry. This argument was put forward on a number of occasions,

Richard: I mean once the terrorism thing runs out there's going to be just one thing after another it's a slippery slope you start there and it's just, I wouldn't be in favour of anything like that, (pause) I mean there's no evidence there that it works.

Respondents were asked if they would be prepared to give up some of their personal data to the authorities if they were told it could make the country safer and it often led to similar answers:

Pat: I would not believe their explanation quite simply I would, I would expect to see a lot of statistics proof and studies done that me handing, eh essentially signing away some of my privacy would actually be effective in what they claim they're trying to do I would not take their word for it.

The third and final subject position of Harper's (2011) typology is the balancing or trading off position. Sets of given dualisms, for example liberty/security, surveillance/privacy, ideally need to be balanced so as to get the best of both, such as allowing the most liberty without sacrificing security. This metaphor of balance is most commonly used in public and political discourse, and implies a certain level of rationality and reason in its proponents. People who 'balance' see themselves as active and having control over their data and privacy. This was typified by Darren:

Darren: In order to get some things done you have to give up a little bit of your privacy, give away a bit of your privacy, for your own selfish kind of goals, for you to buy something or to get something you have to kind of deliver to them your bit of information, so it's a two way thing really. If you want to be paranoid and kind of worry too much about your privacy then you're not gonna get anything yourself.

Here the onus is on the individual; at a later stage in the interview, when talking about privacy, Darren states that even online, other people only have as much access to his details as he allows – in a definition which has echoes of self-governance and the responsibilisation element of the Risk Society thesis proffered by Beck (1992) and Ericson and Haggerty (1997). In the sense of his self identity as a rational consumer, each instance of accepting a service or product is in his mind a choice, a weighing up of costs versus benefits which he should be able to assess accurately. Darren's statement is similar to what Zimmer (2008) describes as the "faustian bargain of technology" (p. 111) where benefits of technological advances must be tempered with the fact that these benefits come at a price, as Darren states "it's a two way thing". The problem with this however is that of information and power asymmetry. It is highly unlikely that in all instances of data gathering, Darren knows that it's happening, the identity of the person or organisation gathering the data, or the ultimate destination of this data. In this case it is not possible to strike a meaningful balance or make a truly informed decision.

A smaller number of respondents were quite indifferent to surveillance and saw it as something which worked in their favour. In these cases, there was common recourse to the phrase "I've got nothing to hide" (see above) and increasing levels of transparency were seen as positive and desirable aspects of modern life which could be used to hold others to account. Patrick noted how he actively sought a GPS tracker on his van from his employers so he could prove he was working at all times.

> **Patrick:** I had a phone alright but they couldn't keep track, I remember eh because they wouldn't give me overtime because they said drivers don't get overtime because they said some drivers used to pull in by the side of the road apparently and they assumed that all drivers would be guilty of that so any overtime they wouldn't pay it… So I kind of suggested you know look if you want to put something on the van you know like a GPS tracker or something like that so you know I'm not pulling in by the side of the road you know, I want my extra eh wages you know.

Surveillance is used for Patrick to claim his entitlements, to prove he was operating within the terms of his employment and to hold his employers to account. Not being monitored had in this case tangible disadvantages for him. This position was echoed by Hannah who worked in a call centre where all calls are recorded; every week a call is picked at random and reviewed by her manager. Instead of feeling constantly under potential supervision and feeling in a panoptical sense the need for self correction, Hannah spoke of how she found it reassuring to know that if a dispute ever arose, she would have a recording to fall back on and as such welcomed the recording of her working life.

The phrase 'I've nothing to hide' recurred across the interviews with such frequency as to warrant calling it a default position. While this view has been explored in detail above, it is worthwhile to further examine the ramifications of such a widely held belief. This common retort has been used to counter arguments against a number of surveillance technologies, from identity cards and CCTV systems to DNA databases among a multitude of others. This view – which is approaching the status of hegemony – clearly benefits those who have the most to gain from surveillance, such as the large bureaucracies of the state and the private sector. The hegemony of a view which benefits powerful interests raises interesting questions: how has such widespread diffusion of this view been achieved? How has this view been inculcated and internalised by so many people? This view creates a dualism in common consciousness between 'us' who obey the law and thus have 'nothing to fear', and 'them', drawn from the class of the criminal 'other' who stand to lose from whatever surveillance measure is in question. By creating such a positive collective identity, proponents of surveillance assure its social desirability and thus mass adherence. Furthermore, this belief inoculates proponents of surveillance against any discussion about the necessity or validity of any surveillance measure. When surveillance is characterised as targeting only those with something to hide, by extension the same characterisation is applied to those who reject surveillance measures. Thus there are positive associations with compliance, and negative associations with resistance.

In the course of the interviews, a common thread was the use of social networking. In a number of cases, interviewees spoke in terms of their pages being not just a means of communicating with friends but a means of broadcasting. Patrick explained how he used his *Facebook* page as a means of telling jokes which he posted everyday in his status updates. These jokes were often ridiculous retellings or parodies of current events into which he put a lot of time and effort, actively courting an audience. Sean is active in Irish politics, and when he was asked how he uses privacy settings on social networking sites he said:

> **Sean:** Most of what I say is for public consumption, I don't use my facebook to keep in touch with my family, or friends either, I have a lot of my friends that are on it but anything that's on it is of a political nature and is generally for public consumption and I want people to see it, I use facebook as a propaganda tool for my work you know, it's not eh even though I set it to private there's over a thousand people who are on it most of whom I wouldn't know.

These two instances show social networking not as being a method of two way communication like a telephone, but instead being a means of broadcasting, a means of display which allows users to claim particular identities such as in these two cases the humorist and the social commentator. Other respondents noted that they used social networking to display cultural or consumptive preferences in order to bond with others of similar interests, in what Castells (2001) refers to as "networked individualism" (p. 129). Using the internet and particularly social networking sites as material supports for networked individualism, respondents build what Castells (2001) calls "portfolios of sociability" (p. 132) where multiple but weaker ties are created and maintained, centred around choices of lifestyle, consumer, or cultural preferences. These ties often correlate to offline networks - online communication and sociability is matched in the 'real' world. Yet there was significant mention of sociability in the "space of flows" (Castells, 1996, p. 408) where communication is global, technologically mediated and spatial differences are compressed to nothing. Peter, 45 year old and heavy user of the internet in this manner states:

> **Peter:** We live more separately, but we don't, you know, we live more separately to our next door neighbour, but we live closer to the guy across the world.

The usage of electronically mediated communication raises interesting questions regarding the nature of contemporary community. It is not just the case that we use globally interconnected digital networks to communicate free from the constraints of geographical location with people from all over the world. Locally based peer groups use technologically mediated means of communicating, even when there is no significant geographical divide. As we have seen above such means of communication leave behind records which are valuable commodities. Local communities thus become monitored and mediated by numerous third parties such as social networking sites as they go about the routine process of communicating amongst themselves. Conversations which once would have taken place over the garden fence now occur across digital networks, which make them amenable to capture, as a valuable resource.

4.   Conclusion

One of the more striking findings of this study is the changing nature of privacy which is best exemplified by Bauman (2010):

> "In our days, it is not so much the possibility of betrayal or violation of privacy that frightens us but in fact it's the opposite: shutting down the exits from the private world, turning the private domain into a site of incarceration, a solitary confinement cell" (p. 31).

Bauman (2010) characterises privacy as having changed, from being a valued inviolable space within which personal development and thought can occur free from the eyes of the world, to being a prison which prevents people from being seen or being on display. This change could be seen as a reversion of meaning to the Latin etymological roots of the word 'privare' which meant to deprive "as the connotation of privacy for classical thinkers was very much to do with deprivation rather than voluntary withdrawal" (O'Hara & Shadbolt, 2008, p. 21). Privacy in this sense was the domestic realm, where very little happened, as opposed to public realm of the polis where all governance, trade, commerce and public discussion occurred. Networked communications in general and social networking sites in particular bring the outside world of the polis directly into the domestic realm, blurring the boundaries between the two. In another article Bauman (2010) rewrites Descartes proof of existing 'I think therefore I am' to "I am seen, therefore I am" (p. 20). As shown above, users of social media often see it as being more than a means of direct communication; it is used as a means of presentation management, where identities are constructed, presented and maintained. The assertion of such identities is carried out through online displays, and their validation occurs through interaction or feedback from viewers. As has been shown above, this culture of display has been synoptically normalised through the mass media in general and reality television in particular. This synoptic normalisation has had the dual effect of increasing the social desirability of being on display via social networking sites, and of minimising apprehensions around the loss of privacy and concerns over surveillance. The social desirability of being on display is further compounded by a common feeling that surveillance measures are aimed at those who have 'something to hide' and so by extension, transparency is aligned with the law abiding. To resist or dissent against surveillance, and to stake a wider claim for privacy has negative connotations. These two parallel processes can partially explain the seeming paradox between notions of privacy and the prevailing trends of networked communication. Moreover, these processes serve to explain exactly why there is seemingly a general indifference towards surveillance and the ever increasing colonisation of the private sphere by digital enterprises.

As communication is becoming technologically mediated; there are questions about levels of surveillance built into these networks which are privately owned, for profit enterprises. These virtual, mediated public spaces make a permanent record of interactions, consumer preferences, political beliefs and opinions. These records are valuable commodities that are packaged and sold across the global marketplace. Thus it can be claimed that this process commodifies social interaction which is becoming more routine with the ever increasing popularity of electronically mediated communication. While there is an elementary level of knowledge regarding the potential for surveillance and the threats to privacy built in to contemporary technologies; this knowledge is tempered by the broader cultural processes which have normalised practices of transparency and display.

References

Agamben, G. (2005). *State of Exception* (Translated by Kevin Attell). Chicago: The University of Chicago Press.

Altman, I. (1975). *The Environment and Social Behaviour: privacy, personal space, territory, crowding*. Monteray, CA: Brooks/Cole.

Amárach Research. (2011). *The Smart Future: An Amárach Briefing May 2011*. Retrieved from http://www.amarach.com/assets/files/The%20Smart%20Future.pdf

Andrejevic, M. (2002). The Work of Being Watched: Interactive Media and the Exploitation of Self-Disclosure. *Critical Studies in Media Communication, 19*(2), 230-248. doi: 10.1080/07393180216561

Andrejevic, M. (2004). *Reality TV: The Work of Being Watched*. New York: Rowman & Littlefield Publishers.

Barter, C., & Renold, E. (1999). The Use of Vignettes in Qualitative Research. *Social Research Update, 25*(2). Retrieved from http://sru.soc.surrey.ac.uk/SRU25.html

Bauman, Z. (2010). *44 Letters from the Liquid Modern World*. Cambridge: Polity.

Beck, U. (1992). *Risk Society: Towards a New Modernity*. London: Sage Publications.

Bentham, J. (1787/1995). *The Panopticon Writings* (Edited and introduced by Miran Božovič). Ann Arbor: Verso.

Bryman, A. (2008). *Social Research Methods* (4th ed.). Oxford: Oxford University Press.

Castells, M. (2001). *The Internet Galaxy: Reflections on the Internet, Business, and Society*. Oxford: Oxford University Press.

Castells, M. (1996). *The Information Age: Economy, Society, and Culture* (Volume 1). The Rise of the Network Society. Sussex: Wiley-Blackwell Publishers.

Clarke, R. A. (1988). Information Technology and Dataveillance. *Communications of the ACM, 31*(5), 498-512. Retrieved from www.cse.unsw.edu.au/~se4921/PDF/CACM/p498-clarke.pdf

Comscore. (2011). *The 2010 Digital Year in Review*. Retrieved from www.comscore.com/Press_Events/Presentations_Whitepapers/2011/2010_Europe_Digital_Year_in_Review

CSO. (2011). *Information Society and Telecommunications in Households 2009-2011*. Retrieved from www.cso.ie/en/media/csoie/releasespublications/documents/informationtech/2011/isth2009-2011.pdf

Ericson, R. V., & Haggerty, K. D. (1997). *Policing the Risk Society*. Toronto: University of Toronto Press.

Finch, J. (1987). The Vignette Technique in Survey Research. *Sociology, 21*(1), 105-114. doi: 10.1177/0038038587021001008

Foucault. M. (1977). *Discipline & Punish: The Birth of the Prison* (2nd ed.). Knopf Doubleday Publishing Group.

Goffman, E. (1959). *The Presentation of Self in Everyday Life*. Edinburgh: University of Edinburgh.

Harper, D. (2011). Paranoia and Public Responses to Cyber Surveillance. *Paper Presented at Cyber-Surveillance in Everyday Life May 2011 University of Toronto Canada*. Retrieved from http://www.digitallymediatedsurveillance.ca/wp-content/uploads/2011/04/Harper-Paranoia-and-public-responses.pdf

Ipsos MRBI. (2012). *Social Networking Quarterly Survey May 2012*. Retrieved from www.Ipsosmrbi.ie/social-networking-quarterly-survey-may-12.html

Jenkins, R. (2004). *Social Identity*. New York: Routledge.

Lester. T. (2001). The reinvention of Privacy. The Atlantic Monthly, 287(3), 27-39.

Lewis, A. (2010, August 26). *User-driven discontent* [Web log post]. Retrieved from www.metafilter.com/95152/Userdriven-discontent

Lyon, D. (1994). *The Electronic Eye: The Rise of Surveillance Society*. Cambridge: Polity Press.

Lyon, D. (2007). *Surveillance Studies: An Overview*. Cambridge: Polity Press.

Manes, S. (2000). Private Lives? Not Ours! *PC World, 18*(6), p. 312. Retrieved from http://www.pcworld.com/article/16331/article.html

Martin, K., & Freeman, R. E. (2003). Some Problems With Employee Monitoring. *Journal of Business Ethics, 43*(4), 353-361. doi: 10.1023/A:1023014112461

Mathieson, T. (1997). The Viewer Society: Michel Foucault's 'Panopticon' Revisited. *Theoretical Criminology, 1*(2), 215-234. doi: 10.1177/1362480697001002003

McNealy, S. (1999). Presentation at an event launching Sun Microsystems's Jini technology.

Moore, B. (1984). *Privacy: Studies in Social and Cultural History*. Armonk: M.E. Sharp.

Nissenbaum, H. (2010). *Privacy in Context Technology, Policy and the Integrity of Social Life*. Standford: Stanford University Press.

O'Hara, K., & Shadbolt, N. (2008). *The Spy in the Coffee Machine: The End of Privacy as We Know it*. Oxford: Oneworld Publications.

O'Hara, K., & Stevens, D. (2006). *Inequality.com: Power, Poverty and the Digital Divide*. Oxford: Oneworld Publications.

Orwell, G. (1948). *Nineteen Eighty-Four*. Retrieved from http://gutenberg.net.au/ebooks01/0100021.txt

Oxford English Dictionary. (2012). 7th edition. Oxford, England: Oxford University Press.

Poster, M. (1996). Databases as Discourse; or, Electronic Interpellations. In D. Lyon & E. Zureik (Eds.), *Computers Surveillance and Privacy* (pp. 175-192). Minneapolis: University of Minnesota Press.

Schneier, B. (2008). *Schneier on Security*. Indianapolis: Wiley Publishing.

Solove, D. J. (2011). *Nothing to Hide: The False Tradeoff Between Privacy and Security*. London: Yale University Press.

Steeves, V. (2009). Reclaiming the Social Value of Privacy. In I. Kerr, V. Steeves, & C. Lucock (Eds.), *Lessons from the Identity Trail: Anonymity, Privacy and Identity in a Networked Society* (pp. 191-208). Oxford: Oxford University Press.

Van Dijk, J. (2006). *The Network Society* (2nd ed.). Thousand Oaks, CA: Sage Publications.

Veal, W. R. (2002). Content Specific Vignettes as Tools for Research and Teaching. *Electronic Journal of Science Education, 6*(4). Retrieved from http://ejse.southwestern.edu/article/view/7687/5454

Wall, D. S. (2006). Surveillant Internet Technologies and the Growth in Information Capitalism: Spams and Public Trust in the Information Society. In K. D. Haggerty & R. V. Ericson (Eds.), *The New Politics of Surveillance and Visibility* (pp. 340-362). Toronto: University of Toronto Press.

Warren, S., & Brandeis, L. D. (1890). The Right to Privacy. *Harvard Law Review, 4*(5), 193-220. Retrieved from http://faculty.uml.edu/sgallagher/Brandeisprivacy.htm

Westin, A. F. (1967). *Privacy and Freedom*. New York: Atheneum.

Zimmer, M. (2008). Privacy on Planet Google: Using the Theory of "Contextual Integrity" to Clarify the Privacy Threats of Google's Quest for the Perfect Search Engine. *Journal of Business Technology and Law, 3*(1), 109-126. Retrieved from http://digitalcommons.law.umaryland.edu/cgi/viewcontent.cgi?article=1094&context=jbtl

Zuboff, S. (1988). *In the Age of the Smart Machine: The Future of Work and Power*. New York: Basic Books.

Section 3.

Research and Reflections on Educational Practices

14 Digital Divide in Post-Primary Schools

Ann Marcus-Quinn[1] and Oliver McGarr[2]

Abstract

This research study developed curricular specific open educational resources (OERs) for the teaching of poetry at Junior Certificate level in Irish post-primary schools. It aimed to capture the collaborative design and development process used in the development of the digital resources and describe and evaluate the implementation of the resources by teachers in different educational contexts. The research employed a case study approach as it was seen as the most suitable methodological approach to capture the richness of the design and implementation of the resource, which was developed in collaboration with six practicing teachers and implemented in three different schools with various classroom settings. Through the use of semi-structured teachers interviews, student questionnaires and classroom observations the research methodology employed aimed to capture the richness of the experience from the participants' perspective. The study found that the resource was adopted in very different ways across the participating schools. The study raises questions about the use of digital resources in schools and the possible emergence of a second digital divide, which is not defined by access to technology as was previously the case, but defined by the use of the technology and the extent to which it is used in a constructive and meaningful way to enhance the students learning experience.

Keywords: open educational resources, poetry, second digital divide.

1. National Digital Learning Resources Service, University of Limerick, Limerick, Ireland; ann.marcus.quinn@ul.ie

2. Department of Education and Professional Studies, University of Limerick, Limerick, Ireland; oliver.mcgarr@ul.ie

How to cite this chapter: Marcus-Quinn, A., & McGarr, O. (2013). Digital Divide in Post-Primary Schools. In C. Fowley, C. English, & S. Thouësny (Eds.), *Internet Research, Theory, and Practice: Perspectives from Ireland* (pp. 277-303). Dublin: © Research-publishing.net.

1.   Introduction

"Today's explosion in media technologies has brought new literacies into being [...] even if our schools have been one of the last places to recognise this" (Goodman, 2003, p. 1).

While the degree to which information and communication technologies (ICT) will impact on education is unknown, the development of ICT is having a profound impact on modern life. In a relatively short period of time the rapid development of ICT has radically changed our methods of communicating and accessing information. This diffusion of technology into all aspects of society has seen the emergence of what is commonly referred to as the information age, and while it is difficult to predict the long-term impact of this rapidly evolving technology, it is evident that the emergence of the information society brings with it the need for new skills and competencies not previously considered a priority in state schooling. Key skills in the information age are associated with the access, manipulation and application of information. Therefore the expansion of digital technologies has placed demands on citizens to become competent effective users of new technologies.

"Just as the industrial societies set themselves the aim of ensuring that all citizens were properly versed in the three Rs[1], the emergence of the knowledge-based society implies that every citizen must be 'digitally literate' and basic skills in order to be on a better footing in terms of equal opportunities in a world in which digital functions are proliferating" (European Commission, 2000, p. 4).

The importance of this type of literacy has raised the issue of the digital divide – a concern that not all students will have appropriate access to this technology and therefore will be disadvantaged. It is now seen as critical that schools address these skills and ensure that no student is left behind. As Davis et al. (1997) claim, "one of the most important challenges to an educational system is to empower

---

1. Reading, 'riting (writing), and 'rithmetic (arithmetic).

the young with the intellectual tools of the culture" (p. 16). The emergence of a possible 'digital divide' sparked governments to address the problem through school-based intervention which led to many high profile initiatives launched towards the end of the 20th century. Ireland was no exception and in 1998 began investing in ICT infrastructure for schools. However, the extent to which this has addressed the digital divide is unknown. Mulkeen (2003) importantly highlights that information literacy does not simply entail access to computers but that "the real digital divide may not be between those who have used a computer and those who have not, but between those with different types of ICT experience" (p. 17). Defining the digital divide is therefore problematic and goes beyond distinguishing between those with access to technology and those who don't. Hawkins and Oblinger (2006) discuss the notion of the 'second-level' digital divide and this is where the hidden and very real divide lies. This digital divide is caused by several issues: age of the machine, connectivity, online skills, independence and freedom of access, and computer-use support. The definition of digital divide must therefore include all of these other issues. It can also be argued that this second-level digital divide also encompasses the type of use of the technology as indicated by Mulkeen (2003), where one school advocates some use of the available technologies but in a very superficial manner, whereas another school's ICT policy champions the meaningful and constructive integration of technology into their teaching and learning. The challenge for schools has therefore shifted. Access to the technology no longer appears to be a significant issue. The main challenge for the future is to develop meaningful activities and resources that foster important digital literacies amongst students. Open educational resources can play an important role in addressing this as they can be tailored to meet the needs of specific students and curricula (UNESCO, 2012).

This chapter reports on an ICT initiative in a number of Irish post-primary schools and examines how a teacher-designed multimedia resource for the teaching of English poetry was used by a number of teachers. The project raises a number of important questions relating to national ICT policy and the future use of ICT in schools. Before outlining the project, the following sections will set the study in context by outlining the background to the study.

1.1.   ICT in Irish post-primary schools: setting the context

In order to understand the context of the study it is important to highlight the key aspects that have shaped how ICT is used and perceived in schools and what the prevailing pedagogical practices are, as both of these issues significantly shape and determine the successful integration of any ICT initiative across the curriculum.

Computer use in Ireland has had a long history. However the rationale for its use in schools has changed over the decades. Early justifications for its use were motivated by an early group of pioneers, coming mainly from a mathematics background and they saw the computer as a machine to be studied (McGarr, 2009). This influenced early computer usage where students learned about the operation of the computer and developed programming knowledge. However, throughout the 1980s computer use in schools appeared to organically develop into a separate subject that focused on basic computer skills such as the use of word processing, spreadsheets and other standard applications. Therefore rather than moving towards a specialist area of study, it instead emerged largely as a standalone subject (Drury, 1995; McKenna, Brady, Bates, Brick, & Drury, 1993).

The launch of the Schools IT2000 initiative, the first large scale attempt to integrate ICT across the curriculum in 1998, also had a strong focus on the need to equip all students with basic ICT skills. This was particularly important in a system that did not have a compulsory ICT experience for students at post-primary level. Therefore, when one looks at the past three decades of ICT usage in schools, it is evident that the rationale for use is strongly based on what could be described as a social rationale, that is, a focus on ensuring all students have a basic level of ICT competence and literacy (DES, 2012). Ultimately, it remains in general a subject to be taught. This is done mainly through the provision of skills courses aimed at developing competence in standard software applications. There are some pockets of ICT integration but this appears to be quite limited (DES, 2008a) and the predominant use of ICT across the curriculum appears to be as a presentation aid for the teacher where presentation software such as *PowerPoint* is used.

A second aspect of post-primary education pertinent to this study is the nature of teaching and learning in most Irish classrooms. Classroom teaching practices in Ireland have long been criticised for their teacher-centred nature and the didactic nature of the learning experience. As far back as 1991 the organisation for economic cooperation and development (OECD) found that teaching and curriculum were largely determined by examinations requirement and that there was a strong emphasis on "a didactic approach" (OECD, 1991, p. 55). Later studies in the same decade by Callan (1997) and Mackey (1998) also reported a largely teacher centred approach to learning. More recent research by Lyons, Lynch, Close, Sheerin, and Boland (2003) into mathematics classrooms revealed similar results reporting that "[c]lasses were strongly teacher directed, with teachers generally using a didactic approach to the presentation of material [...with a lack of] student participation in the organisation of their own learning" (p. 147).

The recent teaching and learning international study (TALIS) report on Ireland, published in 2009, supports these earlier findings reporting that "[t]eachers in Ireland were somewhat less supportive of constructivist beliefs, and somewhat more supportive of direct transmission beliefs than their counterparts in all five comparison countries" (Shiel, Perkins, & Gilleece, 2009, p. 6). Therefore, the multimedia OER developed, with its emphasis on student participation and a non-linear approach to learning, was perhaps not in congruence with either the dominant pedagogical approaches employed in Irish classrooms or with how ICT is generally used as a presentation aid to support such teacher-centred lessons. This research was therefore particularly interested in how it would be adopted by the participating teachers.

The primary aim of the Junior Certificate English curriculum is to build on what has been taught at primary level. The Junior Certificate curriculum for English is varied and expects that all students will develop their language and literacy skills. There is no set teaching methodology for Junior Certificate English. Instead the Department of Education and Science (DES, 2012) provides teachers with a set of guidelines from which they can choose the best approach to suit their students' needs. However, the Junior Certificate English curriculum requires that students sitting both the higher and ordinary level examination be examined on the following:

- Reading;
- Writing;
- Functional writing;
- Media studies;
- Drama (unseen and studied);
- Poetry;
- Fiction.

For the purposes of this research, subject inspection reports were consulted. Subject inspection reports present findings based on observations of practice in schools and classrooms. The purpose of these reports is to make a positive contribution to the teaching and learning of English, and they are therefore intended to be of particular relevance to teachers of English and to school managements. The aims are fourfold:

- To inform and encourage professional dialogue;
- To assist schools and subject departments in the process of self-review;
- To suggest areas for improvement;
- To share exemplars of good practice.

These reports are, according to the DES, a measure of what is actually taking place in schools as they are evidence-based and are informed by a variety of activities.

1.2.   Problematic areas

The subject inspection reports call attention to a number of problems associated with the teaching of English at post-primary level, which include the lack of exposure of some students to a wide variety of literature, including poetry (DES, 2006, p. 24). The lack of audio visual material has also been identified as a problem. Where material is available it should be used as part of the lesson. Where inspectors observed such material being used they commented that it was of great benefit to students (DES, 2008b, p. 30).

The inspectors also identified the teaching of the basic mechanics of language as problematic in some schools and suggested that ICT be used to combat this:

> "The second concern arose where language skills, in particular grammar and syntax, were treated as a separate issue in textbooks. In practice this led to the teaching of language skills in isolation, whereas they should be grounded in the texts the students are reading. The practice of taking English classes to the computer room was observed in a few schools but is much less widespread than is desirable" (DES, 2008b, p. 33).

2.   The project

2.1.   Courseware development

As part of the present study to explore how multimedia and digital learning objects can be used to foster critical thinking, a multimedia rich resource for teaching poetry at post-primary level was developed. The poetry course was selected as it provided the opportunity to explore broad themes within the syllabus. It also enabled the development of research skills, critical thinking and analytical skills, which are required in dealing with ambiguous meaning and the multiple perspectives and interpretations of material. The learning object comprised seven individual lessons: six poems taken from the Junior Certificate syllabus and one lesson focusing on poetry terms. This digital resource was developed in collaboration with English teachers at post-primary level. Teachers in the greater catchment area of the University of Limerick were invited to participate in the research study. Eight teachers expressed an interest in the study and contributed to the development of the courseware. A number of the participating teachers had begun to explore alternative pedagogical approaches to the teaching of poetry but none had explored the potential of ICT. The teachers that participated in the needs analysis for this courseware described how they normally approached a poem with their class. Based on this, we created a wish list for the multimedia lesson. Biographical information on the poet, plenty of images, a background for the social context of the poem were all deemed to be appropriate content. Having a specific objective with measurable outcomes ensures that courseware design was not compromised by the availability of extra features. Deciding on specific learning objectives guarded against the inclusion of bells and whistles for their own sake.

The lack of curriculum relevant ICT materials is a common concern raised by teachers considering using ICT in their lessons. This issue is exacerbated in Ireland due to its relatively small population. This often makes it unfeasible to commercially produce curricular relevant learning material of a high standard. Within this context, tailor-made curricular resources developed in collaboration with practicing teachers using 'easy to use' authoring tools may sound like an impossible task. However, as this small scale research has highlighted, the availability of easy to use authoring tools that produce courseware of a professional quality has enormous potential for innovation in Irish schools. The potential for collaboration and sharing of these resources makes the development of these small scale resources attractive if seen as part of a larger community of courseware developers. There is a growing online community of centres and institutions with material freely available for use both in the classroom and at home. For instance, *BBC Schools* has commissioned a number of digital learning objects that present traditional material in a manner that appeals to a digital generation. In Ireland a number of online educational courseware portals are facilitating the sharing of this technology. Information is presented in attractive visual layout, comprising short pieces of text, often accompanied by spoken readings, thereby removing the often tedious task of decoding written texts. Sharing resources produced in this manner can overcome the problems of bandwidth which often inhibits use in schools.

It is also worth noting that many departments within third level institutions are now developing digital learning objects which they can then upload to a central repository where they may be shared with colleagues at other institutions and may be reused or redeveloped (Marcus-Quinn & Geraghty, 2009; Pegler, 2012; Wiley, 2010; Yuen, Chow, Cheung, Li, & Tsang, 2012). Some international secondary schools have also recognised the potential of collaboratively developed material and have developed similar repositories to share learning resources among staff and students (Driesche, 2011). Such digital resources may also be incorporated into teaching materials distributed to distance learners (Wilson, 2008). Irish post-primary schools should consider similar strategies.

This study was conducted over one academic year. The pilot group participated from October to December. There were three post-primary schools involved. The schools varied in size and type:

- School A is a co-educational school with a population of some 600 students. Improvement was predominantly seen in terms of recent infrastructural developments. As a result of a fire in 2006 the PC lab had to be refurbished. Consequently the PC lab was brand new at the time of this study. Computers are being used in technical/vocational subjects and the integration of ICT as a teaching and learning tool in other subject areas is at an early stage of development;

- School B is a girls' secondary school with a population of 400 students. While the school did not have a history of ICT use, a substantial investment from the *Schools IT2000* initiative has enabled the school to start some developments in this area;

- School C has some 1047 students. The school has used computers since its opening in 2000. The integration of ICT in different subject areas is now being attempted and is more advanced in some areas (Technical Graphics) than others (Humanities).

The teachers involved in this research did not have a history of ICT use. The schools themselves all have ICT facilities as a result of recent state investment in ICT.

2.2.   Participants

Overall, there were 154 students and 13 teachers involved in this study. Table 1 and Table 2 show the breakdown of students and teachers, respectively.

Table 1.   Breakdown of students

Usability group*	1st and 2nd year students Pilot group 2 classes from school A	School A 1st year 1 class	School B 1st year 1 class	School C 2 x 2nd year Learner support groups
24	58	26	30	16

*The Usability group was crucial to identify any issues with the digital resources.

Table 2.   Breakdown of teachers

Teachers consulted for development of resources	1st and 2nd year students Pilot group 2 classes from school A	School A 1st year 1 class	School B 1st year 1 class	School C 2 x 2nd year Learner support groups
8	2	1	1	1

3.   Implementation in the three schools

3.1.   Data collection sources and procedures

This study adopted a case study methodology, drawing evidence from as many sources as possible. Data collection tools included interviews with teachers (pre-use, during use and post-use), student focus group interviews and observation, online questionnaires, and opportunistic elements as they arose. This study was conducted in compliance with the institutional ethical policy. Consent was obtained from the participants following a detailed description of the research project and its aims. Confidentiality and anonymity were guaranteed to all participants where requested.

In this section of the chapter, the methods that were used in order to analyse each data source are presented. All of the data sources were analysed according to specific methods in order to best answer the questions that guided the data collection and analysis for this study in an effort to answer the main research question: How do students use the learning object within the context of the traditional classroom?

3.2.   Interviews with teachers

After reading the available reports pertaining to ICT use in Irish schools, it was necessary to speak to teachers to get an insight into the realities of incorporating ICT into the classroom. Interviews with the teachers contributed directly to the content, design and development of the learning object. Notes from these interviews were recorded with the aid of a Digipad, a device which captures handwritten notes and illustrations using an ink filled rechargeable digital pen and folder on normal paper. The notes can then be uploaded via USB cable to PC and converted into a recognised typed text typeface.

3.3.   Student focus group interviews
and observation

For the purposes of this study it was decided to speak with the students in a focus group setting before they used the learning object. In order to gain a deeper understanding of the practicalities using the technology from a student perspective, student groups were invited to share their thoughts and opinions about the learning object. Students were interviewed in focus groups, as opposed to individually, so that group members could contribute to each other's ideas and responses and therefore more useful information could be gathered (Morgan, 1997). Some of the questions in the focus group interview protocol were replicated in the online student questionnaires. Observation was another key apparatus of the case study toolkit "to see things as those involved see things" (Denscombe, 1998, p. 69).

3.4.   Online student questionnaires

This method of data collection was practical as it is cost effective, anonymous, can reach respondents in distant locations and is mainly written for specific purposes, based on a set of standardised questions (Dörnyei, 2003). Online surveys were administered using *SurveyMonkey*[1] in order to measure student attitudes to English and specifically poetry as a subject, use of learning objects to aid schoolwork, and computer use outside the classroom including games like the *SIMs*. To provide additional background information on type of use, students were also asked about their use of other Web 2.0 technology, such as social networking websites. While most filled out the questionnaire individually in one class, we observed a number of students reading the computer screen beside them, copying each other's answers. This meant that their questionnaires had to be given out in hardcopy in subsequent weeks. The students were more protective of their handwritten work and did not allow other students to copy from their individual work.

3.5. Opportunistic elements of the case study

The case study researcher is likely to be sensitive to opportunistic as well as planned data collection (Hartley, 2004; Stake, 1995). By remaining flexible and allowing for some changes in direction, new ideas could develop. Therefore when the opportunity presented itself to incorporate some usage of the university's virtual learning environment (VLE) into the study, the project embraced it rather than saying it was outside of the original project scope.

As part of the research study, a project site within Sakai (the university's VLE) was set up for the group of 30 students at School B to join. As the school had not issued each student with an individual email/login, the teacher set up one email address for the entire class to use. The teacher did not want students using their personal email addresses for privacy reasons. The students were told that for this reason, their comments would have a level of anonymity that would not usually be the case with a VLE. Students were told that they could type their name at the end of their comments if they wished to reveal their identity. The majority signed their name and took ownership of their contributions. The

---

1. Retrieved from http://www.surveymonkey.com/

student who was deemed to have contributed the most to the online discussion received an *iPod* as a prize. The event logs from the project site 'Poetry Corner' were analysed and all of the log activity was included in the study and copied to a spreadsheet for analysis.

In one of the schools, students were given the option to design their own multimedia poem. This was completely voluntary and was done in the students' own time outside of the classroom. A total of 5 out of 30 emailed a *PowerPoint* presentation on a poem of their choice to the researcher. While this is a very small number this work was completely voluntary and of a high quality. They also contacted the researcher directly to share that they had really enjoyed the experience of using the software in the classroom.

3.6. Post use interviews with teachers

The focus of these interviews was primarily on the student use and impact of the learning object developed. The feedback from these interviews was largely positive; only one teacher expressed concern about moving away from the more traditional poetry lesson.

4. Data analysis

Once the data had been collected, a software package, *Weft*, was used for analysis as it was deemed most appropriate to this research project. *Weft Qualitative Data Analysis* is a graphical user interface package for the analysis of unstructured textual data such as interviews and notes from observations. *Weft* is a freeware tool and in the spirit of freeware, is available for use at no cost to the researcher. It is possible to import documents directly from a word processing package and code these documents easily on screen. *Weft* was suitable for this project as there was no need to work with rich text (italicised, bold, etc), the project was not working with audio or multilingual documents nor was there any need for paid support. This tool crucially facilitated easy data management and retrieval.

5.   Findings

5.1.   School A

In school A, three teachers used the resource. Use of the software varied across the cooperating teachers. The initial use of the software by two of the teachers appeared to mirror the educational practices that have been commonly reported in relation to the Irish classrooms (Callan, 1997; Lyons et al., 2003; Mackey, 1998; OECD, 1991; Shiel et al., 2009). The software was used in one of the two computer rooms in the school. The computers were arranged on a bench that ran along the circumference of the room in a U shape. The teacher's computer, at the top of the room, was projected to a large white screen. This arrangement led to the students working independently on individual workstations. In these lessons, the teacher tended to control the students' use of the software and no student exploration or independent work was allowed. The teachers directed the students to items on the screen and asked individuals to read from the screen aloud. This pattern was repeated for much of the observed lessons. For example, the teacher would navigate to a new screen on the projected screen and request a student to read its content, normally from the student's own computer screen, before discussing the extract, providing an explanation to the class and pointing out aspects of note relevant to the syllabus aims.

Within this controlled approach, the students were not allowed to navigate through the resources without direction. Several messages and reminders reinforcing this approach were given throughout the lesson, with the students being reminded that they were not to progress independently with the software. High levels of surveillance of the students also took place to monitor this compliance; this was evident through the continuous circulation around the classroom by the teacher. Speaking about her approach to the use of the software after one of these observed sessions, the teacher explained;

> **Teacher from School A:** I get them to talk through the poem. We read it together and then we go through the theme and get them to discuss it as a class. I think that I could really use this.

In many respects the software was being used as an electronic textbook/ workbook. Within these lessons, where there were up to 30 students, the researcher noted that the levels of student interest varied significantly. Some students appeared highly engaged and motivated by the novel visit to the computer room and paid full attention to the instructions given to them by their teacher. However, others showed low levels of interest, reflected in the high levels of off-task activities. For example, it was observed during many sessions that students opened a second internet browser to view other websites such as sports websites. When such 'off task' activities were identified by the teacher the student was reprimanded with a verbal warning. Following these exchanges, this off task behaviour switched to less identifiable defiance of the teacher's orders. This behaviour included playing with the technology, such as manipulating the size of graphics from the software or copying them into a word processing document.

Despite the various levels of engagement, an analysis of the completed student work revealed that all students completed the exercises and tasks set by the teacher, albeit to varying degrees. For example, when the completed student responses were analysed, the responses to the questions set on each student worksheet varied to a large extent. Some provided detailed responses to the questions posed while others filled in 'nonsense' words or copied the answers from other students. As a result of teacher intervention, when the teacher explained how the tasks were related to their end-of-term examination, this level of engagement did improve as the project progressed. Although the level of engagement was mixed, the teacher did indicate in one of the final interviews that student interest and engagement had increased.

> **Teacher from School A:** They are all poems that we would cover anyway. They liked using this. They liked finding the extras and reading more about the poet. We will probably use this for the TL21 project.

The third teacher to use the software in this school appeared to take a very different approach, enabling the students to explore the resources and work independently in small groups to complete a project. These lessons took place on a Friday afternoon when the majority of the students in the class were participating in school sports events and therefore the remaining students were there by choice. As a result, there appeared to be very high levels of student interest and engagement, reflected in much lower levels of 'off task' behaviour and viewing of other websites. The students took notes in their copybooks and talked to each other about the information presented to them.

During informal discussions with the teacher after one of the observed sessions, it emerged that the teacher was using the time spent in the computer room as an opportunity to catch up with administrative work, which explains the lower levels of surveillance and monitoring of student work. It was also evident that the students were highly motivated to complete the task. In many occasions there was almost complete silence amongst the group as they worked on the task and, unlike the other groups, all student tasks were completed to a high level. To a certain extent, despite the presence of the teacher, the lessons observed with this group had the appearance of students working independently on the tasks in the absence of a teacher.

> **Teacher from School A:** It's great that they can work away on it themselves... It gives me a chance to fill out the forms... they're very motivated anyway especially if they know that it's coming up on the exam.

5.2. School B

The second school, school B, was a very large urban community college and the software was used as part of two small learning support groups (8 students). Each group varied in age from 12 to 15 years and were a mix of both native and non-native English speakers that had been identified as requiring remedial support for language development. Within this more intimate classroom setting, lessons tended to be more participatory and discussion based. The teacher did not use a textbook with the group and instead chose to select material and resources that best suited the needs of the group. In explaining the pedagogical approach adopted by her and the aims of her practice, the teacher explained:

Teacher from School B: A book would intimidate them. They only need a few poems so I try to have a good variety of themes in a few poems. They have everything they need there for the exam but it's not too much. They know that what they have done is enough and they don't worry because they can do it. All of the themes that are in the poems we cover are common exam questions so they know that they are prepared for the exam (Junior Cert)... I'm always looking for ways to engage with them and get them to talk about the poetry. We play word games. We also talk about what's in the news and what's on TV. Anything to get them talking and discussing in class. It's important that they are confident to talk in the group. They're good to talk now but some of them can be quiet.

Within this context, the teacher, using one computer in the small room, guided the students through elements of the software that she had selected as suitable. The teacher tended to focus on the visual elements of the software to engage the students and promote discussion. In many respects the resource was being used as an alternative to a *PowerPoint* presentation and the lessons remained largely teacher-centred.

Teacher from School B: It's great that the poem could be read aloud for them and having all of the new words explained to them is useful too... They find the theme difficult. They know what it is but they still find it hard to describe... the help with that is good. 'Base Details' is the hardest one for them because there's so much in it but then they have a really strong question to work with so that is definitely great for them.

Since the teacher did not enable the students to use the software individually, the opportunity to collect the students' completed worksheets was not possible. However, six lessons were observed with these groups in order to try to gauge the level of student interest and engagement. Overall the visual dimension of the software seemed to have a positive effect. The visual elements appeared to stimulate quite a significant level of discussion and the teacher used this opportunity to explore aspects of the poem. The teacher's comments in one of the interviews supported this:

Teacher from School B: I would like to use some kind of technology with them (the class) but there's nothing there for them. As a class they are quite weak I teach the support groups as you know and they're very weak. They need a lot of extra encouragement and support. I don't use a text book as it just doesn't suit them. It was great for them to see what the poet looked like. It made it more real for them.

5.3. School C

School C was an all-girls private voluntary secondary school located within an affluent suburb of a city. In this school, the cooperating teacher described the group of students that used the software as a mixed ability group, although they appeared to have a much higher academic ability than the other participating groups. The school had a strong academic ethos and this was reflected in the nature of extra-curricular activities that the students participated in. For example, this group were involved in debating as an extracurricular activity. Within this school, the resource was uploaded to an online learning environment and students accessed the content via a shared login created by the teacher.

A notable difference observed in this school was the level of autonomy afforded to the students. Students were given a very high level of autonomy as they were allowed to work independently on the tasks both within and outside of school. The level of teacher interest in the initiative was also very high. The teacher created creative writing tasks that complemented the digital resource and the students were also provided with weekly writing tasks in which the software assisted them. Students were encouraged to discuss the content, theme and style of each poem via online asynchronous discussion boards. Although participation in these discussion boards was voluntary and anonymous, many chose to sign their contributions and some initiated separate discussion threads on related issues (see Figure 1).

Overall the level of student engagement was very high and the ability and willingness of the group to take ownership of their individual learning was remarkable. This level of interest was also observed by the teacher that noted:

Teacher from School C: The class enjoyed using the computer. They said that they liked using the computer for a change... No one had any difficulty using it. The student teacher got on fine with them. They'd like to use it again.

Teacher from School C: They like using the VLE. I think that because they knew it was the same one that students at the University use they enjoyed it more and of course they're already used to using social networking sites... that kind of online space. They were good to discuss the questions in much the same way that they would do in class. I was very happy with the whole thing.

Figure 1. Topic posted by student "Could the man have been saved?"

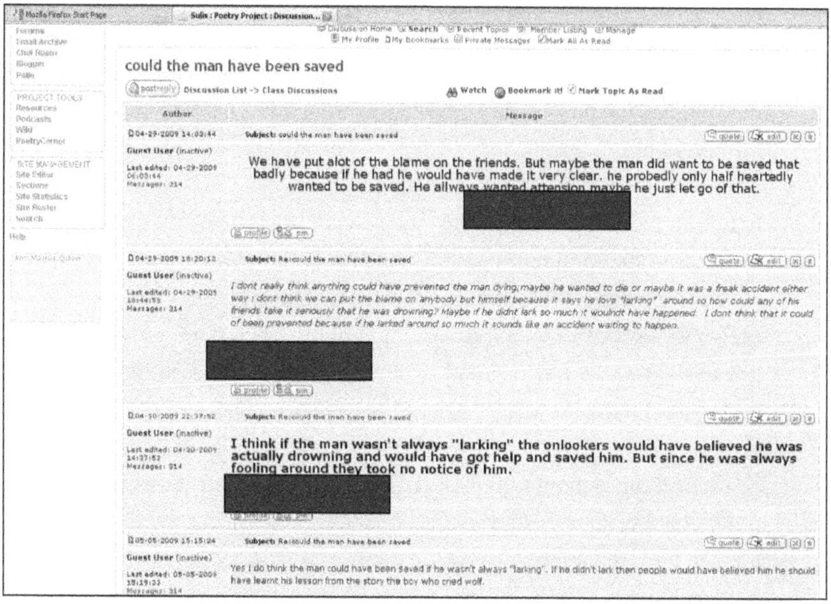

Further evidence of the level of student engagement and satisfaction also surfaced in in student comments at the end of the experience. In response to the question: "What did you like most about using these online resources?" many of the girls stated that they liked listening to the authentic voice. Where this audio was provided they particularly enjoyed listening to the actual poet reading their work:

> **Student from School C:** It had the poet's voice speaking instead of a teachers which I thought was nice because their accents made it more interesting than the same voice over and over again.

> **Student from School C:** In these multimedia resources we are given a background to each poem and poet which I feel gives us a better understanding of the poems.

> **Student from School C:** My normal surroundings when we study poetry is a classroom with twenty-nine other students and one teacher the good thing about the online poetry is its kind of one on one even though the rest of the class are doing it too you have your own computer and your own thoughts on the poem instead of getting notes which sometimes you don't properly understand.

> **Student from School C:** My normal poetry lesson involves a poetry discussion but online we don't have to listen to everyone else and it gets things done a lot faster. Also we got to hear how the poems are meant to be spoken which gives a feel to the tone of the poems. We also got to look at the background of the each poem and poet which helped understand more.

> **Student from School C:** I loved using this online learning as it was fun... unlike the boring environment of the classroom, this online resource was a great way to learn poetry by great poets. It gave me a lot of insight into how technology can help learning.

In reflecting on the experience, the cooperating teacher felt the resource was a valuable addition and that it appeared to meet the learning needs of all students regardless of their level of ability;

Teacher from School C: Both the weaker and the stronger students liked using the resources. The weaker ones liked that they got the prompts on the poetic terms and the stronger ones liked that they got the biographical information.

The teacher further commented that greater value could be obtained from the resource if it was integrated more seamlessly into the students' experience over an extended period of time;

Teacher from School C: I would use it again but over a longer period... so maybe I'd use it once a month or once every fortnight and have some more class activity then built into it. We used it quite intensively this time over the few weeks. If we used it over a longer time I think we might get even more out of it.

6.   Discussion

This study was largely concerned with students in first and second year of their post-primary education. These students had not yet been divided groups based on what level exam they would take at Junior Certificate (higher or ordinary level English). Initially it was intended to only use this type of mixed ability group. However, due to difficulty in recruiting participants two small groups of eight students in a learner support class were also included. Consequently, this study reports on the use of an OER in three very distinct settings with different outcomes and expectations by teachers and students. The learning object was designed to be used by an individual student working on their own, and on their own PC, thus engaging in a personal learning experience. However, the schools involved in the study could not accommodate this. In many cases there were a number of students sharing computers.

The research revealed considerable differences in how the resource was used across the three schools. As has been highlighted earlier, the digital divide is no longer defined by one's access to the technology but rather the actual use of it.

As was evident from the three schools that participated in this study, the nature of the student activities ranged from lower order passive tasks to more higher order challenging activities which gave the students considerable autonomy. It is noteworthy that the autonomy was given to the students in the more affluent schools (as defined by the socio-economic background of the students attending the schools) and to the classes of the more 'able' students. Therefore the use of such resources, rather that addressing the digital divide, may instead widen the gap as it is debatable as to whether the activities and tasks provided to the students in the more teacher-directed lessons provided any benefit to the learners. Indeed it could be argued that such restrictions caused a level of student frustration and subsequent disengagement with the experience. On the other hand, in the schools where students were encouraged to take ownership of the experience, it appeared to have increased motivation and caused greater engagement in the tasks. In fact the resource seemed to have a catalytic effect, causing spin-off projects and tasks.

It appears that the issue of the digital divide is therefore not ICT related but instead points to a broader issue of the nature of the students' learning experience and how they are perceived by the teacher and school. In some instances, they are given a level of responsibility and autonomy which they use to great effect. This then adds to their learning experience and creates more positive attitudes to school and learning. In others (and unfortunately perhaps the majority) the excessive control over the content and the teacher-directed nature of the experience has the opposite effect, causing greater resentment and disengagement. One could argue that in one setting the students are developing the important information literacy skills outlined by Berthelsen, Halliwell, Peacock, Burke, and Ryan (2000) while in the other, because of the restrictions placed on their opportunities to interrogate and evaluate the material presented, these skills are not provided. Berthelsen et al. (2000) encapsulate this claiming that

> "[w]hile information literacy skills are usually considered in relation to the use of information technology, such technology does not, in itself, provide a means for developing other important skills related to information literacy. Information literacy involves specific behavioural skills (e.g.,

using technology) but also processes of critical evaluation of information. While information technology provides students with opportunities to gain access to a wide range of information that can be the catalyst for more critical thinking, a critical perspective is unlikely to develop unless opportunities are provided to support students in being able to evaluate information" (p. 2).

Irish schools have overcome the initial barriers that hinder the integration of ICT in schools. They include suitable resources and teacher ICT skills and knowledge but as Ertmer (2005) argues, the greatest challenges have yet to be overcome. The challenge for schools is to now consider how the technology will be used to best effect. Will it be used to support the existing didactic system as a tool to enhance the teacher's presentation or will it be used as a tool to support more independent learning and exploration amongst students? The history of ICT integration to date would point to the former. In looking at schools over the decades Hargreaves (2003) identified a "basic grammar" of schools that appears to survive societal changes and attempted innovations in schools;

"[b]ehind all the autonomy, attempted innovation and educational expansion, a basic 'grammar' of teaching and learning persisted where most teachers taught as they had for generations, from the front, through lecturing, seatwork and question-and-answer methods, with separate classes of age-like children, evaluated by standard paper-and-pencil methods" (p. 4).

The historical legacy of teacher-centred approaches to lessons and an emphasis on control and examination preparation was also evident in a number of the classes observed in this study. The technology appears to have been selected to serve the 'system's' needs and other aspects were ignored. In this context, in relation to the digital divide and the need to equip students with the important literacies of the future, it could be argued that schools are part of the problem rather than the solution.

"One thing that has struck me in my work with urban kids is the odd congruence between two very different systems: the system of global media that wants young people to be spectators and consumers rather than social actors, and a factory system of schooling that wants young people to be passive and willing vessels for a prescribed set of knowledge and skills" (Goodman, 2003, p. 2).

Before concluding, it is worth briefly examining some of the limitations of the study. This research was small in nature and only encompassed three schools. With this in mind, one must be conscious of the limitations of such as small-scale study and the generalisations drawn from it. However, despite the sample size, the value of this study is that it reveals the vastly different approaches adopted.

Since this study was carried out, new technologies such as rapid authoring tools have become more readily available. However, technologies may change and evolve but, as this study has highlighted, the response from educators will vary significantly. An understanding of this variation in adoption is important for how OERs are developed in the future.

7.   Conclusion

In conclusion, as this chapter has highlighted, the digital revolution has brought new opportunities and challenges for schools. It is understandable that schools' reaction to these demands is to expose students to information and communication technologies. However, the mere use of ICT will not address concerns over the digital divide and indeed may cause a greater divide in the long-term. This divide may occur between students that have acquired critical analytical skills in using ICT in a purposeful manner and those that use ICT in a superficial manner. This use is characterised by a focus on the acquisition of basic skills and the recreational use of social media and gaming. It is therefore critical that future use of ICT goes beyond the basic skills-based emphasis that has characterised its use in post primary schools since its introduction. Greater integration across the curriculum also needs to take place to facilitate the acquisition of these higher order skills.

References

Berthelsen, D., Halliwell, G., Peacock, J., Burke, J., & Ryan, I. (2000). Information literacy: Implications for early childhood teaching. *Paper presented at the Australian Association for Research in Education Conference, 4-7 December 2000.* University of Sydney, Sydney, NSW.

Callan, J. (1997). Active Learning in the Classroom: A Challenge to Existing Values and Practices. In Á. Hyland, O. O'Leary, P. Hogan, & B. Farrell (Eds.), *Issues in Education* (Volume 2) (pp. 21-28). Dublin: ASTI.

Davis, N., Desforges, C., Jessels, J., Somekh, B., Taylor, C., & Vaughan, G. (1997). Can quality in learning be enhanced through the use of IT? In B. Somekh & N. Davis (Eds.), *Using Information Technology effectively in Teaching and Learning: Studies in Pre-Service and In-Service Teacher Education* (pp. 13-26). London and New York: Routledge.

Denscombe, M. (1998). *The Good Research Guide.* Open University Press.

DES. (2006). *Looking at English Teaching & Learning English in Post-Primary Schools.* Retrieved from http://www.crisp.ie/slss/Looking%20at%20English.pdf

DES. (2008a). *ICT in Schools.* Brunswick Press, Dublin.

DES. (2008b). School Subject Inspection Reports. Report prepared by the Department of Education. Retrieved from http://www.education.ie/en/Publications/Inspection-Reports-Publications/Subject-Inspection-Reports-List/report2_71080B.htm

DES. (2012). *ICT Action Plan.* Report prepared by the Department of Education. Retrieved from http://www.education.ie/en/Publications/Policy-Reports/ICT-Action-Plan-Meeting-the-high-level-skills-needs-of-enterprise-in-Ireland.pdf

Dörnyei, Z. (2003). *Questionnaires in Second Language Research.* Mahwah: Lawrence Erlbaum Associates.

Driesche, van den, K. (2011). What do teachers expect when sharing learning materials in an open online environment? *Design, Development and Research, 2011.*

Drury, C. (1995). *Implementing Change in Education: The Integration of Information Technology into Irish post-primary schools.* Unpublished M.Sc. Thesis, University of Leicester.

European commission. (2000). *Communication from the Commission: eLearning - Designing tomorrow's education.* Retrieved from http://ec.europa.eu/education/archive/elearning/comen.pdf

Ertmer, P. A. (2005). Teacher pedagogical beliefs: The final frontier in our quest for technology integration? *Educational Technology Research and Development, 53*(4), 25-39. doi: 10.1007/BF02504683

Goodman, S. (2003). *Teaching youth media: A critical guide to literacy, video production, and social change.* New York: Teachers College Press.

Hargreaves, A. (2003). *Teaching in the knowledge society: education in the age of insecurity.* Philadelphia, PA: Open University Press.

Hartley, J. (2004). Case Study Research. In C. Cassell & G. Symon (Eds.), *Essential Guide to Qualitative Methods in Organizational Research* (pp. 323-333). London: Sage Publications.

Hawkins, B. L., & Oblinger, D. G. (2006). The myth about the digital divide. *Educause Review, 41*(4), 12-13. Retrieved from http://www.educause.edu/ero/article/myth-about-digital-divide

Lyons, M., Lynch, K., Close, S., Sheerin, E., & Boland, P. (2003). *Inside classrooms: The teaching and learning of mathematics in social context.* Dublin: Institute of public administration.

Mulkeen, A. (2003). What can policy makers do to encourage integration of information and communications technology? Evidence from the Irish school system. *Technology, Pedagogy and Education, 12*(2), 277-293. doi: 10.1080/14759390300200158

McGarr, O. (2009). The development of ICT across the curriculum in Irish schools: A historical perspective. *British Journal of Educational Technology, 40*(6), 1094-1108. doi: 10.1111/j.1467-8535.2008.00903.x

McKenna, P., Brady, M., Bates, P., Brick, J., & Drury, C. (1993). *New Information Technology in the Irish School System.* Luxembourg: Office for Official Publications (EC).

Mackey, J. (1998). Teaching methodology in the junior certificate. *Irish Educational Studies, 17*(1), 284-291. doi: 10.1080/0332331980170124

Marcus-Quinn, A., & Geraghty, B. (2009). Design and development of a digital learning resource to deliver online content to teach Japanese syllabaries. In R. Donnelly, J. Harvey, & K. C. O'Rourke (Eds.), *Critical Design and Effective Tools for E-Learning in Higher Education: Theory into Practice.* Hershey, Pennsylvania: IGI Publishing.

Morgan, D. L. (1997). *Focus groups as qualitative research* (2nd ed.). Thousand Oaks, CA: Sage Publications.

OECD. (1991). *Review of National Education Policies: Ireland.* Paris: Organisation for Economic Cooperation and Development.

Pegler, C. (2012). Herzberg, hygiene and the motivation to reuse: Towards a three-factor theory to explain motivation to share and use OER. *Journal of Interactive Multimedia in Education*, Special Issue on Open Educational Resources, 1-18. Retrieved from http://www-jime.open.ac.uk/article/2012-04/pdf

Shiel, G., Perkins, R., & Gilleece, L. (2009). *OECD Teaching and Learning International Study (TALIS): Summary report for Ireland*. Paris: Educational Research Centre. Retrieved from http://www.sdpi.ie/Policy_Issues-International_Trends/talis_summary_report_for_Ireland_2009.pdf

Stake, R. E. (1995). *The art of Case Study Research*. Thousand Oaks, CA: Sage.

UNESCO. (2012). Retrieved from http://www.youthsummit2012.com/

Wiley, D. A. (2010). Identifying Concrete Pedagogical Benefits of Open Educational Resources. *Paper presented at Open Ed 2010: Seventh Annual Open Education Conference, 2-4 November, Barcelona.*

Wilson, T, (2008). New ways of mediating learning: Investigating the implications of adopting open educational resources for tertiary education at an institution in the United Kingdom as compared to one in South Africa. *The International Review of Research in Open and Distance Learning, 9*(1), 1-19. Retrieved from http://www.irrodl.org/index.php/irrodl/article/view/485/1000

Yuen, K. S., Chow, L., Cheung, S. K. S., Li, K. C., & Tsang, E. Y. M. (2012). Overcoming Copyright Hurdles in the Development of Learning Materials in the Digital Era. In K. C. Li, F. L. Wang, K. S. Yuen, S. K. S. Cheung, & R. Kwan (Eds.), *Engaging Learners Through Emerging Technologies, International Conference on ICT in Teaching and Learning, ICT 2012, Hong Kong, China, July 4-6, 2012. Proceedings* (pp. 190-200). London: Springer.

15 The Use of a Task-Based Online Forum in Language Teaching: Learning Practices and Outcomes

Marie-Thérèse Batardière[1]

Abstract

This chapter investigates students' reported patterns of use and perceived outcomes of an online intercultural exchange. It is hoped that the study will inform our understanding of the students' language learning process on an online discussion forum and consequently will help us maximise the educational potential of computer-mediated communication (CMC). It first considers the pedagogical benefits of CMC, paying particular attention to the specificity of an asynchronous CMC environment and the role of task-based language learning. It then briefly presents an online collaborative task integrated in a larger project which promotes a three phase approach and which has been carried out for five years. Drawing on qualitative data collected from a cohort of approximately 25 Irish undergraduate students after a six-week online experience with their French partners, it examines students' self-reported coping strategies when faced with challenges of a technical, cross-cultural and personal nature. It also explores students' perceived learning outcomes, namely building cultural knowledge, fostering critical thinking, improving language accuracy and encouraging further study. In light of these findings, it argues that a meaningful and 'authentic' learning task is essential to allow 'real life' online exchange to take place and to engage students in their own learning.

Keywords: computer-mediated communication, task-based learning, intercultural interactions, authentic use of language.

---

1. School of Languages, Literature, Culture and Communication, University of Limerick, Limerick, Ireland; marie-therese.batardiere@ul.ie

How to cite this chapter: Batardière, M.-T. (2013). The Use of a Task-Based Online Forum in Language Teaching: Learning Practices and Outcomes In C. Fowley, C. English, & S. Thouësny (Eds.), *Internet Research, Theory, and Practice: Perspectives from Ireland* (pp. 305-323). Dublin: © Research-publishing.net.

---

1. Introduction

For the past decade online discussion forums have been gaining popularity in educational settings. As part of the current interest in Web 2.0 tools for language teaching, online discussion boards have become a common component in both distance and blended[1] courses in higher education (Cummings, Bonk, & Jacobs, 2002). When students are provided with an appropriate induction and support programme, these virtual platforms are perceived as easy to use (Lockley & Promnitz-Hayashi, 2012) and can offer an electronic environment that is accessible to participants who are otherwise separated by physical distance. In most language courses, the purpose of introducing an element of online discussion is to enable a collaborative construction of knowledge. Previous research on the use of CMC in language teaching has shown that when learners write in a foreign language, task design plays a fundamental role in fostering this collaboration (Kuteeva, 2007). Thus, in order to help maximise the educational outcomes of a task-based online discussion forum in foreign language learning, this study investigates students' patterns of learning and behaviour outside their classroom setting. More specifically, the following research questions are addressed: what kind of challenges do students encounter in this new learning environment and what coping strategies do they develop? What are the perceived learning benefits of task-based online interactions? What factors seem to influence the success of computer-mediated communication in university teaching?

This chapter first presents an online discussion forum task which is integrated in an undergraduate business and language course at the University of Limerick (UL). In doing so, it explains a number of pedagogical choices that were made to accommodate students' learning needs and practices in a virtual learning environment. Drawing on qualitative data collected from a cohort of approximately 25 Irish students throughout their six-week experience of CMC with their French partners, the paper then examines students' self-reported coping strategies and explores students' perceived learning outcomes. In the light of our

---

1. Blended courses consist of a combination of online and face-to-face tuition.

empirical findings, we make some recommendations about factors that should be considered when designing and implementing an on-line discussion forum.

2.   Online discussion forums: theoretical background

2.1.   The use of technology to mediate communication in second language acquisition

With the increasing use of CMC, new learning environments are emerging that generate meaningful interactions amongst learners and encourage students' strong involvement in the language learning process (Sotillo, 2000). Among these online learning platforms, the discussion forum offers a shared space in which students can exchange information, negotiate ideas, and construct knowledge in an interactive way. The asynchronous or 'delayed' nature of the discussion allows time for critical thinking (Kol & Schcolnik, 2008) and deeper learning (Garrison, Anderson, & Archer, 2000) as it enables students to make connections with past learning and to understand new concepts.

In language courses, CMC is considered an innovative way to expand students' use of a second language and improve students' reading and writing skills while exchanging messages (Little & Ushioda, 1998). Online forums generally provide a framework for text or topic discussion through the target language. Such activity requires students to organise their thoughts, challenge others' views, and take linguistic risks. Researchers in second language acquisition (SLA) put forward the argument that by facilitating the combination of two main language functions, namely interaction and reflection, CMC can promote language learning (Blake, 2000) as "students need to stretch their linguistic resources in order to meet the demands of real communication in a social context" (Ortega, 1997, p. 83).

Some recent studies on text-based CMC interactions have found that specific task design and implementation account for differences in quantitative and qualitative language production (for a comprehensive review, see Ortega, 2009) whereas the mode of communication – under synchronous (e.g., chat rooms and video conferences) or asynchronous conditions (e.g., emails and discussion forums) – plays a minor role on language output (Brandl, 2012).

2.2. The role of task-based teaching in eliciting learner interaction

There is a general consensus among SLA researchers that task-based language teaching (TBLT) provides learners with opportunities to produce the target language in meaningful context, as it moves away from the traditional approach which focuses on the language per se, to a more communicative approach which encourages 'real' interaction between learners (Ellis, 2003). Proponents of collaborative learning stress that a task should be goal-oriented, should have more than one possible outcome and should allow learners to interact with one another over information beyond their repertoires (Pellettieri, 2000) – that is to say, beyond their current level of knowledge of the target language and culture – to ensure that students are actively involved in the process.

The effectiveness of task-based CMC, both synchronous and asynchronous, as a tool for second language teaching has been widely examined (e.g., Blake, 2000; Lee, 2002). While there is no conclusive evidence that interactive negotiation leads to language acquisition, it is widely accepted that this type of interaction among L2 learners is beneficial for L2 development. Smith (2004) illustrates the positive effects of task-based computer-mediated negotiated interaction on second language acquisition. These include: an *increased participation* among students, an *increased quantity* and *heightened quality* of learner output, an *increased attention* to linguistic form, and an *increased willingness* to take risks with their second language (my emphasis).

In such linguistically rich interactions – including some with native speakers (NS) of the target language – technology mediated contexts offer unexplored multi-dimensional perspectives to task-based activities and call for new teaching-learning practices that extend beyond the familiar 'classroom boundaries' (O'Dowd & Waire, 2009). New multifaceted and less predictable patterns of communication may ensue and in turn, prompt teachers to adopt a more flexible approach to the implementation process of the task (Dooly, 2011). Ultimately these new contextual parameters may lead both researchers and practitioners to deconstruct the traditional roles of teacher and learner (Thomas & Reinders, 2010).

3.   Methodological overview

3.1.   Project outline

The online discussion forum is integrated in a larger project which promotes a three-phased approach. Language learners have to select a current French socio-political issue of their choice, retrieve information on the topic from online newspapers and magazines, and analyse it with a view to producing a piece of work demonstrating a thorough understanding of the topic. This individual project aims to broaden students' knowledge of Francophone current affairs, to deepen their awareness of the target culture and to advance their competence in the target language (see Appendix 1 for the project outline).

The CMC task starts mid-way through the project (week 6 of a 12-week course) and runs for 4 to 6 weeks depending on the group dynamic. Each L2 learner submits his/her assignment online and is paired with a native speaker who has expressed an interest in his/her topic. Students then have to engage in debate with their respective partners. In addition, at the end of the project, they have to reflect and report on their learning experience.

3.2.   Participants' profile

A total of 24 Irish undergraduate students and 12 native speakers of French participated in the project. The Irish students (15 female and 9 male students) were between 21 and 22 years of age and were enrolled on a fourth year undergraduate business and French course; the French module represents 1/5 of their programme and four contact hours per week. All Irish students had taken part in a collaborative blog the previous year. The native speakers (NS) were recruited among UL Erasmus and French postgraduate students (2/3) and among French colleagues and fellow-researchers (1/3); they were based either in Ireland or in their country of origin (metropolitan France or French overseas departments). Their voluntary participation was solicited through an email invitation. Their age ranged from 20 to 50. The majority of them were unknown to the learners or their real identity was kept from the learners (in the case of current tutors in the institution for example). They accepted to interact with two Irish students and were asked to post a minimum of three messages (per partnership) over the course of their exchanges. Their involvement was not rewarded in any way.

3.3. Task description

The discussion forum was set-up on the learning management system (LMS) of the institution for their specific module. In this case, the LMS is called *Sulis* and is powered by Sakai. Prior to the start of the exchanges, a discussion thread was created for each topic to facilitate both students and native speakers' assignment and not to burden participants with irrelevant information (see Figure 1 below for the list of topics).

Students were given a 20 minute training session on how to use the forum whereas the native speakers were sent written instructions (including their username and password if needed). The asynchronous communication task was open and non prescriptive, the only clear requirements being that the learners' target language (French) be used at all times in the exchanges and that a minimum of three messages be posted by each participant over the course of the online task with no constraint of frequency.

As previously mentioned, the Irish students had to post their project work on the discussion forum and start the exchange by asking their partner a (controversial) question on their chosen topic. Participants were free to express their views and opinions and the dialogue was not restricted to the topic selected. In the closing stages of the project, the Irish students were asked to give their overall impression of the online exchange experience and explain whether or not they had changed their views on the topic after their interactions with a native speaker. It is important to note that even though the teacher involved in the project had full access to students' postings, she never directly intervened in the exchanges. Any communication with the participants (technical support, gentle reminders, etc.) was carried out via email (see Figure 2 for an email sample).

Figure 1. Topics of discussion (snapshot of the virtual platform)

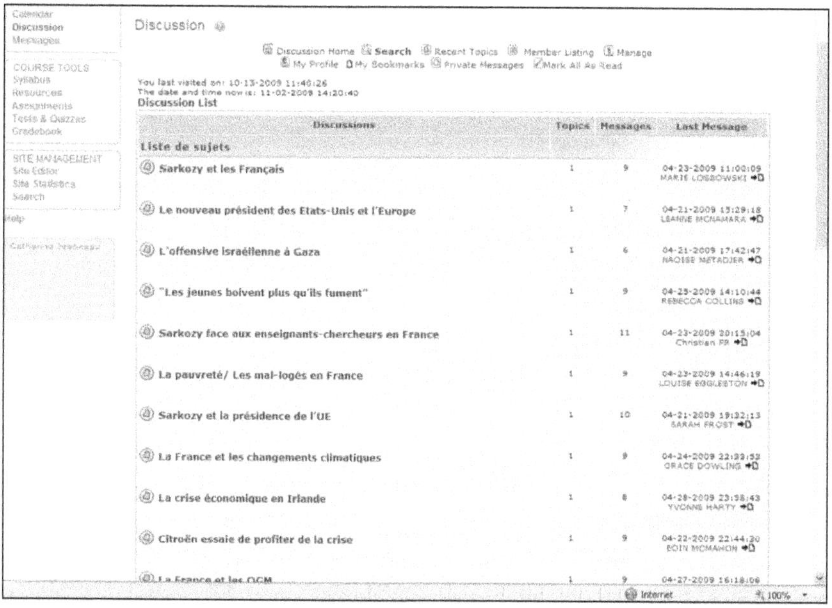

Figure 2. Student-teacher communication (email sample)

From : Marie-Therese.Batardiere	Sent : 24 March 2009 15:15
To : ULStudent:LOUISE XXXX	Subject : Forum de discussion FR4928

Bonjour Louise, Nous avons recherché et trouvé une autre correspondante pour toi. Mais tu dois encore patienter car elle ne pourra se connecter que demain. Merci de ta compréhension. Marie-Thérèse

Fro : ULStudent:LOUISE XXXX	Sent : 24 March 2009 15:04
To : Marie-Therese.Batardiere	Subject : Forum de discussion FR4928

Chere Marie-Therese, Je suis sur Sulis regulierement mais je n'ai recu aucun réponse sur le site. Je comprends que je dois finir les échanges en semaine 10. Est ce-que vous pouvez m'aider? Merci, Louise.

3.4.   Pedagogical changes made to the overall project

This type of project has been running for the last five consecutive years. The researcher has been guided by the methodological principles of action research which promote the development of understanding and the improvement of practice through the cyclical process of action and reflection (Reason & Bradbury, 2001). To inform further action, students were required to fill in a feedback questionnaire at the end of their learning experience. Analysis from the data collected during the first two years of the project led subsequently to a series of changes to the next cohort of students' project work (the one presented here):

- **Timing of the online exchange**: the exchange used to take place at the latter end of the project (the last four weeks), but is now introduced midway through the project in order to extend the period of interactions with the foreign partner and to give students more time for reflection.

- **Simplification of the analytical task**: the first task of the overall project has been shortened to ensure that students are ready to post it on the forum at an earlier date and engage more actively in the discussion forum task.

- **Choice of topics**: students used to have to write about a town or a region where they had sojourned during their Erasmus experience. This made the pairing with a native speaker more difficult (i.e., the necessity to find a NS who knew the town/ region picked by the L2 learner). In addition, the choice of a current French socio-political issue was deemed more controversial and should spark a debate between exchange partners.

- **Adoption to a new platform**: previously, we had used Internet classroom assistant (ICA), commonly referred to as *Nicenet* but this time, the discussion forum feature available in the learning management system of our university was used as students are familiar with this platform (i.e., they visit it on a daily basis for other courses). It was thought that this change might impact on their level of participation.

- **Reflection task**: students were asked to reflect and report on the exchange with the native speaker as part of their overall project. This evaluation task was seen not only a valuable source of feedback for the teacher/ action researcher, but also as a retrospective task for the students on the relevance (or lack of thereof) of an online experience to their campus-based language study.

All these changes were implemented to stimulate the exchange between the L2 learners and the native speakers. In addition, a higher proportion of the overall project grade was allocated to the online task as it was considered central to their (inter)cultural language learning (see Appendix 1 for details).

4. Data analysis and discussion of main findings

Figure 3. Online questionnaire (snapshot sample)

4 8 What factors motivated you to post messages on Sulis? (please rate each element from 0 to 6)	0 (=not at all motivating)	1	2	3	4	5	6 (=very motivating)	Rating Average	Response Count
Compulsory as part of the internet project	0.0% (0)	0.0% (1)	6.3% (0)	0.0% (0)	18.8% (3)	25.0% (4)	50.0% (8)	6 13	16
Interesting to exchange ideas with another person	0.0% (0)	0.0% (0)	12.5% (2)	12.5% (2)	31.3% (5)	25.0% (4)	18.8% (3)	5.25	16
Authentic opportunity to communicate in French	0.0% (0)	0.0% (0)	6.3% (1)	6.3% (1)	31.3% (5)	25.0% (4)	31.3% (5)	5.69	16
Interesting to communicate with a French person	0.0% (0)	0.0% (0)	0.0% (0)	6.3% (1)	25.0% (4)	50.0% (6)	18.8% (3)	5.81	16
Useful to improve your French	0.0% (0)	0.0% (0)	6.3% (1)	25.0% (4)	6.3% (1)	18.8% (3)	43.8% (7)	5.69	16
Good way to get information about French culture	0.0% (0)	0.0% (0)	6.3% (1)	18.8% (3)	37.5% (6)	25.0% (4)	12.5% (2)	5.19	16
Good way to get information about your topic	0.0% (0)	6.3% (1)	0.0% (0)	25.0% (4)	12.5% (2)	25.0% (4)	31.3% (5)	5.44	16
Interesting to get the viewpoint of a French person	0.0% (0)	0.0% (0)	0.0% (0)	12.5% (2)	25.0% (4)	43.8% (7)	18.8% (3)	5.69	16
Interesting to know the point of view of your partner	0.0% (0)	0.0% (0)	12.5% (2)	12.5% (2)	25.0% (4)	37.5% (6)	12.5% (2)	5.25	16
Exciting to use new technologies to communicate with someone	18.8% (3)	0.0% (0)	0.0% (0)	50.0% (8)	12.5% (2)	18.8% (3)	0.0% (0)	3.94	16
Curious to get to know your partner	12.5% (2)	31.3% (5)	18.8% (3)	31.3% (5)	6.3% (1)	0.0% (0)	0.0% (0)	2.88	16

The data analysed in this study was obtained through student feedback collected from three sources: i) student comments on the exchange (as part of the overall project and completed by 21 out 24 students), ii) student questionnaire (filled two weeks after the end of the project and completed by 16 out of 24 students; see Figure 3 above), iii) student interview (to which 3 students agreed to take part as a follow-up from the questionnaire).

Both quantitative and qualitative data were examined with the aim to highlight salient patterns of behaviour adopted by students to complete the online task and to determine what they perceived as the benefits of the Franco-Irish online exchange.

4.1.   Students' coping patterns of behaviour

While a majority of the students (62.6%) stated that they undoubtedly enjoyed the online discussion task, they underlined the fact that they found it quite challenging. The challenges – and the subsequent steps taken to circumvent them – can be broadly categorised as follows: technical, cross-cultural and personal 'obstacles'.

A few technical glitches occurred at the onset of the project. These were mainly due to the complicated way of accessing the institution virtual learning environment (VLE) by the native speakers and the time delay for a few postings to appear on the forum. They consequently made the beginning of the exchange difficult for a few students. However, once the teacher (who could call for extra technical support during the project) was made aware of these problems by students, she intervened to solve them. Some students also complained that they did not receive any email alert when a new message was posted on their thread and had to log on the forum to check it. Unfortunately, their request has yet to be accommodated on the university virtual learning environment.

Regarding the cross-cultural collaborative process, there were particular challenges posed by the lack of interaction between dyad partners. From the Irish student perspective, the reason for their problems was twofold: a lack of queries from the French partners (making it difficult to sustain a lively discussion) and a lack of responses to their questions (limiting the opportunity to get a 'French viewpoint'). In both cases, students coped by adopting a new communication technique and learning approach; when faced with a lack of queries, they introduced a new claim to revive the discussion, and when confronted with a deficit of information, they researched the requested topic themselves.

For some students, the actual performance of the task posed a challenge. They had to overcome the anxiety to write to a French native speaker whom they did not know for a 'real' purpose. A few students stressed that they were self-conscious about their level of French and were afraid that their language ability would impede the depth of the discussion. Interestingly, they affirmed that their fear lessened with usage and with new learning strategies: they observed the native speakers' argumentative style, picked up some useful vocabulary and expressions, read other threads of discussion to assess their own contribution, etc.

From the above reflexions we can contend that, when faced with a new task, students had to learn to overcome new challenges. In doing so, they developed a new set of learning and communicative strategies and consequently new patterns of behaviour.

4.2.   Students' perceived benefits of the online discussion task

In their feedback, students identified the various benefits drawn from their participation to the online exchange. These benefits were grouped into four main areas, namely building cultural knowledge, fostering critical thinking, improving language accuracy and encouraging further study; in each of the four areas several students' comments are included to illustrate their views.

Students first stated that they had become *more knowledgeable on their selected topic*. In the comments section of the project, over two thirds of the students said that they had vastly improved their understanding of the current issue studied. Moreover, 68.8% of the questionnaire respondents selected 'to get information on the topic' as one of the main benefits of the exchange, while another 68.8% added that their 'interest in the topic increased during the exchange'. They particularly valued having access to a different (sometimes new) viewpoint on the topic, especially from a French native speaker as they believed that it gave them an 'authentic' socio-cultural perspective.

> **Student S:** C'était inestimable aussi d'avoir l'occasion d'apprendre la perspective française[1] (Reflection task).

> **Student Y:** As my French partner expressed her ideas it encouraged me to find out more about the subject (Questionnaire).

> **Student F:** It [the exchange] gave a more realistic account rather than reading about it in a newspaper (Questionnaire).

Moreover, students explained that they had become *more assertive about expressing opinions*. In the questionnaire, the majority of the respondents (75.1%) declared that the exchange often challenged their initial beliefs. They mentioned in their comments that they found the discussion demanding because they had to present a clear line of reasoning and integrate the others' viewpoints in their argument. It would seem that the exchange provided them with a platform for critical thinking.

> **Student A:** La discussion a vraiment contesté la validité de mes opinions préconçue[2] (Reflection task).

> **Student R:** Good to get a French persons perspective. Provoked debate (Questionnaire).

> **Student J:** Once you had made-up your own mind on the topic, it was good having the other side of things (Interview).

---

1. English translation: It was also invaluable to get a French perspective.

2. English Translation: The discussion has really challenged my preconceived views.

When questioned on the linguistic value of the exchange, students claimed that they had become *more fluent and accurate in the target language*. All the students who filled up the questionnaire said that they paid more attention than usual to their French and in the reflection task, many of them referred to the linguistic gains of the exchange. They particularly highlighted the amount of writing produced, the access to authentic language – vocabulary related to their topic, expressions and phases, sentence structure, etc. – as well as their substantial efforts to produce better French than usual in order to be understood by their partner.

> **Student K:** ...très avantageux pour moi parce qu'il aide mon niveau de vocabulaire[1] (Reflection task).

> **Student F:** I learned about sentence structure, etc. from partner's postings (Questionnaire).

> **Student L:** ...idioms and things like that that I read from my partner [...] I used them in other areas as well, like in my exams and orals (Interview).

Lastly, one third of the students indicated that the discussion forum had made them *more autonomous and more responsible for their own learning* thus, more inclined to take initiatives to carry out extra work, either by reading other dyads' postings, or by undertaking extra research on the topic. This extra work always came as a strategy to compensate for a deficit such as a lack of information provided by their partner, a lack of knowledge on their behalf to produce a valid argument, or as previously pointed to, a lack of appropriate vocabulary or expressions.

> **Student N:** J'ai reçu seulement une réponse mais ca ma poussé de faire plus de recherche indépendant[2] (Reflection task).

---

1. English translation: [...] very beneficial for me because it helps enrich my vocabulary.

2. English translation: I received only one reply but it pushed me to do more independent research.

Student M: I did a lot of research on the topic to get new ideas and I followed regularly the French news (Questionnaire).

Student R: It motivated me to work harder and read further (Interview).

These findings would seem to suggest that, for some students, the incomprehension or frustration experienced with online intercultural communication motivated them to become more autonomous in their learning.

5. Implications

In this chapter, we set out to identify the challenges posed by virtual exchanges on a discussion forum and the ways students chose to tackle them. It was found that when faced with 'obstacles' of a technical, cross-cultural and personal nature, students responded positively and resorted to a new range of communication and learning strategies. We then sought to examine the perceived learning outcomes of a task-based discussion forum. Four main benefits were highlighted by the students, namely, building cultural knowledge, fostering critical thinking, improving language accuracy and encouraging further study. Finally, regarding the potential factors influencing the online task educational outcomes, we posit that, on the strength of students' positive perceptions of, and attitudes towards asynchronous CMC, the authenticity and complexity of an online task are paramount to the degree of students' enthusiasm and commitment to task.

This goal (i.e., to create a challenging authentic task) was achieved by taking the following steps: at the onset of the project, by allowing students to select and research their own topics of interest rather than working from a teacher-determined list of topics; by involving students in a cognitively challenging real-world activity; later on, by inviting 'real people' into the virtual classroom to assist students' inquiry; and finally, by encouraging students to take more responsibility for their learning (Hanna & de Nooy, 2003, 2009).

Furthermore, in terms of course design, our results bear out that a combination of factors such as, the integration and careful structuring of the online task, the clarity of the marking criteria (see Appendix 1) and the ease of participation, can affect favourably students' involvement in the task. It is worthy of note that in the retrospective interviews, these business students stressed that they gave prime importance to their online language exchange (O'Dowd, 2010).

6.   Limitations and conclusion

The findings presented in this paper are to be taken cautiously due to the relatively small number of participants (24), the nature of the data (i.e., the study is based on self-reported perceptions of students), and given the context in which the asynchronous online communication took place (i.e., the participants were university students, quite motivated, with an intermediate to high level of French); results should therefore be regarded as indicative only of patterns that might be found with other L2 learners working in a CMC environment. Indeed, a replication of our study with a larger number of subjects coming from a more varied array of backgrounds would certainly contribute to understanding the extent of the role of native speakers (as opposed to interactions between non-native speakers of the target language) in an online discussion forum.

Nonetheless, the present study adds to a growing body of research on the added value of CMC on students' intercultural and language development. It underlines the benefits of a well-designed and fully integrated online forum as a learning space where undergraduate students can acquire a range of transferable skills as well as improve their linguistic and intercultural competence. Indeed, it shows that the Irish students were not deterred by challenges which paved the way to the completion of the online project but, instead, took on a proactive and constructive role in the online forum.

Another notable side finding of this study was the quasi-invisible role of the teacher during the online task (as perceived by the students). Indeed, her role which was decisive in the design and implementation of the task, became less active – and more 'responsive' – during the actual performance of the task as student peers shared the 'teaching presence' online (Anderson, Rourke, Garrison, & Archer, 2001) with her. Students' *teaching behaviour* was evidenced in their on-line contributions (postings); the peers' assistance was usually given in the forms of scaffolding and feedback (Ab Jalil & Rahman, 2010).

This latter finding emphasises the role of human agency in a mediated (online) environment and supports the view that the key to successful use of technology in language teaching lies not in hardware or software but in "humanware" (Warschauer & Meskill, 2000, p. 307).

References

Ab Jalil, H., & Rahman, F. (2010). Teaching as assisting others' performance. In L. Dirckinck-Holmfeld, V. Hodgson, C. Jones, D. McConnell, & T. Ryberg (Eds.), *Proceedings of the 7th International Conference on Networked Learning 2010, Aalborg, Denmark* (pp. 1-8). Lancaster: Lancaster University. Retrieved from http://www.lancs.ac.uk/fss/organisations/netlc/past/nlc2010/abstracts/PDFs/Ab_Jalil.pdf

Anderson, T., Rourke, L., Garrison, D. R., & Archer, W. (2001). Assessing teaching presence in a computer conferencing context. *Journal of Asynchronous Learning Networks, 5*(2), 1-17. Retrieved from http://sloanconsortium.org/sites/default/files/v5n2_anderson_1.pdf

Blake, R. (2000). Computer mediated communication: a window on L2 Spanish interlanguage. *Language Learning & Technology, 4*(1), 120-136. Retrieved from http://llt.msu.edu/vol4num1/blake/default.html

Brandl, K. (2012). Effects of required and optional exchange tasks in online language learning environments. *ReCALL, 24*(1), 85-107. doi: 10.1017/S0958344011000309

Cummings, J. A., Bonk, C. J., & Jacobs, F. R. (2002). Twenty-first century college syllabi: options for online communication and interactivity. *Internet and Higher Education, 5*(1), 1-19. doi: 10.1016/S1096-7516(01)00077-X

Dooly, M. (2011). Divergent perceptions of telecollaborative language learning tasks: task-as-workplan vs. task-as-process. *Language Learning & Technology, 15*(2), 69-91. Retrieved from http://llt.msu.edu/issues/june2011/dooly.pdf

Ellis, R. (2003). *Task-based language learning and teaching*. Oxford, UK: Oxford University Press.

Garrison, D. R., Anderson, T., & Archer, W. (2000). Critical inquiry in a text-based environment: computer conferencing in higher education. *The Internet and Higher Education, 2*(2-3), 87-105. doi: 10.1016/S1096-7516(00)00016-6

Hanna, B. E., & de Nooy, J. (2003). A funny thing happened on the way to the forum: electronic discussion and foreign language learning. *Language Learning & Technology, 7*(1), 71-85. Retrieved from http://llt.msu.edu/vol7num1/pdf/hanna.pdf

Hanna, B. E., & de Nooy, J. (2009). *Learning language and culture via public Internet discussion forums*. Basingstoke, New York: Palgrave Macmillian.

Kol, S., & Schcolnik, M. (2008). Asynchronous forums in EAP: assessment issues. *Language Learning & Technology, 12*(2), 49-70. Retrieved from http://llt.msu.edu/vol12num2/kolschcolnik.pdf

Kuteeva, M. (2007). The use of online fora in language teaching: the importance of task design. *IADIS International Conference Proceedings: E-Learning, 6-8 July, Lisbon, Portugal* (pp. 305-308). Lisbon: IADIS.

Lee, L. (2002). Synchronous online exchanges: a study of modification devices on nonnative discourse interaction. *System, 30*(3), 275-288. doi: 10.1016/S0346-251X(02)00015-5

Little, D., & Ushioda, E. (1998). *Institution-wide language programmes: a research-and-development approach to their design, implementation and evaluation*. London: CILT.

Lockley, T., & Promnitz-Hayashi, L. (2012). Japanese university students' CALL attitudes, aspirations and motivations. *CALL-EJ online, 13*(1), 1-16. Retrieved from http://callej.org/journal/13-1/Lockley_Promnitz-Hayashi_2012.pdf

O'Dowd, R. (2010). Online foreign language interaction: moving from the periphery to the core of foreign language education? *Language Teaching, 44*(3), 368-380. doi: 10.1017/S0261444810000194

O'Dowd, R., & Waire, P. (2009). Critical issues in telecollaborative task design. *Computer Assisted Language Learning, 22*(2), 173-188. doi: 10.1080/09588220902778369

Ortega, L. (1997). Processes and outcomes in networked classroom interaction: defining the research agenda for L2 computer-assisted classroom discussion. *Language Learning & Technology, 1*(1), 82-93. Retrieved from http://llt.msu.edu/vol1num1/ortega/default.html

Ortega, L. (2009). Interaction and attention to form in L2 text-based computer-mediated communication. In A. Mackey & C. Polio (Eds.), *Multiple perspectives on interaction in SLA: research in honor of Susan M. Gass* (pp. 226-253). New York: Routledge.

Pellettieri, J. (2000). Negotiation in cyberspace. The role of chatting in the development of grammatical competence in the virtual foreign language classroom. In M. Warschauer & R. Kern (Eds.), *Network-based language teaching: concepts and practice* (pp. 59-86). Cambridge: Cambridge University Press.

Reason, P., & Bradbury, H. (2001). Introduction: Inquiry and Participation in Search of a World Worthy of Human Aspiration. In P. Reason & H. Bradbury (Eds.), *Handbook of Action Research. Participatory Inquiry & Practice* (pp. 1-14). London: Sage.

Smith, B. (2004). Computer-mediated negotiated interaction and lexical acquisition. *Studies in Second Language Acquisition, 26*(3), 365-398. doi: 10.1017/S027226310426301X

Sotillo, S. M. (2000). Discourse functions and syntactic complexity in synchronous and asynchronous communication. *Language Learning & Technology, 4*(1), 82-119. Retrieved from http://llt.msu.edu/vol4num1/sotillo/default.html

Thomas, M., & Reinders, H. (Eds.). (2010). *Task-based language learning and teaching with technology*. London: Continuum.

Warschauer, M., & Meskill, C. (2000). Technology and second language learning. In J. Rosenthal (Ed.), *Handbook of undergraduate second language education* (pp. 303-318). Mahwah, New Jersey: Lawrence Erlbaum.

Appendix

Appendix 1.   Project outline

FR4928 Recherche sur <u>la presse française</u> via Internet 30%

1. REGARDS SUR L'ACTUALITE

Semaines de 2 à 5 / *Travail individuel* / 15%

-Vous rechercherez plusieurs articles traitant d'un même sujet d'actualité et tirés de journaux/ magazines de différentes tendances – *Le Monde, Le Figaro, Libération, l'Express, la Croix, le Nouvel Observateur, etc.*, les lirez, et les référencerez.

-Vous sélectionnerez un seul de ces articles pour l'analyser.

-Vous rapporterez succinctement l'information/ les faits (75 mots environ / **5%**)

-Vous analyserez – sous forme de commentaire – certaines prises de position du journaliste (2 au minimum/ 250 mots environ / **10%**)

2. ECHANGES D'OPINION SUR L'ACTUALITE /<u>3 contributions minimum</u>/

Semaines de 6 à 10 / *Travail en tandem avec un(e) francophone sur SULIS* / 10%

-Vous mettrez votre commentaire sur le forum de discussion

-Vous choisirez l'un des points controversés que vous aurez abordés pour en discuter avec votre correspondant(e) et, pour lancer la discussion, vous soumettrez une question qui sera postée sur le forum, à la suite de votre commentaire.

-Vous lirez les réactions –à vos affirmations- de votre partenaire.

-Vous défendrez vos arguments et en avancerez de nouveaux.

3. AUTRE PERSPECTIVE SUR L'ACTUALITE

Semaines 11 & 12 / *Travail individuel* / 5%

Suite à vos interactions – en ligne – avec un(e) francophone, vous expliquerez, d'une part, si et de quelle façon, votre regard/ perspective sur la question d'actualité étudiée, a changé (150 mots environ) et d'autre part, vous évaluerez la valeur (ajoutée) de l'échange en ligne.

---

16 Using Facebook in an Irish Third-Level Education Context: A Case-Study

Catherine Jeanneau[1]

Abstract

Social networking sites such as *Facebook* or *Twitter* have become social phenomena, and educators are increasingly experimenting with these new tools in order to find out if they can be used for teaching and learning. However, we can question if the use of social media is really in the process of changing teaching and learning practices and whether Irish students are ready to adopt these new tools. We can also query whether social networking sites can contribute to connecting students and developing the feeling of belonging to a learning community amongst them. In order to investigate these various issues, this chapter offers the findings from a case-study where a *Facebook* page was introduced in a learning context. Based on the comparison and analysis of student and staff participation and usage patterns between a virtual learning environment (VLE) and a *Facebook* page, as well as feedback questionnaires, this study highlights that the social networking site led to a greater level of interactivity amongst students, who enjoyed the informality and accessibility of the page. Yet, preconceptions associated with social media continued to prevail, with students failing to appreciate the educational potential of the site.

Keywords: social media, social networking sites, online learning community, Facebook.

1. School of Languages, Literature, Culture and Communication; Centre for Applied Language Studies (CALS), University of Limerick, Limerick, Ireland; catherine.jeanneau@ul.ie

How to cite this chapter: Jeanneau, C. (2013). Using Facebook in an Irish Third-Level Education Context: A Case-Study. In C. Fowley, C. English, & S. Thouësny (Eds.), *Internet Research, Theory, and Practice: Perspectives from Ireland* (pp. 325-347). Dublin: © Research-publishing.net.

1.   Introduction

Web 2.0 technology facilitates participation and information-sharing on the Internet and has led to the advent of a new era for the Internet: 'the social Web' (Kárpáti, 2009). This sharing of content occurs both in the private and public spheres and at a personal and professional level. Ireland has embraced this new age of communication. *Facebook* and *Twitter* are highly present in Irish society. Teachers – and students alike – want to be connected and take advantage of the huge potential given to them by social media. It is thus not surprising to find that they are increasingly adding this technology to their teaching/learning arsenal.

Due to the social nature of these new tools, their successful integration in a teaching and learning context should lead to a higher level of participation from students. Yet, this integration raises a number of questions, especially in the Irish context. Are students and educators ready to change their teaching and learning practices? Are Irish students prepared to adopt these new tools for learning purposes? And can social media really reinforce the bounds between learners in order to strengthen learning communities?

In an attempt to address these issues, this chapter examines a case-study. It observes and analyses online practices of staff and students in a language-learning support context at the University of Limerick where a social networking site (a *Facebook* page) was introduced by support staff to complement an institutional virtual learning environment in an attempt to increase students' participation by using a media platform which is popular amongst them. The study presents how this addition was received by students. The participation study is complemented by the results from student surveys. The feedback questionnaires focused on students' perceptions of both platforms and more specifically on their views on the pedagogical values of the sites and of their sense of 'community belonging' in both learning settings.

The findings and the ensuing conclusions form the basis for recommendations for further applications of social networking sites in an educational context and initiate a dialogue on the use of these sites for language learning and for community building in an Irish context.

1.1. Social media and social networking sites

The advance in computer technology, allowing for instant online communication and the easy creation and sharing of user-generated content via web-based and mobile applications, enabled the advent of social media (McLoughlin & Lee, 2007). This interactive dialogue on the net has become a societal phenomenon, entering our lives in various forms and for a range of functions and purposes. Kaplan and Haenlein (2010) established a classification scheme for social media types containing six categories: collaborative projects (e.g., *Wikipedia*), blogs and microblogs (e.g., *Twitter*), content communities (e.g., *YouTube*), social networking sites (e.g., *Facebook*), virtual game worlds (e.g., *World of Warcraft*), and virtual social worlds (e.g., *Second Life*). For the purpose of this research, we will concentrate solely on social networking sites. Boyd and Ellison (2007) define the latter as "web-based services that allow individuals to (1) construct a public or semi-public profile within a bounded system, (2) articulate a list of other users with whom they share a connection, and (3) view and traverse their list of connections and those made by others within the system" (p. 211).

Since they first emerged, the popularity of social networking sites has grown rapidly, as shown by the Alexa global user ranking list[1] – a listing of all sites on the Web, sorted by traffic – where *Facebook* is in second place just behind *Google*. The penetration rate is especially high amongst young people. A survey carried out in 2008 at the University of Limerick amongst 75 language students revealed that 97 per cent of the respondents had a presence on these platforms and that 51.5 per cent had a profile on more than one networking site (Murray, Hourigan, & Jeanneau, 2008). In recent years, *Facebook* has become the overall 'winner' in the popularity race. Hew (2011) highlights that its use is "nearly ubiquitous amongst students" (p. 663).

---

1. Retrieved from http://www.alexa.com/

Over the past few years, research on the academic and pedagogical use of *Facebook* is starting to emerge (Hew, 2011; Lampe, Wohn, Vitak, Ellison, & Wash, 2011; Lamy, 2011). This site is often presented as a platform to organise group activities or to discuss course or assignment details (Bosch, 2009; Lampe et al, 2011). Hew's (2011) research review concludes that, although learning purposes are stated by students as a motive for using *Facebook*, in reality its use remains essentially social and the educational function is still very marginal amongst students. The present study will attempt to determine whether these findings can be verified in our research context.

1.2.   Community building

The popularity of social networking site relies heavily on their propensity to initiate a feeling of belonging (Arnold & Paulus, 2010). McMillan and Chavis (1986) have been influential in their studies on defining the concept of 'sense of community'. They highlight four key elements which help build this feeling: (1) membership (the feeling of being part of a defined group which holds boundaries); (2) influence (the reciprocal influence of members on each other, the fact that they all have something to bring and take to the rest of the group); (3) integration and fulfilment of needs (the elements that bind the community together, even though the needs of each member might not be the same, each one expresses what they gain from his/her participation); and (4) shared emotional connection (the feeling of closeness experienced by members, this is often linked to shared history and experience). McMillan and Chavis (1986) establish that there is a link between sense of community and the "ability to function competently in the community" (p. 6); the more developed the sense of community is, the higher the level of participation is. Similarities can be found in the definitions of communities which develop in an online environment. Rotman, Golbeck and Preece (2009) state that online communities are "characterized by being groups of people brought together by a shared interest, who create, through interaction on an online platform, a joint repertoire and common culture" (p. 42). These elements are thus crucial when studying participation on social networking sites and when trying to establish whether community building can occur on these sites.

In the context of this study, it was established that reinforcing the sense of community belonging was a key aspect. As highlighted by Pavlenko and Norton (2007) the sense of belonging has an impact on motivation: "The process of imagining and reimagining one's multiple memberships may influence agency, motivation, investment, and resistance in the learning of [languages]" (p. 669). Aceto, Dondi, and Marzotto (2010) go even further in emphasising the impact of online communities in the learning process by stating that they "provide the context, resources and opportunities to expand the members' horizons and awareness of themselves and of other members" which in turn leads to "other forms of learning, such as knowledge and skill acquisition for practical and professional aims" (p. 6). Finding the most appropriate platform to foster this type of learning and to encourage involvement and participation was thus paramount to our study.

1.3.   Social and educational
context of the study

Located at the heart of the Languages Building, and a key feature of the School of Languages, Literature, Culture and Communication, the Language Resource Area (LRA) at the University of Limerick offers all language learners opportunities for learning activities (Language Partner Programme, discussion groups...) as well as a range of resources in the six languages taught in the School and at all the levels represented (from ab initio for some undergraduate courses to advanced level, especially for some postgraduate courses). These are provided on a self-access and voluntary basis.

The role of the LRA is mainly to support language learning, to increase learners' autonomy by fostering meta-cognitive thinking about language learning, to encourage the development and transfer of skills across languages and disciplines, and to facilitate the creation of a community of language learners. The underlying principles for the development of this resource centre were borrowed from research in the field of language advising/language counselling (Mozzon-McPherson & Vismans, 2001) with an emphasis on "helping learners acquire the knowledge and skills to manage their own learning" (Rubin, 2007, p. 1).

A virtual learning environment was initially developed in 2007 on the institutional learning management system called *Sulis* to add flexibility to the services already offered. This proved to be challenging as this VLE – unlike VLEs set up for online courses, designated modules or specific cohorts of students – had to address the needs of a wide audience ranging from first years to postgraduate students, from language specialists to non-specialists. The established VLE (Figure 1) contains an extensive resource repository, a calendar of events, an announcement space for events and various discussion forums (one for each of the six languages and some for specific topics such as language exchange partners).

Figure 1.   Sulis - virtual learning environment - screenshot

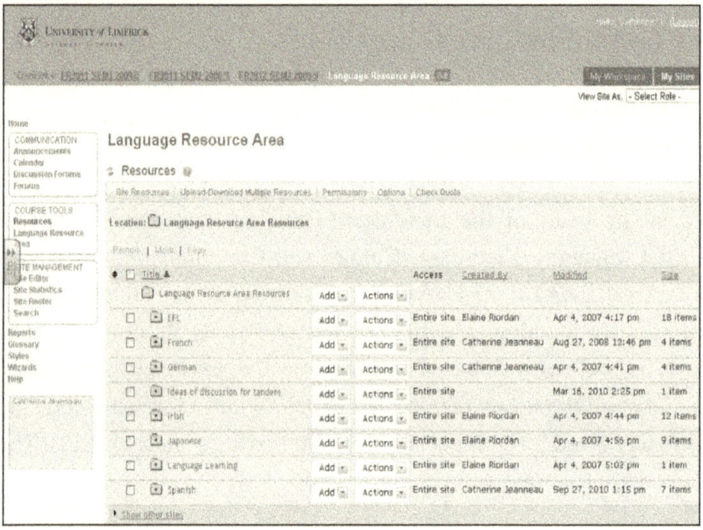

Even though the VLE has remained open, a *Facebook* page for the LRA was created in September 2010 (Figure 2). The main objectives of this page are to reach a wider audience and to offer students a platform where they might feel more at ease communicating. The page is maintained by the administrator of the LRA and is frequently updated with information about the language-learning activities (both inside the university and outside the institution), links to useful resources on the Internet, pictures of events, discussions on language-learning material or popular foreign films. Students are free to 'join' the page by becoming a fan or just visit it whenever they like. They can participate by liking a post, commenting on a message or posting a new contribution. The messages posted on the *Facebook* page have progressively replaced the information which was posted on the communication tools of the VLE, where only the resources function is kept updated. In the second year of the study, students were able to access and use either or both platforms.

Figure 2.   LRA Facebook page

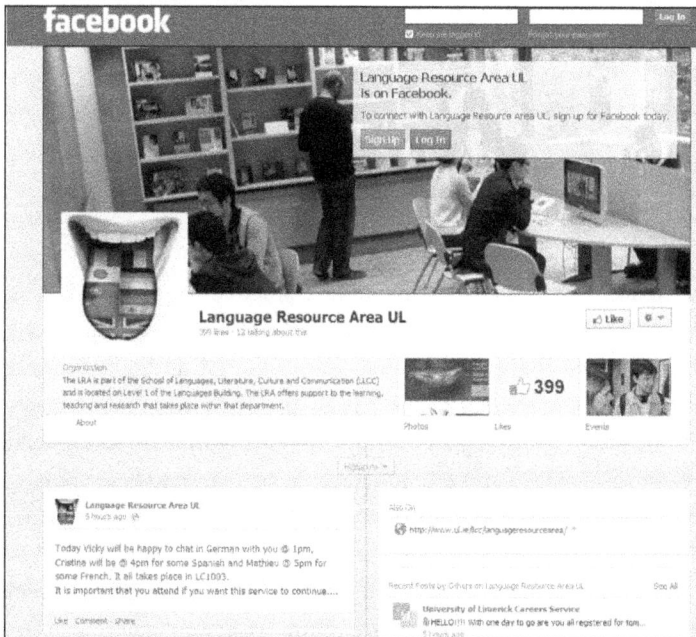

1.4.   Rationale and research questions

In a society where social networking is ubiquitous amongst students, we can question whether the use of social media can affect teaching and learning practices and whether Irish students are ready to adopt these new tools in this new context. We can also query whether social networking sites can contribute to connecting students and developing the feeling of belonging to a learning community.

In an effort to find answers to these queries, this chapter presents the results of a case-study which focuses on the following questions:

- What are the patterns of use and participation of both staff and students on the institutional VLE and the Centre's Facebook page?

- How do these two platforms impact on students' sense of community?

- What are the Irish students' perceptions of these sites and of their pedagogical value?

2. Data collection and methodology

In order to address these issues, the online practices of staff and students on two different platforms (the VLE and the *Facebook* page set-up for the LRA) were observed and analysed. The data was collected during two consecutive years, namely February 2010 to 2011 for the *Sulis* site and February 2011 to 2012 for the *Facebook* page. The general quantitative data (number of users, visits, activities…) were collected from the statistical tools on both platforms. A qualitative study of the content of the sites was then carried out (including a study of the posts, likes…). In addition to the data analysis, two online surveys were carried out using *SurveyMonkey* to get feedback from students. The questionnaire pertaining to the VLE was undertaken in Spring 2011 and was accessed by 60 respondents. The questionnaire concerning the *Facebook* page ran at the beginning of February 2012 and was completed by 64 respondents. The latter included a question asking students to compare the usefulness of both platforms. As 55% of the respondents had used the VLE in the first year of the study and the *Facebook* page in the second, or had accessed both in the second year, they were in a position to offer their opinion concerning both platforms.

3.   Data analysis and results

3.1.   Overall use of the platforms

Figure 3.   Number of users/'fans' and visits/page views

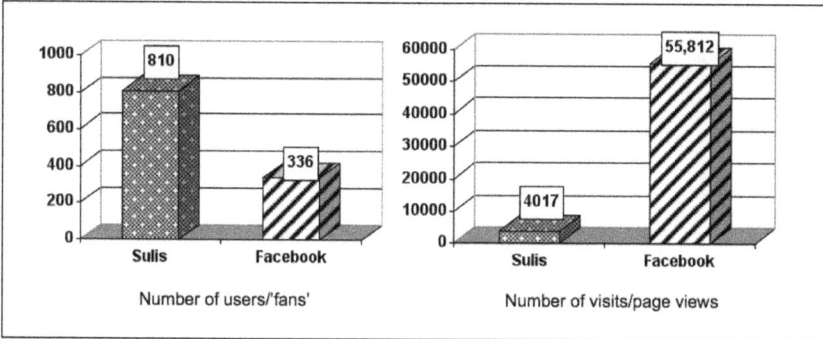

When we observe the overall use of the two platforms (Figure 3), the differences are striking. Even though there are over twice as many users on the VLE, the *Facebook* page was viewed over 55,000 times, as opposed to just over 4,000 visits over a similar timeframe of a year for the *Sulis* site. Some of these divergences in results can be explained by the set-up of the sites.

The higher numbers on the VLE can be explained by the fact that the site was manually populated by the staff of the centre with all the students learning a language in the School. Although access to the site does not automatically equate to use of the site, a vast majority of the students who were given access to the VLE logged in to check it out. However, out of the 810 actual users, 30% accessed the site only once; we may assume they did so out of curiosity.

Conversely, the number of 'fans' on *Facebook* does not truly reflect the number of users of the Facebook page, as users do not need to have 'liked' a page to be able to visit it. The actual number of users is thus more difficult to ascertain. The data from Figure 4 shows how some posts were 'reached', i.e., accessed, over a one-month period. The 'organic reach' line corresponds to the number of unique people, fans or non-fans, who saw the post in their news feed or directly on the *Facebook* Page whereas the 'viral reach' data refers to the number of unique people who saw this post from a story published by a friend. This graph thus highlights the 'viral' nature of *Facebook*: the information passes from user to user via their 'Wall'. This can explain the high number of page views, as the information was transferred from user to user.

Figure 4.   "Reach" of the Facebook page over a one-month period

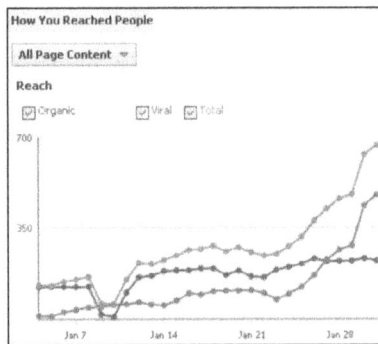

Moreover, we can also speculate that a page viewed does not necessarily equate to a page read. So we cannot assume that the information, while displayed on students' profile, is taken on board.

Figure 5.   Frequency of use of both platforms over a one-year period

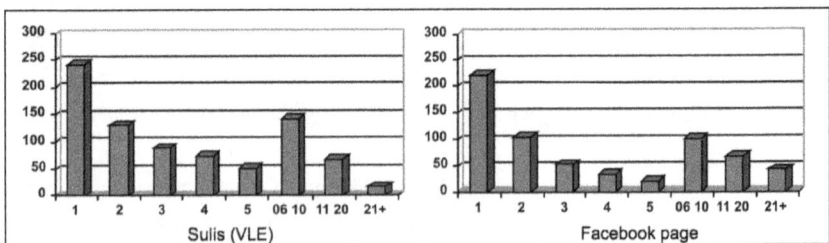

Interestingly, the graphs on Figure 5 reveal that overall, the pattern of use is similar on both platforms, with a high percentage of unique visits, a steady

decrease in numbers up to 5 visits, and a significant proportion of users who can be classified as frequent users (6 visits or more). The only noteworthy differences in this pattern of use are the higher ratio of 6-10 visits on the VLE and the larger amount of users with more than 21 visits on *Facebook*. But overall, the frequency of use is not significantly higher on *Facebook*, as it could have been expected from a medium so widely used by the target audience.

3.2. Details of activities on the platforms

We can note that the VLE is primarily accessed to read content and the other activities (adding content, updating the calendar, posting information) are restricted to staff even though the setting of the VLE allowed students to post as well (see Figure 6).

Figure 6.   Types of activities on Sulis - total: 5283

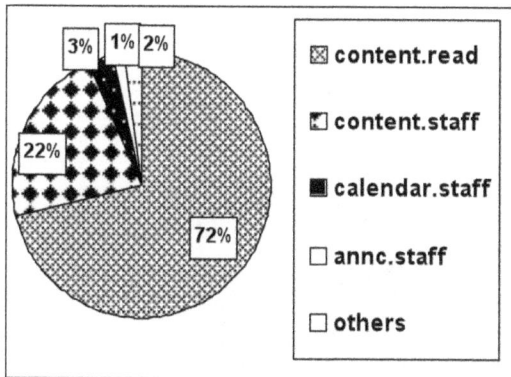

This tends to show that from a student point of view, both the *Sulis* and *Facebook* sites are used in a similar way, mainly to access and read content. However, differences appear when we observe the types of activities and interactivity on both platforms (Figure 7, Figure 8, and Figure 9).

The most salient feature when observing Figure 7 is the discrepancy in the level of staff participation between the two platforms. This can be explained by the nature of the participation on both sites. On the VLE, staff frequently shared useful resources for students (links, material...). This represented 83.5% of all the staff participation on the site.

Figure 7.   Staff and student participation

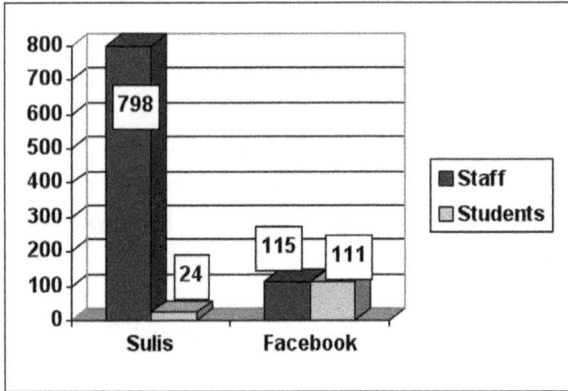

Figure 8.   Types of staff participation

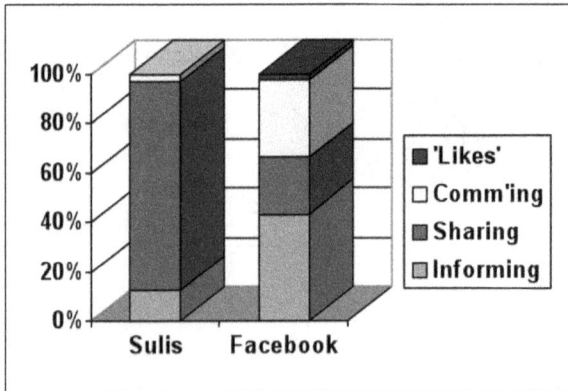

As detailed in Figure 8, this function is far less developed on the *Facebook* page (22.5% of all posts) which is used more extensively to inform students (e.g., events in the School, language-related events in the country, new material acquired by the centre, funding opportunities...) and to communicate with them (e.g., queries about future material to be purchased, survey of favourite foreign movies, response to students posts or comments...). *Facebook* thus seems to hold a more dialogic function. This observation is reinforced by the overall level of student participation, which is five times higher on the social networking site (Figure 9). Even though 70% of the student participation is limited to a 'like', it shows an involvement and a certain level of engagement with the content of the page. Furthermore, the number of comments is also four times higher on *Facebook*, which supports the idea that *Facebook* contributes to a higher level of communication.

Figure 9.   Types of student participation

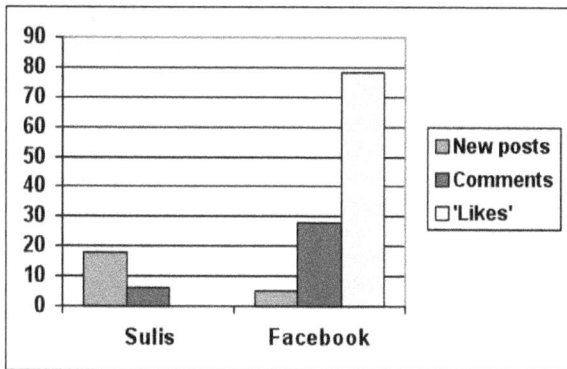

It is revealing to examine in detail the types of posts which elicite the highest level of participation amongst students. On the *Sulis* platform, students react mostly to messages about ways to improve their language learning, about useful resources and their access. Figure 10 provides an example of these messages, with the particularity of being a message initiated by a student. On the *Facebook* page, pictures of events and messages linked to cultural aspects seem to get the highest number of 'likes' and comments. Figure 11 illustrates this point. It would tend to show that *Sulis* is used more as a pedagogical tool whereas *Facebook* is used as a social and cultural tool. The study of the students' feedback will confirm this remark.

Figure 10. Sample of exchanges on Sulis

02/22/2010 11:07:42 PM	Subject: MUSIC!....FRENCH STYLE!
STUDENT Last edited: 02/22/2010 04:07:42 PM Messages: 10	Hey Guys, Some of you may have already heard about it, but "Deezer" is a brillaint website I came across while I was in France over the holidays. Basically its like Youtube but just for music, and the sound quality is excellent. In France, you can play virtually any song you like, its almost like a dj and will learn what type of music you like depending on what you select. You can play all the current top chart music. Its already a big success across Europe (God, it sounds like they're paying me to write this!) **Anyway, my point is this site is a great way to listen to new FOREIGN MUSIC which is a good idea for all us Language Learners! e.g if you select "BEST NEW FRENCH" playlist it will play lots of french songs that are popular at the moment. If you create a profile on the site, you can then create playlists to which you can save new songs as you come across them. You'll then have them to play whenever you want! Heres the address .... :** www.deezer.com/ Believe me, its well worth a look at least. **This is the fun side of language learning!** If you find music you like in a language you are studying, then thats definitely an incentive to improve your level. Definitely a site to add to your favourites. Sorry for the long-winded message! Have fun, David
02/23/2010 09:52:23 AM	Subject: Re:MUSIC!....FRENCH STYLE!
STAFF Last edited: 02/23/2010 09:52:53 AM Messages: 17	Merci David, I am on Deezer all the time! I think you put your finger on a great topic: music for language learning. So come on people (especially those of you who are just back from Erasmus/coop), tell us what music/artists you discovered! Catherine
02/25/2010 09:32:24 PM	Subject: Re:MUSIC!....FRENCH STYLE!
STUDENT Last edited: 02/25/2010 01:32:24 PM	Merci David, J'adore la musique francais sur l'internet! A mon avis, c'est tres interesant. Malachy

Figure 11. Sample of exchanges on Facebook

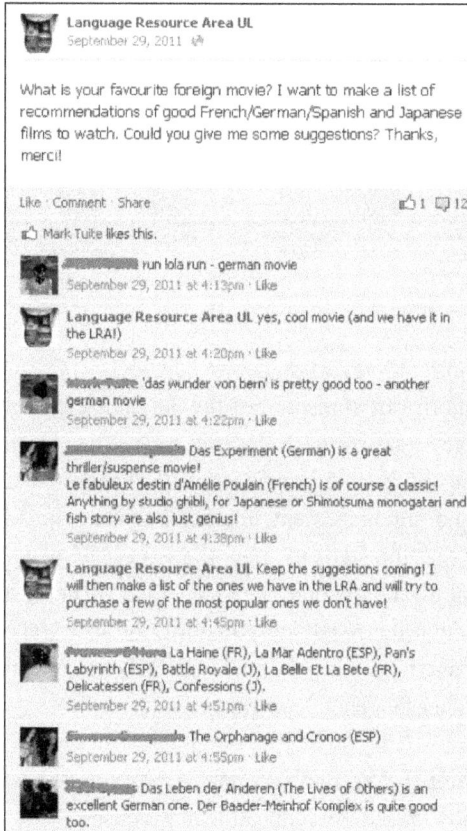

3.3.   Feedback from online users

To complement the data analysis from the two sites, two surveys were carried out to get feedback from students. The first survey focused on the VLE and the second on the *Facebook* page with an extra question asking students to compare the two sites if they used both. The results from these questionnaires can be divided into three broad categories: usefulness of the sites, participation on the sites and sense of community or community building.

3.3.1. Usefulness of the sites

Figure 12. Usefulness of both platforms (in %)

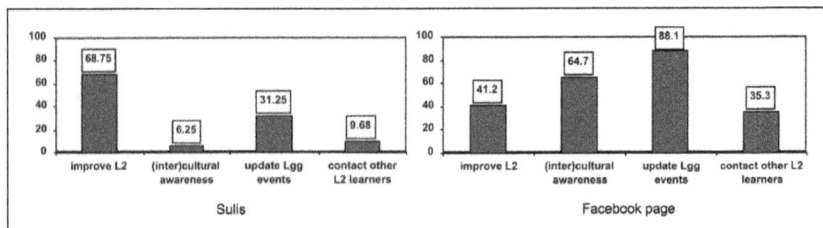

The data from Figure 12 reveal students' perception of the usefulness of the two sites. The majority of students opt for the educational value of the VLE and the informative value of the *Facebook* page. The informative role of the VLE also represents a sizeable proportion of the replies; it could be explained by the calendar and announcement functions of the site. More interestingly, it is worth noting that the students view the *Facebook* page as a good tool to raise (inter)cultural awareness and the educational function of the page is also acknowledged, though not receiving a majority of approval. The social aspect of the *Facebook* page is also highlighted with 35% of students stating that it is useful to contact other language learners.

When asked to compare the two sites and express their preferences, students place *Sulis* strongly ahead for educational purposes (73% against 27% for *Facebook*) citing the larger availability of learning resources as the reason for their choice: "*The Sulis page provides access to many more resources which I find very helpful*", "*there is more information on Sulis to help language learning*".

Preconceptions concerning the two platforms also influence their choice: "*I use the Sulis page as I associate that with college work. I use Facebook as a social site, I do not use it for educational purposes*". When it comes to ease of use, ease of access and overall enjoyment of the platform, the trends are reversed, with *Facebook* topping the poll (77% versus 23% for the VLE): "*Facebook, as it feels socialable [sic] and more enjoyable rather than Sulis*", "*Facebook is easier to* access and gives you info fast, without having to search for it". Finally, we can also notice that several students recognise the value of both platforms but for different functions: "I suppose they are both good, but for different purposes", "Sulis is more useful for serious revision, but the LRA page [on Facebook] is something I would check regularly", "Sulis is a better source of academic resources so I prefer this".

3.3.2. Participation on the sites

Only 12.8% of respondents to the questionnaire concerning the VLE acknowledged they had posted a contribution to the site as opposed to 31.1% of respondents of the *Facebook* survey.

Figure 13. Reasons for not contributing to the sites (in %)

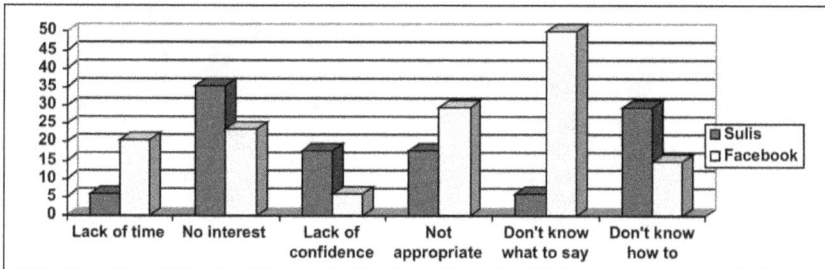

A comparison of the reasons for not posting on the sites reveals some noteworthy differences (Figure 13). While lack of confidence and technological know-how does not seem to be an issue on *Facebook*, students do not seem to know what to say (50% of respondents) and do not feel it appropriate to post contributions (29.4% of respondents). The comments offered by some students shed some light as to the reasons why these feelings prevail: "I haven't found anything worth sharing I guess" and "sometimes I feel afraid to post on it but I do feel it is useful". It would be interesting to explore whether students might feel that they do not have enough expertise to post on a page 'owned' by someone they might perceive as an expert (administrator of the centre) and open to all the other language students. In parallel, students suggested more interactions between students as a way to improve both sites ("*not enough people are getting involved in it which is such a great pity*"), though several added that they did not know how this could be achieved: "*It a great source of new and interesting information but unlike the ULSU [student union] page, people don't communicate as much - I don't think it's really able to bring people together that much. Anyways, the work that is done besides that is amazing. It's a great promoter of the events and meetings so I don't think there is much else to be doing!*".

3.3.3. Sense of community and community building

Figure 14. Contribution of the sites to building group identity (in %)

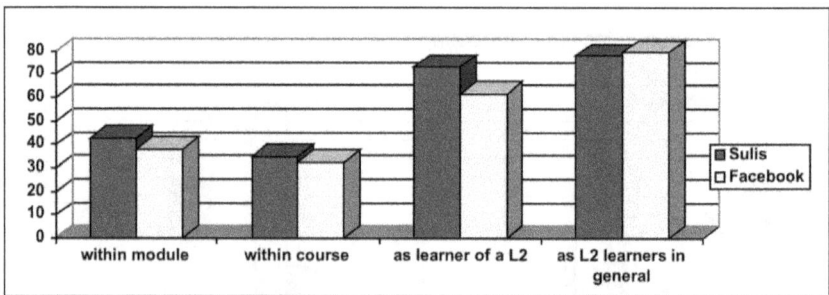

When asked about their perception of the sites' contribution to the 'building of a sense of group identity', we can observe no notable differences between the two platforms (Figure 14). The *Facebook* page receives a slightly lower percentage for the 'specialised' category, such as group identity within a module or as learner of a specific language. This might be explained by the existing groupings per language in the resources and forums section of the VLE site on *Sulis*.

The students' comments once again bring some insight into their way of thinking. For the VLE, one student remarks that: "*Sulis is too impersonal to get any sense of group identity*". As for the networking site, students state that "*most language courses have already established their own Facebook Groups*" and "*each major option sets up their own Facebook that builds a group for us. [...] Any queries are usually put on these pages"*. It would suggest that students do not feel the need to post on the sites put in place by the institution as they already have their own site, where they feel more comfortable communicating. Finally, amongst students' suggestions on how the sites could be improved, several students mentioned that a more 'specialised' approach would be beneficial: *"maybe a tab for each language so quick access for each student in respective fields of study"*, *"by having posts in different languages"*.

4. Discussion and limitations

Overall, it is possible to say that the students surveyed enjoy having access to a *Facebook* page and prefer the informal feel of the social networking platform, especially when it comes to the sharing of information on events and cultural aspects. The study of the participation patterns indicates that *Facebook* tends to encourage more communication from students (even if their involvement is often limited to 'likes') and that it generally promotes activities of a dialogic nature with a focus on social aspects, which proves positive in a language learning context.

The analysis of the data reveals no strong opposition to the adoption of these new tools in a different context. On the contrary, the high rate of access to the *Facebook* page shows that students are, at the very least, curious about the use of the networking site for a different purpose than the one they are familiar with. The general trend of this case-study, including the various comments by the surveys' respondents, suggests that students reacted positively to the integration of a *Facebook* page in their learning environment.

However, preconceptions pertaining to each site continue to prevail. Students perceive the virtual environment as an adequate study tool and the *Facebook* page as a social one. Our study brought similar results as Hew's (2011) findings concerning students' perception of the educational value of *Facebook*, as some of the students' comments on our survey point out to the fact that a proportion of them fail to appreciate the educational potential of the social networking site.

Furthermore, while the *Facebook* page encouraged a higher level of participation from learners, the level of student to student communication was nevertheless not as high as originally anticipated. As this case-study was carried out in a language-learning support context, there was no scope to introduce and explain to students the educational value of the social networking site while running the experiment. Despite being familiar with these technologies, most students have not used them for educational purposes. Therefore, it seems important that educators facilitate the integration of these new tools by showing students how they can be applied more in educational endeavours and how students can benefit from this use.

The findings from our case-study also confirm that the value of social networking sites such as *Facebook* in the creation and development of online learning communities is not to be underestimated. A high number of students indicate that the *Facebook* page contributed to building their sense of community belonging as learners of a foreign language. This can be explained by the fact that social networking sites increase the opportunities for staff-student communication, but more importantly student-student communication. They also provide an environment where all the factors contributing to community building can be gathered: defined boundaries (with the list of fans visible on the page), influence (with the various postings contributing to increase students' knowledge and know-how), fulfilment of needs (with the possibility for students to post queries or find information on the page), and connection (with the ubiquity of *Facebook*, its viral nature and its affordance – with the 'likes' for example). In the field of language learning where community building is an important factor in developing the skills required to speak a language, social networking sites thus have a pedagogical value which cannot be ignored.

However, it is important to highlight that definitive conclusions cannot be drawn from this case-study as the sample of students surveyed was narrow and the study context was limited to one learning scenario. Further investigations in this field would be encouraged to substantiate the findings from this study.

5.   Conclusions and future recommendations

This case-study shed some light on the integration of social networking sites in a learning environment, and specifically in a language-learning context. It highlights that, while Irish students are not resisting the introduction of this new media in their learning arsenal, they fail to fully grasp the educational value of these new tools. A greater involvement from teaching staff, both in terms of promotion and participation on the site, could change these views. If educators were to change their practices, students would be more inclined to follow suit. It also seems important to introduce students to the pedagogical value of social media so that they can approach it with a different frame of mind.

A different approach would be encouraged to promote a higher level of participation amongst students. Indeed, feedback from students emphasises that the 'one site fits them all approach' adopted by the LRA might not suit all students, as some would find it more comfortable to participate in a more 'specialised' community of practice. Therefore, a *Facebook* page set up in the context of a module or a course would probably be easier to manage and could be better perceived.

It would also be worth investigating whether students' lack of contributions could be linked to the fact that they did not feel that they 'appropriated' the site, as the communication on the site is dominated by the administrator of the centre who also 'owns' the sites. This can be inferred from the fact that students created their own pages where course issues and problem-solving take place at a more 'manageable' level. The surveys also show that students attributed their poor posting record to the fact that they did not know what to say. It would be interesting to find out whether they did not feel they had the authority or the knowledge to contribute, or if they were afraid to 'lose face' as they were unaware of the level of expertise of the other users. A smaller-scale *Facebook* page would thus be probably less daunting and could potentially lead to a higher level of participation.

To finish on a positive note, several students have highlighted the prospective value of *Facebook* within this learning context, pointing out that: "*Facebook has lots of potential!*" (Student questionnaire, February 2012).

References

Aceto, S., Dondi, C., & Marzotto, P. (2010). Pedagogical innovation in new learning communities: an in-depth study of twelve online learning communities. In K. Ala-Mutka & A. Ferrari (Eds.), *JRC Scientific and Technical Reports*. Luxembourg: Publications Office of the European Union. Retrieved from http://halshs.archives-ouvertes.fr/docs/00/59/30/45/PDF/JRC59474.pdf

Arnold, N., & Paulus, T. (2010). Using a social networking site for experimental learning: appropriating, lurking, modelling and community building. *Internet and Higher Education, 13*(4), 188-196. doi: 10.1016/j.iheduc.2010.04.002

Bosch, T. E. (2009). Using online social networking for teaching and learning: Facebook use at the university of Cape Town. Communicatio: *South African Journal for Communication Theory and Research, 35*(2), 185-200. doi: 10.1080/02500160903250648

boyd, d. m., & Ellison, N. B. (2007). Social Network Sites: Definition, History, and Scholarship. *Journal of Computer-Mediated Communication, 13*(1), 210-230. doi: 10.1111/j.1083-6101.2007.00393.x

Hew, K. F. (2011). Students' and teachers' use of Facebook. *Computers in Human Behavior, 27*(2), 662-676. doi: 10.1016/j.chb.2010.11.020

Kaplan, A. M., & Haenlein, M. (2010). Users of the world, unite! The challenges and opportunities of Social Media. *Business Horizons 53*(1), 59-68. doi: 10.1016/j.bushor.2009.09.003

Kárpáti, A. (2009). Web 2 technologies for net native language learners: a "social CALL". *ReCALL, 21*(2), 139-156. doi: 10.1017/S0958344009000160

Lampe, C., Wohn, D. Y., Vitak, J., Ellison, N. B., & Wash, R. (2011). Student use of Facebook for organizing collaborative classroom activities. *Computer-Supported Collaborative Learning, 6*(3), 329-347. doi: 10.1007/s11412-011-9115-y

Lamy, M-N. (2011). Entre les "murs" de Facebook et le forum institutionnel: nouveaux espaces d'expression en langue cible. In C. Dejean, F. Mangenot, & T. Soubrié (Eds.), *Actes du colloque Echanger pour apprendre en ligne (Epal 2011)*. Grenoble: Université Stendhal. Retrieved from http://w3.u-grenoble3.fr/epal/dossier/06_act/pdf/epal2011-lamy.pdf

McLoughlin, C., & Lee, M. J. W. (2007). Social software and participatory learning: pedagogical choices with technology affordances in the Web 2.0 era. *Proceedings of the ascilite conference, Singapore* (pp. 664-675). Retrieved from http://www.ascilite.org.au/conferences/singapore07/procs/mcloughlin.pdf

McMillan, D. W., & Chavis, D. M. (1986). Sense of community: A Definition and Theory. *Journal of Community Psychology, 14*(1), 6-23.

Mozzon-McPherson, M., & Vismans, R. (Eds.). (2001). *Beyond language teaching towards language advising*. London: CiLT.

Murray, L., Hourigan, T., & Jeanneau, C. (2008). The re-evaluation of MFL learners' objectives in re-orientating social media usage from leisure activities to educational purposes. Invasion or invitation? *Paper presented at the 2008 CALL conference. University of Antwerp, August 2008.*

Pavlenko, A., & Norton, B. (2007). Imagined communities, identity, and English language learning. In J. Cummins & C. Davison (Eds.), *International Handbook of English Language Teaching* (pp. 669-680). Dordrecht, Netherlands: Springer.

Rotman, D., Golbeck, J., & Preece, J. (2009). The Community is Where the Rapport Is - On Sense and Structure in the YouTube Community. *Paper presented at the 4th International Conference on Communities & Technologies, University Park, Pennsylvania, USA* (pp. 41-49). Retrieved from http://www.iisi.de/fileadmin/IISI/upload/2009/p41.pdf

Rubin, J. (2007). Introduction to special issue: language counseling. *System, 35*(1), 1-9. doi: 10.1016/j.system.2006.11.001

17 Internet-Based Textual Interventions and Interactions: How Language Learners Engage Online in a Written Task

Sylvie Thouësny[1]

Abstract

Computer and Internet literacy is often taken for granted in the case of young adults born into the digital world; it is generally assumed that they can all use technology effectively. However, as mentioned by Fowley (2011), "it is easy to forget that in Ireland for example, many of the young people whom we routinely call digital natives have only lived online since 2005 or 2006" (p. 20). This situation is considered a drawback, especially when making use of Internet-based applications such as word processors in an educational setting. This chapter investigates learners' use of *Google Drive*, and more precisely *Google Documents*, an Internet-based word processing tool, while engaging in a written task. More specifically, it observes how twenty learners of French at university level intervened and interacted with their teacher, after being provided with comments on their written performance, while completing a "bilan", i.e., a written account of their autonomous learning activities and a reflection on their learning outcomes. Findings show that although Internet-based tools are useful in theory to assist learners during a written task, in practice, their functionalities are not systematically exploited by learners who are occasionally reluctant to engage and collaborate.

Keywords: internet-based word processing tool, intervention, interaction, language learning, corrective feedback.

---

1. Independent Researcher, Dublin, Ireland; sylvie.thouesny@icall-research.net

How to cite this chapter: Thouësny, S. (2013). Internet-Based Textual Interventions and Interactions: How Language Learners Engage Online in a Written Task. In C. Fowley, C. English, & S. Thouësny (Eds.), *Internet Research, Theory, and Practice: Perspectives from Ireland* (pp. 349-366). Dublin: © Research-publishing.net.

1. Introduction

The constant increase of technology in our everyday lives has attracted much attention from researchers interested in understanding how technology interacts with educational practice with a special focus on human-to-human communication and language learning (e.g., Garratt, 2012). The use of technology not only requires knowledge of the tools' affordances, but also suggests the development of additional skills, such as computer literacy.

As Levy and Hubbard (2005) noted, "[o]ver many hundreds of years we have moved from a finger in the sand (where writing is technology-free) through hammer, chisel and stone, quill and vellum, typewriter and paper to the keyboard and screen" (p. 145). Internet-based technology in educational settings is commonly acknowledged as a positive attribute that enhances learning in general, and language learning in particular.

While Internet users went from a readable to a writable web (Kárpáti, 2009), language learners, over time, experienced various learning "from" and learning "with" technology environments (Reeves, 1998). A *learning from* Internet-based technology implies a relative passivity from the learners, whereas a *learning with* technology infers an up-to-date competence in the use of computers and the Internet. This should allow learners to take an engaged role in learning activities, as well as an active participation.

According to Woods and Baker (2004), "[i]nteraction is at the heart of the online learning experience" (p. 2). Interaction has been categorised into three distinct components: learner-content, learner-learner, and learner-teacher interaction (Moore, 1989). A learner-content interaction designates the learners' internal conversations they have with themselves when reflecting on the content of the study. A learner-learner interaction illustrates the interactions occurring between learners with or without the presence of the teacher, alone or in group settings. Finally, a learner-teacher interaction characterises the teacher's intention to stimulate the learners' interests as well as the learners' opportunities to clarify misunderstandings.

While the use of technology in current research is depicted as "rewarding for both learners and teachers in second language learning classrooms" (Thouësny & Bradley, 2011, p. 3), Hillman, Willis, and Gunawardena (1994) have long claimed that to understand how the use of technology impacts learning, one must consider a fourth category of interaction between the learner and the computer; this is still relevant. More specifically, a learner-interface interaction, "in which the learner must interact with the technological medium in order to interact with the content, instructor, or other learners" (Hillman et al., 1994, p. 33), denotes the learners' process of understanding, handling and using the various tools when attempting to complete their learning activities.

Years ago, Moran (1983) accurately predicted that tools such as word-processors were not going to disappear despite the many issues one could encounter when using – what he called – the new technology (p. 115). He added that these tools would "become the norm at colleges and universities" and that they would and "should, become part of the writing classroom" (Moran, 1983, p. 115). Indeed, while most students are familiar with word processors and their editing tools, they now have to face a new generation of web applications that enables users to create and edit documents online while collaborating with others synchronously or asynchronously. However, since writing in higher education may be challenging for first year students, as they may have to adapt themselves to methods of learning and assessment they perhaps did not encounter before, asking them to intervene and interact online with their teacher during a written task may represent a difficult endeavour for some of them. For instance, while 82 percent of Irish young adults aged 16-24 years old knew how to copy and move a file to a folder in 2011[1], only 36 percent of them were able to create an electronic presentation (e.g., *Keynote* or *PowerPoint* presentation) during the same year. These figures unveil the fact that students are not all technologically literate. As recently discussed by Lockley (2012), some digital natives may be more fluent in certain technological aspects than others, mostly depending on their educational level, professional experience, and idiosyncratic differences.

---

1. Data on university graduates in computing and computer skills of individuals retrieved from Eurostat, the statistical office of the European Union at http://ec.europa.eu/information_society/newsroom/cf/itemdetail.cfm?item_id=7932 and http://goo.gl/DvIfl.

Through the lens of a sociocultural theory, this chapter observes how twenty language learners of French intervened and interacted online with their teacher after being provided with corrective feedback on their written document, i.e., a written account of their learning activities and learning outcomes. Learners' questions and responses to the teacher's interventions, while using *Google Documents* – an Internet-based word processing tool –, were observed and analysed both qualitatively and quantitatively, so as to provide a better understanding of the learners' use of technology with respect to participations in terms of content and frequency.

2.   Educational setting and participants

The study took place in Ireland at university level during the winter of 2011. Students were enrolled in various Bachelor degrees, such as international business or accounting finance, in which French language was either an obligatory or a facultative subject. The whole class counted fifty-one first year students learning French as a foreign language. Their language level ranged from high to low B1[1].

As part of their assignment, students were asked to experience the French language on their own and to write an account of the learning activities they undertook as well as to reflect on their learning outcomes; the document was called the *bilan*. These activities could include watching a movie, reading a book, or any other leisure activities as long as French language was a prominent part of the activity. The aim was to give students the opportunity to enhance their independent learning based on their own passions. They were therefore expected to become more autonomous and to engage in the language learning activities that suited them the most.

In addition, students were encouraged to write a weekly report on their activities, which was the basis for their end of semester assignment. The criteria for

---

1. The Common European Framework of Reference for languages divides learners into three broad classifications which can be further divided into six levels: A1, A2, B1, B2, C1, and C2, where an A level identifies learners as beginners, a B level characterises individuals as intermediate, and a C level recognises learners as proficient.

the assignment were a minimum of eight hundreds words with at least eight different entries, and with no maximum word limit. They were free to write as much as they wanted and were equally free to use whatever software they liked for their typed submissions. They were nevertheless encouraged to use *Google Documents* as their editing tool in order to be able to interact with their teacher during the writing process. While the reflective document was produced as an institutional request, the continuous assessment on *Google Documents* was facultative. Learners had the option to submit their assignment at the end of the semester without showing parts of it beforehand to their teacher.

Furthermore, the concept of autonomous learning was brought to the group through in-class discussions of the activities the students had undertaken. The aim was to provide ideas to those who did not know how to approach the task. In parallel, workshops were independently proposed at the university[1] to help teachers and students alike use *Google* tools. As none of the students had previously used *Google Documents* either for academic or personal purposes, they were strongly advised to participate in these free workshops. However, as students had to register to attend these independent workshops, it became clear that no student in this class took part in them. A short training on how to create, rename, edit, and save a document was nevertheless given during the second week of the semester.

Out of fifty-one students enrolled in this course, thirty of them chose to create and write their assignment in *Google Documents*, the remaining students simply handed in their assignment on paper at the due date. In the event of choosing *Google Documents*, students were aware that the online learner-teacher collaborative work would be stopped before the deadline. Given the fact that this project was intended to be a continuous activity from beginning to end, i.e., from week two to week twelve, stopping the collaboration at the end of the ninth week was believed to motivate students to write their project early. Yet, ten students chose to start composing their document in *Google Documents* during the last week. As a consequence, these students were not provided with

---

1. The workshops, conducted by Dr. Cathy Fowley, were intended to provide students and teachers alike with information about the advantages of using new technologies in educational settings.

corrective feedback on their written language, and the asynchronous learner-teacher interaction was not initiated. In total, twenty participants created their document with *Google Documents* at the very beginning of the semester, of which seven were female and thirteen were male, all of them Irish students between eighteen and twenty years old.

3.   Analysis

From an educational perspective, feedback is more effective "when it focuses on patterns of error, [...] rather than dozens of disparate errors" (Ferris, 2002, p. 50). Lee (2003) further points out that "selective marking" is more suitable for learners than "comprehensive marking" (p. 228). Within this study, learners' written documents were assessed according to five criteria carrying equal weights: (1) content, (2) vocabulary, (3) syntax, (4) conjugation, and (5) reflection. The first category identified whether the texts provided were adapted to the task and whether the instructions were respected. The diversity of the activities undertaken by learners while learning French on their own was also considered. For example, one student confused the meaning of the word *bilan* with the one of a diary. She kept a weekly report in which she described her new experiences at the university and narrated her nightlife without any references to the French language. Other students reported activities that were in fact proposed by other teachers in other courses. One of these tasks, for instance, was to listen to Edith Piaf[1] to try to reproduce the sound that causes one of the most difficulties for English learners, in other words, the uvular trill [R] or uvular fricative [ʁ] sound. The second criterion of assessment acknowledged lexical diversity, whether the vocabulary was sufficient to explain the chosen activities, and whether students used synonyms to express themselves. The third criterion evaluated the syntax of the sentences, whether the structures were simple, including for instance, only one independent clause, or whether they were more complex. The fourth criterion identified whether the verbs were correctly conjugated in an appropriate tense, as there had been a special focus on this grammatical aspect throughout

---

1. Edith Piaf was a popular French singer in the 50's who is well known for rolling her r's.

the semester. Finally, the last criterion examined the breadth of the learners' reflection on their learning outcomes; whether it was thoughtfully considered as opposed to just saying that they were "learning a lot".

The scale of assistance dispensed within this study for the incorrect lexical and grammatical features was designed from implicit to more and more explicit, as advised by sociocultural researchers such as Nassaji and Swain (2000), who demonstrated that "help provided within the [zone of proximal development] was more effective than help provided randomly" (p. 48). Based on this researcher's previous work, the assistance was designed in accordance with a four level scale of mediation: (level 1) the incorrect word or group of words is highlighted, (level 2) the error type is provided for each incorrect word or group of words, (level 3) detailed explanations about the nature of the incorrect form is given, and (level 4) the correct form is provided (Thouësny, 2011, p. 91). As requested by the learners, the comments were generally provided in English, especially at level 2 assistance. However, if students interacted in French, replies to their interactions were also given in French.

The learners' interventions and interactions after each move from the teacher were observed and counted. A learner's intervention is the action taken by him or her to rework the linguistic input directly after being provided with suggestions at any level of assistance. The action is reflected by a modification of the text. A learner's interaction, on the other hand, shows the two-way flow of information between the learner and the teacher, no matter who started the discussion. Learners' moves, i.e., interventions and interactions were not only counted, but also qualitatively considered in order to appreciate whether, when, and how the mediation was negotiated.

4.   Results

No student wrote more than 8 entries in the final document they handed back to their teacher and the amount of words for each entry was roughly comprised between 100 and 200 words. As previously stated, learners' texts were no longer read and corrected by the teacher after the ninth week of the semester. By the end of the activity, 10 students, for instance, created content for only one entry, while 4 others were able to complete the whole assignment. During the period of observation, learners produced a total amount of 64 entries. Out of 20 participants considered for this study, 11 of them chose to complete their written task with *Google Documents* after week 9. The remaining 9 students stopped using this facility. Another fact worth mentioning is that 14 participants did not use the Internet-based word processing tool to directly type their words in it; rather, they copied the text from another word processor and pasted it into *Google Documents*. This was monitored with the *see revision history* feature of the application, in which the text appeared all at once without any possibilities of tracking changes.

4.1.   Learners' interventions

Table 1 below illustrates the amount of interventions performed by the teacher and the learners at all four levels of mediation (L1, L2, L3, and L4), as well as the help given to students on their text content (C) and learning reflection (R).

A first reading of the values shows that most students responded up to levels 1 and 2, incorrect forms highlighted and error types provided, respectively. For example, 41 incorrect forms were highlighted in student #15's text at level 1. The student intervened for 35 of them, the remaining 6 incorrect forms were left unchanged in the text. Since the teacher followed up with 27 incorrect forms at level 2, one can deduce that 8 of the replacements proposed by the learner at level 1 were correct. At this stage, learner #15 was now provided with the types of error for 27 incorrect forms at level 2, for which he suggested replacements to 23 of them. The teacher continued with the third level of assistance and gave detailed information on the 5 forms that were still incorrect, implying that the learner was able to edit 18 incorrect features after being provided with the error types. Since the student did not propose any corrections (0) at level 3, the interventions stopped there; a dash (-) indicates that the teacher could not regulate the assistance further, although it was still needed. In addition, learner #15 received 5 comments on the text content as well as 3 on his reflective learning; all of these were taken into consideration by the learner, and the text was changed accordingly.

Table 1.   Descriptive table of learners and teacher's interventions
            at all levels of assistance

Students		Entries	Teacher's interventions						Learners' interventions					
			L1	L2	L3	L4	C	R	L1	L2	L3	L4	C	R
1	M	1	8	4	-			1	6	0				1
2	F	2	8	6	1	1		1	6	1	1	1		1
3	F	1	4	3	2	1		2	4	2	2	1		2
4	F	8	63	14	1	-		3	14	7	0			3
5	M	1	8	2	-			1	8	0				1
6	M	1	8	2	-		1		7	0			1	
7	M	1	7	3	-			1	5	2	0			1
8	F	1	8	4	-			1	5	0				1
9	M	1	10	3	-		1		10	3	0		1	
10	M	1	5	-			1		0				1	
11	M	8	37	25	7	-		3	37	25	0			3
12	F	4	59	13	3	1	2	2	31	9	3	1	2	2
13	M	8	36	27	2	0	4	2	36	27	2		4	2
14	M	3	22	18	-		1	1	22	7			1	1
15	M	4	41	27	5	-	5	3	35	23	0		5	3
16	F	8	45	29	7	-	4	2	45	29	0		4	2
17	M	1	7	1	-		3	3	1	0			3	3
18	F	7	0				1						1	
19	M	2	23	12	-		2	2	18	0			2	2
20	M	1	17	-			1		0					1
Total		64	416	193	28	3	25	29	290	135	9	3	25	29

Table 2 below demonstrates that learners responded to almost 70 percent of the teacher's interventions at levels 1 and 2, but that the percentage dropped to 29 percent at level 3. In addition, it shows that all learners who were provided with the correct answer at level 4 adopted the teacher's correction in their final version. Moreover, while most students (16 out of 20) did not consider the detailed assistance to push further their editing process, they all without exception took into account the assistance provided about the content of their entries as well as their learning reflection.

Table 2.   Percentage of learners' interventions
            after receiving assistance at all levels

Interventions at Level 1	Interventions at Level 2	Interventions at Level 3	Interventions at Level 4	Interventions at content and reflection level
69.71%	69.95%	28.57%	100%	100%

4.2.   Learners' interactions

Besides interventions, the learners' moves were also examined to determine
how the teacher's assistance was discussed and negotiated. Table 3 lists all
learners' interactions and classifies them into different categories, namely (1)
non-feedback related question, (2) feedback agreement, (3) response to query,
(4) feedback clarification, (5) replacement confirmation, and (6) feedback
negotiation. Seven students demonstrated their willingness to interact with the
teacher; a total amount of 17 interactions were recorded. It is worth mentioning
that one participant did not use the comment thread to interact asynchronously.
Rather, she discussed some of the feedback face-to-face during the class.

Table 3.   Descriptive table of learners' interactions

St.	Non-Feedback Related Question	Feedback Agreement	Response to Query	Feedback Clarification	Replacement Confirmation	Feedback Negotiation
1						1 (Level 1)
2				1 (Level 2)		1 (Reflection)
3			1 (Level 3)			
4			1 (Level 3)			
12	2	5 (Level 2)	1 (Level 3)		2 (Level 2)	
14						1 (Level 2)
15				1 (Content)		
Total	2	5	3	2	2	3

A **non-feedback related question** is an independent query asked by the learner,
which has no connection to any of his or her incorrect forms. Student #12, for

instance, utilised the Internet-based word processor as a forum discussion tool to ask questions about technology use. In one of her questions, she exposed her embarrassment at not being able to comprehend the tool and asked for a demonstration. The student's query was briefly answered in *Google Documents*, stating that a short presentation on how to use it would be performed in class.

A **feedback agreement** is a form of interaction in which the learner agrees with the teacher on the content of the assistance. Student #12, for instance, let the teacher know that she understood and agreed with the assistance provided at level 2, where the error type is provided. She used short statements such as 'all right', 'I understand', and 'OK'.

A **response to a query** is a learner's return after being asked a question in relation to a specific incorrect form. The teacher generally raised questions at level 3 when providing detailed explanations on the incorrect form. Student #3, for instance, in the case of an incorrect agreement between a pronoun and its antecedent, was asked to reflect on what the pronoun was supposed to replace.

A **feedback clarification** indicates that the feedback may be too complicated to understand and that the terminology used may not be fully adapted to the learner. Student #2, for instance, asked for clarification about the meaning of the term "lexical" in "incorrect lexical choice", an error type which was used to describe an inappropriate selection in terms of word choice.

A **replacement confirmation** reflects a learner's request for approval before in-line editing. Student #12, for example, after being provided with the error type at level 2, suggested replacements in the comment thread and waited for the teacher's approval before including them in her text.

A **feedback negotiation** not only reveals a learner's intention to discuss the assistance, but also demonstrates the idea that the teacher's feedback is not always taken for granted. In such an event, an agreement through discussion must be reached between the learner and the teacher. For instance, student #14 argued that one of his phrases marked as incorrect – as it was incomprehensible to the teacher – was indeed perfect French. This student further explained that he had had the opportunity to experience the language from Quebec and that what was marked as incorrect was in fact a perfectly correct French-Canadian phrase which was unknown to the teacher. As a result of the negotiations, the learner's expression was accepted.

4.3. Learners' evaluation of the content of the class

As part of the end of semester, students received a questionnaire with the aim to evaluate the content of the class. While the questionnaire was not designed to assess the use of *Google Documents*, it is nevertheless known that some of the students enjoyed the interactional aspect of the tool. To the question "What elements of the course did you find most interesting?", some of them replied in an anonymous way:

-Enjoyed doing the bilan, learning something new on my own every week.

-Enjoyed working with GoogleDocs. Great to get feedback from lecturer that way.

-Bilan – Weekly help from Sylvie using Google Docs.

-I like the assistance I received. Like the bilan etc.

5. Discussion and future developments

Writing activities have considerably evolved with the introduction of web-based technologies in our everyday lives, especially in terms of attitudes towards creating and sharing content. Common challenges in textual authorship and ownership of online collaborative writing, such as understanding "what it means [...] to read and write together" (Hunter, 2011, p. 55), are not precisely applicable within this research, since (1) the document was created and written by one individual only, and (2) the text, if in-line edited after interventions from the teacher, was exclusively updated by the student. Furthermore, documents listed in *Google Drive* clearly indicated the name of the owner, in other words, the student's name.

On the whole, the *bilan* activity was not totally successful as learners experienced difficulties in getting organised and acting independently with respect to language learning. Recently, Eneau and Develotte (2012) investigated the relationship that links autonomy and identity and pointed out that "autonomy for adult learners learning foreign languages [...] is constructed through a process of exchange and sharing that depends largely on the resources and the environment" (p. 5). This implies the use of "meta-skills" such as the capacity for learners to identify their own strengths and weaknesses, i.e., knowing themselves as a learner and having the ability to learn from others (Tremblay, 2003, cited in Eneau & Develotte, 2012, p. 5). The observations undertaken within this research do not suggest that the students of this particular class, at the time of the study, saw themselves as independent learners as most of them had great difficulties in learning autonomously. It is important to remember that almost all participants were first year students coming directly from secondary school. It may be the case that asking for learning autonomy might be inappropriate at this stage as students may not be ready yet. One possible reason for this could be the fact that they were extremely disappointed not to have grammar drill exercises anymore like in the "good old days", as one student said during an informal meeting. Another explanation could be that they were, in university, facing too many types of independence they had never experienced before. Most of them were now living for the first time without their parents; they were allowed to wear the clothes they wanted (no more uniforms), they could skip classes (attendance is not mandatory), and so on and so forth. Self-directed learning during first year at university might be too much freedom for students.

Nevertheless, the results show that learners intervened during their writing process: they responded to the teacher's corrective feedback by updating their texts in accordance to the assistance provided. While learners corrected or attempted to correct almost 70 percent of the incorrect forms flagged by the teacher at levels 1 and 2, they followed up with only 29 percent of them at the metalinguistic feedback level. It may be the case that detailed explanations on the incorrect forms were on some occasions too complicated to decipher in terms of linguistic jargon. As found by Lee (1997), teachers often used "a wider range of metalinguistic terms than students could understand" (p. 471). Although some researchers such as Hwang, Ang and Francesco (2002) have pointed out that electronic feedback was perceived as a suitable alternative for shy students who tend to avoid face-to-face feedback for fear of asking the wrong questions in front of the class, only one student asked for feedback clarification through the use of the Internet-based word processing tool. The others might have decided to avoid potential embarrassment by merely skipping the correction process in order not to show their lack of knowledge. It is worth mentioning that participants were Irish students and that Irish students through their educational system, either in primary or secondary school, do not receive any specific tutoring in linguistic knowledge, and tend to have a deficit in terms of metalanguage. To remedy this lack of knowledge, a session dedicated to the explanation of the terminology in use when providing feedback should suitably prepare the students for the comprehension of the language descriptors. Future research should adjust more precisely the level of the meta-linguistic annotations to each individual to ensure a proper understanding of the feedback itself.

Furthermore, the results demonstrated that learners did not interact with their teacher much as only 17 interactions were recorded over the 694 interventions of the teacher. More specifically, only 2.5 percent of the teacher's moves triggered an interaction from the learner. One reason that learners did not interact with an equivalent enthusiasm, aside from the possibility that they did not require any further explanations, could be associated with their different learning styles and preferences, given the fact that computer literacy can be related to students' approach to learning, and that their approach to learning might influence the way they perceive computers and technology (Jelfs & Colbourn, 2002). In investigating the effect of learning styles on course completion in an online learning environment, Terrell (2002) finds that students with preferences for abstract conceptualisation were more likely to complete the program than students with preferences for concrete experience (p. 345). From a language learning perspective, Felix (2004) demonstrates that some learning styles correlate with the way learners are using the web materials. A future study could first examine learning styles as a means to better understand learners' approach in online text writing and editing, as well as intervening and interacting. Although this study proposed to observe a very limited sample of learners' interactions, a classification of the learners' moves could nevertheless be proposed: non-feedback related question, feedback agreement, response to query, feedback clarification, replacement confirmation, and feedback negotiation. This classification needs to be refined as the data was insufficient to draw any conclusive decisions.

6. Conclusion

In light of a dynamic assessment framework encompassing learner-teacher interactions, this study analysed the interventions and interactions of twenty students – 39 percent of the class – who decided to use *Google Documents* as their main editing tool when drafting a report on their activities and learning outcomes. The remaining 61 percent might have felt uncomfortable with the use of a new application, or it may be the case that the level of user-friendliness of the Internet-based tool did not reach their expectations. While most of the participants copied and pasted their texts into *Google Documents*, using it as a repository instead of a tool to create their assignment, a large majority of them intervened by modifying their ill-formed written language in accordance with the teacher's corrective feedback, mostly at levels 1 and 2 when the incorrect form is highlighted and the error type is provided, respectively. Amongst them, a few demonstrated their willingness to interact with the teacher, but their attempts were rather sparse. Whereas the web has been described as a "viable environment for language learning" (Felix, 2004, p. 246), Hubbard and Romeo (2012) point out that, according to the literature to date, "it is common practice to offer little if any [...] training before turning students loose on a [computer-assisted language learning] software application, task, or activity" (p. 35). Although it is frequent to find in research publications that younger generations have some advantages in terms of computer literacy over older people (e.g., Rahimpour, 2011), one could posit that a technology enhanced classroom fostering interactions between students and teachers may not be immediately suitable for every language learner, as students might have different levels of digital literacy, as well as different levels of willingness to interact. As Lam and Pennington (1995) commented nearly two decades ago, instructors must show patience with their students in terms of technology use, as the latter will "need time to adapt successfully to any innovative teaching strategy" (p. 65). Depending on the learners' degree of comfort in using technology in general and *Google Documents* in particular, stimulating learners' asynchronous interactions between themselves and their teacher when using online interactive tools is definitely a challenging endeavour that needs further investigations.

References

Eneau, J., & Develotte, C. (2012). Working together online to enhance learner autonomy: Analysis of learners' perceptions of their online learning experience. *ReCALL, 24*(1), 3-19. doi:10.1017/S0958344011000267

Felix, U. (2004). A multivariate analysis of secondary students' experience of web-based language acquisition. *ReCALL, 16*(1), 237-249. doi:10.1017/S0958344004001715

Ferris, D. R. (2002). *Treatment of error in second language student writing.* Ann Harbour: University of Michigan Press.

Fowley, C. (2011). *Publishing the confidential: an ethnographic study of young Irish bloggers.* Unpublished PhD dissertation. Dublin City University, Dublin.

Garratt, D. A. (2012). *Students' perceptions of the use of peer-to-peer ESL text chat: an introductory study.* Unpublished PhD dissertation. The University of New Mexico, Albuquerque, New Mexico.

Hillman, D. C. A., Willis, D. J., & Gunawardena, C. N. (1994). Learner interface interaction in distance education: an extension of contemporary models and strategies for practitioners. *American Journal of Distance Education, 8*(2), 30-42. doi:10.1080/08923649409526853

Hubbard, P., & Romeo, K. (2012). Diversity in learner training. In G. Stockwell (Ed.), *Computer-Assisted Language Learning: Diversity in Research and Practice* (pp. 33-48). Cambridge: Cambridge University Press.

Hunter, R. (2011). Erasing "Property Lines": A Collaborative Notion of Authorship and Textual Ownership on a Fan Wiki. *Computers and Composition, 28*(1), 40-56. doi:10.1016/j.compcom.2010.12.004

Hwang, A., Ang, S., & Francesco, A. M. (2002). The Silent Chinese: The Influence of Face and Kiasuism on Student Feedback-Seeking Behaviors. *Journal of Management Education, 26*(1), 70-98.

Jelfs, A., & Colbourn, C. (2002). Do students' approaches to learning affect their perceptions of using computing and information technology? *Journal of Educational Media, 27*(1/2), 41-53.

Kárpáti, A. (2009). Web 2 technologies for Net Native language learners: a "social CALL". *ReCALL, 21*(2), 139-156. doi:10.1017/S0958344009000160

Lam, F. S., & Pennington, M. C. (1995). The computer vs. the pen: a comparative study of word processing in a Hong Kong secondary classroom. *Computer Assisted Language Learning, 8*(1), 75-92. doi:10.1080/0958822950080106

Lee, I. (1997). ESL learners' performance in error correction in writing: Some implications for teaching. *System, 25*(4), 465-477. doi:10.1016/S0346-251X(97)00045-6

Lee, I. (2003). L2 writing teachers' perspectives, practices and problems regarding error feedback. *Assessing Writing, 8*(3), 216-237. doi:10.1016/j.asw.2003.08.002

Levy, M., & Hubbard, P. (2005). Why call CALL "CALL"? *Computer Assisted Language Learning, 18*(3), 143-149. doi:10.1080/09588220500208884

Lockley, T. (2012). Native Speaker "digitalians", we just don't speak your dialect. Yet. "digital/keitai native" Culture and CALL in Japan. In J. Colpaert, A. Aerts, W.-C. V. Wu, & Y.-C. J. Chao (Eds.), *Fifteenth International CALL Conference, The Medium Matters, Proceedings, 24-27 May 2012* (pp. 473-476). Taichung, Taiwan: Providence University.

Moore, M. G. (1989). Editorial: three types of interaction. *American Journal of Distance Education, 3*(2), 1-7. doi:10.1080/08923648909526659

Moran, C. (1983). Electronic Media: Word Processing and the Teaching of Writing. *The English Journal, 72*(3), 113-115. Retrieved from http://www.jstor.org/stable/816146

Nassaji, H., & Swain, M. (2000). A Vygotskian Perspective on Corrective Feedback in L2: The Effect of Random Versus Negotiated Help on the Learning of English Articles. *Language Awareness, 9*(1), 34-51.

Rahimpour, M. (2011). Computer Assisted Language Learning (CALL). *International Journal of Instructional Technology and Distance Learning, 8*(1), 3-9. Retrieved from http://espace.library.uq.edu.au/eserv/UQ:238741/Rahimpour2011.pdf

Reeves, T. C. (1998). The Impact of Media and Technology in Schools: A Research Report prepared for The Bertelsmann Foundation. *The Bertelsmann Foundation*, 1-44. Retrieved from http://it.coe.uga.edu/~treeves/edit6900/BertelsmannReeves98.pdf

Terrell, S. R. (2002). The effect of learning style on doctoral course completion in a Web-based learning environment. *The Internet and Higher Education, 5*(4), 345-352. doi:10.1016/S1096-7516(02)00128-8

Thouësny, S. (2011). *Modeling second language learners' interlanguage and its variability: A computer-based dynamic assessment approach to distinguishing between errors and mistakes*. Unpublished PhD dissertation. Dublin City University, Dublin. Retrieved from http://doras.dcu.ie/16559/

Thouësny, S., & Bradley, L. (2011). Introduction on views of emergent researchers in L2 teaching and learning with technology. In S. Thouësny & L. Bradley (Eds.), *Second language teaching and learning with technology: views of emergent researchers* (pp. 1-8). Dublin: Research-publishing. net. Retrieved from http://research-publishing.net/publications/thouesny-bradley-2011/

Tremblay, N. A. (2003). *L'autoformation, pour apprendre autrement*. Montréal: Presses de l'Université de Montréal.

Woods, R. H., & Baker, J. D. (2004). Interaction and immediacy in online learning. *The International Review Of Research In Open And Distance Learning, 5*(2). Retrieved from http://www.irrodl.org/index.php/irrodl/article/view/186

18 Information and Communication Technology in Foreign Language Teaching: Leveraging the Internet to Make Language Learning Real

Etáin Watson[1]

Abstract

The internet is the largest communications network in the world. It has become the virtual backbone of all communication. Therefore, it seems natural to leverage it as a major tool in any education involving communication skills, especially language skills. This chapter outlines a practitioner's experience on how this can be done in a foreign language classroom. It outlines the reasoning for use of various tools, and the practical aspects linked to language learning. The methodology of this investigation follows the pattern of Action Research outlined by Stringer (2007), an informal recursive approach that allows the researcher to select a research question and a method for testing it, then to analyse the results, change the method of testing or modify the question and test again until a satisfactory result is reached. Examples used are for *ab-initio* Italian, and all suggested activities were used with the author's students in live classes.

Keywords: information and communication technology, foreign language teaching, action research, ab-initio Italian.

1. Dublin Institute of Technology, Dublin, Ireland; etain.watson@dit.ie

How to cite this chapter: Watson, E. (2013). Information and Communication Technology in Foreign Language Teaching: Leveraging the Internet to Make Language Learning Real. In C. Fowley, C. English, & S. Thouësny (Eds.), *Internet Research, Theory, and Practice: Perspectives from Ireland* (pp. 367-378). Dublin: © Research-publishing.net.

1.   Introduction

Language must be used or it is not learned. Though application and sharing is necessary for all learning to take place, this is doubly true of language. We acquire our first language without instruction by simply listening and trying to communicate (Brown, 1973; Levine & McCloskey, 2008). However, we often try to learn a second language in a totally artificial manner where even application and sharing in the classroom is not perceived as real. Therefore, learning a second language often becomes laborious and slow. In the past, the only way to change this was to travel to a new environment and learn the local language. Information and communication technology changed this, notably in the last twenty years which saw the advent of personal computers, the internet and the World Wide Web, plus digital audiovisual tools and materials.

The reality of the internet, although technologically created and virtual, is underpinned by the presence of 'real' people. This gives virtual spaces a feeling of reality close to that of being in the country of origin of the language. It seemed natural for the author to use this 'near-reality' aspect of the internet with Italian classes to create a virtual reality for students to use, to learn, test and practice. The theoretical basis for the near reality of movies has been established (Technology & Innovation, 2010) and the literature supports this. Petchko (2011) mentions that the internet World Wide Web has the same characteristic, less than actual reality, but far more than just text, pictures and video.

The classroom is removed from reality. Activities done solely in and for the classroom simply do not register as real for the students (De-Obfuscation of Piaget, 1989). Because of its nature, using the internet registers as a real activity for most students, even though it is acknowledged that the persons with whom one communicates may or may not be exactly as represented (Viadero, 2006). The human brain does not really recognise the difference between reality, dreams, movies, and activities into which one is totally immersed whether real or not (Technology & Innovation, 2010). Therefore, using any of these as part of a lesson tends to give it more reality. This has the end result that the information thus acquired is stored into long-term memory with attachments to whatever connections have been made during the lesson (Brandt & Brandt, 2005). The foreign-language teacher can leverage content on the internet, use internet applications and involve students in internet communities within the context of language lessons for the benefit of the students (Quinn, Rutherford, & Osher, 1999).

Technologies which can be used very effectively include articles, news items, blogs, viewing videos, animations, documentaries and presentations, webquests, web scavenger hunts, participation in social networking sites, having a class *Facebook* page, to name but a few (Carpenter, 2007). These are, of course, all done in the target language, thus increasing vocabulary and understanding. The more connected the activities are, the more benefits students will accrue (Marston, 2011). One very useful way to plan is to create a road map for class activities, almost like plotting out a board game (Wheeldon, 2011). This can be displayed on the classroom wall to help students keep track. Ideally, most class members will become interested in most or all of the activities.

2.   Where and how to begin

This chapter documents some conclusions reached from using the internet for the author's *ab-initio* Italian classes. In order to create a fully functional environment the class was divided into groups of 5-7 people. Each group was mixed for ability, after an initial assessment. The classes were highly successful, and were certainly exciting and interesting.

Sets of activities were created to promote learning in different ways or cater to different learning styles. Each set indicated the time element expected for the activity (daily, once or twice weekly). These were adjusted on a continuous basis to enable change, and the total time required as well as the point value for each activity plus the required deliverables (proof of completion) were determined in advance. Activities were based upon how we use language:

communication for social reasons, finding information, business transactions, entertainment, persuasion, laughter, cooperation on a project or hobby and learning other things.

3.   Vocabulary development

A grammar based approach generally limits vocabulary, but this also limits the students' ability to communicate, thus limiting acquisition (Allen, 2007; Krashen & Terrell, 2000, p. 155). The best way to develop vocabulary is to use it, not as responses to tests, but in real situations for real purposes (Allen, 2007). Development of vocabulary thus included several different strategies in order to cover the various learning styles of the students. Krashen and Terrell (2000) state that students engaged in natural vocabulary learning activities can acquire between 15 and 25 lexical items per hour (p. 156). It made perfect sense, therefore, to begin with fun vocabulary acquisition activities. After all, grammar cannot be learned until vocabulary is acquired (Allen, 2007). Krashen and Terrel (2000) suggest that not only should the activities be fun and natural, but that if the students communicate their meaning that should be all that is necessary in the beginning. This creates a safe learning environment in the classroom. Grammar was graded towards the end of the semester after a generous amount of vocabulary had been learned.

Vocabulary development is best done as an integrated activity rather than separated out as a chore. However, since the students are not in the same language environment as the language they are learning, this has to be simulated and augmented. Hunt and Beglar (2002) recommend the combination of both explicit instruction and incidental learning and add that "learners need to be taught strategies for inferring words from context" (cited in Ketabi & Shahraki, 2011, p. 729). Ketabi and Shahraki (2011) further point out that there is a consensus among researchers "that strategy training warrants time and effort both in and out of the classroom (see, among others, Fan, 2003; Macaro, 2001; Takeuchi, [Griffiths, & Coyle], 2007)" (p. 729). In other words, the internet is a vast resource for language development, as it can supply huge amounts of exposure to the second language in real context, huge amounts of practice materials and connection to a virtual reality in a safe learning environment.

In addition to in class vocabulary lessons, there are numerous video lessons on *YouTube* for beginners. Just a quick search for 'Italian' will turn up dozens. It was thus easy to assign these for students to find and report on each week. A short written report in order to share what was found and a short in class presentation of the site presented an opportunity for continuous assessment. The written reports were put into a monthly or bimonthly class newsletter. As the class *Facebook* was established and the students acquired more facility the reports were shared with a public link to the newsletter.

In addition to vocabulary instruction and practice, students need regular testing of vocabulary in order to help them identify what they know and what they need to learn. This is one chore that students found worked really well when done at home over the internet. The tests were quick and fun. Different strategies can be used to add interest and humour, such as making up silly sentences that are nevertheless correct. For cumulative tests, a random number generator can be used to select previous vocabulary from a database, and any vocabulary selected was marked so as not to duplicate too often. There are online free test creators that are easy to use. Perhaps the easiest with which to begin is a combination of free *Slideshare* and a free survey system[1]. While they are not integrated this combination has one very distinct advantage for learning: it is highly flexible and free. This is only one of the available choices. If the school or college has a portal or website, any presentation can be posted on the site and answer sheets can be made with one of the many free survey systems offered on line.

The internet itself is a vast treasure trove of interesting things and communication opportunities. Computer-aided language learning was found to produce more positive attitudes with the author's classes, especially with students studying vocabulary. A variety of tools and materials was used in order to provide a match for every learning style.

---

1. Upload & Share PowerPoint presentations and documents, retrieved from http://www.slideshare.net/.

Many institutions around the world are beginning to provide internet-based lectures that can be used as learning materials in their local language. These make excellent language learning materials for those who are learning the base language (McCormick, 2000). Advances in learning and teaching have continued to develop across the internet and to be shared (Kuo & Chen, 2004). Demiray and Sever (2009) state that "online distance learning has gained reliability in recent years" (n.p.). According to Holmberg (2005) "[t]here is no tenable reason why any language should be considered unsuitable for distance teaching and learning; rather, there is much evidence of the effectiveness of distance teaching of foreign languages" (pp. 166-167). This is an environment that is especially useful for task based language learning. The teacher can create matched sets of tasks for a number of groups, each with slightly different materials and tasks and each becomes a reusable template.

Task-based language learning is ideal for use on the internet. Students can practice language in a virtual context while completing tasks that are "authentic, pragmatic, contextual, and functional use of language" (Ali, Mukundan, Baki, & Mohd Ayub, 2012, n.p.). Students in the author's classes were expected to learn the language while completing the assigned tasks, during which they engaged in and negotiated meaning. Webquests are excellent group activities, rather like an informational scavenger hunt.

News gathering and reporting was another activity that worked well for groups. A class newsletter was created from the materials, and the students also made their own podcasts. Each group chose one topic, generally something 'how-to', and then created a podcast script and recorded it in Italian, either in video or just audio. By mixing topics in such a way as the students have to use a mixture of English and Italian sites, both translation and communication are promoted. This kind of exercise created a situation where the students could consider the context as real, because they created a real product which was distributed further than just within the classroom and to families. The author's students were completely engaged with this activity and made great progress while trying simply to communicate.

Another vocabulary exercise was used as a webquest for nouns and verbs. For these the class vocabulary database was used or added to by requiring that each student looks for illustrations, animations or video clips that demonstrate the meanings of a certain number of words. They could use free clipping tools to copy them from the web, and the locations were also noted for each as a citation. From a copyright point of view, a vocabulary database for a language class can be considered fair use as long as the sources are documented. By giving each student or pair of students certain letters of the alphabet to work with, duplication could be avoided.

Once the students were a bit more at ease with the language and technology, a version of *Compare the Maps* was used. This can be made with any HTML tool that can create thumbnails. One inexpensive set of tools is made by *Techsmith*[1]. Different operating systems may have other capture tools built in. Most photo organisation tools can also make both covers and thumbnails for these maps. Some simple representations of buildings, doors, shaded windows were used to make clickable covers for hidden illustrations or video clips, and all video clips or text were in Italian. Each student or group got one map and every map had similarities, differences and parallels to others. For example, one map may had the same video clip as another, but words under different covers were placed in different places on the map. After distribution, the students or groups could compare their maps and talk about and record the differences, similarities and parallels in Italian. Virtually anything which might be compared can be used, and once some artefacts are made, they become easier to use and they can be reused for future classes. The creation of these maps could indeed become another group project.

Within the classroom the use of video clips for vocabulary practice are opportunities for training and discussion. Much of language is ambiguous. Different languages invite the creation of ambiguity in different ways. Some of these uncertainties can be disambiguated by a well-constructed powerful artificial intelligence agent. However, there are many that simply depend

---

1. Products such as *Snagit*, *Camtasia*, and *Jing* have discount prices for government, non-profit and education and can be found at http://www.techsmith.com/index.html.

upon human understanding of possibly dozens of shades of meaning and possibilities. These are only learned by using the language, generally by making mistakes. The following example from Italian (Nespor, 2001, p. 132) displays an ambiguous sentence with two possible phonological interpretations:

La vecchia spranga la porta

a. [(la vecchia)f (spranga)f (la porta)f] - *"the old lady blocks the door"*

b. [(la vecchia spranga)f (la porta)f] - *"the old bar carries it"*

The only way to tell the meaning of this is by the context. A really good artificial intelligence engine might be programmed to understand most possible uses of this phrase. However, there are so many possibilities that even the most sophisticated artificial intelligence agent can decipher them all. For this reason using language in real situations is necessary.

4.   Inference of meaning

There are a number of different factors which can help language learners to infer meaning. Once the learner has acquired enough vocabulary to build a structure of context of the target language, it is possible to begin to infer meaning from context. At this juncture communication must be encouraged, along with interesting reading and viewing of videos in order to provide as much material in as large a variety as possible. It is at this point that the internet became much more useful. For example, there is a country site for Italy on *Facebook*, and the students were able to create a page for their module group. Games, puzzles and exercises, such as *Compare the Maps*, could thus be shared.

In class lessons were created in order to point out the methods for inferring meaning when it is not known. This could for example involve using the meanings of surrounding words, the narrative that precedes or follows the words or phrases and in the many different ways it is used, by identifying the subtle class of the words or phrases. For example, we have words which identify family members and relationships, words which introduce, words that define, and as many more classes as the speaker can find some way of separating from the rest. The students were asked to discuss how they might infer meaning. For example, are there adjectives that give clues? If something has colour it is almost always a noun. Does it have sound, smell or texture?

A search for Italian on *YouTube* will net a whole array of videos, some language, some cooking, travel and many more. Video presents visual and sound cues in addition to what is found in text and the students could thus watch short videos in a group and then discuss what they saw. A search on the terms 'Italian TV' or 'Italian television' brings up dozens of choices[1]. As a simple method for sorting through these, reviews of these sites for possible use were assigned. Criteria were set and a template was made for the students to fill in and pick numbers which correspond to the numerical link on the search results in whatever search engine was chosen.

5. Finding new tools

As students progressed, they became involved in finding new tools. Some of those available include the following communications tools:

- *Quipper* is a tool for sharing and trading quizzes. Once students begin participating in creating their own lessons there is a double bonus above the actual learning. Firstly, the student who creates the quiz has actually made something useful and secondly for the student receiving and resolving the quiz. It is an *Android* tool free to download and there are many shared quizzes already created that others have shared (http://www.quipper.com/);

---

1. For instance: Italian TV - Watch Internet TV from Italy (http://wwitv.com/television/104.htm); Free Italian TV - Watch Online TV Channels - Free Internet TV (http://beelinetv.com/free_italian_tv/); BBC - Languages - Italian - TV - Online programmes (http://www.bbc.co.uk/languages/italian/tv/onlineprogs.shtml).

- Italian video sites: a search using the terms Italian Video brings up both learning sites, such as *Yabla Italian Video* Immersion (http://italian.yabla.com/) and *Italian YouTube for Schools* (http://www.fandor.com/) which stream Italian films and dozens of others;

- This online article points out and reviews six free sites for making animated cartoons. Some can be displayed on the site, some on *YouTube* or on the class *Facebook*. Some use text while others sound bites (http://mashable.com/2010/10/).

Almost any digital camera is now capable of making short videos and these can go on YouTube or Facebook. The students picked their topics from a list and worked in pairs or small groups.

Considering this extremely small sample, a discussion with the class of what sites they may want to use was found to be a good idea, as each student could bring in a report on one site and present it and the class then checked them out and voted for a few.

6.   Putting it all together

This chapter presented a small part of what is available for language learning on the internet. It covered the places where the lecturer in the Italian classes was able to find vocabulary, materials and tools. It presented a variety of ideas on how a lecturer was able to use the internet for language learning. One can simply use the content for vocabulary, such as Italian learning sites, *YouTube* and social networking sites.

In short, the internet offers a virtual world that is as real as the participants desire. One can move around the world instantly and connect to people everywhere in any written language. There is a wide variety of sites available for vocabulary practice and for connection to other people using the same language. Basically the use of the World Wide Web is only limited by the combination of the imaginations of the teachers and their students. A virtual tour of Roma in Italian is even available online among dozens of other useful and fun tools. The internet has thus created a short step from the book to the world.

References

Allen, J. (2007). *Inside words: Tools for teaching academic vocabulary, grades 4-12*. Portland, ME: Stenhouse Publishers.

Ali, Z., Mukundan, J., Baki, R., & Mohd Ayub, A. F. (2012). Second Language Learners' Attitudes towards the Methods of Learning Vocabulary. *English Language Teaching, 5*(4), 24-36. doi: 10.5539/elt.v5n4p24

Brandt, L., & Brandt, P. A. (2005). Cognitive poetics and imagery. *European Journal of English Studies, 9*(2), 117-130. doi: 10.1080/13825570500171861

Brown, R. (1973). *A first language*. Cambridge: Harvard University Press.

Carpenter, S. (2007, November 28). Shoot First, Ace Geometry Later. *Scientific American Mind*. Retrieved from http://www.scientificamerican.com/article.cfm?id=shoot-first-ace-geometry

Demiray, U., & Sever, N. S. (2009). *The challenges for marketing distance education in online environment*. Eskisehir: Anadolu University.

De-Obfuscation of Piaget. (1989). *Education, 109*(3), 343-345.

Fan, M. Y. (2003). Frequency of use, perceived usefulness, and actual usefulness of second language vocabulary strategies: a study of Hong Kong learners. *The Modern Language Journal, 87*(2), 222-241. doi: 10.1111/1540-4781.00187

Holmberg, B. (2005). Teaching Foreign Language Skills by Distance Education Methods: Some Basic Considerations. In B. Holmberg, M. Shelley, & C. White (Eds.), *Distance Education and Languages: Evolution and Change* (pp. 166-177). Clevedon: Multilingual Matters.

Hunt, A., & Beglar, D. (2002). Current research and practice in teaching vocabulary. In J. C. Richards & W. A. Renandya (Eds.), *Methodology in language teaching: An anthology of current practice* (pp. 258-266). Cambridge: Cambridge University Press.

Ketabi, S., & Shahraki, S. H. (2011). Vocabulary in the Approaches to Language Teaching: From the Twentieth Century to the Twenty-first. *Journal of Language Teaching & Research, 2*(3), 726-731. doi: 10.4304/jltr.2.3.726-731

Kuo, R. J., & Chen, J. A. (2004). A decision support system for order selection in electronic commerce based on fuzzy neural network supported by real-coded genetic algorithm. *Expert Systems with Applications, 26*(2), 141-154. doi: 10.1016/S0957-4174(03)00115-5

Krashen, S. D., & Terrell, T. D. (2000). *The natural approach: Language acquisition in the classroom*. London: Prentice Hall Europe.

Levine, L. N., & McCloskey, M. L. (2008). *Teaching learners of English in mainstream classrooms K-8: One class, many paths*. Boston: Allyn and Bacon.

Macaro, E. (2001). *Learning strategies in foreign and second language classrooms*. London: Continuum.

Marston, P. (2011). Emotion, ambiguity and telling stories: The role of neuroscience in using computer games for learning. *Psychology of Education Review, 35*(1), 16-20.

McCormick, J. (2000, April 24). The new school. *Newsweek*, 60-62.

Nespor, M. (2001). About parameters, prominence, and bootstrapping. In E. Dupoux (Ed.), *Language, Brain, and Cognitive Development: Essays in Honor of Jacques Mehler* (pp. 127-142). Cambridge, MA: The MIT Press.

Petchko, K. (2011). The role of cognitive, phonological, and linguistic comprehension abilities in early reading development in the Russian language (pp. 2328-2337). In INTED2011 Proceedings, 5th International Technology, Education and Development Conference, Valencia, Spain.

Quinn, M. M., Rutherford, R. B., Jr., & Osher, D. M. (1999). *Special Education in Alternative Education Programs. ERIC Digest E585*. Reston, VA: Eric Clearinghouse On Disabilities And Gifted Education.

Stringer, E. T. (2007). *Action Research*. Thousand Oaks, California: Sage Publications Inc.

Takeuchi, O., Griffiths, C., & Coyle, D. (2007). Applying strategies to context: the role of individual, situational and group differences. In Cohen, A. D. & Macaro, E. (Eds.), *Language learning strategies: Thirty years of research and practice* (pp. 69-92). Oxford: Oxford University Press.

Technology & Innovation Management Conference Paper Abstracts. (2010). *Academy of Management*. doi: 10.5465/AMBPP.2010.54509556

Viadero, D. (2006, August 30). Cognition Studies Offer Insights on Academic Tactics. *Education Week*, 12-13.

Wheeldon, J. (2011). Is a Picture Worth a Thousand Words? Using Mind Maps to Facilitate Participant Recall in Qualitative Research. *Qualitative Report, 16*(2), 509-522. Retrieved from http://www.nova.edu/ssss/QR/QR16-2/wheeldon.pdf

Research and Reflections on Irish Resources

19 The Born Digital Graduate: Multiple Representations of and Within Digital Humanities PhD Theses

Sharon Webb[1], Aja Teehan[2], and John Keating[3]

Abstract

This chapter examines the production and utilisation of digital tools to create and present a born-digital theses, and in so doing, considers the changing function of traditional theses. It asks how (relatively) new technologies and methodologies should affect the representation and function of graduate scholarship in the Digital Humanities (DH), and moots an alternative to the print thesis, proposing instead two alternative texts: one a static PDF (representative of a traditional print thesis), and another enriched version, congruent with DH methods and tools, which incorporates functional boundary objects such as interactive timelines, and also explicitly documents the use of historical sources. These objects serve both to enhance the readers' experience, and to expose the scholarly process. An overview is provided of the methodology used to generate the multi-format digital thesis – derived, modified, transformed and visualised from XML – encoded scholarship. As such, we consider the implications of the creation of this single base XML encoding that, combined with software processing tools, can generate multiple representations of research. This chapter is based upon the working methodology of Webb's (2011) PhD thesis.

Keywords: digital humanities, digital scholarship, born digital graduate, XML, XLST, XLS-FO.

1. Department of History, National University of Ireland, Maynooth, Co. Kildare, Ireland; sharon.webb@nuim.ie

2. An Foras Feasa Research Institute, National University of Ireland, Maynooth, Co. Kildare, Ireland; aja.teehan@nuim.ie

3. An Foras Feasa Research Institute, National University of Ireland, Maynooth, Co. Kildare, Ireland; john.keating@nuim.ie

How to cite this chapter: Webb, S., Teehan, A., & Keating, J. (2013). The Born Digital Graduate: Multiple Representations of and Within Digital Humanities PhD Theses. In C. Fowley, C. English, & S. Thouësny (Eds.), *Internet Research, Theory, and Practice: Perspectives from Ireland* (pp. 381-404). Dublin: © Research-publishing.net.

1.   Introduction

Given the digital humanities place within traditional research, this chapter asks, if a digital approach is used to create research, why should its presentation be limited to the traditional, static representation of that research. Here, we discuss one approach or methodology to present scholarship online that takes advantage of the digital medium and its inherent functionality, moving beyond static scholarly texts. Webb's (2011) thesis examines procedures and strategies for conducting humanities research using digital tools and applications within a historiographical system. Thus, this chapter is central to a reflective and reflexive process resulting from, and in, the critical self-evaluation of such theses and their outputs. As Webb's (2011) PhD indicates, we use digital humanities methodology to create or formulate knowledge, but how do we adequately represent such a digital humanities thesis? It should embody the digital humanities principles and research that helped to create it. In an effort to address this, we have instead used XML and XSLT along with software libraries to create a framework, encapsulated in a Bundle Object, to add dynamic functionality to an otherwise static text (see Figure 1).

Figure 1.   Visualisation of the Bundle Object, taken from Webb's (2011) thesis

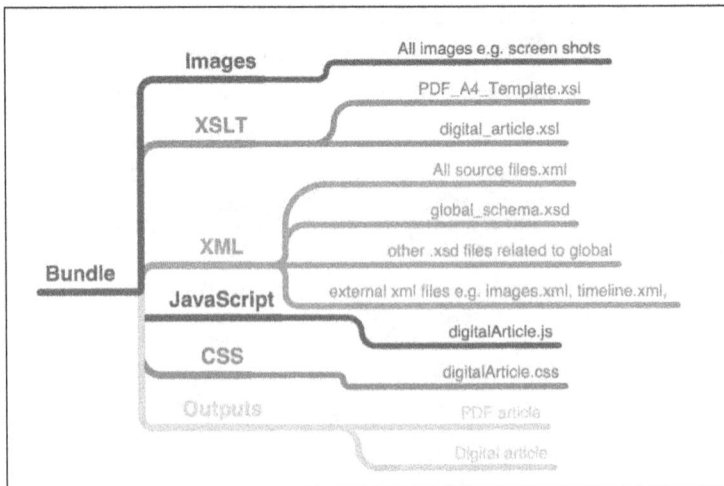

Generic characteristics are encoded, which enable the use of the described framework. The digital thesis proposed here takes multiple formats depending on user needs and reading environment. The two formats we will discuss are a static, printable, electronic version – a PDF – and a dynamic, interactive, enhanced version. Both of these are generated from a single, base XML encoding of the research; the thesis is both polymorphic and dynamic. Polymorphism refers to an object's ability to take many possible forms; the form to be taken is chosen at instantiation depending upon the conditions extant within the environment at the time. It is dynamic in the sense that the form can change, even after instantiation, upon interaction with the user and in response to their actions within the environment.

2.   Literature review

This new means of presenting the research output from a digital humanities PhD has been long heralded. The last few decades have seen a noticeable shift in the way we represent, codify and present knowledge. Theorist such as Nelson, who coined the phrase hypertext in the 1960s to refer "to non-sequential writing...[or] text that branches" (Nelson, 1981, cited in Landow, 2006, p. 2), and Landow, whose 1992 and 2006 editions discuss the paradigm shift in writing in response to technological changes, provide an historical account of these changes while demonstrating the impact digital media have on our consumption and production of text and narrative. Nelson's (1974) publication *Computer lib/Dream machine* is a liberal manifesto that considers the personal computer and information technology to be a means to promote knowledge creation and dissemination. Nelson's (1974) hypertext can be described as "the deep connections and entanglements in human knowledge" (Webb, 2011, p. 341). He states that "everything is deeply interwingled"; human knowledge is intertwined and connected, and indeed linked (Nelson, 1974, p. 307). It is this characteristic of human knowledge that is reflected in his idea or concept of hypertext.

Landow (2006) discusses Nelson in-depth, and in his publication refers to hypertext essays and new types of academic writing, namely blogs (p. 77). More recently Fitzpatrick's (2011) *Planned obsolescence, published, technology and the future of the academy* discusses the changes in scholarly communication, focusing on topics such as peer review, authorship and preservation. This text also refers to hypertext and the reconfiguration of academic writing in line with this form of electronic publishing. Fitzpatrick (2011), however, discusses "the difficulties in readerly engagement" and the readers' "desire for fuller participation that hypertext could not itself satisfy" and suggests that we need "to think differently about the networked relationships among our texts and, and among the readers who interact with them" (p. 99). It is in this sense that we consider DeStefano and LeFevre's (2007) article to inform the method and production of the digital articles presented in this chapter as they discuss the cognitive effects of hypertext on readers and users alike. In our case, the cognitive load can be adjusted (lower in the static, higher in the dynamic version) by the reader depending on the level of complexity at which they wish to read. Thus, the enriched, dynamic version is not a 'better' version of the thesis while the static printable one is a 'lesser' one; rather they each have a context (reader or environment) to which they are more suited.

In its polymorphic multiplicity of presentation (depending upon reader and environment), our e-thesis exemplifies the 'born digital' object. As Armstrong (2008) indicates about born digital e-books:

> "a book may be first created for use only in a digital form, having no previous version existing on paper – the term 'born- digital' has been coined – and this may be typified by a much greater use of the design features available. If, from its inception, a book has been planned and designed for reading electronically the author and publisher are both able to take advantage of the medium to add value to plain text [...]. However, if it has the essential qualities of a book [...] and is accessible to be read on computers or on e-book readers, the origin does not affect its classification" (p. 6).

Our scholarly e-thesis is very much designed to take advantage of the digital medium to add value to plain text, and has no previously existing paper version; in this sense, it is born digital. Despite this, it is still essentially an e-thesis; it is designed to communicate research, following a novel methodology, and existing in multiple possible final formats.

While this project engages with the desires and concerns articulated by Nelson (1974), Landow (2006), and DeStefano and LeFevre's (2007) as discussed above, it also serves as an example of the problematising nature of born digital scholarly documents. Vanhoutte (2007) outlines the difficulties associated with categorising 'electronic editions' of texts; the various types of taxonomic categorisations that can be employed complicate the typology of editions. These can be predicated upon, for instance, an underlying textual theory, the method of editing, or the format used to present the final text (Vanhoutte, 2007, p. 159). The fractured nature of the evolving typologies makes it difficult to categorise an 'electronic edition' of an existing traditional text, let alone one that is born within, and designed to take advantage of, the digital. While an e-print or e-thesis can be considered a surrogate of a traditional document, it is produced using a single method, and uses one format to present the final text; this born digital thesis does not. This object has multiple, reconfigurable versions of itself, differing in format depending on user and environment. Thus, even as it addresses the concerns of some scholars, it adds to those of others.

The first representation of the PhD theses is the print ready document, rendered as a PDF. The generation of this print based document satisfies academic requirements and is part of the examinable component of a thesis. The PDF document also caters for different user activities and learning requirements, which include the novice reader or the traditionalist and is used to scaffold the user's learning and comprehension requirements. The digital articles (the web delivery format) described here are markedly different from the electronic PDF version (the printable format) many Irish universities now require to be deposited into institutional repositories such as NUI Maynooth's ePrints and eThesis archive. The digital articles move from the electronic, though still static printable PDF format, to an interactive web delivery format dynamically created using HTML and accompanying technologies. Although any printed thesis can take a static electronic form, such as a PDF, it would offer no functional benefits or advantages beyond basic search, which in the context of digital humanities, does not adequately reflect the use or creation of new digital tools and artifacts as part of the research process. Our digital articles are generated from a Bundle Object, which adds dynamic functionality to otherwise static-research output, presenting the research in an online environment. This online environment presents an enriched version of the chapters: for instance, a referencing model in XSLT automatically generates a dynamic bibliography for each chapter, including features such as "intertextual links" (Samraj, 2008, p. 55) between the text and source material. In addition, software libraries can be used to support the innate variability of a boundary object – defined as an object with user dependent functionality and meaning (Thomas, Sargent, & Hardy, 2008) – which can take the form of diagrams, tables, timelines, etc. Thus, depending on the user's activity and perspective, the presentation of the boundary object will change.

3.   Documents as products of praxes

Traditional humanities doctoral research in any number of disciplines, such as history or literary studies, all produce a print thesis despite their markedly different praxes. The print medium has been exploited in various ways in order to encode research, resulting in the development of a variety of boundary objects capturing the process or results of enquiry. For instance, history research may require the use of timelines, as traditionally represented in print. These timelines have evolved in response to the 2-D material nature of paper. Their digital counterpart, rather than merely representing a print-bound flat timeline, could seek to better represent the underlying historical data, perhaps in a dynamic timeline. However, these mechanisms for expression of research are often generic enough to be implemented in any discipline; the methodology is generalisable.

The same is not true of the process of research itself, which often develops into quite distinct praxes, depending on the discipline. Researchers will all be familiar with the community 'rules' that guide the production of their scholarly outputs. For instance, the rules of production that scholarly editors follow will differ from language to language, and even within language but between historical period. Consequently, though the Bundle Object developed here utilises generalisable expressions of research (for instance digital or non digital boundary objects), it is specifically supportive of the historical research praxes. In order to reuse this Object within a literary studies discipline, for example, changes would be required in the hosting system, and the interaction mechanisms with the sources.

Traditionally, research outputs codified as chapters or sections can be seen as the final manifestation of a PhD thesis and reflect the use of print or static technology. The functionality of these outputs varies according to different headings and ranges from literature reviews, general narrative and concept generation, to the development of structured arguments based on theory and source material and to the provision of essential referencing and bibliographic material. These functions are referred to as "generic characteristics of academic discourse" in linguistic structural analysis (Mingwei & Yahjun, 2010, p. 95). Chapter functionality represents and reflects the original research statement and provides the means to convey and articulate traditional scholarship within the medium of print. However, the product of a digital humanities thesis, which describes a process of digitally-influenced scholarship, should not be restricted to a printed document.

This approach reflects the innate capability of the digital medium to layer extra functionality over that of printed works. Rather than creating a single representation of scholarly output, the use of XSLT, an XML based language which adds functionality and form to XML encoded files as it incorporates languages such as HTML and JavaScript, and software libraries generates and encourages a reflexive process between text, argument, narrative and source material where multiple representations co-exist. Furthermore, it reflects the changing praxes of the digital humanities scholar, manifest in the nature of the documents used to record that scholarship.

4.   Methodology

This chapter is based upon the working methodology of Webb's (2011) PhD thesis, which applies a digital humanities approach to historical research at each stage of investigation into *A study of associational culture in Ireland and the development of Irish nationalism, 1780-1830, with the construction of a software information environment*. Webb's (2011) thesis, funded by the HEA under the PRTLI4 Humanities, Technology and Innovation award to An Foras Feasa (NUI Maynooth), includes a discussion of the creation of factlets and subsequent visualisation of factoids, as described in Webb and Keating (2009).

Factlets are defined as structured annotations which prompt users to follow the functional and genre specific steps taken to produce historical writing, specifically argument development regarding narrative, deduction and consequence. They provide a means to preserve transparency between "facts of the past" and "facts of history" (Elton, 2002, p. 50). Factoids are used as a method to connect "different kinds of structured information" (Bradley & Short, 2005, p. 9) and are a visual representation of the connections between different factlets and cultural objects or digital cultural objects. Factoids are presented as a network of factlets and primary sources. These digital artefacts fulfill two functions. In the first instance they inform historical research and support argument development, in the second, they provide the means to open up scholarship and the historical interpretation contained therein, as they can be reused to present the scholarly process on-line.

The creation of Webb's (2011) historical thesis is supported by a digital humanities methodology and demonstrates the use of digital technology as an essential feature of humanities research. This digital methodology includes the use of XML, a mark-up language designed to structure data, XSLT and XQuery, the querying language associated with XML. It also included software development, using the Adobe's Flex framework, which realises the creation and implementation of factlets and factoids within an interactive online environment created at An Foras Feasa. Webb's (2011) research is focused on a traditional historical question but relies upon a digital methodology to support source management, argument development and research presentation, the result of which is the creation of new research outputs, as digital artefacts, as well as scholarship contained in the traditional written thesis.

This approach changes reader and user activity – one user may read the article while another may interact with the digital records of scholarly process. In order to realise the born digital thesis we used an existing framework, an interactive repository developed at An Foras Feasa. This environment, which is a highly interactive, front end driven, Fedora based repository (Fedora is an open source repository system to manage and store digital content), was previously used to manage the digital objects or collections linked to the historical research. Within this system we realised the factlet and the factoid model which informed the creation of the historical narrative contained in the born digital thesis and transformed through the Bundle Object. Functionality in the system includes annotations, discussion forums, automatic relationship graphing, media hosting and digital archiving and preservation. The use of this existing system allowed us to extend the functionality of the Bundle Object and the XSLT templates contained therein. This activity realises the importance of data reusability and supports the creation and presentation of the multiple representations of research. While part of an existing framework at An Foras Feasa, the products now described can be realised in a number of environments and they are not specific to this system or indeed to the historical context of the research.

Transformation of a born digital text (a thesis) into both the print and digital media relies upon the existence of a single, defining text-model. Figure 2 shows the process involved in creating new research objects. The first stage, the XML encoding, which creates the master document, makes possible all subsequent processes. Creating a unifying model allows the generation of XML schema and subsequent XML encoding in order to manifest the new research objects (the various chapters in a research thesis). The model considers presentation properties (chapter, paragraph, section), which allows for transformations specifically for presentation purposes, as well as semantic properties which encode the 'textual semantics' (Eggins, 2005) of the text – its logical class (Teehan & Keating, 2010a). This approach makes the text reusable and ensures "a single lexia can function very differently" (Landow, 2006, p. 107) in different environments.

Figure 2.   The process or stages involved in creating multiple representations of scholarship and new digital objects based on specified use cases – the dynamic generation of a static PDF document, the traditional thesis, and a dynamically generated interactive digital article delivered over the web

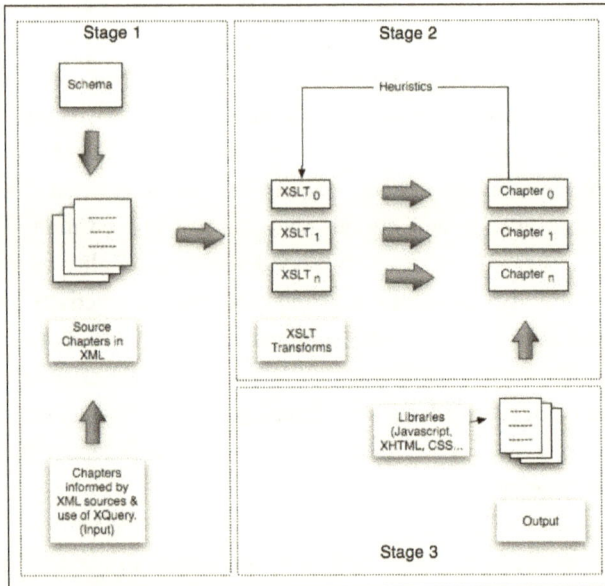

The model is translated into a schema which allows us to mark up the content of the scholarship, including narrative, which in historical research pertains to 'logical' rather than 'ideological' content. Stages 2 and 3, as illustrated in Figure 2, are the realisation of the various Use Cases. The XSLT transforms, which translate the XML files (the input) into HTML files (the output) and software libraries are templates from which text from different sources, (different sections of a thesis) can be modified and transformed. This essentially creates a suite of tools that support (different) user activity.

These various macros support the creation of multiple representations of the text. Our encoded texts reflect the functions embedded in standard print theses, but augment those capabilities for these born digital theses. Here, two specific Use Cases address (i) the creation of a dynamic bibliographic referencing model, and (ii) the context-dependent presentation of boundary objects.

These low-level Use Cases (the implementation) support our higher level ones (the features or functions), that is the dynamic creation of static or interactive versions of a base text-model. The print model transforms the original text to a print ready text, and can account for various institutional templates. Embedding references to the various primary sources used in the XML encoding instructs an XSLT to create a hypertext of linked resources and creates 'intertextual links' and boundary objects for user interaction between the narrative and various digital objects within the digital medium.

The research activities which contribute to the development of Webb's (2011) historical thesis are methodologically oriented within a digital humanities framework. This framework includes support for historical research activities such as source gathering and management, source querying, argument development and visualisation and formal write up of narrative, argument and conclusions. While these activities help create scholarship, the creation of multiple representations focuses on research presentation and dissemination, and as such the PDF and digital article cater to this specific activity. These multiple representations also consider the digital artifacts that are created and generated as a result of this research e.g., factlets and factoids.

Figure 3.   A visualisation of the interaction beween the different technologies used

The XML source file (the input, the master document) is translated into HTML (the output) using the XSLT transform, of which multiple templates can be

created. The XSLT contains all HTML and references to JavaScript, CSS, etc. XSL-FO is used within an XSLT template but uses a different processor to create the PDF.

An XSLT transform, incorporating the use of XSL-FO, a formatting language for XML, was created (see Pawson, 2002). XSL-FO is used to format XML documents and can output high quality, print ready documents in PDF and as such is described as a typesetting language or specification. Unlike XSLT which has no formatting rules, but essentially converts the XML to a different format (e.g., HTML, a different XML schema, TEI, etc.), XSL-FO has specific rules associated with design and layout. As such the XSL-FO style-sheet formats and controls all content design, formatting and organisation. This enables us to create multiple templates that cater to different institutional demands but use the same master document (see Figure 3). Using XSL-FO within an XSLT transform enables the dynamic generation of content. The print ready text, created using the XSLT XSL-FO template, dynamically generates the table of contents, footnotes, the bibliography and a glossary of terms from the master document (see Figure 4 – an extract of a XSL-FO/XSLT template). Bi-directional internal links create a navigational document and any figures, images, etc., are also handled. This template can be used for all chapters of a thesis, or other encoded articles, to create standardised print documents which adhere to institutional and academic formatting requirements.

Figure 4.   An example of XSL-FO which controls the layout of a biblography

```
<!-- bibliography -->
<fo:page-sequence master-reference="bibliography" format="1">

    <fo:static-content flow-name="xsl-region-after">
        <fo:block text-align="center" font-family="Times">
            <fo:page-number id="bibPage"/>
        </fo:block>
    </fo:static-content>
    <fo:flow flow-name="xsl-region-body">

        <fo:block>
            <xsl:apply-templates select="/" mode="bib"/>
        </fo:block>
    </fo:flow>
</fo:page-sequence>
```

The 'page sequence' stipulates where the bibliograhy will appear in the final document or PDF and the call to '<xsl:apply-tempaltes/>', controls the extraction of content for the bibliography from the XML input file.

The second use case, the creation of an interactive digital article, based upon the same master document, also contains footnotes, table of contents, etc., but its online environment allows for the inclusion of boundary objects, such as interactive time lines, key stones or tool tips. These are encoded in a separate XML file and provide extra contextual information to the reader, rendered as hover text (only visible when the user interacts with the text). Boundary objects within the digital article also include references to sources within the digital repository. Interactive spring graphs also demonstrate the relationships between factlets and their sources through a factoid and alerts the user/reader to the existence of these objects. This second representation of the source document also uses an XSLT which includes HTML, CSS and JavaScript. Both the printed article and the digital article consider different user requirements and scaffold the user. The inclusion of boundary objects described within the digital article takes into account increased cognitive load and effects on working memory which can impact different users when interacting with hyper texts (DeStefano & LeFevre, 2007). As DeStefano and LeFevre (2007) state, multiple interruptions in hypertext reading e.g., leaving the main text, can affect a reader's comprehension. It is in response to this that we included additional contextual information within the main text, through key stones: rendered as a hover text, they reduce the user's need to leave the main text or follow external links.

5. The Bundle Object within an interactive repository

While these two representations, the PDF (printable format) and the digital article (web delivery format), can exist independently of each other and other systems, their inclusion in an interactive environment further improves their functionality. The use of an existing online repository, which utilises Fedora and handles various digital objects including bespoke objects, namely the Bundle Object, enabled us to load and render the representations of the thesis chapters, the PDF and the digital article, as described above. The Bundle Object, which functions as a wrapper for all the XML, XSLT, XSL-FO, JavaScript, CSS etc. files, enables the system to dynamically generate and host the PDF and the digital article (or other templates produced). Importantly, it also provides access to the master document which created these representations which are essentially derivates of this underlying encoding. The XML schema does not belong to a standard such as TEI (Text Encoding Initiative), which develops and provides guidelines and schemas for text encoding, instead a custom schema was developed to "encapsulate the process" described above (Teehan & Keating, 2010b, p. 385).

Figure 5.   Visualisation of the relationship between various digital objects and the Bundle Object

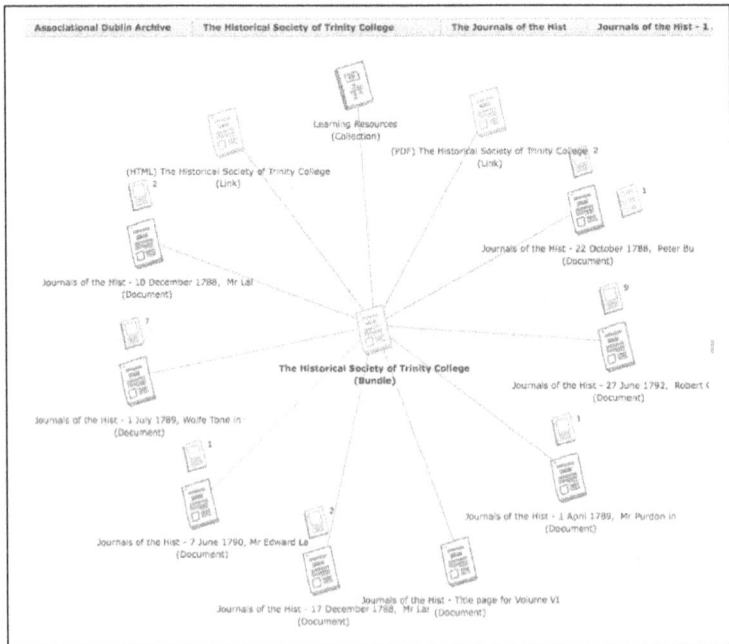

Figure 5 is the Bundle Object as it is presented in the online environment. As the central node in a relationship graph it maps all the digital resources in the

thesis chapter to the PDF and digital article. It graphically represents the thesis chapter and demonstrates its intrinsic link to the digital sources. The master document (in XML) contains the historical narrative and, through our templates, we can create the traditional narrative, but most importantly we can develop new representations with additional boundary objects, contextualisation and functionality. We use the Bundle Object to create different perspectives of the thesis. Aspects of the PDF and the digital article are illustrated in Figure 6, Figure 7 and Figure 8.

Figure 6.   Dynamically generated table of contents in the PDF representation of 'The Historical Society of Trinity College and radical politics leading to the 1798 Rebellion

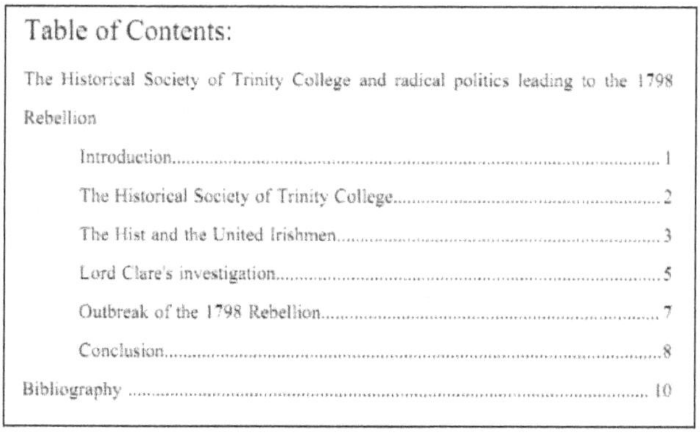

Table of Contents:

The Historical Society of Trinity College and radical politics leading to the 1798 Rebellion

Introduction.. 1

The Historical Society of Trinity College.. 2

The Hist and the United Irishmen... 3

Lord Clare's investigation... 5

Outbreak of the 1798 Rebellion... 7

Conclusion... 8

Bibliography 10

Figure 7.   The same table of contents in the digital article

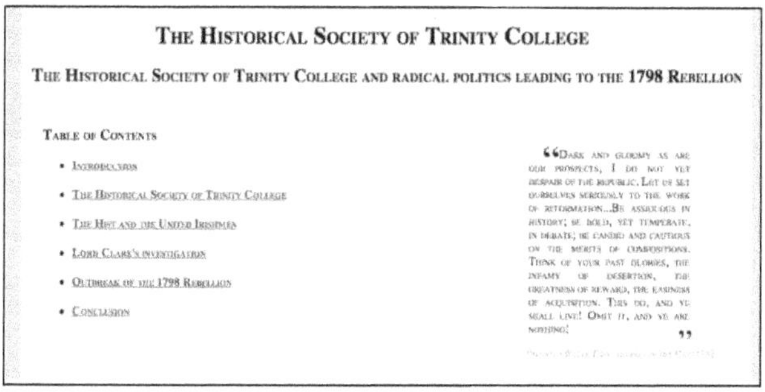

Figure 8.   Screen shot of the digital article and key stone which provides contextual information about John Wilson Croker

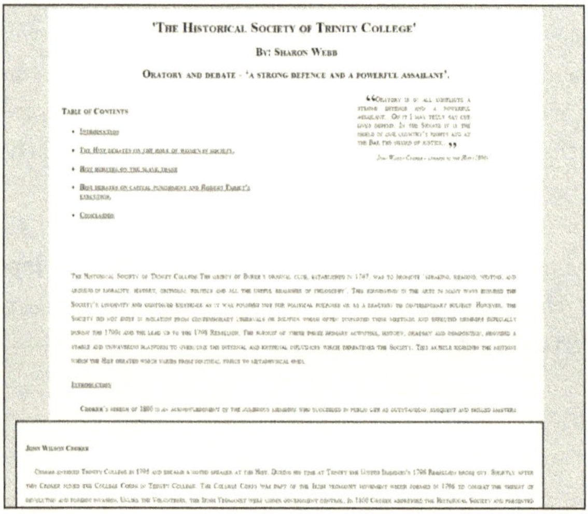

Further representations of the thesis were enabled through the use of Mediasite, a webcasting technology. A recording of a lecture on *The Hist and Radical Politics* was uploaded along with related slides. This lecture, available in the interactive environment, also generated a number of discussions and reflects the ability to create dynamic scholarship as the system engages users and scholars in open dialogue and discussion. This audio-visual version, although not dynamically generated, provides another access point to scholarly dialogue and discussion which caters to different user needs and requirements.

6.   Impact

As illustrated in Figure 5 this repository includes collections containing digital objects and learning resources, such as slides and presentations. It also supports user and source interaction through online discussions and annotations. This environment, which hosts the various digital objects including the Bundle Object, allows users to add and view factlets and factoids, promoting user interaction with primary source material and the scholarly articles which are derived from these cultural artefacts. The provision of a discussion forum generates and encourages debate between users as well as engagement with scholarly content which can focus on primary sources as well as learning resources, e.g., digital articles or online lectures.

Within this type of environment the PDF version of the scholarly article transforms from a functional requirement, satisfying an academic need, to an object which caters to different user and learning requirements. The PDF, as well as the digital article which provides extra contextual information through key stones or hover text, provide users, scholars and students with different access points to knowledge and content. These representations consider issues born from hyper-textual forms of reading which can impact user comprehension and working memory, or cognitive load, and relies on different levels of user expertise, both in the knowledge domain and hypertext engagement and experience.

The *Associational Dublin Archive* within the digital repository is specific to Webb's (2011) historical thesis on associational culture and Irish nationalism, and contains a number of different digital objects related to this work. The collection includes primary sources, digitised from records at the manuscript department at Trinity College and the Russell Library at NUI Maynooth, as well as factlets and factoids which relate directly to the historical research statement. Factlets are linked to digital primary sources and demonstrate the historical interpretations specific to the research topic. It is within this environment that the XML encoded chapters of the PhD thesis, contained in the master document, are transformed using the XSL-FO and XSLT templates and where both versions, the PDF and the digital article, are uploaded, effectively becoming boundary objects in the online collection.

Other boundary objects are presented in the digital article, including a dynamically generated spring graph which demonstrates the relationship between digital primary sources and factlets that are directly related to the scholarly content in the article (Figure 9). The digital article also supports the inclusion of an interactive timeline which more usefully visualises the topics of debate for the Historical Society of Trinity College than an equivalent static, print timeline (Figure 10).

Figure 9.   Dynamically generated spring graph in the digital article which visualises the links between the primary document, the central node and the factlets which are utilised in the scholarly article

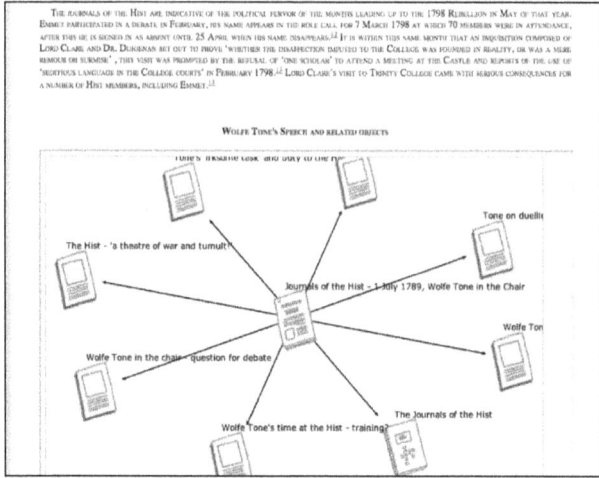

Figure 10. Dynamically generated timeline which chronologically maps the debates of the Historical Society of Trinity College and provides access to the Society's response

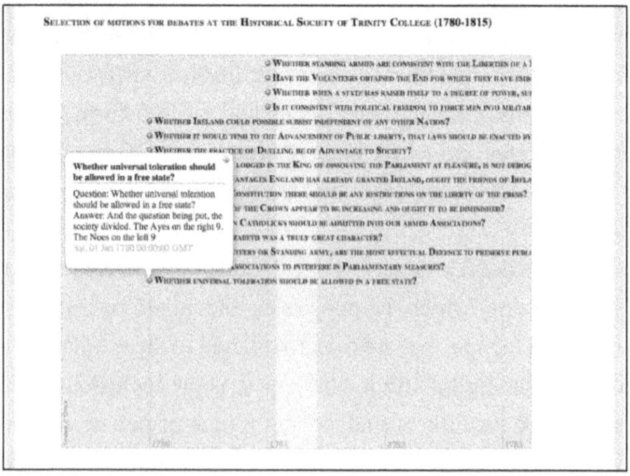

The online environment at An Foras Feasa supports scholarly research but the ability to upload the Bundle Object, which contains all the code required to produce the PDF article and the digital article, enables the user to present their research in its multiple forms. In this sense the environment, or system, supports scholarly research but also supports the presentation of the products of that research. Hosting digital humanities research in an environment which directly links back to the primary sources that informed the research presents scholarly interpretation and argument development through factlets and exposes associative thinking through the factoid visualisation, engaging users and readers alike in new explorations of scholarly research. It also creates transparency in research as it facilitates and encourages user or reader engagement with research content as well as sources and immerses users (within this example) in historical debate and inquiry.

The Bundle Object specifies the multiple representations of scholarly content. It contains all the XML, XSLT, CSS and JavaScript files which enable the production of multiple representations. The PDF and the digital article are but two representations which include personalised features of research. Yet these templates can be modified, extended and reused for new research by new users. Indeed, three M.A. students at An Foras Feasa have already reused these templates to present aspects of their thesis, both in a historical and literary perspective.

The production and use of multiple representations of scholarship, encapsulated in the Bundle Object, takes advantage of the possibilities offered by the digital medium and challenges the author to think in 3-D, real-time, dynamically and audio-visually. This process can improve readability and accessibility for various readers and users and allows the author to control the presentation of the work in response to a perceived audience, including the digital artifacts created through research. It also enables the reader to choose the version most suitable to their level of expertise and, in this sense, aligns the appropriate medium to the appropriate audience.

The digital article (web delivery format) offers advantages over the printable, static, format (the PDF), not only for accessibility but because it can include different tools for users to engage and interact with content. It can include peripheral or contextual information, but also gives direct access to primary source material. As Fitzpatrick (2011) points out, the value of online scholarship or publishing "is the means of interacting with the content, rather than the content itself" (p. 47). It is in this sense that pursuing new ways to present and enhance online scholarship can add value to content. The methodology to create multiple representations of a digital humanities thesis, described above, enables us to dynamically generate the examinable component of a thesis. The same methodology allows us to dynamically generate the digital article but offers new ways to present the same scholarly content. The development of keystones, the inclusion of interactive timelines and the spring graph visualisation allow the reader/user to engage with the content in whole new ways. The functionality of the digital article, however, is extensible as we can add new features by simply changing the templates. Yet, the printable format is not made redundant by this process, as it can provide a sustainable method of access.

We may ask if our process is respectful of or subversive to the print or PDF version of scholarly content? The PDF may serve a specific functional purpose, but we must examine its contribution to knowledge engagement and its utility as a means of access to content for different users and their cognitive or pedagogical requirements. This format also serves as a simple tool or mechanism for preservation of online content, as the scholarly content does not rely upon the existence of the digital or interactive representation. The PDF can exist in its entirety without reference to the online environment. So, while this process may be subversive to the print article as a means to represent born digital theses, it is respectful of the gains and benefits of this traditional format which cater to different user requirements working within an interactive online environment.

Sustained access to and maintenance of functionality within the digital article requires more work in comparison to the printable format presented as a PDF. Fitzpatrick (2011) remarks that "the digital may be more prone to a material obsolescence than [the] print" (p. 6), a fact that enforces our first use case described above, the generation of a printable format, and supports the creation of multiple representations of scholarship using the master document – one source XML.

The inclusion of these representations within an online environment, such as that developed at An Foras Feasa, not only supports and enhances user engagement with content but offers solutions to the 'material obsolescence' described by Fitzpatrick (2011). Institutional support can help with digital sustainability but national developments, namely the creation of a national trusted digital repository by the Digital Repository of Ireland (DRI)[1], are also important in terms of preservation and access to scholarly content. DRI's mission, to develop a trusted digital repository, is inherently concerned with producing a technical framework that provides access to content and shares it, but which is also fundamentally concerned with the long-term preservation of that content. Within a national technical framework then, what other use cases can we satisfy in terms of multiple representations of a thesis?

7.   Conclusion

This chapter demonstrates the process and production of support tools for digital scholarship, and how the creation of appropriate templates can make manifest various representations of digital humanities PhD theses from a single model. The use cases are reliant on the ability of the encoding and the schema to encapsulate both the functions of the text and the various transformations and software libraries.

Multiple representations of and within PhD theses pose new problems and issues for the individual researcher but also for academic evaluation. There are no rules or regulations on how to present digital theses which go beyond an e-version of a printed one, which in effect mimics the print version. It also challenges the idea of published theses, especially in terms of the prestige attached to being

---

1. DRI is a four-year PRTLI 5 funded project which aims to develop an interactive trusted digital repository for contemporary and historical, social and cultural data held by Irish institutions. It is a research consortium lead by the Royal Irish Academy. Partners include National University of Ireland Maynooth, Trinity College Dublin, Dublin Institute of Technology, National University of Ireland Galway and National College of Art and Design. See www.dri.ie for more details.

'published' in an academic career. How do you 'publish' an interactive article in the same way you would publish a monograph? How is the work involved in creating these representation credited?

The products (PDF, digital article) of the methodologies discussed which use XML, XSL-FO, etc., impact not only the presentation of scholarship but how that scholarship is perceived and used. Presenting a chapter of a PhD with access to source content within an interactive environment creates dynamic scholarship. It exposes the interpretations embedded in the scholarship explicitly as the factlets reveal the connections between the sources and the interpretations. As a visualisation then, the factoids can move the user/reader away from the final product, the thesis chapter, which may be perceived as static scholarship. Factoids enable the user/reader to interact with the essence of the scholarship – the sources, the interpretations, etc., and not just the final product of it – the static article.

The various representations, the PDF, the digital article with boundary objects, and the video and slide show concerned with direct content of the PhD, held within the digital repository with direct access to primary sources and their interpretations, bring the user back to the original history, as it stands with and without interpretation, the difference between 'facts of the past' and 'facts of history'. This is the essence or fundamental reason for the creation and use of factlets and factoids as it creates transparency between primary sources and historical interpretation. The online environment allows the reader/user to return to the sources which informs the scholarship and the user's ability to create new factlets, start or enter discussions provides the user access to, and the opportunity to engage with, historical debate. The result of this interaction with primary source material and historical debate is the creation of dynamic history. It allows users to 'do' history, not only read it, and encourages debate and questioning of the interpretations presented in the final products of scholarship (e.g., the document).

The use of factlets and factoids are specifically employed for historical research but the Bundle Object is a generalised expression of research and as such can be modified, extended and reused within different disciplinary contexts. However, given the historical context of Webb's (2011) thesis further work on the production or extension of the Bundle Object for a literary environment may be necessary. Other areas of development include additional boundary objects, two of which have already been identified since the finalisation of Webb's (2011) thesis: a geographical visualisation to map the various clubs and societies discussed on associational culture and social networking graphs to view relationships between clubs and their members.

Current research students in digital humanities constitute a newly born digital generation, the nature of whose outputs differs markedly from earlier generations. Reflections on this changing process should also include an analysis of new methods and techniques to create dynamic scholarship. The encoding of the final phase in a PhD thesis allows scholarship to be reused, modified, visualised and transformed, allowing for greater distribution and accessibility of digital scholarship. Thus the dissertation, in its multiple representations, can not only remain central to the discipline of Digital Humanities but shape its future development.

References

Armstrong, C. (2008). Books in a virtual world : The evolution of the e-book and its lexicon. *Journal of Librarianship and Information Science, 40*(3), 193-206. doi: 10.1177/0961000608092554

Bradley, J., & Short, H. (2005). Texts into Databases: The Evolving Field of New-Style Prosopography. *Literary and Linguistic Computing, 20*(Suppl), 3-24. doi: 10.1093/llc/fqi022

DeStefano, D., & LeFevre, J. (2007). Cognitive load in hypertext reading: a review. *Computers in Human Behavior, 23*(3), 1616-1641. doi: 10.1016/j.chb.2005.08.012

Eggins, S. (2005). *An Introduction to Systemic Functional Linguistics* (2nd ed.). London: Continuum.

Elton, G. R. (2002). *The Practice of History* (2nd ed.). Oxford: Blackwell Publisher Ltd.

Fitzpatrick, K. (2011). *Planned obsolescence: Publishing, technology and the future of the academy*. New York: New York University Press.

Landow, G. P. (1992). *Hypertext 2.0: the convergence of contemporary critical theory and technology*. Baltimore: The Johns Hopkins University Press.

Landow, G. P. (2006). *Hypertext 3.0, Critical Theory and New Media in an Era of Globalization*. Maryland: The John Hopkins University Press.

Mingwei, Z., & Yajun, J. (2010). Dissertation Acknowledgements: Generic Structure and Linguistic Features. *Chinese Journal of Applied Linguistics, 33*(1), 94-109.

Nelson, T. (1974). Computer Lib/Dream Machines. Republished in N. Wardrip-Fruin & N. Montfort (2003) (Eds.). *The new media reader* (pp. 301-338). Cambridge: The MIT Press. Retrieved from http://www.newmediareader.com/book_samples/nmr-21-nelson.pdf

Nelson, T. (1981). *Literary Machines*. Swarthmore, PA: Self-published.

Pawson, D. (2002). XSL-FO. California: O'Reilly & Associates.

Samraj, B. (2008). A Discourse Analysis of Master's Theses Across Disciplines with a Focus on Introductions. *Journal of English for Academic Purposes, 7*(1), 55-67. doi: 10.1016/j.jeap.2008.02.005

Teehan, A., & Keating, J. G. (2010a). A Digital Edition of a Spanish 18th-century Account Book, Part 1: User-Driven Digitisation. *Jahrbuch für Computer-Philologie, 10*, 169-187.

Teehan, A., & Keating, J. G. (2010b). Appropriate Use Case modeling for humanities documents. *Literary and Linguistic Computing, 25*(4), 381-391. doi: 10.1093/llc/fqq026

Thomas, R., Sargent, L. D., & Hardy, C. (2008). *Power and Participation in the Production of Boundary Objects*. Cardiff Human Resource Management Working Papers. Retrieved from http://goo.gl/WxFMI

Vanhoutte, E. (2007). Traditional editorial standards and the digital edition. In E. Stronks, P. Boot & D. Stiebral (Eds.), *Learned Love. Proceedings of the Emblem Project Utrecht Conference on Dutch Love Emblems and the Internet* (November 2006) (pp.157-174). The Hague: DANS Symposium Publications.

Webb, S., (2011). *A study of associational culture and the development of Irish nationalism, 1780-1830, with the construction of a software information environment*. Unpublished PhD dissertation. NUI Maynooth.

Webb, S., & Keating, J. G. (2009). *MIHS - Text Mining Historical Sources using Factoids*. Paper presentation at Maryland University, DH2009.

20 DHO: Discovery – Stargazing from the Ground Up

Niall O'Leary[1]

Abstract

In 2008, the Digital Humanities Observatory was charged with creating an all-island gateway to Irish digital collections and resources. A key factor in the achievement of this goal was the development of the web application, *DHO: Discovery*. This chapter will describe what *DHO: Discovery* was intended to be and to what extent it achieved this end. In particular it will detail the infrastructure upon which the system is based and explain how external and internal factors affected the choices made in its development. It will describe the approach taken to the data harvested for the system, recounting how it was gathered from a variety of national repositories and showing how the responses of providers to the project shaped its development. *DHO: Discovery* stresses the importance of strong metadata and highlights the importance of best practice and standards-compliant development. Through the use of internationally recognised standards, *DHO: Discovery* can be used as a basis for further development. The development of several innovative data visualisations demonstrates how some of this potential has already been realised. The design of these tools will also be described. In charting the development of *DHO: Discovery*, it is hoped that lessons learnt might contribute to the future development of digital humanities in Ireland.

Keywords: digital humanities, repository, Fedora Commons, SOLR, metadata, Europeana, sustainability, visualisations.

1. Digital Humanities Observatory, Dublin, Ireland; n.oleary@dho.ie

How to cite this chapter: O'Leary, N. (2013). DHO: Discovery – Stargazing from the Ground Up. In C. Fowley, C. English, & S. Thouësny (Eds.), *Internet Research, Theory, and Practice: Perspectives from Ireland* (pp. 405-426). Dublin: © Research-publishing.net.

1. Introduction

The Digital Humanities Observatory (DHO)[1] was established in 2008 as part of the Humanities Serving Irish Society (HSIS)[2] consortium. The DHO was established to

- identify standards and advise on best practice in the area of digital humanities;
- store, preserve and provide access to the increasingly complex range of e-resources available to the humanities in Ireland;
- enable the fullest exploitation of existing national research collections and data repositories.

Reporting to the Royal Irish Academy, the unit (initially comprised of nine people with skills ranging from data encoding to project management) encourages the innovative use of technology in what has traditionally been a pen and paper domain, promoting internationally accepted standards and best practice.

Key to the DHO's work is its website (http://www.dho.ie) which it uses to disseminate news and promote its activities. This website is also the access point for many of its online developments. The DHO has collaborated with other projects to build several high-profile websites such as the Saint Patrick's Confessio Hyperstack[3] and the Doegen Records Web Archive[4], but in pursuing its own remit it has striven to create its own suite of services. For instance, in an effort to promote existing digital humanities projects across Ireland, one of the first online services the unit developed was *DHO: Drapier*[5]. This interactive database, available from the main DHO website, surveys current activity in Irish digital humanities and documents the methods, formats and standards that are being used. New projects can learn to use similar techniques, or established

---

1. Digital Humanities Observatory, http://dho.ie/

2. Humanities Serving Irish Society, http://hsis.ie/. The HSIS consortium is comprised of the Royal Irish Academy, six of the seven Irish universities, Queen's University, Belfast and the University of Ulster.

3. Saint Patrick's Confessio Hyperstack, http://www.confessio.ie

4. The Doegen Records Web Archive, http://www.dho.ie/doegen

5. Drapier: Digital Research And Projects in Ireland, http://dho.ie/drapier/

projects can locate related work in their field. However, *DHO: Drapier* does not provide access to existing data repositories or make collections of digital material available for analysis. To achieve this, the Digital Humanities Observatory set about developing another online service, *DHO: Discovery*.

The development of *DHO: Discovery* was initiated when the Observatory had a full contingent of staff and a number of years to run. In 2010, I joined the DHO as IT Projects Manager and became involved in the project. In many ways it provided a practical opportunity for me to further my understanding of digital humanities and contribute to the area. However in 2011, the fortunes of the Observatory itself changed radically. Initially given a three-year lifespan, it was hoped that the DHO might acquire additional funding (and maybe even staff) over time. This was not to be. By June 2011, all DHO staff had reached the end of their contracts with little prospect of renewal. Funding stopped in August 2011, but fortunately enough was left to maintain a staff of two. In this reduced form, the unit will continue until August 2013. This has created obvious pressures and has forced the DHO to be creative and extremely cost-effective in developing *DHO: Discovery*.

In this chapter, I would like to describe *DHO: Discovery*, chart its development and share some of the lessons learnt from my experience of the project. In charting its development, I will address the creation of the infrastructure, the gathering of data, and the subsequent innovations the system made possible.

2. What is DHO: Discovery?

On a very basic level, *DHO: Discovery* is a search engine. It allows a user to find related items from many different online sources using one integrated interface. However, it has many differences to traditional search engines such as *Google* or *Bing*. Concentrating on data from national cultural and academic sources, it only deals with online digital objects suitable for primary research. Such objects include texts, images, video and audio. It uses accepted standards, such as Dublin Core, to allow faceted searching, i.e., searching on the basis of fields such as creator, subject matter, date of creation, etc., not always available on the original websites. *DHO: Discovery* provides several ways to navigate content, but always provides links back to the original websites. This makes it easier to create new connections between heterogeneous content from multiple sources. For instance, rather than having to go to the individual websites of Trinity College Dublin (TCD), University College Cork, etc., for information on Michael Collins[1], a search through *DHO: Discovery* will find all relevant digital objects from the principal research repositories of these institutions, and a variety of cultural institutions, displaying these results with descriptions, thumbnails, rights details, spatial data, and other information. Users can discover Ireland's many online treasures by visiting this one online service. In addition *DHO: Discovery* offers researchers new ways to visualise data and hopefully gain new insights into old content (Figure 1). Indeed this is one of the key functions of the system. *DHO: Discovery* tries to demonstrate some of the exciting possibilities available when internationally accepted standards are applied to digital content and explore new methods of processing humanities data.

There are some precedents to *DHO: Discovery*, the most obvious being Europeana[2], a huge online database of European art and culture. With over twenty million objects, including a lot of Irish content, this allows faceted searching on a grand scale. However, despite a small amount of work on visualisation (Europeana4D[3], for instance), Europeana has predominantly concentrated on its search tool. Its Irish content is also somewhat limited, coming mainly from large Irish providers such as the National Archives and the National Library, but ignoring many universities and smaller institutions.

From an American perspective, some moves are afoot to replicate the Europeana service with the Digital Public Library of America[4], but this is still in development. The principal competitor to such initiatives is of course *Google*. *Google* has its

---

1. Michael Collins (16/10/1890 – 22/08/1922) was an Irish revolutionary leader and politician. Collins was shot and killed during the Irish Civil War.

2. Europeana, http://www.europeana.eu/portal/

3. Europeana4D, http://wp1187670.wp212.webpack.hosteurope.de/e4d/

4. Digital Public Library of America, http://dp.la/

own Google Books and Google Art projects[1], each of which covers large and important collections of works. Again though, it has tended to concentrate on the search and display of its content, generally ignoring the potential of metadata. It also seems to be dealing with each type of media in isolation; books and artworks are treated differently[2].

Figure 1. Detail on a document from the Documents on Irish Foreign Policy collection, displayed in DHO: Discovery

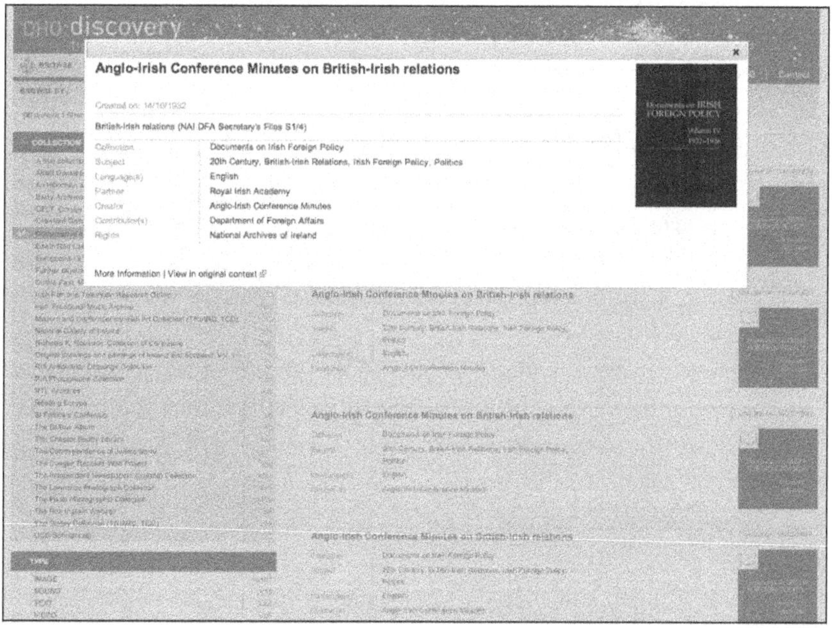

In Ireland, there are also some notable developments that deal with some of the issues *DHO: Discovery* set out to address. Trinity College Dublin has used the TARA institutional repository to store much of its digital resources[3]. Effectively

---

1. Google Books (http://books.google.com) and Google Art (http://www.googleartproject.com).

2. In October 2012 *Google* launched its Cultural Institute (http://www.google.com/culturalinstitute/#!home) which addresses this shortcoming to some extent.

3. Trinity's Access to Research Archive (TARA), http://www.tara.tcd.ie/. More recently the Digital Resources and Imaging Services Department at Trinity College Library Dublin launched its own digital repository, http://digitalcollections.tcd.ie/home/

this is a database of images, texts, and other media, stored with appropriate metadata. There is sufficient metadata associated with each object to satisfy the requirements of several recognised digital library formats, for instance Dublin Core or METS, and the objects can be found using a search engine responsive to this information. University College Dublin (UCD) takes a similar approach with its repository, the UCD Digital Library[1]. Repositories such as these also act as hosting mechanisms, making the data they hold available on the Internet. However in each case these services are restricted to the university's own collections (or even subsets of those collections). In addition, there has been little work done on alternative approaches to navigation and visualisation of the data held in these repositories.

In 2008, the DHO set out to address the shortcomings of the systems mentioned above, or at least indicate how they might be addressed. To do this it decided to develop a system that would
- allow users to find content of research interest in an easily navigated way;
- provide a unified interface for national digital resources of digital humanities interest;
- demonstrate the potential of technologies available for digital humanities;
- allow for the serendipitous discovery of objects in disparate collections, creating new connections;
- use the platform as the basis for the development of visualisations that reveal more than any one site can do by itself.

In revealing the many data collections available throughout Ireland it was hoped that it would increase the visibility of these research resources and, as a by-product, drive the growth of digital humanities scholarship.

Given the DHO's national remit, and taking a cue from the work at UCD and TCD, it was decided to develop a national digital repository that would hold the nation's digital objects and associated metadata. In tandem with the development and population of this repository, a website, *DHO: Discovery*, would be

---

1. UCD Digital Library, http://digital.ucd.ie/

developed, accessible from the DHO main website. This website would allow a user to navigate and make sense of the repository's contents. Once the main site had been created, a series of visualisations would be developed to showcase what was possible using the data.

3.   Building the infrastructure

A digital repository stores, manages and provides access to digital content. In 2008, two of the leading open-source repository solutions were Fedora Commons and DSpace[1]. The limited resources available to the DHO called for a development framework that was flexible, powerful, standards compliant, and allowed for rapid development. It should also be cheap (preferably free). While Fedora Commons and DSpace, both satisfied many of these needs, Fedora Commons provided more flexibility (Gourley & Viterbo, 2010) and was adopted as the technology set for this repository.

Fedora Commons is not a repository in its own right, but is instead a digital asset management (DAM) architecture. It provides the foundation upon which many types of digital library might be built. Unlike a package such as Microsoft Word, it is not a complete application itself, but is instead built from distinct modules. A developer must choose these modules and put them together himself. In this way, the final product reflects the needs of the individual system. For instance, out-of-the-box searching is achieved using a search engine module developed by a third party, the company Lucene, but this can be swapped with other more powerful modules. In our case, we swapped it for Lucene's own enterprise solution, Apache SOLR[2].

The decision to use the SOLR module was not an arbitrary one. SOLR provides a powerful full-text search tool, allowing faceted searches, scalability, and a lot of opportunities for integration with other systems. Crucially though, the

1. In 2009, the Fedora Commons organisation and the DSpace Foundation, providers of these software products, amalgamated to create Duraspace.

2. Apache SOLR, http://lucene.apache.org/solr/

website that would give users access to Fedora was being developed using a programming language called JavaScript, specifically a library of JavaScript code called JQuery. JavaScript is a programming language used extensively for the web. It is predominantly a client-side language (works on a user's own machine), but can be used in other ways. Many JavaScript libraries, such as JQuery, are available that make development easier, providing ready-made functions for common tasks. The JQuery library supported the use of SOLR, which made the search engine key to the website. In essence SOLR connected the website to the repository.

Towards the end of 2009, the website was progressing well and Fedora was installed. DHO staff began to turn their attention to content. As well as looking for digital content for the repository, they began to devise a data model to reflect the objects that would populate the system. As important as the technologies used, the model by which one maps one's data is crucial. In order to properly index a digital object within a repository, one must enumerate the various fields, or facets, by which a user might categorise that object. There are obvious metadata elements that should be recorded: the title of a painting for instance, or the author of a particular book. However, a richer model is required when allowing users to search and browse resources from across different collections. Though it is tempting to create a bespoke model, this can be dangerous. A facet might be left out at the outset that proves necessary as the project grows (what about an alternative title for the object?). Some terms might be too ambiguous, not allowing enough specificity. Without the right data model, a project cannot be integrated with similar projects. Adopting an arbitrary model might doom your project from the outset by restricting its scalability or flexibility. A recognised model, by contrast, ensures that your data can be understood internationally. In the case of *DHO: Discovery*, it was important that the system could be developed by other parties and integrated with other systems.

As has been mentioned, other initiatives had already addressed these issues, for instance Europeana. As it happens, the DHO was working with the Irish Manuscripts Commission to aggregate content for Europeana and it was highly likely that content harvested for *DHO: Discovery* might eventually find its way into Europeana as well[1]. Using a variation of the Europeana data model would allow us to benefit from their expertise, future-proof *DHO: Discovery* and allow for future interoperability between the two systems[2]. In addition, the Europeana data model adopts many terms from Dublin Core, a model established by the Dublin Core Metadata Initiative (DCMI) for the very purpose of describing resources for discovery[3]. By using Europeana's model we ensured future compatibility with other Dublin Core compliant systems. For all these reasons, with very little tweaking, Europeana's data model was adopted as our own.

4. Gathering content

In 2010, as the data model was being finalised, I began work at the DHO as IT Projects Manager. It soon became apparent that getting actual data for the system was proving problematic. There were many reasons for this. For instance, some content providers did not have the resources to contribute digital objects to the repository. For some of the other providers the notion of an external organisation hosting their images, video and audio, even one with which they were a partner, seemed to represent too much of a loss of control. Overall, providers were more disposed to giving information about their objects rather than the objects themselves. Without those objects though Fedora could not be populated and *DHO: Discovery* could not become the rich platform we envisaged. Another approach had to be found.

Fortunately the modular nature of Fedora Commons proved useful in tackling this problem. It was SOLR, not Fedora, that the website depended upon, and, as a self-contained module, it could be used by itself. Indeed we could supply it with data directly as spreadsheets. This presented a new model. Rather than store the objects in a repository like Fedora, we could simply store the metadata

1. Irish Manuscripts Commission, http://www.irishmanuscripts.ie/

2. Europeana Semantic Elements v3.2 XML Schema. Europeana's current data model, backwards compatible with version 3.2, is Europeana Data Model Definition v5.2.3.

3. Dublin Core Metadata Initiative, http://dublincore.org/

associated with those objects in SOLR itself, as a search index. With Fedora Commons and digital objects no longer required, the DHO: Discovery website was back on track. However, we still needed content, even if only in the form of spreadsheets.

There are many ways to gather content from contributors. An automated approach might use the Open Archives Initiative Protocol for Metadata Harvesting (or OAI-PMH) to harvest content on a scheduled basis, ensuring data is always up to date[1]. However, to use this protocol the data provider must also use their own OAI-PMH compliant system and few institutions have the resources to do this. The flip-side of this is that few institutions have the resources to make frequent changes once the initial effort to publish a collection has been made. More realistic is a manual approach. Metadata for indexing can be supplied via manually generated text files. The format for these text files is XML, a language that allows free text to be encoded in a structured way and is used to build customised markup languages like the Text Encoding Initiative (TEI)[2] language. A spreadsheet can be converted into an XML file very successfully using the column headings to label the content. A suite of web forms was developed to take spreadsheets and other files, transform them into the files SOLR needed and submit them directly to the index. A collection could be added to DHO: Discovery within a matter of minutes. It was not entirely automated, but it wasn't too far from it.

Content providers find spreadsheets a lot easier to create and supply. Where databases are used, it is often possible, with relatively little difficulty, to create a report of data directly as a spreadsheet. We decided to give each of our contributors template spreadsheets listing all the fields that could be populated and asked them to complete it. Many contributors were happy with this approach. What made them especially happy was the fact that we did not need their digital objects.

---

1. OAI-PMH, http://www.openarchives.org/OAI/openarchivesprotocol.html

2. "Extensible Markup Language (XML) is a markup language that defines a set of rules for encoding documents in a format that is both human-readable and machine-readable" (XML, 2013, para. 1). TEI is used to encode a wide variety of primary texts, such as novels, letters, journals, etc.

Why did we not need the digital objects after all? The Internet allows websites to display files hosted on other servers; the files don't have to belong to the website. Now that we no longer needed to populate Fedora, we could use this property to our advantage. By including the web addresses of the contributors' objects in the spreadsheets, *DHO: Discovery* could display their images etc. without actually hosting them.

Even with this new approach collecting content proved difficult. As part of the Humanities Serving Irish Society project, most Irish universities were obliged to submit content to *DHO: Discovery*. However, not all were in a position to do this. One institution was re-organising its own repository and did not feel their metadata was of a sufficient quality to be submitted. Others had no content or else did not have enough resources to prepare it. Nevertheless we approached all our consortium partners in an attempt to get at least one representative collection from each and largely succeeded. We also approached cultural institutions. From our work aggregating content for Europeana, we had already forged many relationships with these, and given the similarity of the two data models, had metadata in a format that could be harvested quickly with very little manipulation required. We contacted these institutions and got their approval for content to be included in *DHO: Discovery*.

5.   Going live and going forward

By 2011, we had enough content to populate *DHO: Discovery* and on March 30th, Deputy Seán Sherlock, Minister of State for Research and Innovation, launched the site. The site as launched provided a faceted browse and search service for around 6,000 digital objects and three basic visualisations, i.e., a treemap, a basic tag cloud, and a node-link graph. The DHO's efforts could now concentrate on acquiring more metadata and developing new visualisations. Unfortunately 2011 also saw the departure of much of the DHO's staff and by July 2011, only two remained; one for outreach, one for IT.

Content destined for Europeana had provided metadata before. Now it seemed feasible to reverse the process and take data from Europeana. In September 2012, all metadata held by Europeana was made publicly available under a creative commons license, but it had been available for non-commercial purposes for some time beforehand. In essence, this meant that a developer could use any of the metadata stored by Europeana, provided any rights associated with the original object (e.g., use of the thumbnail or original image) were respected. With this in mind any Europeana Irish data not already in *DHO: Discovery* was imported, helped by the fact that our common data model meant that this data was already in the format needed. A program was developed making it possible to select and harvest collections contained within Europeana directly from that system's index. A wealth of content became available and at time of writing *DHO: Discovery* has indexed 20,701 objects from 30 collections.

When dealing with many collections from diverse sources, one quickly becomes aware of the varied vocabularies used by different curators to describe similar objects. For instance, a collection of architectural drawings might use the term 'Gothic Vaults (Architecture)' while another might use the term 'Gothic Architecture'. Developing a number of online tools for submitting data to SOLR allowed me to incorporate some filtering of these terms. Without removing anything, common terms were added to some objects with similar subject terms (e.g., 'Gothic'). However, this involved a huge manual effort and the issue could only be addressed at the most basic level. Ultimately the use of diverse vocabularies by different providers highlighted the importance of using common standardised ontologies[1]. This can only happen if curators work together.

Despite these inconsistencies, the value of good metadata, particularly subject terms, was clear. One of the earliest collections to be indexed was correspondence from the Documents on Irish Foreign Policy project[2]. Using key phrases such as 'Anglo-Irish Treaty' or 'British-Ireland Relations', it was possible to collate all documents pertaining to the Anglo-Irish Treaty of 1921. This formed the basis

---

1. Organisations such as the Getty Research Institute are actively developing such ontologies.

2. Documents on Irish Foreign Policy, http://www.difp.ie/

for an e-book produced by the DHO in collaboration with the Documents on Irish Foreign Policy and the National Archives of Ireland (Crowe, Fanning, Kennedy, Keogh, & O'Halpin, 2012).

Regardless of improvements and new content, site usage statistics suggested the service was not being used. Admittedly given the reduction in staff at the DHO, promotion of the site was limited, but there was a more fundamental problem. It was not appearing in search engines. Initially *DHO: Discovery* was developed using HTML and JavaScript (specifically the AJAX-Solr and JQuery libraries), which meant that all the processing of search queries was made within the user's browser. The content of a page was created when a user made selected facets or entered a search term, but the address of the page remained the same. Effectively the site was made from one page and without human interaction this page was blank. Search engines, such as *Google*, follow the links on unique pages to index content. Despite the thousands of objects indexed by *DHO: Discovery*, there were no links to follow and no unique pages, at least not without human interaction. All *Google* could 'see' was a blank page. *DHO: Discovery* was in danger of never being discovered.

Search engines need pages to index, preferably ones with appropriate keywords. The DHO had those keywords – the objects' metadata – it just needed to expose them. Obviously pages for every single object could not be created manually, but a program to automatically generate those pages when a link was followed could be developed, and following a link was the very way search engines interact with a site. One link on the main page – 'Collections' – led to this program. This generated a 'Collections' page linking to an individual 'Collection' page that in turn listed links to all the objects in that collection. Each object now had its own page detailing all its related metadata (Figure 2).

In this way a website of one page (as far as *Google* or *Bing* were concerned), suddenly became a site of thousands of pages. In addition each object page gave further utility, presenting the object's location on a map and offering customised links to, for instance, *Wikipedia*. Search engines began to index *DHO: Discovery* and in September 2012, there were over 730 visitors from 52 countries.

Figure 2.   An object page describing an item of Irish content in Europeana 1914-1918

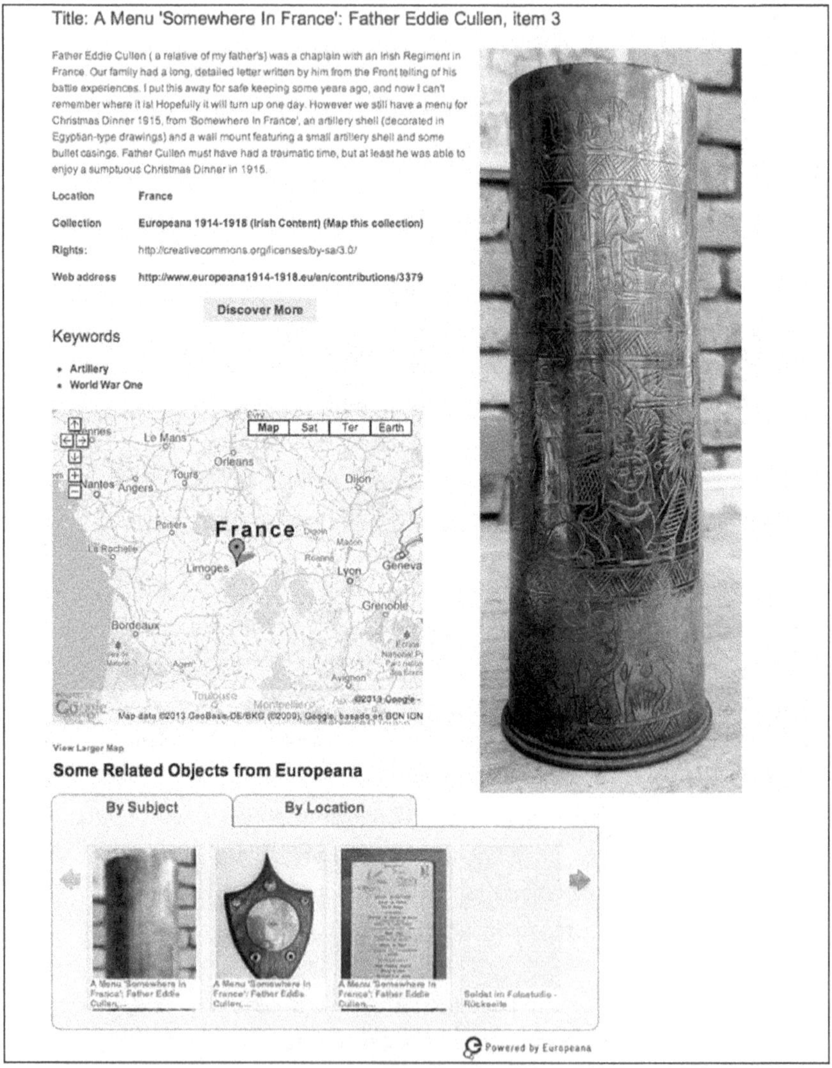

Title: A Menu 'Somewhere In France': Father Eddie Cullen, item 3

Father Eddie Cullen (a relative of my father's) was a chaplain with an Irish Regiment in France. Our family had a long, detailed letter written by him from the Front telling of his battle experiences. I put this away for safe keeping some years ago, and now I can't remember where it is! Hopefully it will turn up one day. However we still have a menu for Christmas Dinner 1915, from 'Somewhere In France', an artillery shell (decorated in Egyptian-type drawings) and a wall mount featuring a small artillery shell and some bullet casings. Father Cullen must have had a traumatic time, but at least he was able to enjoy a sumptuous Christmas Dinner in 1915.

Location   France

Collection   Europeana 1914-1918 (Irish Content) (Map this collection)

Rights: http://creativecommons.org/licenses/by-sa/3.0/

Web address   http://www.europeana1914-1918.eu/en/contributions/3379

Discover More

Keywords

- Artillery
- World War One

Some Related Objects from Europeana

Metadata proved useful in creating pages suited for search engines, but it also provided the data needed to create search queries to external websites. Just as

DHO: Discovery built queries for SOLR automatically, with a little customisation these queries could be tailored for Europeana[1]. For instance, the value in the 'Creator' field, i.e., who wrote, painted or generated the object, could be used to explicitly query Europeana on the basis of 'Creator', safe in the knowledge that their use of the field corresponded with our's. The results they returned, formatted as XML, could be readily transformed into HTML and integrated into each object page to show related objects from around the world[2].

6.   Exploiting the data

DHO: Discovery was intended to provide insights into humanities data that could only be done because of:

- the large number of aggregated objects available;
- the standardised nature of the metadata collated;
- the specialised skillset available in the DHO.

Above all, the value of a standards-based approach to data needed to be highlighted. The different ways of navigating the collections, and the added value provided by the individual object pages, achieved this in part. Using a common data model meant a common approach to programming could be adopted. Throughout 2012, this concept was further exploited in the development of a wide range of innovative visualisations employing open source libraries and software. From a personal perspective, these developments gave me an opportunity to explore the possibilities of structured data and experiment with new approaches to data analysis. I would like now to discuss some of them in more depth.

Scholars in the digital humanities field will be familiar with a variety of tools for visualising large datasets, whether those datasets are the words in a text,

---

1. Europeana uses OpenSearch protocol to pass queries to their system. OpenSearch, http://www.opensearch.org/Home

2. More recently a widget returning results from the Digital Public Library of America was also developed using this approach.

or the complete oeuvre of an individual author. There are, however, relatively few online applications that process content on-the-fly[1]. The huge amount of metadata within *DHO: Discovery* provided an excellent dataset to explore this approach.

At time of writing there are 10 visualisations, all to be found at http://discovery. dho.ie/discover.php. They include:

- Exhibit Visualisations
- Google Maps
- Google Charts
- Image Galleries
- Wordle-style Word Cloud
- Raphaël Visualisations
- Europeana4D
- Treemap Visualisations
- Tag Cloud
- Node-Link Visualisations

Key to these developments is SOLR. It can provide results in several formats including JSON and CSV[2]. For the DHO's purposes though the most powerful format it delivers is XML. XML is a crucial technology in the world of digital humanities. If one understands the schema of a particular XML format, one can transform it into almost any other text format using Extensible Stylesheet Language Transformations (XSLT). XSLT is a language for transforming XML documents into other XML documents, or other objects, such as web pages. The DHO's approach to visualisations was to take the SOLR results in XML format and convert them into a format that could be used by a particular web application, e.g., Google Maps. To minimise the dependence on client-side programming (browsers can be fickle in their support for this), and to maximise the toolset available, the decision was made to combine client-side

---

1. A notable exception is TAPoR, http://www.tapor.ca/

2. JavaScript Object Notation (JSON), is a text-based open standard designed for representing simple data structures and associative arrays. Comma-separated values (CSV) files are used to store tabular data in plain-text form.

technologies, such as JavaScript, with the power of server-side programming (mostly using a language called PHP).

7.   Developing the visualisations

Other DHO projects employed the Exhibit framework to add a rich database-like experience to websites[1]. Developed by MIT, Exhibit is a collection of JavaScript files that can be integrated into web pages to create timelines, tables, maps and faceted searching. When the browser loads the page,

> "the Javascript reads in one or more JSON data files and builds a local database in the memory of the machine running the browser. Data can then be filtered and sorted directly in the browser without having to re-query the server. The design of Exhibit is optimised for browsing faceted data" (Exhibit, 2012, section "Overview", para. 1).

Exhibit sites are normally created manually, but here was an opportunity to generate customised 'exhibits' dynamically based on a user's selected criteria.

Although SOLR can deliver JSON automatically, its format is not suited to Exhibit. Instead an application was developed that

- created a SOLR query dynamically from user choices selected on a web form;
- submitted the query and received the results as an XML file;
- used XSLT to rewrite the XML results into the required Exhibit-specific JSON format;
- created the Exhibit web pages dynamically from this automatically generated JSON content.

By having an intermediate script take the results and reformat them, the resulting web pages would be assured of getting the data exactly as needed.

---

1. For other examples of Exhibit, see http://research.dho.ie. For more information on Exhibit, see http://www.simile-widgets.org/exhibit/

This 'proxy' approach proved to be a successful model and formed the basis for many further developments.

Maps are an especially effective way of conveying data. Exhibit is capable of displaying Google-like maps, but only when it has the appropriate geo-spatial coordinates. To explore the possibilities of online maps directly meant developing explicitly for the Google Maps platform[1].

Google Maps uses an XML file format called KML in which place names, geo-spatial co-ordinates (e.g., '53.3473,-6.2591') and even web addresses can all be encoded. Much of this metadata was in *DHO: Discovery*. Indeed some providers had even supplied the geo-spatial co-ordinates needed to pinpoint a place on a map. Unfortunately these providers were the exception rather than the rule. It was necessary to pair a place name with its co-ordinates.

Fortunately much of our content was to be found in Ireland. Co-ordinates for many Irish towns and cities are easily available and so a database of the most common Irish places was set up. This had the added benefit of allowing the DHO to make entries for places and geographical features that were specific to some of our objects, but for which current information was not easily available (e.g., Dun Laoghaire was once called Kingstown and was referred to as such in many 19th century images). Each visualisation that required a map (remember Exhibit has a mapping tool) could use this database. Obviously countries and major world cities were also added to account for collections (such as that of the Chester Beatty Library) that had a more international dimension.

Another benefit of this database was that there was now a resource against which programs could check for place names. Many of our providers simply didn't populate the location field. However, the location was often referred to in either the title of the object or its subject terms. A filter was developed for the data input tool that checked the title and subject fields of new collections for any words that corresponded with the place names in the database. If there

---

1. Google Maps, http://developers.google.com/maps/

was a match the place was added to the location field. While not foolproof, once combined with a brief manual check, this opened a lot of collections up to mapping.

The Exhibit application provided a web form that built up a SOLR query which could now be re-used. Now instead of converting the results into JSON, they were formatted them into KML (the file format recognised by *Google*), and this KML file was supplied directly to Google Maps. In addition, because the pathways to the thumbnails of the objects were available, the 'pins' used to locate places on the map could be customised, or if more than one collection was involved, the objects colour-coded by their collection.

As well as its map application programming interface (API), *Google* has provided tools for developing other web features. One of the most powerful is Google Charts[1]. As with Exhibit and Google Maps, the key to developing charts is to supply the data in the format required by the application code. Formatted as a JavaScript array, the data could be rendered as, for instance, pie-charts or barcharts. It is not the only API available though. Other graphics libraries, such as Raphaël, can be used to created alternative displays of large datasets. Using visualisation, a user can tell at a glance the subject matter of a collection, the frequency of topics, the time range covered and much more. Data visualisation is not a replacement to standard methods of study, but it is a powerful addition (Figure 3).

Again and again, the same basic web form could be used to generate a SOLR query and then use XSLT to convert the results to a format recognised by a JavaScript library. This library along with the formatted results were embedded in a dynamically created web page delivered to the user by a server-side program. Even the formats could be re-used. For instance, Europeana4D, an application that charts geographical and spatial data together, uses KML files. There was no reason why this method could not be re-used and further developed over time.

---

1. Google Chart, http://developers.google.com/chart/

Figure 3.   A graph illustrating a collection's subject matter over time, created using Raphaël

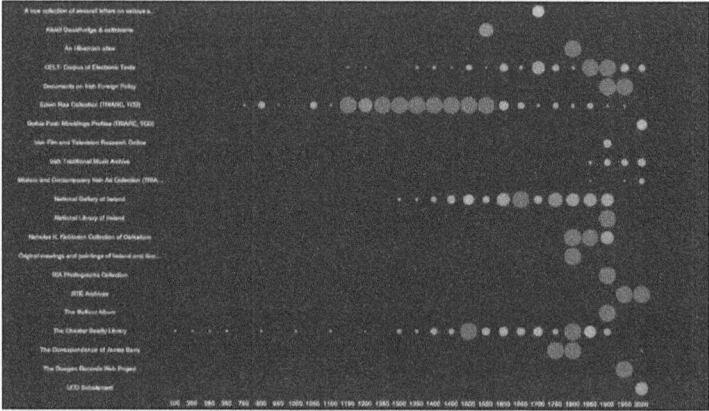

8.   Conclusion

The Digital Humanities Observatory has satisfied its remit of exposing Ireland's rich online resources to the digital humanities community. It has done so using best practice and open standards. With *DHO: Discovery* it illustrates how a disciplined, structured approach to primary digital data can open up a vast array of research opportunities. With minimal expenditure, using open-source software, and building on the rich resources Ireland has to offer, it has transformed existing digital data into new material for scholarship . However, what it achieved is only a beginning. At this point, the lessons learnt in its development are as important as the service itself.

Ireland is a small country. There is no need for isolated silos of data or overly proprietary attitudes to its curatorship. Particularly in the case of public bodies, there is an obligation to open Ireland's digital heritage to all. *DHO: Discovery* demonstrates how easily this can be achieved, and, despite the downturn in the economy, how it can be re-purposed cost-effectively. Properly done, Ireland can become a shining light in the world of digital humanities.

In 2011 the Digital Repository of Ireland was created to develop a national digital repository[1]. This presents a valuable opportunity to achieve that to which *DHO: Discovery* aspired. However, all owners of important digital content need to work together to make this happen. With a holistic vision and appropriate funding, such repositories will be essential to the future of digital humanities in Ireland.

Acknowledgments. The Digital Humanities Observatory and the work described in this paper are funded by the Irish Higher Education Authority (HEA) under the Programme for Research in Third Level Institutes Cycle 4 (PRTLI-4). The DHO was established under the auspices of the Royal Irish Academy. Additional support for repository hosting and programming is provided by the Dublin Institute for Advanced Studies (DIAS) and the Irish Centre for High-End Computing (ICHEC). The author would like to acknowledge the contributions of all the staff at the Digital Humanities Observatory, past and present, especially Randall Cream, Emily Cullen, Shawn Day, Don Gourley, Kevin Hawkins, Faith Lawrence, Katie McAdden, Dot Porter, Susan Schreibman, Paolo Battino Viterbo, and Bruno Voisin.

The image of an object page (Figure 2) incorporates images drawn from Europeana (http://www.europeana.eu/portal/) and made available under the Creative Commons Attribution-ShareAlike 2.0 Generic license (CC BY-SA). Arthur Mathews was the original contributor of the photographs used. It also includes a map image supplied by Google Maps (incorporating map data ©2013 GeoBasis-DE/BKG (©2009), Google, basado en BCN IGN).

References

Crowe, C., Fanning, R., Kennedy, M., Keogh, D., & O'Halpin, E. (Eds.). (2012). *The Anglo-Irish Treaty, December 1920 - December 1921* [Adobe Digital Editions version]. Retrieved from http://research.dho.ie/1921treaty.epub

---

1. Digital Repository of Ireland, http://www.dri.ie/

Exhibit (web editing tool). (2012). *Wikipedia*. Retrieved from http://en.wikipedia.org/wiki/ Exhibit_%28web_editing_tool%29

Gourley, D., & Viterbo, P. B. (2010). A Sustainable Repository Infrastructure for Digital Humanities: The DHO Experience. In M. Ioannides, D. Fellner, A. Georgopoulos, & D. Hadjimitsis (Eds.), *Digital Heritage: Third International Conference, EUROMED 2010 Lemessos, Cyprus, November 8-13, 2010 Proceedings* (pp. 473-481). New York: Springer.

XML. (2013). *Wikipedia*. Retrieved from http://en.wikipedia.org/wiki/Xml

21 Database in Theory and Practice: The Bibliography of Irish Literary Criticism

Sonia Howell[1]

Abstract

Focusing on *The Bibliography of Irish Literary Criticism* (BILC, 2010), a bibliographical database of Irish literary criticism developed by humanities and information and communications technology (ICT) researchers in NUI Maynooth, this chapter investigates the opportunities and implications afforded the field of Irish literary studies emerging from and enabled by electronic advances. Unlike earlier accounts of database technology that have emerged from the humanities community (Dimock, 2007; Folsom, 2007), this chapter provides a more practical and more critical account of the new medium. It is argued that while the relational structure of databases such as BILC, combined with appropriate interface design, can yield interesting insights into Ireland's literary history, "the optimism and the excitement about new possibilities for rethinking the texts, canon, and creation" offered by digital resources such as BILC are "ahead of the actual development work" (Dalbello, 2011, p. 496). However, following McGill (2007), it is further argued that an engagement with the BILC database affords an opportunity to identify potential areas for development in resources of this kind. Building on observations made throughout, the chapter concludes with a discussion of how increased attention to issues regarding dissemination and sustainability are vital for ensuring the potency and ongoing viability of digital databases designed for use in humanities scholarship.

Keywords: Irish studies, database, historiography, Colin Graham, sustainability, dissemination.

1. An Foras Feasa and the School of English, Media and Theatre Studies, NUI Maynooth, Maynooth, Co. Kildare, Ireland; sonia.howell@nuim.ie

How to cite this chapter: Howell, S. (2013). Database in Theory and Practice: The Bibliography of Irish Literary Criticism. In C. Fowley, C. English, & S. Thouësny (Eds.), *Internet Research, Theory, and Practice: Perspectives from Ireland* (pp. 427-446). Dublin: © Research-publishing.net.

1.   Database technology and Irish literary studies

Commenting on the relationship between humanities scholarship and digital technology, McGann (2008) provided the following forecast:

> "All around us information technology is moving from paper to digital forms. For humanists, while the need to consult original materials will always remain, our research and scholarly intercourse will soon be carried out primarily in digital media. Our depositories, finding aids, analytic tools, and publishing venues will all be digitally designed and integrated" (p. 80).

In the field of Irish literary scholarship, this move from print to digital forms of knowledge production and dissemination has accelerated in recent years, when an increasing number of projects is being produced in digital form. Yet as Kelleher (2011) has observed,

> "we have yet to examine fully the role of material objects (texts, compilations, compendia) in structuring our access to information and knowledge, and their changing role in light of the new possibilities offered by the digital and the virtual" (p. 12).

Subsequently, important epistemological questions regarding the achievements of these resources have remained unaddressed. Relatedly, in the absence of engaged scholarly critique, we have yet to acknowledge what remains to be realised in works of literary scholarship that appear in digital form.

Within the field of literary studies, perhaps the most commonly produced and most frequently utilised digital resource is the online digital database. Described at the most basic level, a database is "a system that allows for the efficient storage and retrieval of information" (Ramsay, 2004, chapter 15, section "Introduction", para. 1). As Ramsay (2004) usefully summarises, "[t]he purpose of a database is to store information about a particular domain (sometimes called the universe of discourse) and to allow one to ask questions about the state of that domain"

(Chapter 15, section "Database Design", para. 1, emphasis removed). While general purpose databases such as *Project Muse* and *Early English Books Online* have been a common feature in the field of literary studies for almost two decades, more recently, a number of what Farmer and Lesser (2008) have referred to as "analytical databases" (p. 1140) have begun to emerge. According to Farmer and Lesser (2008), analytical databases differ from earlier kinds in that they are "tailored to address the kinds of inquiries that scholars tend to ask in a given field of research" (p. 1147).

The past decade has witnessed the publication of a number of subject-specific databases in the field of Irish studies where established scholars have actively experimented with this new technology and the opportunities it affords those studying Ireland's literatures. From the publication of the CELT[1] database in 1997, a proliferation of online digital databases emerged. However, in keeping with Kelleher's (2011) previously cited observation, to date, little commentary or extended analysis have been produced concerning the opportunities and implications afforded the field or Irish studies emerging from and enabled by electronic advances[2].

Responding directly to this absence, this chapter offers a critique of one of the most recent databases of this type to emerge within the field of Irish literary studies, the *Bibliography of Irish Literary Criticism* (BILC, 2010). Moving beyond the metaphorical and celebratory accounts of the new medium promulgated by critics such as Dimock (2007) and Folsom (2007), it investigates both the content of the database and the searches it permits. Examined in light of the developer's objectives, and in relation to its contribution to current debates in the field of Irish studies, this chapter considers the achievements of the database to date. By highlighting the successes and weaknesses of the database, this chapter simultaneously points towards what remains to be realised by the digital resource and concludes with suggestions for future developments.

---

1. http://www.ucc.ie/celt/index.html

2. This stands in notable contrast to similar projects developed in the US, such as The *Walt Whitman Archive* or *The Rossetti Archive*, where the design and development of the digital resource has not only produced a scholarly tool, but has engendered theoretical discussion.

2.   The bibliography of Irish literary criticism

BILC is a fully searchable and freely available database of Irish literary criticism covering the period from the Irish Literary Revival to the present day. It is a project of the National University of Ireland, Maynooth and was funded by the Irish Research Council for the Humanities and Social Sciences (IRCHSS). The database was developed over the space of four years by the project's editor, Colin Graham, and a post-doctoral researcher, Thomas Hubbard. At various stages in the project, ICT colleagues were employed to develop the technical structure of the database, with consultative advice provided by Damien Gallagher, software engineer with An Foras Feasa, and John Keating, Associate Director, An Foras Feasa[1].

According to BILC's editor, there were two reasons for embarking upon the project: funding and his own academic interests. As previously noted, the project was funded by the IRCHSS; more specifically, it was financed under *Theme 1: Research infrastructures in the humanities and social sciences* of the Thematic Research Grants 2005-2006. The criteria specified by the IRCHSS for this funding strand were as follows:

> "This priority will seek to respond to the challenges of creating a research infrastructure in the third-level system in Ireland, which will underwrite national capacity for top class research in the humanities and social sciences. Project Grants awarded within this rubric will support the creation and development of datasets, digitalisation of archives, surveys and methodologies" (http://www.irchss.ie/awards/scheme-62006).

Interestingly, and significantly for the project, in a personal interview, Graham (2011, July 18) revealed that, "the funding opportunity was there before the idea" indicating that the proposal for the BILC project was at least partially shaped by the criteria sought for by the funding body. Responding to the particular interest in projects of a digital nature, in drafting his proposal Graham stated that a

---

1. The ICT specialist who worked on the project were; Paddy Lyons (NUIM), Damien Gallagher (An Foras Feasa, NUIM) and Danny Fallon (An Foras Feasa, NUIM).

'database' would be created which contained the digitised MAchine-Readable Cataloging (MARC) records of works of Irish literary criticism from the Literary Revival to the present day.

While BILC may have been influenced in part by the criteria required by the IRCHSS, the project also developed out of Graham's own scholarly interests. As the database was designed to address a number of the theoretical concerns raised by Graham throughout his printed publications, it is useful to outline these concerns in detail before moving to investigate how BILC's editor attempts to overcome these issues through the digital medium.

An overview of Graham's oeuvre of work as it has appeared in print form reveals the scholar's preoccupation with literary criticism as it has developed on the island of Ireland. For example, in his seminal monograph, *Deconstructing Ireland: Identity, Theory, Culture*, Graham (2001) offers a critique of the development of an Irish literary historiography by positing, "some of the schemata into which [Irish literary criticism] has repeatedly fallen" (p. 33). In his later essay, *Irish Literary Historiography, 1800-2000*, Graham (2006) traces "some of the major patterns of thought which have critically shaped 'Irish writing' since the Revival" (p. 567) and in so doing, calls attention to the manner in which the field has been mapped as much by literary criticism as by the literature itself.

Notably, in both *Deconstructing Ireland and Irish Literary Historiography*, Graham (2001, 2006) points to the limitations of both projects, calling attention to the fact that neither provides a complete overview of the history of Irish literary criticism. In *Deconstructing Ireland*, Graham (2001) clarifies that the account of Irish literary criticism provided in the book does not chart the exact development history of Irish literary criticism; that, he argues, is "a history still to be authoritatively written" (p. 33). Similarly, in *Irish Literary Historiography*, he accedes that "for reasons of space" the account of Irish literary historiography provided in his essay is "by no means a fully comprehensive survey of every intervention in the field [of Irish literary history]" (Graham, 2006, p. 563). What both *Deconstructing Ireland and Irish Literary Historiography* provide, therefore, are macro considerations of developments in the field of Irish literary criticism which highlight how concerns with nation and identity have dominated the field.

Extending on his earlier work, a driving concern for Graham in developing the BILC database was to enable researchers to engage with the hybrid body of works that constitute an Irish literary historiography in a manner that could eschew the dominant meta-narrative of the nation. Thus, the overall aim of the project was to "construct a critical literary history that was not entirely hidden, but was unacknowledged" (Graham, personal communication, July 18, 2011) and in so doing, to highlight the extent to which critical writing has shaped understandings of Irish literature. Hence, one of the main objectives of the database was to make available the bibliographical records of material previously difficult to access, stored within physical archives, as well as more widely known and readily available critical works and, in so doing, to enable the user to chart the development and trajectory of an Irish literary historiography.

Capitalising on the large volumes of storage permitted by the digital medium, the project developers utilised the possibilities afforded by database technology to include previously unknown material relating to an Irish historiography. For example, among the 1,215 publications listed in the database, a number of these are obscure or previously unheard of titles. These include older publications such as *The American Traveler and The Freeman's Journal*, or more recent, but also rarely considered, titles such as *The Tuam Herald and The RTE Guide*. Within these titles, the user of the database finds entries by writers writing outside of the academy.

While the content of the database was compiled, at least in part, to challenge the canon of Irish literary criticism, the structure of the database was also designed with the intended aim of disrupting any linear narrative of an Irish literary historiography. As stated on the *About* page on the BILC website, the database was designed to permit 'multiple entry points' to the materials listed in its domain by enabling the user to search according to author, title, date, publisher and by subject keyword (BILC, About). Additionally, the BILC database enables users to browse or search by the 1,755 'subject keywords' assigned to the MARC records in the database. It also provides the options of browsing, searching or conducting an advanced search.

In the *Editorial Policy* outlined on the BILC website, the editor proposed that through the varied data contained within the BILC domain combined with the various search functions enabled by its interface, the database "enables users to trace fresh narratives of Irish literary criticism/history" (BILC, Editorial Policy, section "Uses for BILC", para. 1). It is further claimed that owing to the presence of works relating to the reception of Irish literature in Europe and America and the reception of international works by Irish critics, the database "enhances the international dialogues favoured by the Ireland of today" (BILC, Editorial Policy, section "Uses for BILC", para. 2). The aspirations for the digital resource expressed in the editorial comments were again reflected in Graham's own comments on the genesis and development of the database. In presenting the user with various modes of accessing the material contained within the database, Graham (2011, July 18) intended that scholars using BILC would be "afforded the possibility to re-formulate the canon but also to re-formulate the syllabus" (personal communication). Moreover, by permitting the user to sift through the material in a number of ways as opposed to a particular linear narrative, Graham (2011, July 18) envisaged that the database would serve to disrupt the 'existing story' of Irish literary historiography. Through these new forms of organisation and access, Graham (2011, July 18) suggested that "the digital format may test the academic assumptions" made in the universities, and in so doing may "ultimately stretch them" (personal communication).

In expressing his aspirations for BILC, Graham's formulations echo some early accounts of database technology emerging from scholars within the wider literary studies community. Perhaps the most notable example of commentary of this sort was Folsom's (2007) account of *The Walt Whitman Archive*, published in a special edition of the MLA. In his controversial article, *Database as Genre: the Epic Transformation of the Archives*, Folsom (2007) draws heavily on ideas postulated by Manovich (2001) in *The Language of New Media* to support his provocative claim that database technology provides a means of overcoming the linearity of narrative which is both demanded and enforced by the codex form. He notes that, for Manovich (2001), databases are "collections of individual items, with every item possessing the same significance as any other" (Folsom, 2007, p. 1574). This is a generally accepted understanding of the database form. However, Folsom (2007) goes further by not only referring to, but extending on, Manovich's (2001) controversial claim that "database and narrative are natural enemies" (cited in Folsom, 2007, p. 1574). Folsom (2007) proceeds to argue that the database is the most appropriate environment for storing *Walt Whitman's rhizomatic work* which itself denies the constraints of linear narrative.

While offering a welcome and overdue engagement with database technology from the field of literary scholarship, in his account of the *Whitman Archive* and the significance of the medium for the materials stored therein, Folsom (2007) blurs the boundaries between a metaphorical and a practical account of the database. As McGann (2007) rightly notes in his response to Folsom's (2007) essay, this "loose way of thinking about our paper-based inheritance as well as about these new digital technologies [...] debases our understanding the matters being discussed" (p. 1589). As McGann's (2007) response makes clear, Folsom's (2007) celebration of database technology conveyed through the recourse to metaphor is neither an accurate nor useful way to consider the significance of the new medium for literary scholarship.

More concrete and informed accounts of database technology have been provided by scholars such as Ramsay (2004), Hockey (2006), McGann (2007) and Price (2009). Against claims that databases are tools free from narrative constraints, Price (2009) – Folsom's (2007) co-editor on *The Walt Whitman Archive* – usefully points out that,

> "A database is not an undifferentiated sea of information out of which structure emerges. Argument is always there from the beginning in how those constructing a database choose to categorize information – the initial

understanding of the materials governs how more fine-grained views will appear because of the way the objects of attention are shaped by divisions and subdivisions within the database. The process of database creation is not neutral, nor should it be" (para. 21).

Considered from a practical rather than a metaphorical perspective, it becomes apparent that contrary to understandings of databases as unadulterated sources of information, relational databases are revealed to be carefully constructed ideological tools. By calling attention to the manner in which information is structured and organised in a database environment, Price's (2009) observations serve to emphasise the fact that these digital resources are, at least potentially, powerful ideological tools. For this reason, these digital resources require sustained and informed scholarly attention rather than metaphorical or idealistic engagements therewith.

3.   Analysing BILC

As identified by Farmer and Lesser (2008), unlike comprehensive databases, analytical databases such as BILC are tailored to accommodate more specific research concerns. This is achieved through both the careful selection of material to be included in the domain – what McGann (2007) has referred to as "an initial critical analysis of the content materials" (p. 1588) – and the design of an interface which enables searches relevant to the research concerns being catered for by the database. Hence, in analysing the value of the BILC database it is useful to focus on the material it contains, the searches permitted by the interface and the accounts of Irish literary historiography generated by a combination of the two in order to establish what new forms of knowledges are or can be generated through an engagement with the resource.

As previously noted, BILC contains works relating to an Irish literary historiography. Significantly, as stated on the BILC *Editorial Policy* page, "while work by academic critics predominates […] it has been [the editor's] policy to include a wealth of non-academic criticism" (BILC, Editorial Policy, section "Bibliographic Data", para. 2). Hence we find that materials from lesser-known regional journals such as *The Freeman's Journal* are listed in the database, as are articles from more contemporary publications such as the *RTÉ Guide*. Another significant editorial decision was to ensure that commentary on the canonical figures in Irish writing such as Yeats and Joyce did not dominate in the database, privileging instead the records by and relating to lesser-known authors.

While both the inclusion of material published in sources other than academic journals and a shift in focus away from the canonical figures in Irish writing provide welcome developments in the history of the Irish literary criticism, it is important to note that the content of the database was compiled through strategic process of selection driven by the research question the resource was designed to address. Inevitably, this initial critical analysis of the content subsequently shapes the types of knowledges that can be generated by an engagement with the database.

Like the content of the database, the user interface was also designed to enable research queries pertinent to the construction of an Irish literary historiography. The most all-inclusive search permitted by the interface is one conducted according to 'bibliographical records'. This allows the user to search for a particular word or phrase across the entire collection. For example, if we search contemporary Irish author Colm Tóibín, the database brings back 35 results, where Tóibín features as an author, a subject key word or in the title of an entry (Figure 1). If a more specific focus is desired, the author's name can also be searched by 'author/editor', 'subject keyword' or 'title' only. As the works listed in the database all relate to Irish literary criticism in some way, searching a particular writer as an author provides an interesting insight into how Irish authors have not only produced the nation's literary corpus but have been actively involved in mediating the reception thereof. For example, if we search Colm Tóibín as author, we see that the author has published essays in the public media and elsewhere reviewing the work of other contemporary Irish writers as well as providing commentary on earlier writers such as Henry James and J. M. Synge (Figure 2). He has also provided more general commentary on topics such as *how to read a novel* and *homosexuality in literature*. The results of such a search serve to validate Graham's (2011, July 18) claim that "criticism is not separate [but …] intertwined with [Ireland's] literature" (personal communication) and open up interesting new avenues for investigation into Tóibín not only as writer, but as critic. Alternatively, if we search for Colm Tóibín as subject, we discover the extent to which his own writing is mediated by critical commentary (Figure 3). In ways analogous to Tóibín's commentary on the works of other contemporary Irish authors, Belinda McKeon and John Banville have provided reviews of Tóibín's novels. Commentary has also been provided by established academics such as Terry Eagleton, Tom Herron and Eve Patten.

Figure 1.   A selection of the results from a search of Colm Tóibín
under 'bibliographical records'

Authors	Title	Year
Toibin, Colm (1955 -	The Belfast test [on Bernard MacLaverty] / Colm Toibin	1981
Wallace, Arminta	In the shadow of a playwright [interview-article with Colm Toibin] / Arminta Wallace	1994
Kelly, Shirley	[Interview with Colm Toibin] / Shirley Kelly	1994
Harmon, Maurice (1930 -	[Review of Colm Toibin, The heather blazing] / Maurice Harmon	1994
Whelan, G.V.	[Review of Colm Toibin, The sign of the cross: travels in Catholic Europe] / G.V. Whelan	1995
Murphy, Hayden (1945 -	[Review of talk given by Colm Toibin at the 7th biennial Edinburgh Book Festival, September 1995] / Hayden Murphy	1995
Toibin, Colm (1955 -	Introduction [to Francis Stuart, Black list, section H] / Colm Toibin	1996
Dunne, John	[Review of Colm Toibin, The story of the night] / John Dunne	1996
Eagleton, Terry (1943 -	[Review of Colm Toibin, The Blackwater lightship] / Terry Eagleton	1999
Herron, Tom	Contamination: Patrick McCabe and Colm Toibin's pathologies of the Republic / Tom Herron	2000
Kelly, Shirley	Colm Toibin reassessed the old lady of Coole [interview] / Shirley Kelly	2002
Frazier, Adrian	The double life of a lady [review of Colm Toibin, Lady Gregory's toothbrush] / Adrian Frazier	2002
Banville, John (1945 -	Homosexuality [review of Colm Toibin, Love in a dark time] / John Banville	2002
Toibin, Colm (1955 -	Introduction [to L.P. Hartley, The go-between] / Colm Toibin	2002
Toibin, Colm (1955 -	Love in a dark time and other explorations of gay lives in literature / Colm Toibin	2002
Toibin, Colm (1955 -	[Review of Vincent Banville, An end to flight] / Colm Toibin	2002
Harmon, Maurice (1930 -	[Review of Colm Toibin, The master] / Maurice Harmon	2004
Clark, Alex	Songs of experience [interview-article with Colm Toibin] / Alex Clark	2004
Kenny, John	[Review of Colm Toibin, The master] / John Kenny	2005
Toibin, Colm (1955 -	Synge: a celebration / edited by Colm Toibin	2005
Sussler, Betsy	Chris Abani and Colm Toibin in conversation [interview-like format] / edited by Betsy Sussler	2006
Toibin, Colm (1955 -	Henry James for Venice / Colm Toibin	2006
Toibin, Colm (1955 -	Hinterland: the public becomes private / Colm Toibin	2006
Walshe, Eibhear	The vanishing homoerotic: Colm Toibin's gay fictions / Eibhear Walshe	2006
Toibin, Colm (1955 -	Single minded [a 'rereading' of Henry James, The lesson of the master] / Colm Toibin	2007
Broderick, John (1927 - 1989)	Stimulus of sin: selected writings of John Broderick / edited by Madeline Kingston; with a foreword by Colm Toibin	2007
Ryan, Matthew	Abstract homes: deterritorialisation and reterritorialisation in the work of Colm Toibin / Matthew Ryan	2008
Toibin, Colm (1955 -	How to read a novel / Colm Toibin	2008
Delaney, Paul (1948 -	Reading Colm Toibin / edited by Paul Delaney	2008
Toibin, Colm (1955 -	Selling Tara, buying Florida / Colm Toibin	2008

Figure 2.   Results yielded by a search of Colm Tóibín as 'author/editor'

Authors	Title	Year
Toibin, Colm (1955 -	The Belfast test [on Bernard MacLaverty] / Colm Toibin	1981
Toibin, Colm (1955 -	Henry James for Venice / Colm Toibin	2006
Toibin, Colm (1955 -	Hinterland: the public becomes private / Colm Toibin	2006
Toibin, Colm (1955 -	How to read a novel / Colm Toibin	2008
Toibin, Colm (1955 -	Introduction [to Francis Stuart, Black list, section H] / Colm Toibin	1996
Toibin, Colm (1955 -	Introduction [to L.P. Hartley, The go-between] / Colm Toibin	2002
Toibin, Colm (1955 -	The living breath of things [review of Seamus Heaney, Human chain] / Colm Toibin	2010
Toibin, Colm (1955 -	Love in a dark time and other explorations of gay lives in literature / Colm Toibin	2002
Toibin, Colm (1955 -	[Review of Vincent Banville, An end to flight] / Colm Toibin	2002
Toibin, Colm (1955 -	Selling Tara, buying Florida / Colm Toibin	2008
Toibin, Colm (1955 -	Single minded [a 'rereading' of Henry James, The lesson of the master] / Colm Toibin	2007
Toibin, Colm (1955 -	Synge: a celebration / edited by Colm Toibin	2005

Figure 3.   Results yielded by a search of Colm Tóibín as 'subject'

Wallace, Arminta	In the shadow of a playwright [interview-article with Colm Toibin] / Arminta Wallace	1994
Kelly, Shirley	[Interview with Colm Toibin] / Shirley Kelly	1994
Harmon, Maurice (1930 -	[Review of Colm Toibin, The heather blazing] / Maurice Harmon	1994
Whelan, G.V.	[Review of Colm Toibin, The sign of the cross: travels in Catholic Europe] / G.V. Whelan	1995
Murphy, Hayden (1945 -	[Review of talk given by Colm Toibin at the 7th biennial Edinburgh Book Festival, September 1995] / Hayden Murphy	1995
Dunne, John	[Review of Colm Toibin, The story of the night] / John Dunne	1996
Eagleton, Terry (1943 -	[Review of Colm Toibin, The Blackwater lightship] / Terry Eagleton	1999
Herron, Tom	Contamination: Patrick McCabe and Colm Toibin's pathologies of the Republic / Tom Herron	2000
Kelly, Shirley	Colm Toibin reassessed the old lady of Coole [interview] / [Shirley Kelly]	2002
Frazier, Adrian	The double life of a lady [review of Colm Toibin, Lady Gregory's toothbrush] / Adrian Frazier	2002
Banville, John (1945 -	Homosexuality [review of Colm Toibin, Love in a dark time] / John Banville	2002
Harmon, Maurice (1930 -	[Review of Colm Toibin, The master] / Maurice Harmon	2004
Clark, Alex	Songs of experience [interview-article with Colm Toibin] / Alex Clark	2004
Kenny, John	[Review of Colm Toibin, The master] / John Kenny	2005
Sussler, Betsy	Chris Abani and Colm Toibin in conversation [interview-like format] / edited by Betsy Sussler	2006
Walshe, Eibhear	The vanishing homoerotic: Colm Toibins gay fictions / Eibhear Walshe	2006
Toibin, Colm (1955 -	Single minded [a 'rereading' of Henry James, The lesson of the master] / Colm Toibin	2007
Ryan, Matthew	Abstract homes: deterritorialisation and reterritorialisation in the work of Colm Toibin / Matthew Ryan	2008
Delaney, Paul (1948 -	Reading Colm Toibin / edited by Paul Delaney	2008
Patten, Eve	The sign of the cross: travels in Colm Toibins Europe / Eve Patten	2008
McCarthy, Justine	Atlantic crossing [review of Colm Toibin, Brooklyn] / Justine McCarthy	2009
McKeon, Belinda	[Interview with Colm Toibin, marking the appearance of his new novel Brooklyn] / Belinda McKeon	2009
McCrum, Robert	You can take the man out of Ireland ... [interview with Colm Toibin, and on his new novel, Brooklyn] / Robert McCrum	2009

It goes without saying, however, that neither the results yielded from searching Tóibín's name as 'author' or as 'subject' include all the works of critical commentary produced either by the author himself or those concerning his own work.

Tóibín is an extremely prolific writer, having published not only an extensive number of fictional works, but also an even larger number of journalistic pieces. Since the 1970s, he has worked as a journalist for *In Dublin, Hibernia* and *The Sunday Tribune,* and as features editor of *Magill, Ireland's current affairs* magazine. In more recent years, he has been a regular contributor to the *Dublin Review,* the *New York Review of Books* and the *London Review of Books.* Between 2007 and 2010, he was art critic for the UK edition of *Esquire* magazine. Which is to say that the author has produced a wealth of critical commentary that is not listed in the BILC database. In his role as art critic for *Esquire* magazine, for example, Tóibín has written essays on a number of international artists including Andy Warhol and Richard Long (http://www.colmToibin.com/essays). Yet the international scope of Tóibín's work is not reflected in the results yield from a search of Tóibín as 'author/editor' in the BILC database. With the exception of the essay on Henry James perhaps, the majority of the critical works that are listed as being authored by Tóibín are on topics relating to Ireland or Irish literature. Rather than enhancing 'international dialogues', therefore, the current selection of Colm Tóibín's critical works included in the database regrettably may conceal the global scope of his oeuvre.

This limited representation of Tóibín's critical writings in the results yielded is indicative of a continued dominance of commentaries regarding the nation and a national literature within the BILC database. The majority of the critical works listed which address Colm Tóibín as subject attempt to situate his work under the rubric of Irish literature. For example, McCrum's (2009) interview with the author following the publication of his novel *Brooklyn* is tellingly entitled *You can take the man out of Ireland.* In the article, McCrum (2009) situates Tóibín within an Irish literary heritage by comparing him to figures such as James Joyce, Flann O'Brien and John McGahern. Furthermore, McCrum (2009), like many of the other critics whose commentaries on Tóibín are listed in the BILC database, reads the author's work through a specifically Irish lens.

While such considerations as McCrum's (2009) are useful and serve to emphasise the degree to which Tóibín's writing is connected to his nation of origins, within the BILC database, considerations of this sort have gained predominance over other possible ways of reading the author's work. This is particularly evident in the 'keyword/subject' searches by which the user can access bibliographical records relating to Tóibín. Given Tóibín's status as a prominent figure in the field of gay literature and the number of commentaries by queer theorists on his work, one might expect that a subject keyword search according to 'queer studies' would bring back works either by or on the author. However, attempting such a search reveals that the term 'queer studies' is not a listed term among the 1,755 subject keywords within the database. While a search of 'gender' brings back results which are pertinent to queer studies, such a lumping together of these issues under the term gender is not desirable. Such a search highlights the extent to which not all trajectories or modes of reading are permitted by the database.

It is important to note, however, that the aforementioned issues of selection and categorisation are not problems unique to the digital medium; they are, in fact, ones which face any collection of Irish writing which inevitably prioritises writings on an Irish subject. But while literary scholars in the field of Irish studies have begun to call attention to the limitations of print based literary collections gathered under the rubric of the nation (Kelleher, 2003; Meaney, 2007), they have not, as of yet, provided similar critiques of digital collections such as BILC. In the absence of any sustained scholarly attention, the ideological trends that inform these resources have gone unquestioned; this absence may in turn give rise to overly celebratory accounts of the new medium such as that offered by Folsom (2007).

As the brief critical analysis of BILC provided here reveals, rather than being an undifferentiated flood of data free from the constraints of narrative, the database is shown to be a significant, though also partial work of literary, editorial and archival scholarship which, despite its desire to enable new narratives, inevitably directs the user according to particular trajectories. Moreover, contrary to Folsom's (2007) claim that database and narrative are 'natural enemies', the account of BILC provided here highlights the extent to which the technical structure of the database is complicit in constructing narratives of Irish literary historiography. Hence, in keeping with Dalbello's (2011) observation regarding digital humanities projects more generally, we find that "optimism and the excitement about new possibilities for rethinking the texts, canon, and creation" afforded by database technology is "ahead of the actual development work" (p. 496).

4.   Making the most of the medium

While the discussion above demonstrates how the digital medium does not overcome all the limitations of the literary collection as it appears in codex form, the aim here is not to make a case against such digital resources. Rather, the purpose of the critique here is to be constructive: as McGill (2007) has noted, "if we misconstrue media shift as liberation, we are likely to settle for less than the new technology has to offer us" (p. 1595). Hence, following McGill (2007), we can argue that it is only by engaging with digital tools such as BILC that we are afforded an opportunity to identify potential areas for future developments in resources of this kind.

Although considering database technology in practical terms provides a more sobering account of the potentialities of the new medium than those hoped for by Folsom (2007), such considerations also encourage us to ask what future developments of analytical databases like BILC can and should be made in order to make the most of the new medium. As the analysis of BILC provided here reveals, the database, at present, remains a predominantly national project. This subsequently limits the extent to which the digital resource enables the 'international dialogues' aspired for by its editor. However, unlike the literary collection as it appears in codex form, owing to the digital nature of the database, it may readily be included within wider networks of digital resources which are international in scope. One such network is the Study Platform for Interlocking Nationalism (SPIN) project (http://www.spinnet.eu/), currently being developed by humanities scholars and ICT specialists in the Netherlands. Included as part of this network, BILC may not only move closer towards achieving its objectives, but will significantly benefit from increased dissemination. As the most successful digital resources are, according to Warwick, Terras, Huntington,

Pappa, and Galina (2006), those which "actively pursued the most determined and varied dissemination strategy" (p. 30), this increased dissemination will also ensure the ongoing viability of the project.

Critiquing the BILC database also calls attention to another wider concern within the field of digital humanities: sustainability. "Sustainability" as it applies to digital resources, "signals a broad set of concerns – they are both technical and institutional – about how to maintain and augment the increasingly large body of information that humanists are both creating and using" (McGann, 2010, p. 1). While many of the debates surrounding digital resources have tended to focus on sustainability in either financial or technical terms, as the European Science Foundation (2011) report on *Research Infrastructures in the Digital Humanities* made clear, sustainability involves the "maintenance and preservation" of both the "content [and the] tools that scholars use to interrogate [digital] objects" (p. 21). Sustainability is thus as much about the maintenance and preservation of the materials stored within a database as it is about the technical structure of the resource.

As the BILC database was a project driven by a literary scholar, it is a work of established humanities scholarship. However, since its publication, to date, no further resources have been available to "maintain and actively update the interface, content and functionality" (Warwick, Galina, Terras, Huntington, and Pappa, 2008, p. 395) of the BILC database. While the technical structure of BILC remains, at present, in good repair, the content of the resource has already begun to date, with an obvious detrimental effect on the functionality of the database. For example, on the BILC *About* page, it is stated that the database provides works relating to Irish literary criticism from the "Revival to the present day" (BILC, About, para. 1); however, the most recent entry listed in the database was published in 2011, thus indicating that the database has already begun to fall out of sync with recent developments in Irish literary criticism. A practical consideration of the BILC database thus highlights the fact that the future viability thereof is most endangered not by the lack of additional funding or technical obsolescence, but by the absence of ongoing resources from the community for whom it was designed.

Literature from the wider digital humanities community informs us that in order to secure the ongoing viability of resources like BILC, it is essential that clear, long term plans are put in place early on in the development of such projects to ensure that they are maintained after their publication (Warwick et al., 2008). As has been established in the case study provided here, this requires considerations that are financial and technical, but also theoretical and disciplinary. Given the subject-specific nature of analytical databases such as BILC, those who take up the responsibility of databases of this kind need to possess expertise in the field for which they are designed. At the same time, owing to the digital nature of databases, the maintenance thereof also requires a degree of technical competence. As few humanities scholars currently possess the technical skills necessary to maintain and update a database, and few ICT specialists possess the humanities expertise required to retain the analytical nature of databases such as BILC, ongoing collaborative work between practitioners in the two disciplines is imperative after the publication of the resource, in order to ensure that both the theoretical and the technical structures are sustained.

Looking further into the future more positively, it is likely that recently emerging practitioners in the emerging field of digital humanities may take responsibility for digital resources such as BILC. Having received hands on training in the technologies required for designing and maintaining databases for humanities scholarship, this new generation of scholars are acquiring both the theoretical and practical competence necessary to keep analytical databases like BILC in sync with developments in both the humanities and the digital humanities. In so doing, they will not only ensure the ongoing viability of digital databases but may drive these valuable projects forward.

5.   Conclusion

By moving away from earlier metaphorical, celebratory and perhaps naïve accounts of database technology to more practical considerations thereof, this chapter demonstrates that digital resources such as BILC are carefully constructed ideological tools which, like literary collections in codex form, face challenges of inclusion, categorisation and narrative. By extension, such considerations also point to the need for sustained critical engagements with resources of this type. By critically analysing both the content and the searches enabled by the BILC database, we can assess what new perspectives on an Irish literary historiography can be generated by an engagement with the new medium. Relatedly, we can determine what search queries are not, as of yet, permitted by the resource, and thus signal towards potential future developments.

A practical consideration of the database also brings to the fore the more general issues of dissemination and sustainability which face all digital resources. By calling attention to the need for increased dissemination and ongoing maintenance of the BILC database, this chapter engenders new considerations regarding responsibility for digital resources: as McGann (2005) has observed "defining it [sustainability] as a practical problem shifts us to ask 'how'. And when we make that shift we realize [...] that the question ultimately comes down to 'who'" (pp. 9-10). As this chapter points out, given the analytical nature of the database, the who must possess both the humanities and technical skills necessary to ensure that both form and content of BILC are developed in a manner which caters to the needs of the community for whom it was designed. At a time when BILC is beginning to show signs of scholarly neglect, it is propitious that practitioners with the dual skill set necessary for ensuring its maintenance have begun to emerge from within the field of Irish Studies.

References

BILC. (2010). *Bibliography of Irish Literary Criticism, 1890-Present: BILC*. Retrieved from http://bilc.nuim.ie/bilc/index

BILC. *About*. Retrieved from http://bilc.nuim.ie/bilc/about

BILC. *Editorial Policy*. Retrieved from http://bilc.nuim.ie/bilc/policy

Dalbello, M. (2011). A Genealogy of Digital Humanities. *Journal of Documentation, 67*(3), 480-506. doi: 10.1108/00220411111124550

Dimock, W. C. (2007). Genres as Fields of Knowledge. Introduction. Special Topic: Remapping Genre. *PMLA, 122*(5), 1377-1388

European Science Foundation. (2011). *Research Infrastructures in the Digital Humanities*. Retrieved from http://www.esf.org/research-areas/humanities/strategic-activities/research-infrastructures-in-the-humanities.html

Farmer, A. B., & Lesser, Z. (2008). Early Modern Digital Scholarship and DEEP: Database of Early English Playbooks. *Literature Compass, 5*(6), 1139-1153. doi: 10.1111/j.1741-4113.2008.00577.x

Folsom, E. (2007). Database as Genre: The Epic Transformation of the Archives. Special Topic: Remapping Genre. *PMLA, 122*(5), 1571-1579. doi: 10.1632/pmla.2007.122.5.1571

Graham, C. (2001). *Deconstructing Ireland: Identity, Theory, Culture*. Edinburgh: Edinburgh University Press.

Graham, C. (2006). Literary Historiography, 1890-2000. In M. Kelleher & P. O'Leary (Eds.), *The Cambridge History of Irish Literature: Volume 2* (pp. 562-599). Cambridge: Cambridge University Press. doi: 10.1017/CHOL9780521822237.014

Hockey, S. (2006). A History of Humanities Computing. In S. Schreibman, R. Siemens, & J. Unsworth (Eds.), A Companion to Digital Humanities [online]. Oxford: Blackwell Publishing. Retrieved from http://www.digitalhumanities.org/companion/

Kelleher, M. (2003). The Cabinet of Irish Literature: A Historical View on Irish Anthologies. *Éire-Ireland, 38*(3-4), 68-89.

Kelleher, M. (2011). From the Anthology to the Database: Old and New Irish Studies. In M. M. Ladrón & J. F. Elices Agudo (Eds.), *Glocal Ireland: Current Perspectives on Literature and the Visual Arts* (pp. 12-25). Newcastle upon Tyne: Cambridge Scholars Publishing.

Manovich, L. (2001). *The Language of New Media*. Massachusetts and London: MIT Press.

McCrum, R. (2009, April 26). You can take the man out of Ireland. *The Observer*. Retrieved from http://www.guardian.co.uk/books/2009/apr/26/colm-toibin-brooklyn

McGann, J. (2005). Culture and Technology: The way we live now, what is to be done? *Interdisciplinary Science Reviews, 30*(2), 179-189. doi: 10.1179/030801805X25918

McGann, J. (2007). Database, Interface, and Archival Fever. *PMLA, 122*(5), 1588-1592. Retrieved from http://faculty.winthrop.edu/kosterj/WRIT510/readings/McGann.pdf

McGann, J. (2008). The Future is Digital. *Journal of Victorian Culture, 13*(1), 80-88. doi: 10.1353/jvc.0.0000

McGann, J. (2010). Sustainability: The Elephant in the Room. In J. McGann (Ed.), *Online Humanities Scholarship. The Shape of Things to Come* (pp. 1-22). Houston: Rice University Press.

McGill, M. L. (2007). Remediating Whitman. *PMLA, 122*(5), 1594-1596. Retrieved from http://www.jstor.org/stable/25501806

Meaney, G. (2007). Engendering the Postmodern Canon?: The Field Day Anthology of Irish Writing, Volumes IV & V: Women's Writing and Traditions. In P. Boyle Haberstroh & C. St. Peter (Eds.), *Opening the Field: Irish Women, Texts and Contexts* (pp. 15-31). Cork: Cork University Press.

Price, K. M. (2009). Edition, Project, Database, Archive, Thematic Research Collection: What's in a Name?. *DHQ: Digital Humanities Quarterly, 3*(3). Retrieved from http://www.digitalhumanities.org/dhq/vol/3/3/000053/000053.html

Ramsay, S. (2004). Database. In S. Schreibman, R. Siemens, & J. Unsworth (Eds.), *A Companion to Digital Humanities* [online]. Oxford: Blackwell Publishing. Retrieved from http://www.digitalhumanities.org/companion/

Warwick, C., Terras, M., Huntington, P., Pappa, N., & Galina, I. (2006). *The LAIRAH Project: log analysis of digital resources in the arts and humanities. Final Report to the Arts and Humanities Research Council* [online]. Retrieved from http://discovery.ucl.ac.uk/189677/1/189677.pdf

Warwick, C., Galina, I., Terras, M., Huntington, P., & Pappa, N. (2008). The Master Builders: LAIRAH research on good practice in the construction of digital humanities projects. *Literary and Linguistic Computing, 23*(3), 383-396. doi: 10.1093/llc/fqn017

22 Digital Humanities and Political Innovation: The SOWIT Model

Vanessa Liston[1], Clodagh Harris[2], Mark O'Toole[3], and Margaret Liston[4]

Abstract

In this chapter we show how a new type of political knowledge can be harnessed from everyday communication flows between citizens to support community and policy development processes. The emergence of this new knowledge will be enabled by an e-supported deliberation process (SOWIT) that aims to improve political communication and deliberation between citizens, civil society organisations, local councils and councillors. To explain the SOWIT project and its innovative approach to political engagement we first outline its motivation with respect to political reform in Ireland. We then discuss the model's framework and features in functional terms. The core innovations are rooted in SOWIT's foundation in the fields of Q-methodology, discursive representation and meta-consensus theory. Finally, we explain how the model departs from the epistemic norms of current political paradigms particularly with respect to public opinion and random selection as a basis for representativeness in deliberative fora. SOWIT is currently being developed as a pilot in collaboration with Fingal County Council in Dublin.

Keywords: political innovation, e-supported deliberation, SOWIT, public opinion.

1. Trinity College Dublin, Dublin, Ireland; vliston@tcd.ie (corresponding author)

2. University College Cork, Cork, Ireland; clodagh.harris@ucc.ie

3. Kilkenny County Council, Kilkenny, Ireland; mark.otoole@kilkennycoco.ie

4. Independent Researcher, Kilkenny, Ireland; margaret.liston@gmail.com

How to cite this chapter: Liston, V., Harris, C., O'Toole, M., & Liston, M. (2013). Digital Humanities and Political Innovation: The SOWIT Model. In C. Fowley, C. English, & S. Thouësny (Eds.), *Internet Research, Theory, and Practice: Perspectives from Ireland* (pp. 447-470). Dublin: © Research-publishing.net.

1. Introduction

Political innovation using technology is not commonly regarded as within the domain of Digital Humanities. Online political discussion fora, mini-publics and deliberative polls have a strong social science basis with design and output framed in positivist terms as indicated by the Discourse Quality Index (Lord & Tamvaki, forthcoming; Steenbergen, Bächtiger, Spörndli, & Steiner, 2003), survey data and representativeness indicators. However, where political innovation is rooted in the democratic norms of inclusion and difference it becomes at its root concerned with extending an understanding of the discursive world. Interpretation versus scientific positivism prevails and the political innovation enterprise becomes fused with philosophical, creative and discursive trajectories.

This goal of discursive understanding (see Dryzek, 2010) is particularly important at a time when citizen deliberation[1], reasoning and judgement are becoming recognised as key to governance in a complex networked society (Barnes, Newman, & Sullivan, 2007; Dryzek, 1987). At the global level, citizen deliberations are increasing integrated to climate management and biodiversity policy. At the national level there is a growing interest in citizen assemblies as a way of debating national referendum issues (British Columbia Citizen Assembly on Electoral Reform, 2004; G1000 Belgian Citizens' Summit, 2011; Ireland's We The Citizens (WTC) pilot, 2011). Municipalities and cities are also experimenting with deliberations and direct democracy through participatory budgeting (Porto Alegre, Brazil; Freiburg, Germany)[2], law making (Municipal Health Councils, Brazil; Iceland's Crowd Sourced Constitution) and citizen initiatives (Finland's Citizen Initative). At the same time, the rise in social media use has led to the rapid emergence of a broad range of online participatory and deliberation experiments such as Fishkin's

---

1. Deliberation is a commonly understand a process in which citizens discuss an issue and provide reasons both for an against an issue with the aim of achieving a mutually acceptable outcome. Processes of deliberation are commonly oriented to Habermas's (1975) ideal speech situation which requires that all participants have equal opportunity to contribute to the discussion, are free from domination, and are motivated by the pursuit of truth in all claims made. The aim is to provide the ideal conditions so that the force of the better argument prevails.

2. In 2008 the city of Freiburg combined online deliberation with the use of a budget simulator, enabling citizens to better assess the impacts of their choices.

Vanessa Liston, Clodagh Harris, Mark O'Toole, and Margaret Liston

(2009) online deliberative polls, the Womenspeak parliamentary consultation on domestic violence in the UK (Smith, 2009), and Community Campaign Creator (Coleman & Blumler, 2009).

Yet, despite the promise that deliberation holds for enabling a more participatory and informed political system, deliberative methods to date rely mainly on Habermasian theories of communicative rationality and discourse ethics. Accordingly, ideal deliberation between individuals should emphasise reason-giving, impartiality and focus on the common good. Difference democrats such as Young (2000), and others (Pennington, 2003; Tully, 2002) however, have argued that these standards can result in exclusion of the most marginalised. In Young's (2000) words they "extend already constituted institutions and practices to people not currently benefitting from them enough […] thereby expecting them to conform to hegemonic norms" (p. 12).

In this chapter we offer a new approach to deliberation that moves from the procedural focus of communicative rationality to a substantive focus on the discursive structure of public opinion. We show how individual subjectivity and judgement can be harnessed to unlock the social structure in public opinion in a way that provides more inclusive information for, and new approaches to, the development of sustainable policy. We root our participatory and deliberative approach in a method for observing individual subjectivity (Q-method), developed by physicist and psychologist William Stephenson in 1953 (Stephenson, 1953). However to date it has not been scaled to enable its use in political processes. The SOWIT model (Social Web for Inclusive and Transparent democracy) is thus entirely novel.

We begin by outlining the motivation for SOWIT with respect to political reform in Ireland. We then discuss the model's core features in functional terms. Finally, we explain how it departs from the epistemic norms of current political paradigms. During our discussion we refer to particular elements of the full SOWIT model (see Liston, Harris, & O'Toole, 2011a) that are relevant to the discussion at hand. The innovation we propose highlights the transformative potential of the growing field of digital humanities in Ireland.

1.1.   Political engagement, reform and deliberation in Ireland

Recent concern with the state of Irish democracy has given rise to bursts of political innovations that touch on the core of democratic values such as free speech, power and voice. Such innovations in Ireland have ranged from the Open Data movement, to citizen deliberations by civil society groups (The Wheel, Claiming our Future, The Second Republic), the WTC assembly[1], as well as online political initiatives (Political Reform Score Card[2]; Fix Our Area[3]). The lobbying techniques of Irish civil society organisations have also evolved to include media campaigns and social media communication strategies in response to the impact of the economic crisis on Ireland's social partnership and corporatist structures (Carney, Dundon, Ní Leime, & Loftus, 2011).

At the macro-level political reform has also become firmly established within national level political discourse. The 2011 general election saw reform addressed in the manifestos of all political parties. The Constitutional Convention is the first opportunity for Irish citizens to deliberate at the national level on constitutional reform and the Local Government Action Plan (Dept. of Environment, Community and Local Government, 2012) promises new structures for enabling greater citizen participation, such as participatory budgeting. As the innovation of social partnership which emerged in the 1990s is replaced by fluid social dialogue processes, a transformation is occurring in the dynamics of participation and decision-making in Ireland.

However, despite this agitation towards reform and citizen engagement, there are challenges for political reform that inhere in the character of the Irish public sphere. Across the spectrum of democratic theory, the public sphere generally describes a plurality of free spaces for the expression of diverse opinions, contributing to a plurality of voices and perspectives on an issue,

---

1. The WTC pilot assembly was an opportunity for a random selection of Irish citizens to deliberate on suggestions that emerged from regional events around Ireland on the future of their country. The deliberation took place on June 25th and June 26th 2011 in the Royal Hospital Kilmainham, Dublin, Ireland. It was made up of 100 citizens selected randomly from a cross-section of Irish citizens, aged between 18-87. For further information see http://www.wethecitizens.ie.

2. http://www.reformcard.com

3. http://www.fixourarea.com

thereby informing and forging public opinion (Dewey, 1927). Arendt (1967) in particular notes that opinion exchange in the public sphere is essential for the discovery of political truth. However, a recent study by Gaynor (2011) suggests that the social partnership scheme in Ireland significantly narrowed the public sphere in the 1990s in particular. She also points to the lack of significant social action on the bailouts of the Irish banks as a symptom of the lack of alternative discourses, voices and interests (Gaynor, 2011, p. 513). This conclusion resonates with Habermas's (1975) concern with the decline of the institutions of public opinion when state and society penetrate each other (O'Brien, 2009). Similarly, O'Carroll (2002) finds that the Irish public sphere is 'stymied', preventing communities from articulating their interests, developing skills and political agency.

We address this concern with the Irish public sphere by outlining a normative design for a hybrid communication and deliberation model that is directly linked to Council decision processes. The model, entitled SOWIT enables citizens, civil society organisations and political representatives to engage directly in discussion, deliberation and policy development on an ongoing basis. Specifically, it responds directly to recent calls for the explicit recognition of "the situated, partial, and constitutive character of knowledge production, the recognition that knowledge is constructed, taken, not simply given as a natural representation of pre-existing fact" (Drucker, 2011, para. 3, emphasis in original).

We present this model and explain its approach to the generation of a new type of political knowledge through the concepts of discursive representation and dynamic visualisation of meta-consensus based deliberation (Dryzek & Niemeyer, 2006, 2008).

2. The SOWIT model

SOWIT is a new model of citizen engagement that aims to respond to the challenges associated with harnessing public opinion for sustainable policy while harnessing the potential of the technology for asynchronous and visualised communication[1]. A core feature of SOWIT is that it is integrated in a supportive capacity to policy decision processes at local authority level. In this way, SOWIT aims to support the impact of the public sphere by having a direct feedback link with local government.

The SOWIT model comprises three spheres:

- A collaboration sphere which enables asynchronous open cross-group and local authority communications;

- A deliberation sphere which provides a space for discourse 'speakers', Councillors and Council officials;

- A decision sphere which is the democratic institution, in this case the County council.

The models design is rooted in the work of Young (2000) on social inclusion and Dryzek and Niemeyer (2006, 2008) on discursive representation.

2.1. The collaboration sphere

The collaboration-sphere is a permanent and open online federated social network for citizens, civil society organisations, councillors and local government officials. Citizens can connect with one another and with elected members on political issues, learn about other citizen views, obtain information, and contribute to the identification of social discourses that can be represented in deliberations. The output of citizen issues and sentiment is publicly available data. SOWIT communications are allocated time at Council meetings for discussion. Feedback from the council meetings is posted to the collaboration sphere. Consistent with the dispersed nature of the general public sphere, the online collaboration space integrated citizen's information from other sources as well as OpenData sets (Figure 1).

---

1. For full details of the model and explanation of these theoretical frameworks see Liston, Harris and O'Toole (2011a).

Figure 1. Proposed integration of SOWIT to support local authority policy development processes

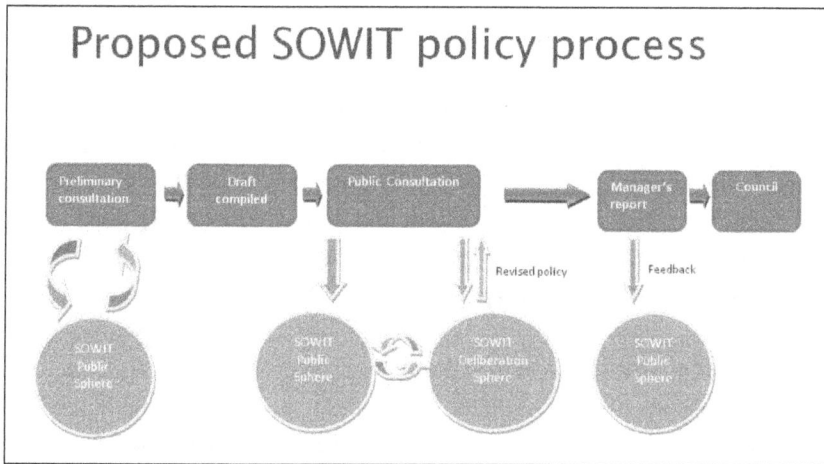

Proposed SOWIT policy process

Attending to the hermeneutical challenges that inhere in a Dewian collaboration sphere of open communication (Dewey, 1927) SOWIT deploys an innovative active listening tool that aims to support citizens to actively create shared meaning. REFLECT software, developed by Kriplean, Toomim, Morgan, Borning, and Ko (2011), assists with the interpretative problem of understanding and converting information. It enables participants in a conversation to summarise and re-state expressions in a stream of discussion, thereby enabling clarification, supporting common understanding and identifying barriers to communication[1]. As such the basis of SOWIT's approach to political communication and knowledge is "centered in the experiential, subjective conditions of interpretation" (Drucker, 2011, para. 13).

The collaboration sphere also acts as an evolving learning space, where citizens have access to the most relevant policy and broad contextual information for formulating and informing their opinions. Such information is presented

---

1. It does so by providing a space for bulleted summaries beside comments in a web forum. Any reader can add a bullet point summarising what the commenter said. These restatements are publicly viewable and the original commenter can clarify whether the summary is accurate. As such individuals in the community are facilitated to listen actively to other members. For further information see http://homes.cs.washington.edu/~travis/reflect/.

in a visualised manner, to which citizens can propose additional relevant information sources.

2.2. The deliberation sphere

The deliberation sphere is activated during the policy development process. In this forum citizens engage with diverse social discourses in a deliberation process with other citizens, civil society organisations, councillors and officials. We define social discourses in Dryzek and Niemeyer's (2008) terms as "a set of categories and concepts embodying specific assumptions, judgments, contentions, dispositions, and capabilities" (p. 481).

In this respect, SOWIT is a radical departure from political discussion fora and current deliberative initiatives because it attends specifically to the discursive struggle that creates and constitutes power relations in society which are the heart of Young's (2000) work on inclusion. This focus on discourse has been pioneered in the innovative concept of discursive representation (Dryzek, 2010; Dryzek & Niemeyer, 2008). In these works the authors provide a comprehensive account of how a discursive approach can enable a scalable method for inclusive citizen deliberations. Citizens are included to the extent that the discourse to which they subscribe with respect to a policy issue is actively represented in deliberations. We adopt this line of reasoning and root the online model in Concourse Theory (Stephenson, 1953) and it's derived Q-methodology as exemplified by Niemeyer (2004, 2011) and Dryzek (2010). We summarise this method with specific reference to SOWIT.

2.3. Unveiling social discourses

Concourse Theory holds that social discourses are expressed in the *concourse of communicability*, which refers to the stream of everyday conversation (Stephenson, 1953). By analysing streams of opinion in normal conversation it is possible to identify underlying structures in public opinion. These structures or patterns in opinion represent expressions of social discourses. Stephenson (1953) developed Q-method for identifying such discourses, and this method formed the basis of the empirical deliberative experiments of Dryzek and Niemeyer (2006, 2008). Q-method has recently been revived in the literature on public policy (Ellis, Barry, & Robinson, 2007) and in a wide number of deliberative experiments in the Netherlands, Australia and Canada (Cuppen, Breukers, Hisschemöller, & Bergsma, 2010; Ray, 2011).

Accordingly, the inclusion of all social discourses relevant to an issue at hand is achieved by collating the widest possible range of statements on a particular policy issue (from the web, print media and stakeholder interviews). Social discourse structure is revealed through citizens' subjective ranking of these statements. The assumption is that these opinion statements, drawn from natural speech, represent a comprehensive view of all opinions on the particular issue within the sample population. These statements are then ranked by a purposive sample of key stakeholders and a random sample of citizens. This method, known as the Q-sort, requires citizens to assess the relative importance of each opinion statement by ranking the statement within a quasi-normal distribution grid (see Figure 2). This is enabled using a drag and drop interface. Forcing preference ranking within this structure necessitates the use of citizen judgement.

Figure 2.   Sample Q-sort grid
in which a diverse range of statements are ranked

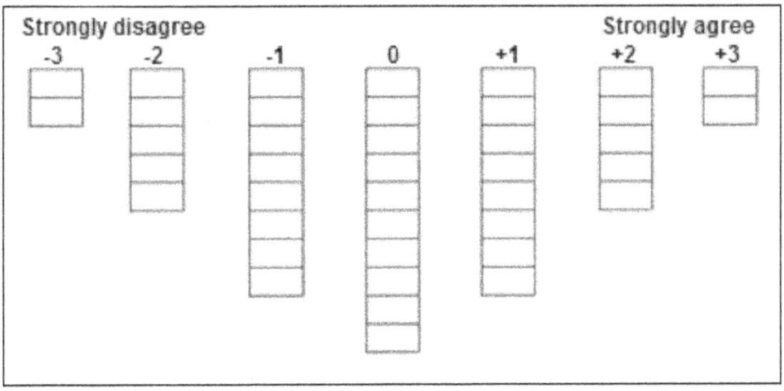

Upon completion of the Q-sort the rankings are correlated and factor analysed to identify underlying commonalities, which are identified as discrete social discourses. For example, in a deliberative research experiment related to wind farm development, the social discourses emerging from a sorting of a broad sample of statements included Rationalising Globally - Sacrificing Locally, Local Pastoralist – Developer Sceptic, Embrace Wind, and Site Specific Supporter – Energy Pragmatist (Ellis, Barry, & Robinson, 2007).

2.4.   New knowledge type

The knowledge that is produced from SOWIT's proposed Q-sort ranking in the collaboration sphere stage is significantly different from current public opinion data which inform public policy and public opinion in Ireland. SOWIT knowledge departs from the objective positivist knowledge extracted from survey methods on which political knowledge is based, to foreground interpretation and public judgement. Our concern with aggregate opinion-based political knowledge (and its data capture methods) is based on a wide literature that emphasises the unstable and manipulable nature of public opinion, particularly relevant in the context of political communication during electoral campaigns. In a recent empirical study, Chong and Druckman (2010) show that when campaign messages are separated in time by days or weeks, individuals give more weight to most recent communications, demonstrating volatility. In contrast, they find that people who deliberate on the information they receive through political campaign communications demonstrate attitude stability and a focus on earlier communications. A further problem with opinion is that inter-subjective understandings of an issue can vary significantly between citizens based on their exposure to the issue and their life-world. Dryzek (2005) states "opinion surveys embody a culture hostile to deliberative democracy" (p. 197).

However, this critique of using survey data as truthful political knowledge does not detract from opinion as the core vehicle through which truth in politics can be found. In contrast to the opposition between truth and opinion raised by Plato, we adopt Arendt's (1967) claim in her essay *Truth and Politics*, that objective truth as a basis for political regimes should be replaced by the ability to make political judgements, which is founded on a plurality of opinion.

Opinion becomes truthful according to Arendt's (1967) reading of Socrates, by means of public debate through which one finds what in one's opinions is true. This approach is directly relevant to Gadamer's (2004) focus on questioning as the path to knowledge. In *Truth and Method* he affirms the "priority of the question over the answer, which is the basis of the concept of knowledge. Knowledge always means considering opposites" (Gadamer, 2004, p. 359). He further states:

> "Someone who wants to know something cannot just leave it a matter of mere opinion, which is to say that he cannot hold himself aloof from the opinions that are in question. The speaker (Redende) is put to the question (zur Rede gestellt) until the truth of what is under discussion (wovon der Rede ist) finally emerges" (Gadamer, 2004, p. 361).

Accordingly Arendt (1967) sees the public space not where already formed opinions are defended but a space which enables the "condition of their formation, articulation, and circulation in a broader process of critical thinking and *judging*. It is through this process of opinion formation that facts come to have truth for us in a politically significant sense" (cited in Zerilli, 2012, p. 68).

Yet, such judgement also requires citizens to have access to knowledge to inform opinions, support the questioning process and enable new issues brought out into the open. The flow of free information both before and during the deliberation process supports the challenge of prejudices, prevents the domination of empty opinion, and the suppression of questions with which Gadamer (2004) was concerned. The availability of such information is prioritised in both the collaboration sphere and during deliberations.

Public judgement is thus central to the SOWIT collaboration sphere and specifically to the policy development processes with which SOWIT is concerned. Normatively, this concern resonates with theorists concerned with the functioning of democratic systems. Leading Federalist Alexander Hamilton in 1788 suggested it is not public opinion that we need to guide us, but public judgment. In his words "[t]he deliberate sense of the community should govern the conduct of those to whom they entrust the management of their affairs" (cited in Hamilton, Madison, & Jay, 2003, p. 436). Kornprobst (2011) states that understanding the emergence of public judgement should be of central concern to modern democracies. Elster (1983) states that "[i]f people are agents in a substantive sense, and not just the passive supports of their preference structures and belief systems, then we need to understand how judgment and autonomy are possible" (cited in Kornprobst, 2011, p. 88). This public judgement focus is at the heart of deliberation which emphasises reason giving and openness to preference transformation when faced with what Habermas (1975) describes as the "forceless force of the better argument" (p. 108).

Although individual judgement has not yet been transformed to public judgement knowledge which will occur during deliberations, the active ranking by citizens of the social concourse of communicability within the online collaboration sphere has enabled the identification and extraction of underlying structure in public opinion.

2.5.　SOWIT deliberations

SOWIT deliberative processes are not orientated to pure consensus which, it is argued, leads to exclusion (Connelly & Richardson, 2004; Young, 2000). To address this challenge all relevant discourses identified are represented within the deliberation sphere. The deliberation process is structured sequentially (Bächtiger, Niemeyer, Neblo, Steenbergen, & Steiner, 2010) so that various forms of communication are supported at various stages (including story-telling, rhetoric etc). Rational deliberation argued to be exclusive by Young (2000) is accorded only one place in the deliberative sequence. Deliberations also aim towards meta-consensus as developed by Dryzek and Niemeyer (2006). Meta-consensus contrasts with pure consensus which can negatively impact minority groups and discourses. It focuses on disaggregating opinion on normative, epistemic or preference dimensions which enables a wider space for deliberation. For example, strong opposition on normative (value-based) grounds may be acknowledged, but such difference does not necessarily block further deliberation on the epistemic dimension (knowledge-based opinion/ beliefs about cause and effect). The distinction made between value-based versus fact-based opinion also supports knowledge and information in the deliberation process. Where citizens' opinions can be based on multiple different sources of 'information', presenting fact-based opinions during deliberation enables the public evaluation of such facts for manipulation through propaganda or 'symbolic politics' (Niemeyer, 2004, 2011). Finally, meta-consensus does not require consensus on a single preference outcome thus enhancing discursive inclusion as presented by Young (2000) and the recognition of diverse life-worlds.

Practically, deliberations are conducted in a face-to-face setting with a group not likely to exceed 15 participants. The participants include 'discourse speakers' which are a sub-group selected from the Q-sort participants according to their stated 'ideal criteria' indicated in survey responses during the Q-sort process (for further details see Liston, Harris, & O'Toole, 2011a). Those citizens that are the best fit with the pre-stated 'ideal' criteria act as temporary speakers for a discourse relevant to a particular policy issue. Participants also include elected representatives and Council officials. Each participant has a laptop/pad/mobile communication device which they use to input statements of opinion during deliberations. Statements are projected to a common overheard screen. Once a set of statements are gathered these are Q-sorted by participants during 'rest-points' in the deliberation. SOWIT technologies support analysis, visualisation and measurement of deliberative progress based on comparative analysis of Q data at various rest-points during deliberations.

In doing so, SOWIT aims to encourage active reflection and judgement of each participant on statements raised by the diverse discourse speakers. The goal of the process is to reduce the initial distance between participants as measured by analysis of their respective Q-sorts, motivating co-operative behaviour rather than competitive lobbying or bargaining.

This judgemental process enables political knowledge to move from being offered as objective data to citizens, through opinion polls designed by professionals, to being *capta* based. This means that information that is understood as important by citizens is offered by participants during deliberations and then ranked by colleagues. What is considered knowledge thus becomes infused with a relevant and shared meaning. As Alexander (2002) states "Capta are richer than data as they are recognised to be relevant (which implies that they are in a context)" (p. 64).

In our approach we specifically attend to Drucker's (2011) call for visualisations to represent subjective understandings of the nature of knowledge. She states that instead of adopting "quantitative approaches that operate on claims of certainty", humanist methods should infuse graphic representations of knowledge (Drucker, 2011, para. 6). From this foundation a new stream of political knowledge flows. In sum, the output of the deliberation stream can thus be analysed for new knowledge, new patterns and new research questions, which are at the heart of the digital humanities project.

2.6. The local Council/policy development sphere

The proposals of the deliberative process and final discourse submissions are passed to the local Council where the final policy decisions are made. A resonance score is calculated between final policy and the output of the deliberative sphere. This is published to the collaboration sphere where the Council provides feedback to citizens outlining how their input was used. As such SOWIT aims to achieve Dryzek and Niemeyer's (2008) concept that policy should 'resonate' with public opinion defined as "the provisional outcome of the contestation of discourses as transmitted to the state or other public authority" (p. 484).

Resonance as such is based on an acknowledgement of the diversity of notions of the common good, the role of public judgement in accommodating claims on public goods and the critical role of interpretation and reflection in this process. In this regard SOWIT overcomes one of the core challenges faced by deliberative projects, as it is integrated into the policy making process in an ongoing and sustainable manner.

3. Challenges to current models

Our discussion so far has focused on the basis of SOWIT in generating a new type of political knowledge based on normative principles (Gregersen & Køppe, 1989). We now turn to compare the contribution of SOWIT to the approach of a significant deliberative experiment at national level in Ireland, the WTC pilot Citizens' Assembly. This pioneering event generated significant awareness among the public for the potential of deliberative judgement, demonstrated the value of deliberative mini publics in engaging citizens in debates on political and constitutional reform, and informed the Irish Government's Constitutional Convention. However, a number of criteria distinguish it from the SOWIT approach. Within the scope of this chapter, we discuss two of these criteria: representativeness and knowledge.

3.1. Representativeness: the issue of random sampling

Citizens' assemblies and deliberative polls address the issue of inclusion mainly within the framework of political representation through the random sampling of citizens (WTC pilot Citizens' Assembly Ireland; G1000, Belgium; the Canadian citizens' assemblies). The assumption is made that the observed population is representative of the entire population. However, a number of authors have critiqued the assumptions on which the random sampling method depends for legitimacy. Davies, Blackstock and Rauschmayer (2005) for example argue that the assumption that individuals hold perspectives attributed to them by their structural group characteristics has not been tested and does not necessarily hold. They specifically identify a 'recruitment problem', 'composition problem', and 'mandate problem' with the sampling method and call for a focus on argument representation based on Concourse Theory and Q-methodology. A further issue raised by Dryzek and Niemeyer (2006) is that random sampling does not account for the fact that citizens occupy multiple discourses which are activated in different contexts.

The SOWIT model challenges current approaches to the epistemic notion of representativeness that inheres in the concept of random sampling citizens. It departs from the assumptions that a select group of random individuals can be regarded as representing the complex patterns of views and judgments of the wider population. Instead, SOWIT investigates the extent to which a deliberating citizen subscribes to the natural social discourses present in society with respect to a particular issue. The fact that the Irish Citizens' Assembly addressed 18 different issues (drawn from themes raised at a number of regional meetings), would require using the SOWIT method: the identification of a statement set that comprehensively captures diversity of opinion in the public sphere on each of these issues, and the engagement of citizens in Q-sorting to uncover discursive structure.

For deliberation SOWIT would also identify participants based on Q-sort characteristics as well as ideal criteria pre-selected by sorting participants. This is a crucial question, as national level deliberative processes to date have not analysed the extent to which selected individuals represent the landscape of discourses that characterise competition and conflict within the given society. In this respect, we endorse Dryzek's (2010) view that the representation of social discourses can provide both more inclusive political process and one which is scalable to the global level.

Yet, random sampling can be a powerful legitimising tool where it is used in the context of the inclusive concourse of communicability, i.e., the stream of everyday conversation in which social discourses inhere. The citizens selected by random sampling are then assumed to offer equal chance to all citizens of being selected to conduct a ranking of the diverse social opinion. The interesting aspect of Q-sorting is that statistically it requires only a small number of Q-sort participants to identify discourses, with increasing numbers of sorts having no significant difference on the underlying structure of opinion. Our point is that giving all citizens an equal chance to rank the diverse range of opinions on a particular issue, (which necessitates only a small number of participants) enriches the ways in which representation occurs in deliberation. These citizens are not automatically required to deliberate but choose among themselves ideal criteria for discourse speakers, for example, the strength with which a participant identifies with a discourse measured as factor loadings (for discussion see Dryzek & Niemeyer, 2008). The random sample thus identifies the social discourses and selects the criteria by which discourse speakers emerge. The speakers align with a core discourse relevant to the issue at hand, thus improved deliberation occurs, and a unique knowledge stream for that particular issue emerges from the sorting process.

3.2. Knowledge: whose knowledge and for whom?

The second way in which SOWIT differs from the WTC pilot Citizens' Assembly is in its approach to knowledge. A final report on the initiative's outcomes (Farrell, 2011) provides the results of a positivist analysis of the deliberative process for which the issues to be deliberated were chosen by the organising and researching team. It is written by academics and the knowledge produced aspires to a level of absolute truth. Specifically, with reference to the 'scientific process' that underlay the WTC pilot Citizens' Assembly it states, "'statistic significance' shows 'real change' in opinion, not change due to chance" (WTC, 2011, p. 42). Yet in producing such knowledge for a diverse Irish public, it inevitably raises the question of the validity of the epistemological basis by which knowledge from the deliberative process was generated.

Furthermore, transcripts and core knowledge from the deliberative processes were not obtained during the event and therefore could not be made publicly available. This has resulted in a reliance on the version of knowledge that was generated by the opinion polls conducted before and after the initiative. This method restricts any inquiry into how, for example, obvious issues of framing and communication style might have influenced the outcome during the course of the citizens' deliberations. Thus, to date, data from these highly significant political events, as in the case with similar experiments (G1000 Belgium; the Canadian citizens' assemblies) are not publicly available.

In contrast, the knowledge base of SOWIT deliberation is derived from the concourse of communicability of every day conversation. Thus the opinions that are deliberated and from which underlying discourses emerge are generated by citizens themselves. It is these opinions that form the well from which deliberations spring.

Furthermore, the SOWIT approach holds that because of the hermeneutic challenges of identifying political knowledge, deliberative processes and their content must be fully public with a full stream of content made publicly available. This enables not one interpretation of the text from one particular epistemological viewpoint only, but the emergence of many alternative views, through examination by citizens. We argue that if deliberation is a common and public project, so too is its interpretation. Indeed, the output of the SOWIT deliberation sphere will be a radically new type of political knowledge that is publicly open enabling new perspectives and a common dialogue on what perspectives and dialogue processes mean from our collective perspective.

3.3. Reality check

The potential of SOWIT to address citizens' demands for improved engagement in politics is not just theoretical. Any such development must be designed in a way that responds to the constraints and challenges of current political behaviour patterns and expectations. To this end, consultations have been a priority of the development process. To date three consultations have been held. The first meeting was held with civil society organisations in the Fingal County Council area. Their feedback was positive and constructive, resonating with the enthusiasm expressed by citizens in the WTC regional meetings for greater voice in their democracy, particularly at local government level. The participants noted that SOWIT could improve their ability to collaborate with each other and to affect a stronger voice in local government. Yet, they also pointed to a number of potential challenges in the implementation of the SOWIT approach. The challenges cited included the need for an inclusion strategy so that marginalised citizens or those not IT literate were not further disenfranchised politically. Citizens' trust in digital technologies also emerged as an issue, they noted that any technical complexity in the system could facilitate manipulation and therefore the system should be fully open to independent inspection (see Liston, Harris, & O'Toole, 2011b, for a full report of the consultation and impact on the SOWIT design).

The second consultation was held with elected members of Fingal County Council. Some Councillors felt that SOWIT was relevant at a national level for deliberative processes on policy. Others noted that it provided a unique forum for counter-balancing the communication distortions of the tabloid media, enabling Councillors to have a voice and respond to negative or incorrect claims. On the other hand, a repeated concern was the potential impact on their workloads and the extent of the power imbalance between elected members and the executive. As such, deliberations would only be effective where they explicitly included the local authority management and where deliberations were framed to have more meaningful impact than competitive individual lobbying by citizens, groups and stakeholders (Liston, Harris, & O'Toole, 2012a). The final consultation was held with the management of Fingal County Council which expressed their support and engagement with SOWIT (Liston, Harris, & O'Toole, 2012b).

As such, while the SOWIT model provides a normative model rooted in political and philosophical theory, and informed by empirical findings on deliberative experiments, its nature necessitates ongoing evolution and adaptation to changing contexts and political dynamics. The rationale for rooting SOWIT at the local level is to support evolution of the public sphere where it is closest to people (see Gaynor & O'Brien, 2012) and respond to citizens' calls for greater participation at local government level.

4.   Conclusion

SOWIT has the potential to be a significant innovation in political engagement in Ireland. It breaks new ground in taking a distinctly new approach to political knowledge and data generation than is currently practiced in the form of public opinion surveys and positivist analysis of deliberative forums. Its foundation in discursive representation and meta-consensus provides a means for a new interpretative approach to citizen participation, one in which the knowledge and opinions of each citizen is recognised as relative, contextual and open to transformation. As such SOWIT, while adopting certain modalities of the positivist approach, aims to be decisively interpretative in its focus on the interpretation of information, the social construction of meaning and the inclusion of all social discourses in deliberation. The outcome will be new digitally-born political artefacts and a new means of political engagement and understanding in the public sphere.

However, we acknowledge that a significant amount of further research is needed from inter-disciplinary and practical perspectives. Firstly, Q-method was developed as a research instrument and not a political process. As such, further research and experimentation is required to fully examine the implications of Q-method on many different aspects of political legitimacy, inclusion and the functioning of the representative system. Secondly, an issue of particular research importance is the way in which citizens communicate across cultures and languages, not only practically but also with respect to the different world views that are argued by Whorf (1956) to inhere in different linguistic systems. Thirdly, an important issue raised by citizens involves the need for an 'active inclusion' strategy so that all citizens, regardless of their level of IT literacy or education, can participate in and understand the knowledge resulting from the SOWIT method of inclusive deliberations. Evidence of the effectiveness of outreach is clear in the Brazilian web based public budgeting process in Belo Horizonte, state of Rio Grande do Sul. This initiative successfully brought online crowd-sourcing via an outreach program to the favelas of Brazil (CDoten, 2012). Not least, critical attention must to be given to the institutional constraints and social and cultural factors that affect the diffusion of innovation.

The SOWIT project raises many questions for further research as it is currently in the very early stages of development. By its nature, it will remain an evolving and changing project, calling for new understandings of our changing political and social world that is driven not only by the myriad of perspectives of the giants of social science and digital humanities but by the 'wisdom of the multitude' (Aristotle, 2000) of Irish and global citizens.

Acknowledgements. We would like to express our gratitude to Fingal County Council, civil society organisations and citizens for their engagement in and support of the SOWIT project. We would also like to thank two anonymous reviewers for their valuable comments on an earlier version of this paper.

References

Alexander, M. P. (2002). *Towards reconstructing meaning when text is communicated electronically.* PhD thesis. University of Pretoria, Pretoria. Retrieved from http://upetd. up.ac.za/thesis/available/etd-08192002-155431

Aristotle. (2000). *Politics* [Translated by Benjamin Jowett: with introduction, analysis, and index by H. W. C. Davis]. New York: Courier Dover Publications.

Arendt, H. (1967, February 25). Reflections: Truth and Politics. *The New Yorker*, p. 49.

Bächtiger, A., Niemeyer, S., Neblo, M., Steenbergen, M. R., & Steiner, J. (2010). Disentangling Diversity in Deliberative Democracy: Competing Theories, their Blind Spots and Complementarities. *Journal of Political Philosophy, 18*(1), 32-63. doi: 10.1111/j.1467-9760.2009.00342.x

Barnes, M., Newman, J., & Sullivan, H. (2007). *Power, Participation and Political Renewal: Case Studies in Public Participation.* Bristol: The Policy Press.

Carney, G., Dundon, T., Ní Leime, Á., & Loftus, C. (2011). *Community engagement in Ireland's developmental welfare state: A study of the Life Cycle Approach.* National University of Ireland Galway: Irish Centre for Social Gerontology.

Chong, D., & Druckman, J. N. (2010). Dynamic Public Opinion: Communication Effects over Time. *American Political Science Review, 104*(4), 663-680. doi: 10.1017/S0003055410000493

Coleman, S., & Blumler, J. G. (2009). *The Internet and Democratic Citizenship: Theory, Practice and Policy.* Cambridge: Cambridge University Press.

Connelly, S., & Richardson, T. (2004). Exclusion: the necessary difference between ideal and practical consensus. *Journal of Environmental Planning and Management, 47*(1), 3-17. doi: 10.1080/0964056042000189772

Cuppen, E., Breukers, S., Hisschemöller, M., & Bergsma, E. (2010). Q methodology to Select participants for a stakeholder dialogue on energy options from biomass in the Netherlands. *Ecological Economics, 69*(3), 579-591. doi: 10.1016/j.ecolecon.2009.09.005

Davies, B. B., Blackstock, K., & Rauschmayer, F. (2005). 'Recruitment', 'composition', and 'mandate' issues in deliberative processes: should we focus on arguments rather than individuals? *Environment and Planning C: Government and Policy, 23*, 599-615.

Dept. of the Environment, Community and Local Government. (2012). *Putting People First: Action Plan for Effective Local Government*. Retrieved from http://www.environ.ie/en/PublicationsDocuments/FileDownLoad,31309,en.pdf

Dewey, J. (1927). *The Public and its Problems*. London: G. Allen & Unwin.

Drucker, J. (2011). Humanities Approaches to Graphical Display. *Digital Humanities Quarterly, 5*(1). Retrieved from http://www.digitalhumanities.org/dhq/vol/5/1/000091/000091.html

Dryzek, J. S. (1987). Complexity and Rationality in Public Life. *Political Studies, 35*(3), 424-442.

Dryzek, J. S. (2005). Handle with Care: The Deadly Hermeneutics of Deliberative Instrumentation. *Acta Politica, 40*(2), 197-211. doi: 10.1057/palgrave.ap.5500099

Dryzek, J. S. (2010). *Foundations and Frontiers of Deliberative Governance*. Oxford: Oxford University Press.

Dryzek, J. S., & Niemeyer, S. (2006). Reconciling Pluralism and Consensus as Political Ideals. *American Journal of Political Science, 50*(3), 634-649. doi: 10.1111/j.1540-5907.2006.00206.x

Dryzek, J. S., & Niemeyer, S. (2008). Discursive Representation. *American Political Science Review, 102*(4), 481-493. doi: 10.1017/S0003055408080325

Ellis, G., Barry, J., & Robinson, C. (2007). Many ways to say 'no', different ways to say 'yes': Applying Q-Methodology to understand public acceptance of wind farm proposals. *Journal of Environmental Planning and Management, 50*(4), 517-551. doi: 10.1080/09640560701402075

Elster, J. (1983). *Explaining Technical Change*. Cambridge: Cambridge University Press.

Farrell, D. (2011, December 12). Tánaiste welcomes the WetheCitizen's findings [online]. *We The Citizens*. Retrieved from http://tinyurl.com/wethecitizens

Fishkin, J. S. (2009). *When the people speak: deliberative democracy and public Consultation*. Oxford: Oxford University Press.

Gadamer, H.-G. (2004). *Truth and Method* (2nd ed.) [Translation revised by Joel Weinsheimer and Donald G Marshall]. New York: Continuum.

Gaynor, N. (2011). Partnership Associations, Deliberation, and Democracy: The Case of Ireland's Social Partnership. *Politics and Society, 39*(4), 497-519. doi: 10.1177/0032329211420081

Gaynor, N., & O'Brien, A. (2012). Because it all begins with talk: community radio as a vital element in community development. *Community Development Journal, 47*(3), 436-447. doi: 10.1093/cdj/bsr058

Gregersen, F., & Køppe, S. (1989). A normative theory of humanist knowledge. *Journal for General Philosophy of Science, 20*(1), 40-53.

Habermas, J. (1975). *Legitimation Crisis*. Boston: Beacon Press.

Hamilton, A., Madison, J., & Jay, J. (2003). *The Federalist Papers*. New York: Bantham Dell.

Kornprobst, M. (2011). The agent's logics of action: defining and mapping political Judgement. *International Theory, 3*(1), 70-104. doi: 10.1017/S1752971910000291

Kriplean, T., Toomim, M., Morgan, J. T., Borning, A., & Ko, A. J. (2011). Reflect: Supporting Active Listening and Grounding on the Web through Restatement. *Proceedings of the Conference on Computer Supported Cooperative Work, Hangzhou, China.*

Liston, V., Harris, C., & O'Toole, M. (2011a). Computer-mediated deliberation for citizen self government: A theoretical design of an integrated policy process. *Paper prepared for presentation at the Political Studies Association of Ireland Annual Conference, 21-23 October 2011, Dublin.*

Liston, V., Harris, C., & O'Toole, M. (2011b). Report on Consultation with Civil Society Organisations in Fingal County. *SOWIT Report.* Retrieved from http://www.sowit.eu/node/2

Liston, V., Harris, C., & O'Toole, M. (2012a). Report on Consultation with Fingal Councillors. *SOWIT Report.* Retrieved from http://www.sowit.eu/node/36

Liston, V., Harris, C., & O'Toole, M. (2012b). Report on Consultation with Fingal County Management Team. *SOWIT Report.* Retrieved from: http://www.sowit.eu/node/39

Lord, C., & Tamvaki, D. (forthcoming). The politics of justification? Applying the 'discourse quality index' to the study of the European Parliament. *European Political Science Review.*

CDoten. (2012). *Digital Connections in the Favelas of Brazil* [Blog]. National Democratic Institute for International Affairs. Retrieved from http://demworks.org/blog/2012/09/digital-connections-favelas-brazil

Niemeyer, S. (2004). Deliberation in the Wilderness: Displacing Symbolic Politics. *Environmental Politics, 13*(2), 347-372. doi: 10.1080/0964401042000209612

Niemeyer, S. (2011). The Emancipatory Effect of Deliberation: Empirical Lessons from Mini-Publics. *Politics and Society, 39*(1), 103-140. doi: 10.1177/0032329210395000

O'Brien, E. (2009). Intellectual Imposters ? – We Should be so Lucky ! Towards an Irish Public Sphere. *Etudes Irlandaises, 34*(2), 101-114. Retrieved from http://etudesirlandaises.revues.org/pdf/1660

O'Carroll, J. P. (2002). Culture lag and democratic deficit in Ireland: Or, 'Dat's outside de terms of d'agreement'. *Community Development Journal, 37*(1), 10-19. doi: 10.1093/cdj/37.1.10

Pennington, M. (2003). Hayekian Political Economy and the Limits of Deliberative Democracy. *Political Studies, 51*(4), 722-739. doi: 10.1111/j.0032-3217.2003.00455.x

Ray, L. (2011). Using Q-methodology to identify local perspectives on wildfires in two Koyukon Athabascan communities in rural Alaska. Sustainability: Science, Practice, & Policy, 7(2). Retrieved from http://sspp.proquest.com/archives/vol7iss2/1011-061.ray.html

Smith, G. (2009). *Democratic Innovations: designing innovations for citizen participation.* Cambridge: Cambridge University Press.

Steenbergen, M. R., Bächtiger, A., Spörndli, M., & Steiner, J. (2003). Measuring political deliberation, a Discourse Quality Index. *Comparative European Politics, 1*(1), 21-48. doi: 10.1057/palgrave.cep.6110002

Stephenson, W. (1953). *The Study of Behavior: Q-Technique and Its Methodology.* Chicago: University of Chicago Press.

Tully, J. (2002). The unfreedom of movements in comparison to their ideals of constitutional democracy. The Modern Law Review, 65(2), 204-228. doi: 10.1111/1468-2230.00375

WTC. (2011). *We the Citizens: Participatory democracy in action - a pilot.* Retrieved from http://www.wethecitizens.ie/pdfs/We-the-Citizens-2011-FINAL.pdf

Whorf, B. L. (1956). *Language, Thought, and Reality: Selected Writings of Benjamin Lee Whorf* (Edited by J. B. Carroll). Cambridge, MA: MIT Press.

Young, I. M. (2000). *Inclusion and Democracy.* New York: Oxford University Press.

Zerilli, L. M. G. (2012). Truth and Politics. In J. Elkins & A. Norris (Eds), *Truth and Democracy* (54-75). Philadelphia: University of Philadelphia Press.

Name Index

McCrum, Robert 439, 445
McCullough, Alexis 140, 154
McGann, Jerome 72, 428, 434, 435, 442, 444, 445
McGarr, Oliver xv, 6, 277, 280, 302
McGill, Meredith L. 427, 441, 446
McKenna, Peter 280, 302
McLoughlin, Catherine 327, 347
McLuhan, Marshall 58, 73, 137, 139, 155
McMillan, David W. 328, 347
McNealy, Scott 246, 272
McQuail, Denis 117, 131
Meaney, Gerardine 440, 446
Méndez García, Jesus 242
Meskill, Carla 320, 322
Meyer, Robert 170, 174
Miller, Carolyn Handler 64, 73
Miller, Daniel 206, 209, 220, 222
Mingwei, Zhao 387, 404
Minnis, A. J. 98, 110
Mitchell, W. J. T. 75, 78, 79, 80, 83, 91, 93
Mitra, Ananda 209, 222
Mohd Ayub, Ahmad Fauzi 372, 377
Mokhtarian, Patricia L. 226, 241
Monfreda, C. 232, 241
Moore, Barrington 254, 272
Moore, Michael G. 350, 365
Moos, Markus 231, 242
Moran, Charles 351, 365
Morgan, David L. 287, 302
Morgan, Jonathan T. 453, 469
Morley, David 137, 140, 155

Morozov, Evgeny 163, 174
Morris, Adalaide 58, 73
Morrison, David E. 118, 132
Morrison, Diane M. 119, 131
Morris, Steven 162, 175
Mozzon-McPherson, Marina 329, 347
Mukundan, Jayakaran 372, 377
Mulkeen, Aidan 279, 302
Munfakh, Jimmie L. H. 184, 196
Murphy, Orla ix
Murray, Craig D. 16, 19, 20, 32
Murray, L. 327, 347

Nagle, Angela xv, 5, 157
Naji, Jeneen xvi, 4, 55
Nassaji, Hossein 355, 365
Neblo, Michael 458, 467
Nedelcu, Mihaela Florina 207, 222
Negri, Antonio 169, 174
Negroponte, Nicholas 137, 138, 152, 155, 164, 165, 175
Nelson, Peter 230, 242
Nelson, Theodore 383, 385, 404
Nespor, Marina 374, 378
Neuman, W. Russell 207, 220
Nevins, Tara 117, 132
Newenham, P. 148, 155
Newman, Janet 448, 467
Niemeyer, Simon 451, 452, 454, 455, 458, 459, 460, 461, 463, 467, 468, 469
Ní Leime, Á 450, 467
Nissenbaum, Helen 16, 31, 51, 53, 255, 262, 272

www.ingramcontent.com/pod-product-compliance
Lightning Source LLC
Chambersburg PA
CBHW022344280326
41935CB00007B/70